NEWSWRITING
IN TRANSITION

NEWSWRITING IN TRANSITION

Ray Laakaniemi

Bowling Green State University

Nelson-Hall Publishers
Chicago

Cover Painting: "Magestic Lady Is A Horse's Name,"
Ned Schwartz, Beret International Gallery

Project Editor: Rachel Schick
Illustrations: Don Lee
Design/Production: Tamra Phelps
Typesetter: E. T. Lowe
Printer: Capital City Press

Library of Congress Cataloging-in-Publication Data

Laakaniemi, Ray.
    Newswriting in transition / Ray Laakaniemi.
        p.   cm.
    Includes bibliographical references and index.
    ISBN 0-8304-1347-2
    1. Journalism—Authorship. 2. Reporters and reporting.
I. Title.
PN4775.L23   1995
808'.06607—dc20   94-20118
                                                        CIP

Manufactured in the United States of America

10 9 8 7 6 5 4 3 2 1

 TM The paper used in this book meets the
minimum requirements of American
National Standard for Information
Sciences—Permanence of Paper for
Printed Library Materials, ANSI
Z39.48-1984.

Contents in Brief

PART III

REWRITE—TURNING A GOOD STORY INTO AN EVEN BETTER ONE

Contents

Putting it off until the last minute.
The critical difference between an idea and a first draft.
Telling a story versus listing everything in the first paragraph.
Understanding the need for revision and rewrite.
Respecting the reader's intelligence but understanding that some words
  and terms can be confusing.

5. Understanding Process in Writing   58

Process theory breaks the act of writing into its component parts so the
  writer can understand which part, if any, needs more work to make a
  better story.
Writing is a disconnected process, seldom following one-two-three step
  order, and writers should realize this.
Writing a news story in many respects is like doing a scientific
  experiment—finding a question to answer, using reliable questioning
  methods, focusing on important answers, etc.
Why a great deal of thinking and analyzing needs to be done by a writer
  before he or she starts to write.
Why and how stories change as they are being written, and how new
  discoveries change the shape and form of the story.

6. Gathering News: Reporting and Writing Go Hand-in-Hand   71

Why you can't write good stories without good information.
Why developing story ideas may be more important than the actual writing.
Specific things reporters watch for—quotes, details, numbers, and specifics.
How to ask people for information, and how to write down what they
  give you.
Why you should always get more information than you need for a story.
The incredibly close ties between reporting and writing.

7. Libel and Privacy: Respect for the Individual   91

Balancing the public's right to know with the individual's rights to protection
  of reputation and privacy.
The growing specter of libel (injury to reputation) as a force in the media.
Steps a reporter can take to minimize, but not eliminate, the threat of libel.
Understanding how truth and privilege (dealing with the public business)
  can be used as defense against libel.

8. Developing Your Own Philosophy of Newswriting   104

The student/writer needs to understand why he or she is writing before
  starting to write. Knowing the purpose of a story makes all the difference
  in putting it together smoothly.
Every story in every newscast or newspaper is not important to everyone.
  But the reporter must act as if every routine story is the most important
  story he or she has ever done.
Why writing is more difficult than many other professions, and how to make
  it easier.

PART II

MEDIA WRITING

interested in reading the rest of the story. The "hook," or "catchy" lead, often takes time to develop.

The feature ending is not like the ending of other news stories. It is a reward to the reader for having read the entire story, and generally has a "bang" of its own. Feature writers save incidents, anecdotes, or examples to use as endings.

Above all, a feature is a story, an example of a person or incident that needs to be retold so society can understand what is happening in other parts of society.

Introduction to the Philosophy of Newswriting: From Prewrite to Rewrite

NEWSWRITING may never be the same again, so this newswriting book is different. It is an introduction to newswriting, with an emphasis on the philosophy of newswriting. It focuses on the subtle and the major transitions taking place in the learning of newswriting that will make writing easier and more meaningful for beginning reporters. It looks to the day when reporters will report (as some are now reporting) directly from the scene with a laptop or other computer, where they must be able to think and compose on a computer screen in minutes.

It also assumes that the media will continue to change and come together in form and function, and that this will have an impact on the form of news stories. The fact that many newspapers are buying 1-900 and other electronic systems and producing facsimile newspapers, that the phone companies would like to run dial-in classified advertising, and that the use of computers is growing exponentially means the media will continue to change.

While the form may change, the essential purpose of the reporter will be the same: to explain events and trends in words and in a way the reader can understand quickly and easily. The message is the heart of any reporting, despite the evolutions in form of message.

This book is unlike the 20 or so others on the market because it focuses on understanding *why* news stories are written the way they are.

By focusing on the problems the student needs to understand *before, while,* and *after* writing news stories, this book provides something new and useful. It focuses on how the reporter thinks his or her way through a story.

This book offers solutions to the most common writing problems students have, based on 20 years of teaching and media experience. It starts with the questions the student asks most, and it goes step-by-step through the most common writing forms.

Something special is added from national writing coach research, in that the student can understand the most common writing problems professionals have—and avoid those problems.

The book builds on writing theory, but does not dwell on it. It progresses naturally from the writing development stage the student is likely to be in at the start, to the stage they need to be in to begin professional newswriting. There is no glossing over the problems students will have in learning a new writing style.

By telling the beginning writer *why* these steps are necessary, and then taking that writer through each step, they will understand why they are writing in this manner. This ought to make a complex writing form easier.

Throughout the book, good writing examples from national and regional newspapers, national magazines, and wire services are used. They have been selected from award-winning stories in national and regional contests and are used to illustrate different points.

Extensive efforts have been made to include writing from all regions, from male and female reporters, and all elements of society. There are some 60 examples in the book from 23 states; 50 percent by male authors, 40 percent by female authors, and 10 percent are group projects. Of the 60 stories, 23 are known to address minority issues or are written by members of minorities.

Chapters on cultural diversity and visual literacy are included. Little progress has been shown in reporting on minorities in this country in the last 50 years, despite the pleadings of the Hutchins and Kerner commissions. Chapter 23 includes statements by minorities on covering minorities and advice on getting student reporters to think about cultures other than their own or the culture of their close personal friends. Visual literacy has been added because writers must not only understand photos, graphics, and other visuals, but also know how to work with designers, photographers, and others for the improvement of the product.

We feel students need to read well-written news stories to understand how to write better news stories, feel the enthusiasm the writer has for the story, and have the satisfaction of reading all the way through a well-crafted story.

It is quite clear that most beginning news writers do not read enough news stories. The 40-plus examples carefully chosen for this book illustrate key points in the newswriting process, and are thoroughly discussed before the articles are presented. Therefore, the student will know what to look for in each article.

The theory that is included is process writing theory, well known to English teachers but all-but-new to journalism. It stresses looking at a story as being made up of component parts, not as an entire "product" or single unit. Understanding that a story comes in parts helps to fix that story when some parts are not up to standards.

Process theory also teaches that rewrites are a normal part of the writing process, not a two-minute penalty whistled by the writing instructor. Students who understand process will be better able to cope with the rewrite needed to polish and improve their copy.

One of the main emphases of this book is on the single greatest problems news writers have—organizing a news story. A national study of writing coaches in the late 1980s indicated that reporters had problems organizing leads, organizing stories—and organizing time.

By stressing process, rewrite, and organization, the book teaches students the beginning-to-end system of writing news stories, both formula and feature. By understanding that it is not a simple sit-down-and-write process, they will be able to understand the different needs of different stories.

The relevant, well-written models of stories at the end of many chapters demonstrate to readers what others have accomplished before them. Writing students need role models. The difference in writing skills between those who have had models to follow and those who have not is significant, in my opinion.

Perhaps the reason reporters have so much trouble organizing stories is that they do not think in terms of the entire story, only the individual parts. If the students of today do not read entire news stories, it is going to be difficult for them to write entire news stories.

For one thing, students cannot understand how a story is organized unless they see how others organize them. Most books offer only snippets of stories, without letting the student see how the entire story is organized.

Further, the power of short words and sentences has to be experienced to be understood.

The concern, confusion, and uncertainty students go through is a part of any writing process, and a significant focus of this book. We try to put that uncertainty into perspective, to show the writer that everyone has uncertainties and that writing is indeed a difficult process.

This book takes a close look at the personal side of newswriting. How should the writer react to the uncertainties encountered? Deal with deadlines? Organize a seeming jungle of information? Know which quotes to use and how many?

The way stories are written stems from reader and viewer habits, which are not what beginning writers think they are. Newswriting is evolving as the news media enters a new era of competition between newspapers and television, and of cooperation in the newsroom. Differences between writing for newspapers and for radio and television may disappear because of changing technologies. What will remain is the importance of understanding information and putting it into a logical form based on the technology being used.

We hope the writer gains an understanding that the first draft will not be as smooth as expected, and that the second and third drafts (depending on time available) will inevitably improve the story. The first draft is basically an exercise in organization, taking the story from the realm of ideas to the realm of the concrete. Following drafts are bound to make the story smoother, better, and more interesting because they build on the strengths of the original draft and eliminate the weaknesses.

Once the philosophy and the process are understood, the writer can then attack building blocks and the news story forms. Building blocks are those elements that are peculiar to newswriting—short sentences, specific words, accuracy, proper quotes, etc. What was passable and praised in an English class may not be acceptable in a Journalism class because of the different audiences. Brevity and conciseness are golden to an audience that, in most cases, devotes as little time as possible to the words the writer has agonized over.

For the purposes of this book, the story forms are divided into two categories—formula stories and feature stories.

Formula stories are those that remain the same in structure each time, but change in content. These include many of what we call the inverted pyramid stories (most important information first in the story). A very important aspect is to know which stories take formulas and how the formulas operate.

Formula stories include obituaries, accidents and disasters, announcements, meetings and speeches, roundup, and multiple-incident stories. Some of these are more complex than others, but understanding the formula for each and why it is used makes the process easier to understand.

Feature stories include the longer story, the background information story, the personality profile, and the success story. It is a formula story with several formulas. Whichever writing technique works in telling the story best is the technique to use. The challenge for the beginning reporter comes in choosing the technique.

Once the basics are understood, the reader is introduced to a special section on story enhancements. The reporter/writer must understand the basics before understanding how to make copy brighter, more interesting, and more saleable.

This book grows out of 18 years of experience in newspapers and college public relations and 21 years of college and university teaching, some of the years overlapping.

It could not have been written even three years ago because of changes in the understanding of the writing process. I owe a debt to those people who are pioneers in the understanding of the complexities of writing, and to literally hundreds of college students who have suffered with me through the mental pains of learning to write in a way the public will understand and the media will accept. The book is writing and thinking combined, two of the most complex and difficult processes known to mankind.

Several short chapters are devoted to important topics that are usually included or imbedded into longer chapters in other texts. By focusing on one major topic at a time, these chapters help a reporter think through important aspects of writing. These topics include attribution, rewrite, dealing with deadlines, reader and writer habits, and developing the body of the story.

Three chapters respond to changing conditions in the media: first-person stories; reporting cultures other than your own; and understanding the relationships between reporting and the visual side of the media—photographs, charts, and visuals. A special effort is made to point out similarities and the need for cooperation between reporters and photographers and graphic artists.

Several references are made in this book to material previously published in *The Coaches' Corner*, a national newsletter for newspaper writing coaches. Persons interested in the newsletter ($7 per year) can write to Paul Salsini, 2230 E. Bradford Ave., Unit G, Milwaukee, WI 53211.

Special thanks to Larry Jankowski, Geoff Haynes, Doug Lillibridge, Dick Hendrickson, Dave Swartz and the Jerome Library Periodicals section, Don Hadd and most of all, Karen, Brian and Jan.

About the Author

Ray Laakaniemi is an associate professor and chair of the Department of Journalism at Bowling Green State University. He earned an A.B. at the University of Michigan and an M.S. and Ph.D. at Ohio University in Athens, Ohio. He conducted the first national study on newspaper writing coaches in the late 1980s. He has conducted writing workshops for newspapers and groups of newspapers in 10 states and Japan. He has 20 years of newspaper and public relations experience, and has been teaching journalists how to write news for 30 years.

PART I

BEFORE YOU WRITE

1
The Nature of News

"Journalism is literature in a hurry." —Matthew Arnold

In This Chapter

What is news, and how do you know?
What are the elements that make up news?
The difference between "hard" news and "soft" news.
Samples of different kinds of news stories.

WRITING a news story can be compared to the first play of a football game. There is anticipation, there is action, and there can be a lot of confusion. Once the center snaps the ball to the quarterback, things go in all different directions.

When a reporter sits down to write a news story, he or she must also rely on months, if not years, of training. The reporter must consider the facts of the story, the needs of the reader, the proper form for the story, and the limited amount of time to complete the story.

Writing a news story contains, as Matthew Arnold indicates, equal parts of literature and hurry. With the pressure of deadlines in the media business, writers tend to forget the literature and focus on the hurry. There are ways of working around this tendency.

Most students taking beginning newswriting will have completed basic college English requirements. Although the form and organization of writing in the two fields are somewhat different, the basics of grammar, spelling, logic, and thought before writing are similar and important. Very important.

Because everything tends to happen at once, as with the opening play of a football game, we need to understand all of the parts that go into writing the first news story. We start by trying to understand what news is, and why we are writing it.

As society continues to change, it becomes more difficult to describe. The changes themselves become the stories, and the reporter needs to understand the basic facts, the changes, and how to report on them clearly. The writer must have a framework established to write stories so that new information can be adapted to news formats quickly and easily.

Definition of News

One dictionary, *Webster's Encyclopedic Unabridged*, defines news in two ways. First, it is a report of a recent event; intelligence; information, as in, "His family had no news of his whereabouts for months."

The second definition is the presentation of a report on current events in a newspaper or other periodical, or on radio or television.

These definitions seem straightforward enough. Why do we even dwell on it? Primarily because the nature of news is considerably different from what beginners may think. Class reports cover a particular subject or a bit of information already known to someone else. English themes can tend to be oriented toward what you think about a subject, thus becoming your opinion backed by facts.

News reports, however, are items of information of interest to someone else. They focus on what is new in a topic or event, rather than what is already known. It is the reporter's duty to separate the new from the old. Because news reports must tell a large number of persons (a mass audience) what is new, they have to be done quickly. Writers do not have a week or two to write most news stories. They need to be done in thirty minutes, or an hour, or a day, so that they will still be "new."

Elements of News

It helps to understand news by looking at the traditional elements of news, called news values. Why is news different from English themes or reports for a psychology class?

Thinking about these components also gives news writers a better knowledge of why news stories are written the way they are. Newswriting is writing with a clear purpose, and the purpose develops from the following news values.

Timeliness

When readers pick up a daily newspaper, they expect to find the latest news. Usually this means reports on meetings, accidents, or appointments that have happened in the last 24 hours. Something that happened more than 24 hours before the paper is printed is considered to be too old to publish, or "out of the news cycle." If the reporter gets the story in too late for the newspaper to use it, it is not used. Period.

Different media have different news cycles. Radio, because it is instant, will have different news stories every hour. Television news will be different in its morning, noon, and evening newscasts. Magazines deal with news up to two or three months after it happens, which makes it even more important that they understand the needs of their audience and how events are important to their readers.

Another set of terms often heard in news is *hard news* versus *soft news*, and these concepts have a lot to do with timing. Hard news is generally about an event that happens during the news cycle, and is one of the "standard" items news media cover—fires, accidents, meetings, earthquakes, etc.

Not all news happens within a specified news cycle. The changing of the industrial nature of cities in "the Rust Belt," the research to discover a cure for AIDS, or the growing popularity of a teacher in the school all take time. These are categorized as soft news, or sometimes *features*, which are background stories that develop through time or have a personal or human interest slant. Features about the history of serious news stories have also been called *hard features*.

Proximity

Each media outlet serves a limited geographical area. A hometown newspaper serves its town, and perhaps much of the surrounding county, but not far beyond that. Circulation areas are determined mainly by government areas (such as school districts) and shopping patterns, among other things. And since there is so much news that it is impossible to include everything, the editors choose topics that are of interest to the largest number of people who live, shop, and work in an area.

Radio and television markets are also largely determined by political boundaries and shopping patterns, although the boundaries are less clear because signals can be transmitted much more easily than newspapers can be circulated.

There are exceptions to the proximity principle, obviously. Some radio or television stations transmit across great distances. And there are newspapers that circulate across the entire country, not just in a limited geographical area.

But for the most part, local newscasts and local newspapers serve a limited geographical area. Since they try to cover news that is of interest to as many persons as possible, they tend to focus on government and schools, which have an impact on every family in the community.

There may also be what has been called *psychological proximity* as well. A person who lives in a college town, a town that makes automobiles, or a farming community is interested in other college towns, auto towns, or farming towns. These communities may have the same kinds of problems, and they may have solved them in different ways. Something that happens in one town may be of interest only because it happened in that town. People in the next county may not care.

Prominence

All people may have been created equal, but some are more powerful or interesting than others. When the mayor of a town or the president of a university says something, it is probably of interest to a lot of people in town. When the president of the United States speaks, everyone listens.

When a rape trial involving local people is held in a town, usually only the persons in the community are interested. But when nationally prominent people are on trial, the entire nation tunes in. The issues may be the same, but the prominence of the people involved is not. When major national figures announce they have the virus that causes AIDS, the entire nation knows it within a few hours. But someone in your block may have it, and you won't know about it.

Conflict

Conflict has been interpreted by many as the media's tendency to focus on arguments between the president and Congress, big business and labor, or entertainment figures and the popular magazines.

If we think of the media as one group of persons informing everyone else about issues in society, or as different parts of society talking to each other, conflict may not seem as negative.

If a public official says the city may have to lay off 300 employees because it is running out of money, is this a conflict between politicians or between the official and the press, or is the media bringing up a point that the public needs to understand?

If the newspaper reports there have been three robberies in one subdivision overnight, is the media reporting negative news, or is it alerting people who live there of a potential danger?

Conflict in ideas may not be the same as physical conflict. It may be airing, or discussing issues that need to be discussed.

Audience

Different people have different interests, and you have to understand the interests of your audience. This often comes into mind when you cover governmental meetings that are of little interest to you, because you may have just moved to town, do not have children in school, or do not own a home. Most newspaper readers *do* have children in school and *do* own houses in an area, so writers have to write with *their* interests in mind. This is difficult for some beginning reporters because their subject does not have an

7

impact on their lives, but it helps to understand that governmental units can change policies, increase taxes, or make rules that make the readers do something they may or may not want to do.

In public relations, the same news may be presented to different groups with several different emphases. The emphasis is changed, not the facts, because different groups want to know different things. For Ford employees, the threat of a strike means different things to workers, administrators, stockholders, trustees, and the communities in which Ford has plants. It is necessary to communicate to all of these groups, in different forms and through different media.

Cable television may have 45 channels, but most people watch only a few. There are thousands of magazines published in the United States for different interest groups, but most people read only a handful of them. Stories have to be relevant to the audience being served. The news does not change, but the facts emphasized are those the audience wants to know.

Uniqueness or Unusualness

People like to know who is or was the first to do something, witness the popularity of the *Guinness Book of Records*. This has a place in local news as well, such as the first person of any group to become a mayor, the first time the city has enforced a new law, or the first person to accomplish a certain feat.

Very often change can be reported in terms of firsts. For example, it may be the first time that industrial income is greater than farm income in County A, or the first time more than one new industry has located in a town in one year.

People also have a sense of humor and a sense of the unusual. Perhaps the oldest saying in journalism is that if dog bites man it is not news; but if man bites dog, it is news. Very few people bite dogs, but if they do, it is still of interest. Perhaps not as much as when it was first stated, but it is still news. Reporters watch for unique or unusual events.

Human Interest

When a baby girl fell into a well in Texas and could not get out by herself, the whole world watched as rescue efforts were made. When the president's cat does something unusual, the country hears about it.

Life is not all seriousness, meetings, and conflicts. People react to the fun things as well as to the problems of other people. News media that do not pursue the human values lose their audiences.

Competition

The way news is used or "played" depends to a great deal on what else is available to the reader. A writer for the afternoon paper must know what the morning paper covered today. If there are several news departments in a radio or television market, each department must keep up with or stay ahead of the others to remain in business. The national networks and the major local television stations watch each other closely so they will not be "scooped" or shut out. When a station says it has an "exclusive," it is going to play it prominently. Newscasters will chuckle to themselves because they were lucky or worked harder than someone else to get the story.

Not all news stories have all of these news values. And the value of going through this is not in memorizing a list but in knowing that certain elements are of more interest than others, and that different audiences have different information needs.

The audience of the 1990s has different interests and needs than the audience of the 1960s or the 1930s. As conditions change, values will, too.

Beginning reporters go through stages. At first, they wonder if they have a good story. They may rely on the old adage: "news is what your editor says it is." Then they begin to recognize certain types of stories, and understand how these stories are different from ones they have used recently. Only after some time will they begin to anticipate news stories, and provide a public service by warning the audience that something of this nature is likely to happen.

In these cases, reporters have become part of the community or the organization they work for, and they understand readers' needs. They have written many stories, come to know the people they write about, and developed their own confidence level. This knowledge and confidence will come, but not right away.

For now, one step at a time. Understand that not all news stories or audiences are the same and that there are definite reasons why news stories are written the way they are.

Look at a campus or city paper, listen to radio news, or watch network news. See which values can be identified. Analyze the lead stories in each medium. The news elements are the same, only the audiences and the actors are different.

Sample News Stories

It is much easier to understand what a news story is after reading several samples. Concluding this chapter are eight different news stories from several different sections of the United States. The topics of these stories are:

- Some people get hooked on drugs while others do not.
- Some people run for judgeships on the basis of their names, which are familiar, instead of their reputations, which are not.
- An important cancer research drug—Taxol—is not being produced because of confusion, red tape, and government inaction.
- At 4:00 A.M., there is an armed robbery at a convenience store—by a tough 11-year-old boy.
- A woman dies in her basement condominium and isn't found until three years later.
- The job market for college students—a topic of interest to all undergraduates.

These stories have most of the elements outlined previously. Not all stories have all elements, and not all stories will be of interest to all readers or viewers. But these stories do have the things that make people want to read stories—they affect the readers personally. How can you not be interested (or shocked) by an 11-year-old boy robbing a store at gunpoint, or by the mysterious disappearance of a woman who left no clues whatsoever.

Read these stories for their news elements. This is only a small sample. There are literally millions of news stories in this country every year.

Watch how the stories are written, but on this reading, ask yourself these two questions. Does this story interest me? Would it be likely to interest a significant part of a typical reading or viewing audience?

Drug Dependency

Beth Francis, health editor of the *Fort Myers (Fla.) News Press*, wrote "Why some get hooked, but others get away." It was judged one of the best news stories in a competition among Gannett papers in 1991 for Specialty Reporting.

Notice what is new in this story; that is, what you would not have known if you had not read the story.

It is cunning and powerful. It tiptoes in and seduces us, pretending to be a friend, smoothing over the hard edges of our

10

lives and shutting out the pain. But as it feeds on itself, it consumes us, propelling us into a frenzy of despair, ruining our relationships, jeopardizing our health and our lives.

Alcoholism and drug use are associated with at least 50 percent of traffic fatalities, 50 percent of murders and 25 percent of suicides...

Researchers now agree that addiction—whether it is to alcohol, cocaine, speed, valium or any other drug—is one disease. Most addicts will switch substances when their drug of choice is not available in a never-ending quest to alter their moods and escape their problem....

The recognition that addiction has a strong psychological component is an important advance, said Dr. Gerard Sager, medical director of the addictive disease unit at Charter Glade Hospital in Fort Myers.

Why do some people become addicts, yet others can easily walk away from occasional drug use?

Most experts believe a person's biological and psychological makeup, combined with their social environment, all play a role in causing addiction.

Having one trait alone does not guarantee addiction. For example, the child of an alcoholic is not automatically destined to alcoholism. But the more high-risk traits a person has, the more vulnerable he or she is. Some common ones include:

- Genetics—Having an alcoholic parent increases your risk of a drinking addiction because of inherited body chemistry. Abuse of other substances may also have a genetic link, but there has been less study in this area.
- Sensitivity to drugs—Some experts believe the exhilaration of a drug's high is felt more intensely in addicts than in other people, because of the differences in the way an addict's body metabolizes the drug.
- Low self-esteem—People who feel poorly about themselves may achieve a feeling of power from using drugs.
- Depression—People suffering from depression often "self-medicate" with drugs. Some theories hold that depressed and anxious people are susceptible to addiction because of an underlying neurochemical imbalance that is temporarily corrected by the drug.
- Environment—Children who are brought up in homes where parents drink or use other drugs are more likely to do the same. Children brought up in poverty or who are sexually or physically abused are also at risk.

A Judge by Any Other Name

One of the responsibilities of the nation's press is to keep the public aware of problems that arise in government. Unless the press brings it to the public's attention, how else will the public learn of any problems?

James McCarty and Ulysses Torassa of the *Cleveland Plain Dealer* point out a problem in an upcoming election—serious confusion over names of candidates. Their Feb. 17, 1992, story was headlined "Judge not by name alone: 92 lawyers crowd ballots for courts." Notice how the reporters add quotes from people familiar with this problem.

> There's nothing like a familiar name to help a lawyer get elected judge in Cuyahoga County.
>
> Lavish fund-raisers, avid supporters and advertising blitzes are fine, but with 92 lawyers pulling petitions to run for 27 judge's jobs this spring, having the right name can work magic where buttons and billboards fall flat.
>
> The early ballot for the May 5 primary shows four Sweeneys, three Corrigans, and—just to see if you're paying attention—a McMonagle, a Gallagher, a Celebrezze and a Calabrese.
>
> Mix them in with those already on the bench—four Corrigans, three McMonagles, a Sweeney and a Gallagher, who are not up for reelection this year—and you are looking at a judicial stew that would boggle the most informed voter on Election Day.
>
> "I have no idea who half of these people are, and I am in the courthouse every day," said Mark A. Stanton, a veteran defense lawyer who ran for judge in 1990.
>
> "There is a mania about being a judge. Anybody with a decent name is throwing their name in. It scares the hell out of me," Stanton said.
>
> Political observers credit the swollen field to an over-abundance of lawyers competing for a dearth of work. For many, a county paycheck would be a big improvement over what they're making now. Another factor is the growing opportunity for women on the bench, the observers say.
>
> What this grab bag means to the people of Cuyahoga County is clear: Voter confusion.
>
> "The ability of the electorate to know who they're voting for is questionable," said Thomas J. LaFond, Cleveland Bar association president. "By the time they get to the bottom of the ballot where the judges are, the number of votes cast usually drops by 50 percent, sometimes more."

The Taxol Mess

Eric Nalder of the *Seattle Times* wrote a three-part series on a promising cancer drug that is in very short supply because of a series of problems and bunglings. The series, which started Dec. 15, 1991, won a National Headliner Award for outstanding news reporting for papers with over 150,000 circulation. The Headliner competition drew 1,500 entries from throughout the United States.

TRIALS OF TAXOL: PROMISING CANCER DRUG IS STALLED IN THE FOREST

It's been called the most important cancer-fighting drug of the decade—so important that the National Cancer Institute has made its development an "emergency priority."

Yet despite evidence more than two years ago that the drug showed promise, it remains in critically short supply—unavailable except to some 600 of the thousands dying of cancer each year.

In fact, at a time when government researchers were discovering reasons to make the drug a high priority, the source of it—the bark of the Pacific yew tree—was being mowed down and burned with a vengeance.

How could this happen? Bureaucratic bungling and good intentions foiled by everything from ignorance to greed.

It's a story—revealed in scores of interviews and government documents— that raises fundamental questions about forestry practices such as clear-cutting and slash burning, about the diversity of our dwindling natural resources, and about the way pharmaceuticals are developed and sold.

The cast of characters is wide-ranging: from a former Walla Walla gun-shop owner who lost his family's fortune by gambling on yew trees to hopeful scientists working at Bristol-Myers Squibb Co., the nation's second largest pharmaceutical company.

A Congressional committee is investigating the exclusive deal the cancer institute gave Bristol-Myers to develop the drug—called Taxol—and a grand jury is investigating what appears to be the widespread theft of yew trees from government lands.

"It's filled with cheating, lying and romance; every element is in this yew business," said Dominic Daley, a forester and sometime gold miner who collected yew bark for a while.

"The whole thing just smells," said Patrick Connolly, the most experienced yew bark collector in Oregon...

The yew is scattered around southeastern Alaska, Washington, Oregon, Idaho, Montana and northern California. Logging eliminated the tree in some areas, greatly diminished it in others.

One U.S. Forest Service document tells how 85 percent of the yew trees disappeared from a forest near Ashland, Ore., where they flourished. In other parts of southwest Oregon, good stands remain where timber companies got sloppy and left them behind.

But the Forest Service doesn't know how many yews are inside its boundaries because only commercially valuable trees were inventoried.

And when a contract to collect yews was let out, it went to someone who had never collected it before and who was not able to fulfill it.

When he learned that his guess of $2.74 was the low bid, the winner of the bid said "Great, what do I do now?"

He was unaware that bark when delivered weighed half as much as when cut, or that bark was easy to peel between April and September when the sap is running but impossible to peel without machinery during the winter months. When he got started in August, he had only one month to collect bark. With all his problems, he delivered only 13,000 of the 60,000 pounds he promised—and six months late.

By June 1990, cancer institute officials saw they were two years behind on their supply...

Part 2

Hazel Roberts of Tacoma died of cancer three weeks ago, having never gotten a promising drug called Taxol that seemed like a life preserver out of reach to her in the final months of her life.

Roberts, 67, nearly qualified among a handful of women chosen to participate in trials with the experimental drug, but by the time limited quantities were available three months ago her ovarian cancer had spread beyond hope.

...To make the drug more available, the government this year granted a near monopoly to one huge drug company, Bristol Myers Squibb. They did it because:

- No company would pursue an expensive drug program without overall control. But Bristol Myers, when asked if it would have done the research to develop taxol without the special government deal, said "We might have; we never had to face that decision."
- Foreign companies might buy up the only approved source of taxol—the bark of yew trees that grow wild in the northwest—and use it for patients overseas. But Bristol Myers is already testing patients with Taxol in Europe this year and Japan next year. It plans to sell Taxol overseas as well as in the U.S.
- The government can't market a drug even when the government scientists discover it.

Eleven-Year-Old Robber

A major part of news is the unusual nature of an event. We have become used to the usual, even when it is negative, like accidents, robberies, or drug deals. But when something out of the ordinary happens, that is clearly news.

Watch how Carolyn Koperdak of the *Lorain (O.) Morning Journal* handles the unusual angles in this Sept. 8, 1992, story.

BOY, 11, HELD IN ROBBERY:
LOADED GUN AIMED AT DAIRY MART CLERK

LORAIN—It wasn't a child's game of cops and robbers when an 11-year-old boy armed with a loaded 22-caliber black steel handgun pulled off the armed robbery of a Dairy Mart early yesterday morning.

"Just when you think you've seen it all, something comes along to shock you," said Police Capt. Cel Rivera. "This is the type of thing you only see in New York, Chicago or LA."

The boy was arrested yesterday at 8 A.M., four hours after reportedly robbing the Dairy Mart at 2808 Broadway. He is being held in the Lorain County Detention Home on two counts of aggravated robbery. He is accused of robbing the same store Sept. 1.

Rivera said the boy, who stands 5-foot-3, was calm and calculating, with the persona of an adult criminal.

"You get other 11-year-olds in here, for petty theft or something, you put them in a holding cell and they're crying. You spend time calming them down or letting them call their

15

moms," said Rivera. "Not this one. He wasn't overwhelmed or impressed about the idea of being locked up or in a holding cell.

"He threatened to kill an officer and said 'Nothing's going to happen to me anyways.' He was calm...but the things he says are very calculated and callous."

Dressed in sneakers, long shorts and a blue shirt, the boy walked into the store at 4 A.M. He had already stolen the steel automatic handgun from his mother and had climbed down a utility pole to exit his bedroom window, Rivera said.

The gun was immediately pointed at the first person he met in the store's front aisle—a 52-year-old sales clerk.

"If you don't give me the money, I'll put a hole through you," the boy was quoted as saying. After the clerk handed over the money from the register in a brown paper bag, the boy went on a shopping spree, Rivera said.

"This is no seasoned armed robber," said Rivera. "He took his time. He asked for two Playboys, two black Malcolm X hats and some cigarettes."

The boy fled the store on foot with a 16-year-old "look out" who was waiting outside. The boys ran to the 16-year-old's home two blocks away and divided the loot—less than $60—on the front porch.

From descriptions and information that the suspect stuttered, Patrolman Larry Meek identified the 11-year-old as the suspect. Police called his mother and searched the West 22nd Street home, but could find no evidence.

At 8:09 A.M., the mother called police and said she was holding her son after chasing him on Broadway. The two boys were coming from a fast-food restaurant on East 28th Street, where they had bought some food. His mother yelled at them to stop.

The boy dropped the gun and took off running. He stopped after his mother told him the police were after him and were going to shoot him, Rivera said.

At the police station, the boy admitted to both robberies. Witnesses said that during the first robbery, Sept. 1, the boy came in and out of the store four times. One time he bought cookies. Another time he played video games. The last time, at 2:40 A.M., he pulled out a gun.

"It was the same clerk who said a male came in, stood in the doorway with a handgun in his hand, and demanded money," Rivera said.

But the clerk described the suspect as a 20-year-old

male, about 160 pounds. When the clerk said the suspect stuttered, officers began to suspect the 11-year-old, Rivera said.

As far as the officers could tell, the boy didn't rob for drugs or for someone else. He has a criminal history since the age of 8 that lists numerous accounts of petty theft, breaking and entering, criminal trespassing and domestic violence, Rivera said.

"This is a young child who developed the idea that whenever he wants something, he has the right to take it," Rivera said. "Now he's elevated to using a loaded pistol. I think they're going to need the wisdom of Solomon over in the Juvenile Court to determine what to do with this one."

The boy will face the charges during a hearing today at the detention home. The 16-year-old was arrested for two counts of complicity to aggravated robbery and receiving stolen property.

Rivera said he believes the boy should serve prison time and get long-term counseling.

"You're not talking about a kid who's remorseful," he said. "You're talking to someone who said 'Nothing's going to happen to me...' a kid with a propensity for violence, well on his way to prison. Yet, you don't want to give up on him."

Mysterious Death

Some stories are sad and pull at your emotions. One of these is "The solitary death of Suzan Carter," reported by Jonathan Heller and edited by Ina Chadwick in *The Fairpress* of Westport, Conn., on Oct. 31, 1991. The paper has since been merged with another local paper.

Follow this main story, which was accompanied by two or three other stories, and note how many sources Heller talks to, and how he handles the mystery of the story. Although reporters usually avoid using questions in their stories (readers want answers, not questions), Heller uses them properly here.

Suzan Carter led a life of solitude in her dungeon-like apartment in Norwalk. One day in January 1989 she laid down on her bed, curled up in a fetal position, and died.

She lay dead in that condominium—tucked away on a side street a few blocks from Norwalk Center—for nearly three years, somehow slipping through society's cracks.

"It's almost like a *National Enquirer* story. It's totally bizarre," said Robert Horowitz, Carter's former boss.

"She was a very quiet, private person. She was going through some personal and physical problems at the same time, and the combination just overwhelmed her," Horowitz said.

It is the story of depthless despair, one that has everyone asking the same questions: How come no one discovered her body for so long? Didn't she have a family? What happened when her bills started piling up?

These things are clear: Suzan Carter, who would be 44 now, was an unhappy woman who suffered severe health ailments. She married three times; two ending in divorce and one in annulment. She was fired from her job as a bookkeeper and had to go on welfare.

A real estate agent and locksmith found her last Monday after opening up the foreclosed, cobweb-strewn condominium at 7-9 Arch Street for sale. Police estimated the date of death by newspapers, a TV guide, an uncashed welfare check and opened mail in her kitchen. Carter's body, however, was remarkably well-preserved because of the cool, almost cave-like atmosphere in the basement dwelling, said Dr. H. Wayne Carver, the chief state medical examiner. The heat and electricity had long since been cut off for non-payment.

"This is only the second time in my career I've seen something like this," Carver said. "She was mummified. It's the same way the Egyptians did it. Sure, they used magic and chemicals, but basically what worked was drying."

The cause of death is difficult to determine after so much time, Carver said, but authorities have ruled out foul play. Sources said Carter suffered from emphysema, a hip disorder and possible diabetes and alcoholism.

Her mother, Ruth Krampitz, was apparently the last relative to speak with Carter. Telephone records show that Krampitz called her daughter Jan. 26, 1989, and the two spoke for 37 minutes.

Then no contact. The family visited the silent apartment repeatedly, called Carter's friends, and even contacted Horowitz, Carter's former employer, to see if she had used him as a reference in a job search. They also tried to trace her by her Social Security number.

Sometime in late spring or early summer of that year, one of her brothers filed a missing persons report with Norwalk police. Police, however, have said they can't find that report.

No one apparently noticed the odor of decomposition, probably because Carter's basement apartment was isolated at the end of a long hall. The storage and laundry rooms are off another wing in the basement.

A neighbor who refused to identify herself said, "I didn't even know there was a condominium at the end of that hallway."

After some time family members ceased visiting the apartment and leaving notes under the door. Jeffrey Tager of Bloomfield, the family lawyer, said they were denied access to the dwelling and were "led to believe" by the Berkeley Square condominium association that the home had been searched by police. It is unknown why the family never insisted on searching the apartment themselves.

Anita Schmidt, the condominium association's president, said the family never contacted the association. "They may have talked to someone who lived here, but not the association." She said she could not have denied them access to the apartment since the association doesn't have keys to any of the units.

In June 1989 Carter's 1975 Pontiac was tagged as an abandoned vehicle and towed to the parking lot of a nearby office building, although its whereabouts are unknown.

Her mortgage company continued to pay the taxes on the condominium, the last payment having been received in July. However, the bank initiated foreclosure proceedings in November 1989.

[The story is also accompanied by three sidebars, one detailing clues that should have told someone that something had happened to Suzan Carter. Another points out that the apartment had been built illegally, with no zoning or code enforcement permits, and therefore was now sealed and closed forever. The third digs into whether missing person reports were filed, and gives family and police sides to the controversy.]

The Placement Puzzle

Students are a significant subgroup in any college town, and the largest "public" (group of people with a common interest) on any campus. Notice how Jane Prendergast of *The Cincinnati Enquirer* covers this subject in the following story, which ran May 8, 1992, p. 1.

Notice especially how she includes several different sources, including students, college officials and industry sources to give a balanced presentation.

GRADUATES BRACING FOR TOUGH JOB MARKET: SOME COLLEGE SENIORS EXPECT THE WORST

Just six weeks before graduation from the University of Cincinnati, Mikki Smith is almost at ease about not having a job.

The job market's uncertainty, her own uncertainty about what to do with an English literature degree and her financial uncertainty have left her with one choice: take some time off to save money, then go to graduate school.

"It's a little scary right now," said the 21-year-old senior from Independence, Ky. "But I think this is the best thing for me."

Beginning this weekend and continuing through the summer, area colleges and universities will unleash more than 11,000 graduates. Among them: Nearly 1,500 people with master's and doctoral degrees; 16 new rabbis; more than 350 medical doctors and lawyers.

Nationally, 1 million people will graduate from college this spring and summer. Some of the graduates know what they will do; 1 in 10 will leave school with job offers, according to a study done at Michigan State University.

But with today's job market—some experts call it the worst they've seen—many will leave school not knowing what the future holds.

"They graduate in June saying 'OK, world, I want a job now,'" said Patrick Scheetz, director of Michigan State's collegiate employment research institute. "Well, this time the world may not have anything for them."

He estimates that hiring of graduates will drop by 10 percent from last year. That's on top of a 9.8 drop last year and a 13.3 drop in 1990.

Yaulonda Carter is one who hasn't landed a job. A March graduate of Ohio University in communication systems management, she has sought employment for almost a year. Finding nothing, she turned this week to a part-time minimum-wage job at a telemarketing company.

"It's very frustrating, a very big letdown to think that I've gone to school for five years, kept my grades up, and still have to take something less than I want," said Carter, 25, of Roselawn. "To have to settle for less is very disappointing."

But she plans to continue to look for a job in the morning while she works in the afternoons and evenings.

"I know there's a job out there for me, I just have to keep looking for it. I have to keep telling myself that."

The new graduates, Scheetz said, are pushing into a market full of people laid off by companies downsizing. The reality for graduates, he said, is that they have less experience than many others competing for the same jobs.

Taking a part-time job related to your field might be a good move, said Katrina Jordan, associate director of UC's career placement office. "That way, the students have just a little more time to look for a permanent position or to come up with another career alternative. And the part-time job may lead to something full time."

Sarah DuMont of Withamsville, Xavier University's valedictorian, has held her 4.0 grade point for four years and will take the summer off before job hunting. A communications art/electronic media major, she works part-time on the switchboard for radio stations WEBN-FM and WLW-AM.

"In this business, you need to have your foot in the door—this job gives me that," DuMont said. She said she'd be willing to go wherever she has to go for a job in promotions or programming.

The local hiring picture is mixed. No specific numbers of hires were available from Procter and Gamble or Cincinnati Gas and Electric, but a P&G spokesman said recruiting and hiring were steady. At CG&E, however, hiring for non-union jobs that would go to graduates with degrees in engineering or computer science is "about as grim as you can get," said Bruce Stoecklin, media services director. "We don't expect to hire anybody in that category this year."

From General Electric, where 2,800 employees at 11 plants across the country face layoffs, a more specific picture: The local Evendale plant hired 66 recent college graduates last year, 42 this year, said spokesman Paula Kolstedt. Virtually all are in engineering or information systems.

Rick Hearin, director of Miami University's Career Planning and Placement Office, says though he does not want to sound "like a Pollyanna," the job news locally isn't all gloom and doom. The biggest difference in the job market this year, he said, is in the level of students just under the top 15 to 20 percent of the class.

The top students "get jobs even in a tough market," Hearin said. "The next tier often do, too, but not always. There just are not enough jobs to go around."

A survey of its 1991 graduates by the College of Mt. St. Joseph showed good job news: of the 250 graduates who responded, 86.8 percent had full-time jobs, were in graduate school or were seeking internships. Professional placement rates were 100 percent in such fields as chemistry, math, nursing, paralegal, secondary and special education.

Anna Fiehler, who graduates from Miami on Sunday with a bachelor's degree in mathematics and statistics, is avoiding the job market for now. After barely making it through Kettering Fairmont High School in suburban Dayton, with a 1.9 grade point average, she's now a math whiz headed for graduate school. She plans to meet the job market in six years with a doctorate in math.

"I don't think I ever wanted to see school again after high school," Fiehler said. "But now, I just don't want to stop. And hopefully the job market will be better in six years."

Miami's placement office made an extra effort this year to coach students against assuming the worst about the job market.

"There's no question that some people are using today's headlines to cop out," Hearin said. "We've been counseling our kids. Don't make it easy for your competitor to get the job by just dropping out."

Things to Remember

- Not everything that happens is news.
- News stories come in different forms, but all should be of interest to readers.
- Not all news stories are of equal interest to all readers. You have to provide all elements of society with news they need.
- All news stories are not the same. There are generally accepted principles for why some stories are more important to a given audience than others. They have to do with timing, how close the story is to you, how many people will be concerned about it, etc.

Exercises

1. Study your local newspaper, a regional newspaper that serves your area, or a radio or television newscast. How many of the stories are of direct interest to you? Can you tell why the editors of each paper or newscast chose the stories they did? Does this story selection indicate they know their audience

well? Which of the stories are "hard news" and which are "soft news"?

2. Be prepared to analyze a section of a newspaper and determine which of the news values listed in this chapter are the most important for each of the stories. Are there stories that include several of the news values?

2
Newsroom Pressures and Pleasures

"I have made the letter longer than usual because I lack the time to make it short."—Blaise Pascal

In This Chapter

Dealing with deadlines.
The importance of accuracy.
Understanding what audiences need.
Working within the structure of a newsroom.
Learning how to manage your time well.
The satisfactions of working in the media.

MAGAZINES have a deadline once a week, sometimes once a month. Dailies have a deadline every day, television station news departments have three or four a day, and radio news can have a deadline every half hour.

Associated Press and the wire services, which service newspapers, radio and television, have a deadline every minute.

The Pressure of Deadlines

Some of you will understand deadlines, because you have worked on newspapers or in the electronic media. Others will be frightened at the prospect of having to do a news story in less than a day. Most beginning writers are used to reports or themes being due in weeks, rather than days.

Deadlines are one of several important facts of life in the news business. They color everything that happens. The public, which picks up its paper when it gets home, or sits down to the evening news, has only the slightest idea of the pressures reporters are under.

Understanding why these pressures are necessary can permit the reporter to operate under them more easily. Knowing that these pressures *will* develop permits the reporter to put them in the back of his or her mind before starting to write. It provides a more complete picture of what the reporter should expect before starting to write.

A deadline is the latest time a story can be completed. It is established by working backward from the time the reader or audience gets its news.

If the newspaper must reach readers by 4:00 P.M. so they can look at it when they get home from work, allow one or two hours for distribution to the homes, an hour or more for printing, and another hour for putting the paper in final form. So the last minute a story could be accepted might be 12:00 P.M., or noon.

And that would be the very last minute any news could be accepted. But since an entire newspaper can't be printed at one time, sports scores from last night's games might be due by 6:00 A.M., and various other departments would have deadlines of 8:00 and 9:00 A.M. Much of the feature material would be done the day before the paper is printed.

Television news is much the same. Stories on the 6:00 P.M. news must be arranged so that all editing and other preparation is done well in advance. There is much to coordinate and organize well before the "opening bell."

The mass media must be organized around mass production to reach a mass audience. This puts pressure on the reporter to fit into the system. And since this is a habit that will not develop overnight, it needs to be practiced at the earlier stages of the reporter's education.

Like other work habits, the ability to deal with deadlines can be developed. The key is organizing the writer's time, and understanding (and accepting) why stories have to be completed long before the public will see or hear them. It requires a mental discipline, which in turn is soothed by the satisfaction of seeing your name in print or your efforts go out over the air. It isn't easy, but then a lot of things aren't.

Newsroom communication is often quite difficult, because several stories are worked on at one time, and deadline pressures mount. The more work done well before deadline the better, because it eases last-minute pressure.

Computers are an integral part of the media, and an integral part of meeting deadlines. Most reporters need not go beyond word processing, but investigative reporters need to know how to use databases and spreadsheets. As computers advance, reporters will be expected to keep up with the advances.

While computers do work with blinding speed, reporters must do a lot of homework to know the particular programs they are working on. Not only must they know how to write, but also they must know how to do it in a computer format, on deadline, and often from a remote site at the last minute.

Computers require the reporter to do more work than before. The reporter must write, edit, set type, and often put headlines or special instructions in the story. It can be done, but it can be very demanding.

The Pressure of Accuracy

Assume for a minute that when you come into the classroom in the morning, the person sitting next to you says, "I see that you have been charged with driving while intoxicated. There's a story in the morning paper."

You would turn pale, your pulse rate would go up, and in a minute you would blush. What makes it worse is knowing it is not true but having thousands of people think it is true.

Obviously, there has been a mistake, but your reputation has suffered nonetheless. In the media, this is known as libel (injury to reputation), and in this case let us assume it was caused by a careless reporter who misspelled someone else's name.

By the time the paper makes a retraction, you are afraid your reputation will never recover. You are likely to sue the newspaper, to give them grief for the grief they caused you.

The cardinal rule of news is get it right the first time. Joseph Pulitzer, whose name is now attached to the famous Pulitzer prizes in journalism, once said that the three most important things in journalism were "accuracy, accuracy and accuracy."

This subject is discussed in the chapter about law, but for the moment remember that in spite of time pressures, there can be no compromise on accuracy. Professionalism and personal pride call for news writers to do it right, to be accurate at all times. It is necessary to double check the spelling, addresses, and facts given by police or other sources, and think everything through carefully.

The Pressure of Completeness

There are one or two other major concerns news writers need to have that come from competitive pressures and the nature of the mass media. Just because something has been accurately reported does not mean it is a solid story. You must check with other sources to verify what the first source told you. Almost never does a one source story get into the paper or onto television if it has any controversial aspects to it.

An incomplete story is just as bad as an inaccurate story. Saying a person has left her job, but not saying she has resigned from it, is not correct. Saying a company has been taken to court without trying to get a public statement from that company is an incomplete report. Saying a candidate for office was arrested for drunk driving 20 years ago without asking him and finding out that he was cleared of all charges is an incomplete story.

Often beginning reporters wonder why editors ask them for additional sources or check that the facts they are using have been verified. With libel judgments running into the millions of dollars recently, every story must be accurate. Fact checking has to be done before the story goes out, not after, because after is too late.

This often means that on investigative stories, editors will require that stories be in several days ahead of the deadline, so that they can check it out with lawyers and ask for rewrites by the reporter if necessary. This adds to the time pressure reporters are under, but it is necessary to be certain the story is accurate.

The Pressure to Interest Audiences

Presidential candidate Adlai Stevenson once joked, "Editors are people who separate the wheat from the chaff—and print the chaff."

At a recent state press convention, a discussion on whether the press was believed by the public was about to end. The last question had to do with credibility as opposed to relevance, and the speaker, a nationally known researcher, said "Relevance is a far greater problem than credibility."

In a world of deadline pressures compounded by legal pressures, reporters and editors have little extra time to plan ahead. Yet if they do not provide information and stories that make the reader stop and read, or the viewer look up long enough to understand the story, they have failed in their mission.

And in the era of the 1990s, with increasing competition between newspapers, radio, and television for the time and attention of the audience, the requirement to make stories as interesting as possible within the facts given is even more critical.

Please understand that there are very few earthquakes, visits by the president to your town, or interviews with persons who have discovered the cure for a major disease. The number of major stories a person handles in a lifetime is very small, while the number of routine stories is in the thousands. The way the reporter handles routine stories and makes them as interesting as possible is very important.

One of the old axioms in news is that headlines must "tell and sell" the story. Stories themselves must be written in a form that is interesting enough to make the reader stop and read the entire story. In many cases, the writer is not going to be successful, but the effort has to be made.

If the mission of news is to help people understand society, and to make the world a little better place in which to live, care must be taken in the presentation to be sure the public understands the main point. Future chapters talk about clarity of writing, making stories interesting, and being sure the audience understands the main point.

Writing for a purpose is not easy. While there is "fun" in writing feature stories, feature stories are only some of the stories the reporter usually writes. Working within the framework of facts and verification takes much of the freedom and creativity out of writers' hands. In years to come, the writer may specialize in features if they have "jumped all of the other hurdles" that face beginning reporters.

Newsroom Hierarchy

In most newsrooms, there are usually more reporters than there are editors. As in any business or organization, many of the decisions are made at the top and then relayed down to the reporters through the editors.

However, because of the time pressures and the complexities of completing stories on time, communication in most newsrooms is not as good as it should be. There is not enough time to explain every decision to every reporter in a full and complete manner. Reporters should understand this, and make their own efforts to ask the questions they feel are important—after deadline.

Pressures on editors at large papers are such that in the mid-1980s, a study (Giles 1983) indicated that 40 percent of managing editors (those who manage other editors) had enough stress to be taking medicine or seeing doctors for answers to their health problems. Understanding the nature of these pressures will make the transition to the newsroom much easier. Few jobs have the daily pressure of a newsroom, whether it is a newspaper, radio station, or television newsroom.

The Pressure for Story Ideas

Each day the newspaper starts with blank pages, referred to in the jargon of the business as number of columns, or newshole. Six to seven days a week, 52 weeks a year, blank news pages every day. The same problem exists in the electronic media, but they usually have even less time to fill their allotted space.

The reporter who comes in with story ideas for the area they are covering, or who quickly and diligently develops story ideas offered by others, is a jewel in a newsroom. He or she is also promoted more quickly than those with less enthusiasm for their work.

Developing story ideas comes from within—within the newsroom and within the reporter. Groups of reporters and editors will get together for "brainstorming" sessions, and reporters are expected to contribute. Personality features are numerous on most beats. Reporters, surprisingly enough, do not always read their own paper, much less competing papers, but these sources are full of ideas worth developing into stories. This is not to mention television newscasts or the many magazines covering almost every imaginable interest a reader might have.

College journalists should consider the courses they take outside of their journalism sequence as sources for story ideas. A campus community has faculty experts in almost every field. The student reporter's job is to find a subject of interest to her readers and get background and comments from someone who is an authority in that field. The professional reporter's task is the same, but finding authorities may not be as easy at first.

Time Management

One editor told of a reporter coming back from a meeting and getting ready to write a story. The reporter asked the same two questions almost every reporter asks: "How long do you want the story and how much time to I have?" The answers were, let us say, 500 words and 90 minutes to complete the story.

The reporter then spent 45 minutes at lunch and 15 minutes talking with other reporters and going through the mail. This left 30 minutes to complete a story, which he did—with barely two to three minutes to spare.

Before you despair, think of your own work habits. When you have a term paper to do, do you complete it with three weeks to spare, or with a day or two left? When you have an exam, do you study a week before the exam, or the last day or two? Unfortunately, we all have the same habits.

But in a newsroom situation, where each part of the team must work together for the product to be done professionally and on time, these habits lead to poor work, frayed nerves, and unnecessary pressure.

Procrastination also removes from the picture the best tool the reporter has for improving his or her story—the rewrite, which will be discussed later. For now, let's just say that any story worth writing is worth rewriting, and a reporter ought to allow time to do the story at least twice (perhaps more) before turning it in.

In my 30-plus years in the news and teaching business, I have yet to see a rewritten story that was not significantly better than the first draft.

Satisfaction

A discussion of this nature would not be complete without discussing why reporters spend the long, pressure-filled hours working in newsrooms. It isn't for the money, which is not great, or the pleasure of facing empty pages and fast-approaching deadlines each morning.

Many reporters would not do anything else. They were born curious, or developed curiosity at an early age, and their reward is knowing what goes on as it happens. These people enjoy explaining to others the things that might make their lives easier or more fruitful.

Some reporters are in it because they "live their beats." Sports reporters, regardless of their age, still enjoy the competition and the buildup before a game. Police reporters enjoy the mystery, the chase, and dealing with the criminal system. Countless specialists in such areas as automobiles, food, medicine, and government are respected for their knowledge and known far and wide for their contributions to the field.

The journalist is society's watchdog, but he or she also knows well that a watchdog doesn't always bite. People need to be warned about pending problems, but they also need to be reminded of the basic goodness of human nature. This is the role of the feature writer, the person who understands human nature, or digs behind the scenes for further interpretation of a breaking story.

Reporters often leave journalism to become novelists, playwrights, or screenwriters. Their work draws national and international attention, and is preserved in libraries and on film.

All of these people are interested in the human condition, in what makes man tick or fall apart, and in what society can learn from the trials and tribulations it undergoes each day. Their satisfaction is helping the rest of us understand what is going on in the world.

Things to Remember

- Deadlines must be met for news to get to the reader or the audience on time. Reporters can and must learn how to handle their time, making use of "slow" times to avoid last-minute rushes.
- What an audience wants and needs is not always easy to determine, and is not always what the reporter or editor thinks the audience wants or needs. News writers have to work at understanding audiences.
- Despite the pressures and the problems of writing for others, rather than for yourself, most reporters and editors would rather be doing this kind of work than anything else.

Exercise

1. Arrange for an individual or group tour of a news medium, or ask if you can "tag along" or "shadow" a reporter during a day's work. See for yourself the pressures—and the satisfactions—of keeping hundreds or thousands of others informed on what is important to them.

3
Reader Habits: Why News Is Written the Way It Is

In This Chapter

"Tell me why this is important to me."
"I have so many other things to do right now."
"I've got to get going. What is the point of this?"
"I'm sorry, could you repeat that? You lost me there."

IT MAY be hard to accept, especially for someone who has spent hours writing a news story, but the audience does not share the same excitement for your story that you do.

Newspaper readers may be watching television, having breakfast, talking to the dog, or any number of other activities while they are reading the newspaper. The average reader spends perhaps 15 minutes a day on a newspaper.

A television viewer flips through the channels, watching parts of one program and going on to another before the first is completed.

Radio is an accompanying activity; you listen to it while you drive, while you are having a picnic, or while you are reading or studying.

Attention Span

It is critical that the writer understand that the audience's attention is not 100 percent, because this has an effect on how the story is written. If the reader is not paying attention, the writer must be very careful to be as direct and clear as possible.

The lead has to be something that makes readers pay attention. It has to catch their eye and make them stop doing the other things they are doing at the time.

Looking at this from "the other side," it also means that if a lead is dull, boring, or so complicated that the reader doesn't understand it, the audience goes back to what it was doing. It is easier to "tune out" than it is to fight a complex sentence or go through something that has been heard or read before. If the audience has to struggle to find the point of the story, it is easier to go on to something else. No one is forcing them to read the story or listen to the broadcast.

Problem Solving

The reader is looking for answers to help make life easier. He wants to know what is happening in the world, but more importantly, what impact it will have. If an out-of-town bank goes out of business, is this going to affect the local bank? If California is suffering from a drought, is this going to increase the price of fruits and vegetables grown there? If the city is thinking about an income tax, how much will that cost him personally?

The audience "scans" the papers and news broadcasts, looking for clues to things that might influence their lives. If the headline doesn't indicate that the reader should be concerned with the story, she goes on to something else. This is not all bad. If a reader finds that the day's news doesn't change her life very much, she can be satisfied that she might be able to rest for another day or two. As one joker said "always check the obits first. If your name is not there, go on to the rest of the paper."

This also explains why newspaper sales are higher after a winning football game. The reader, always uncertain, wants to verify what he saw in person or on television. It makes him feel good to see that he agrees (or disagrees) with the sports writer, and it gives him a chance to check out just how many total yards Barry Sanders had when the game was over. You know the result, you just want to be sure everyone else knows it.

Competition for Time

Assume you have a few minutes free after dinner and before you start studying for the evening. How many things can you consider doing?

There is the day's mail, the newspaper (possibly several of them), radio, television, national news magazines, talking with your friends, the game room, the telephone for a call to friends or parents, perhaps a letter from home. There are many choices to be made.

So it is in the non-college world. People come home from work at night, eat dinner, and choose their evening activity: newspapers, radio, magazine, evening game shows, or 40 cable TV stations. There might be a meeting to go to, a sports event to watch, or calls to friends or relatives. There might be business to conduct or a marketing research phone call to answer. If the family has children, their activities dictate what the parents will be doing.

The point is this: in any person's life, choices must be made. Whether to read the paper or listen or watch the news depends on available time and what other activities are scheduled. And if you do start to read or watch the news, you may be interrupted in the middle of your reading or watching. Life is like that.

The reporter must understand this in order to write news stories that will be read:

- Many stories must be short and direct, or the reader will tune out.
- They must be as relevant to the reader's life as they can be, otherwise the reader will tune them out.
- They must be as interesting as the facts allow, or else the audience goes on to something it considers more interesting.
- They must be "perfectly clear," so the reader doesn't get the wrong impression if he or she is not paying full attention.

Spelling and Grammar

A retired gentleman called the local newspaper once or twice a week to point out grammatical mistakes. He may or may not have been an English teacher, but he was determined that his calls were going to make the paper "shape up."

When he died, his children found an entire drawer full of clippings from the newspaper, with misspellings and factual errors circled. The survivors called the newspaper, asking if the paper wanted the collection.

Perhaps no other single factor is as easy for the reader to identify with as spelling. Readers were all responsible for spelling when they were in school. They expect newspapers and television stations to spell properly and radio announcers to pronounce properly. It may be the audience's way of getting back at the media for reporting news the audience doesn't want to hear or read.

Of the thousands of students I have had over the years, only a small percentage have *not* had their names spelled wrong in a paper. I ask them each semester. It helps to bring home how such inaccuracies feel to others.

Whatever the reason, spelling and grammar have become sore points with readers and editors. Readers take it as a sign of weakness, and will not trust the paper on other things if it does not spell correctly. Editors look at resumes and clippings submitted by job candidates and throw out those that have even one spelling error.

The reporter must check spelling on the final draft before turning in the copy. Go ahead and write, get the facts straight and let the story flow in a natural way. But on the final check before you turn it in, double check the spelling and grammar. Dictionaries should be available at all times.

The reporter must also be conscious that anyone's knowledge of grammar and spelling is always incomplete. No one can be 100 percent sure on all spellings and all matters of grammar. Be willing to double check (or rewrite) before turning in the final copy.

Straightforward Statements

A three-hour governmental meeting can involve a dozen or more discussions. Some will be long and complicated, others will be short and to the point. There may be 10, 15, or more persons involved in various discussions during the meeting.

The job of the reporter is to make sense of this complex activity and to boil it down to one or two statements that summarize the meeting for those who did not attend. Most governmental meetings have very few members of the public in attendance, unless they have a grievance or a point of view to offer. Elected officials rely on the media to tell the public what is happening.

And readers are not concerned that the reporter has 15 people, 12 discussions, and three hours to sort through. They want to know, in the headline if possible, what went on at that meeting that concerns them.

The problem is not in writing straightforward declarative sentences. The problem is in sorting through three hours of meeting to determine what is relevant to the audience and then stating that in a simple declarative sentence. This is not a writing problem, it is a thinking problem.

And with deadlines being what they are, most reporters either write the story immediately after the meeting or very early the next morning.

This means the reporter must *anticipate* what is going to happen so that he or she can make judgments on what was important or relevant at the time the meeting is going on. The task then becomes a matter of judging which of the 12 decisions is the most important and is of the most concern to the most readers.

And once that decision has been made, the reporter has to make a straightforward declarative sentence that tells what was important.

A straightforward sentence is, "There will be no parade at City Park next week because of the fear of protesters."

A complex, improper lead would be "After an hour of often heated debate last night before city council, those who wanted to cancel a proposed parade at City Park got their wish. Council voted 5–2 with one abstention to deny a permit to the Anti-War Protest, Inc. group."

If you get the impression that all of the thought and most of the decisions have to be made *before* you start to write, you are correct.

Readers may want to know about the discussion that went into the decision, but they first want to know what that decision was.

That is what calls for a straightforward statement. Readers expect you to make it easy for them.

Sentence Length

One of the major differences between journalistic writing and theme writing is the length of the sentences and paragraphs.

When you write a term paper, you are taught (quite properly) to use modifiers, to qualify statements that need qualifying, and to set the reasons for each of your arguments. This often leads (again quite properly) to long sentences. In terms of typing on a computer screen or a standard sheet of paper, your sentences may go several lines. Combining several of these sentences into one paragraph, you may have a typed paragraph that goes 10 or more lines.

This does not work in media writing for several reasons, many of which we have already discussed.

The audience wants to know right now and up front what is important. They do not want the history of the event. They do not want all of the qualifying statements first, although they must be included for accuracy. They want a simple declarative sentence so that they can make sense of the news as it pertains to them.

So, in the print media reporters try to come to the point directly. Qualifiers and "weasel words" must be included, but they come later.

The print media, primarily newspapers, also have another problem with sentences that are too long. One typed line in a normal newspaper column becomes two lines of type. Two become four, etc. If you were to run a six-line typed paragraph, it would become 12 lines of "copy" in a news story. Twelve lines without spacing would be more than one and one-half inches of solid copy. To a reader, this looks too long and complex, even if the sentences are short. They may turn away from solid blocks of copy, thinking it looks like a dictionary. This paragraph is already eight, going on nine lines, and you can see how difficult it is to read.

Just think what it would be like if the columns were narrow, as they are in newspapers.

The problem is somewhat similar in the radio and television news field. Just imagine you were "on the air," and had to watch several dials and get ready to insert a cassette. If the sentence is too long, you lose your place—and maybe your breath—and the newscast comes to a grinding halt while you find your place again. Better to use short sentences, keep your focus on the things you have to do, and know where to catch a breath.

How short should short sentences be? The length of a line or the number of lines is not the most important factor.

Don't be too short too often. Watch for this. Too many, too short is silly. It sounds like baby talk.

Say clearly what needs to be said and then stop. A simple, powerful declarative sentence will do it.

> "State Senator Tom Reigleman will retire at the end of his term."
>
> "Anderson Township residents are upset about their new taxes, and want to know why they were reassessed."
>
> "If you live in Green Springs, your taxes will go up about $50 next year."

Notice that none of these sentences have qualifying statements attached to them. Each would be perhaps one and one half or two lines in newspapers. None would cause an announcer to stop for breath halfway through the sentence.

Again, the writing seems easy, but the thinking that goes into this is not easy. It takes experience, but more than anything, it means you must think of the reader first.

Suggested Lengths

For 50 years, people who study writing have been saying that written leads are too long. Most of them are still too long. Leads have not become much shorter, with a couple of exceptions. *USA Today* makes a conscious effort to shorten its leads. The late Harry Stapler conducted a study of leads on 12 major American dailies in 1985, and found they averaged 28 words in their leads and 21 words in the second and third paragraphs.

Stapler said it was obvious reporters and editors were trying to include too much in the leads. They were trying to get all 5 Ws and an H into the leads.

In journalism, the five Ws and an H are Who, What, Where, When, Why, and How. These are the questions a reporter needs to ask to be sure she has gotten all of the important information in the story.

But trying to put everything into the lead means the first sentence of the story is too long. By the time readers get to the end of the sentence, they have forgotten what the first part of it was. This is termed short-term memory. People can only remember so many thoughts or read so many words before their brains become overloaded.

Sentence length is not the only factor. Complex words make a reader stop and think before going on to the next word. Legal terms such as *stare decisis* or *habeas corpus* are everyday talk for lawyers but would stop most readers on the spot.

Short, familiar words strung together into a long, flowing sentence—even 30 or more words—may be all right. If the reader has no trouble going from one idea to the next, the sentence can be longer and still easily understood. See the examples at the end of this chapter.

The solution to overly long sentences is to think the story through before starting to write. Ask what the main point of the story is and why it is being used. Some call this the sixth W—so what?

Unless news writers have determined what the main point of the story is before starting to write, they will try to put it in words while writing. This is why sentences get too long, too many qualifiers are added, and the story may seem to be confused. It is because the reporter is confused, and has not thought it through before starting to write.

Role Models

If you play basketball, you learn by watching the professional stars on television. If you are acting in the senior play, you might watch movies to see what you can learn about acting from the current popular stars. And if you would like to be in television news, you can watch network anchors to see how they handle the news. Finding role models for writing the news is not that easy. But it is very important.

Richard Marius of Harvard University says, "Every good writer I know has been a reader." Aspiring writers need to see how good writing is done so that they can understand what good writing is. It is not easy to define or point out, and the tricks of the trade in writing are many.

So during the time you are learning to write, you ought to be reading stories from others who have had courses like this. There are plenty of resources available to students in any part of the country, including departmental and university libraries and local newsstands, which can show you how professionals in the field write bright and lively stories.

Depending on your field of interest, there are examples of good writing in many magazines available at your bookstore. Choose an area you would like to write about, and see how the magazines develop different styles and personalities to their stories. Watch how stories start, proceed logically, and end. Notice tricks that are used to catch your attention.

Watch local newspapers for how they handle routine stories, which are the bread and butter of most newspapers. Watch Sunday newspapers for how they handle features. Papers with Sunday editions generally have large enough staffs so that they can specialize in feature stories, and their stories may be longer, more elaborate, and more educational than the routine stories found in most daily editions.

Watch especially *USA Today*, which has developed a style of its own in terms of short sentences, short stories, and extended features about selected topics each day. For traditional newspaper persons, *USA Today* is controversial because the stories are generally shorter than most news stories. When you read them, ask yourself if anything is missing, and if you would want longer or more stories. When you read the features, watch closely as to how many specific details are included in each story.

Many homes have copies of *Reader's Digest*. This is a good example of carefully edited stories, each with a clear angle or purpose, with short, direct, to-the-point sentences. This writing may look easy to you, but it has undergone considerable careful editing.

Reader's Digest also does a lot of personalizing, which is using people as the focus of their stories to illustrate a point. The reader feels as though he knows the person and the problem the person is working with. More about this when we discuss writing principles in chapter 21.

For those of you interested in sports, the writing in *Sports Illustrated* is well worth checking into. It is careful, clever, and makes you think. Again, none of this comes easy; these are some of the best writers in America, and most of the stories are written and rewritten carefully to make them as powerful as possible.

Another easy-to-find newspaper is the *Wall Street Journal*, which runs a page one feature each day. This feature, often far removed from the daily pressures of business, has become one of the most read and most awaited stories in newspapers each day.

You can't expect to write like the pros at the beginning, but you have to know what they are writing before you can do what they do. It pays to have a goal, and something to watch and follow as you go.

The Form for Your Copy

Your instructor will have specific suggestions for how your papers should look when they are completed. This will vary according to the medium you write for, but for most beginning classes the form is pretty much the same. Instructions for in-class and outside assignments may differ because of these variations. But the following instructions will apply to most student papers.

Put your name, the date, and a key word for the story (a "slug," such as Accident or Personality feature or Council Meeting) at the top left corner of the page. Do not use slugs that have whimsy, wit, or sarcasm in them because you most often put this on a computer and sometimes these wise remarks slip through. Never type anything on a computer that you don't want someone else to see.

Double space all stories so that corrections and suggestions can be written on the page.

Allow about one-third of the first page for space for your teacher to comment or your editor to make suggestions if you plan on using "hard copy" or paper. Similar provisions can be made on computer stories for the same reason.

An agreed-upon mark at the end of the story should be used. The most common is -30-, an old time printer symbol used on linotypes to indicate the end of a story.

If the story originates in the town you are in, there is no dateline, or name of city line, to start the story. If it comes from another city in your state, use the name of the city in this way: ANAHEIM. If it comes from another state, use the city and the state: MARLBORO, Mass. If it comes from a city well enough known that everyone knows where it is, use the city name alone: NEW YORK. See the *AP Stylebook* under Dateline for more information.

If you are doing a longer paper out of class, put your name on each page, and put More at the bottom of each page to indicate you are not completed. Copy editing symbols are a universal "language" that instructors and editors use to communicate with reporters and students. Since we are in the computer age, you may think you can make your corrections on the screen, but many changes are still made on paper, especially in longer series or in out-of-class assignments.

Copy Editing Symbols

These are the symbols to be used on paper. There are similar and very useful items to be used on most word-processing programs. Some, like the strike-through function in which the computer draws a line through a word or sentence, are not available on all programs.

TABLE 3.1   Copy Editing Functions

Copy Editing Function	On Paper	On Computer
Indent	L	Hit return, and/or Tab
Capitalize letter or word	Underline 3 times	Shift and Type CAPS
Transpose words	Jones Robert	Move one word
Change from word for number to the number	Nine means 9	Retype
Abbreviate	California becomes Cal.	Retype
Spell out in full	N.Y. becomes New York	Retype
Change from Caps to lower case letters	USE SLASH	Retype
Change from lower case to capital letters	three lines under letter or word	Retype
Close up space	astro naut	Delete space
Do not change what you suggested to change	Stet (let it stand) Minneapolis stet	Use original typing or retype as needed
Delete a word or several words	The dog was usually asleep, at this time	Click on word or words and hit delete, depending on program
Insert a word or words	The dog was usually asleep at this time.	

Examples of Well-Written Stories

We conclude this chapter with two articles that are written to be read quickly and easily. They are not simple stories; indeed, they are complex and deep stories. But they read well because the writers and editors understand short sentences and familiar words.

"Kidnaper Foiled"

"Kidnaper Foiled" averages 25 words to a sentence. The important word is averages, because some sentences are as short as six words, some as long as 47.

The key to readability in this story is the use of familiar words. The longest words in the story are yesterday, ignition, millionaire, ferocious, tenacious, and investigators, words that can be easily understood by anyone. The only words that may cause problems are *accosted*, which means to approach or confront, and *assiduously*, which means diligent or persevering. There is a noticeable lack of police terminology.

The story also has a fast pace, and even the long sentences are not hard to read because the parts flow logically. The longest sentence, 47 words, is easy to read. It starts, "I heard someone screaming..." and it is the fourth sentence from the end.

KIDNAPER FOILED—BRAVE NASHVILLE WOMAN FOILS KIDNAPING ATTEMPT
Spot News Individual award, Best of Gannett award
by Robert Sherborne and LaCrisha Butler,
The Nashville Tennessean

Andrea Conte, pistol-whipped and bloody, escaped a kidnaper yesterday by coolly switching off the ignition of her white Lincoln Town Car and jumping to safety.

"She turned off the ignition and while he was fumbling with that, she climbed back into the car and got out the back door," said Conte's husband, millionaire businessman and political figure Phil Bredesen.

Conte, 47, suffered a broken right cheek bone, a broken bone in her left hand, a gash on her scalp which required several stitches and various other bruises and minor cuts in a ferocious struggle with her kidnaper.

But her husband and police both say she was lucky to escape with these relatively minor injuries and credit her tenacious resistance to the well-dressed, middle-aged kidnaper.

"We don't know what his original intent was because his plan was spoiled by her bravery in fighting him off," said Sgt. Robert Moore, supervisor of the violent crimes unit of the Metro Police Department.

The kidnaper was still at large early today, but police had several leads they were pursuing.

The kidnaper accosted Conte as she arrived to open Conte-Philips, a gourmet food and cookware store she owns.

In his struggle with Conte in the parking lot of the Paddock Place shopping center on White Bridge Road, the kidnaper dropped a dress hat, a pair of reading glasses and a revolver-type pellet pistol, which investigators hope will yield fingerprints...

Police also plan to use computers to trace the license number of the late model white Lincoln Town Car with a brown leather interior. Witnesses provided investigators with a license number of the automobile which proved to be wrong.

Conte was resting last night at her spacious home at 1794 Chickering Road.

An independent and intensely private woman who assiduously shied away from the spotlight during her husband's unsuccessful campaigns for mayor and Congress last year, Conte declined to talk with reporters.

Bredesen, emerging from St. Thomas Hospital—where Conte spent five hours undergoing treatment for her injuries and having X-rays and other diagnostic tests—said she was "mad" about the incident.

It began about 9:45 A.M. on what was otherwise a normal winter day for the family.

Bredesen, who is currently working as a Medicaid consultant for Gov. Ned McWherter, left the family's home first and drove their son, Benjamin, to school on his way downtown.

Conte, as she customarily does, left the house shortly after her husband and drove to the gourmet food and cookware store.

When she pulled into the parking lot, there was a white Lincoln Town Car in the adjoining spot, with a bespectacled man reading in the front seat...

When Conte got out of her dark red Buick Somerset and reached into the back seat to get some parcels, the man also stepped out of his car, pointed the pellet pistol at Conte, and ordered her to get into his car.

She refused and instead, began screaming.

"I heard someone screaming and at first thought it may have been a child who didn't want to go to the doctor," said Jerry Strobel, manager of the Grand Ole Opry House, who had been shopping at the Beveled Edge and had just walked out the door.

"Then, I saw that this was more than that. The two people were struggling. She was being dragged into the car."

Number 978

Douglas Pardue, senior writer of the *Roanoke (Va.) Times & World-News*, won a Robert F. Kennedy citation for this January 26, 1985, story and a subsequent series entitled "Forgotten Homes, Forgotten People." It is a simple, solemn, straightforward story about a woman who froze to death at home when the temperature outside fell to 11 degrees below zero and she had no heat in the house.

The section used here averages about thirteen words per sentence. The longest words are companion, relatives, dignified, and electricity.

MADELINE ADAMS TATE: NOW SHE IS JUST A NUMBER

No. 978 was buried shortly before 9:30 Friday morning.

Three people, not counting the gravedigger and the funeral home employees, attended her burial.

One of the mourners didn't know No. 978, and the other two said they knew her only slightly. They'd seen her walking to and from her day jobs in Roanoke and thought they ought to come to the burial to show respect for a good honest woman who had worked hard all her life.

Richard Harris, the chaplain, didn't know her, but he chose a few Bible verses that seemed to apply.

It is better to rely in the Lord than put any trust in flesh, Harris read.

A few minutes was all it took. The three mourners left....

No name was on the small concrete marker on the grave, just the number 978 for the 978th person buried in Coyner Springs Cemetery, the cemetery Roanoke provides for the poor.

No. 978 died Monday. She froze to death in a shack she and a companion rented for $50 a month a few short blocks from city hall.

No. 978 had a name. Madeline Adams Tate. She was 76.

When she dozed off Monday night, the temperature dropped to 11 below zero, the lowest in 73 years.

On Monday morning, relatives of her companion for the past several years, George Williams, called police when no one came to the door. Williams was suffering from frostbite.

Madeline Tate was found on the floor with her feet next to the wood stove. The embers in the stove could barely warm a hand held close. There was no electricity in the house and the kitchen water pipes had burst.

Tate was wearing a red and gray dress, two floral print blouses, a blue sweater, a red bathrobe and black boots...

The city received no call in time to save Tate. But it did what it could: it paid for the funeral.

Madeline Adams Tate's short, dignified funeral cost $255.

Things to Remember

- Despite the fact that you will spend hours on a story, the reader may spend only minutes on it, if that. News media have to adapt to reader's lives, not the other way around.
- People reading newspapers or watching or listening to newscasts are probably doing something else at the same time. You have to come right to the point and be perfectly clear so they will not miss the point.
- Readers expect and deserve accuracy in facts and in spelling and grammar. This is a non-negotiable starting point, and all else comes after this.
- You can't know what good writing is unless you read good writing. Any professional needs to have good examples to follow.

Exercises

1. Check your library for books such as *The Best Writing of 1993* and other years, by the Poynter Institute and the American Society of Newspaper Editors. This volume is especially valuable because the editors talk to the reporters who did the outstanding writing.
2. Watch your newspapers, especially the Sunday metropolitan papers, for examples of features and other stories that show good writing. Don't expect that every story is going to be a prize winner, and learn to be critical in analyzing stories.
3. Watch especially how the writers make an effort to be accurate— but also interesting. Good news stories must have both to catch the reader's attention.
4. Watch for leads in newspapers and opening statements on television. Do these writers make a special effort to point out *your* point of interest first when they report stories?

4
Writer Habits

"Writing is very easy. All you do is sit in front of a typewriter keyboard until little drops of blood appear on your forehead."
—Red Smith, late sports editor of the *New York Times*

In This Chapter

The most common problems news writers have.

We have to get organized.

Putting it off until the last minute.

The critical difference between an idea and a first draft.

Telling a story versus listing everything in the first paragraph.

Understanding the need for revision and rewrite.

Respecting the reader's intelligence but understanding that some words and terms can be confusing.

UNTIL recently, not a great deal was known about how news reporters write. Most editors knew that reporters usually did not get stories done until the last minute, and that editing those stories was usually rushed for time.

The Coaching Movement

In recent years, several studies have looked into how reporters think about their stories, how they go about digging for information, and how writing coaches (persons who help reporters with writing) see reporters and their problems. More research needs to be done, but at least we are starting to have an idea of how reporters work.

Not surprisingly, reporters are much like the general population in several aspects. Understanding their problems before starting to write may be a great help. This is not to be considered as derogatory toward reporters, but to point out where problems exist and what reporters can do to make their writing more interesting.

The writing coach movement on American daily newspapers began in the mid-1980s. As newspapers face ever greater competition, efforts are being made across the country to make stories more interesting and to help writers do their work more effectively.

A study of writing coaches (Laakaniemi 1986) attempted to identify the major writing problems of reporters. The study included all of the persons known at that time to be helping daily newspaper reporters improve their writing.

The coaches said that reporters were not unlike students trying to "get themselves together" for studying and exams. Their greatest problem was organizing—both their material and their time.

The study found three problems that coaches thought needed the most work. (This is not to criticize the way reporters work, but to show how complex writing is and how even professional writers can improve their work and work habits. If beginning reporters can eliminate these problems early in their careers, they can be that much more effective in years to come.)

The three main problems were:

- Reporters don't organize their material before they start writing.
- Reporters don't spend enough time thinking before they start writing.
- Reporters don't read copy carefully before they turn it in.

These problems undoubtedly stem from the fact that the news is a hectic business. Reporters must find people, ask them questions, find others, ask them the same questions, and put this into the context of the news of the day. It is a confusing, roundabout business, filled with unanswered phone calls, wondering who to contact, and dealing with people who are not always willing to answer questions.

Putting information together from two or three sources to make one story takes a lot of thought and considerable time in a business that has less time than almost any other. Small wonder, then, that reporters are not always organized, not always ready to report in a clear and cogent manner.

Small wonder also that a reporter takes time to organize material, time that often goes right up to and after deadlines. It takes time to think through complex material, organize it, and to think in terms of what this means to the reader, not the writer.

Putting it Down on Paper

There may be an answer, although some reporters will always tell you that experience is the best teacher and there are no shortcuts.

One answer is to think the story through before the reporter sits down to write.

But since this is what most reporters already do to some degree, they need to put that thinking down on paper or on the computer screen.

Writing thoughts down on a piece of paper, or perhaps on the top few lines of the computer screen, will help to organize. In effect, writing something down is an act of commitment, a statement that this is what you think or believe at the moment. It ends the period of uncertainty that can lead to delays and poorly written stories.

So, you could use a word outline, with one or two words to represent each thought to be expanded on in the story. This does not mean you will follow this outline without deviation to the end of the story. It just means that at this moment, you think this is the best plan to follow.

By committing to a plan—any plan—you remove the uncertainty that is likely to cause procrastination and disorganization. You can then proceed to write something, which can be improved upon in later drafts. But without writing something, you have nothing to improve upon. Your thoughts are still in your head, and not on paper or the computer screen, where they can be adjusted or modified or edited.

Putting thoughts onto paper or the computer screen also helps you decide which thought is the most important. This, in turn, gives you an idea of where the story will start, where it will end, and what goes on in between. As you write, you may find that the outline needs to be changed, or that new information has come in to the office while you were doing the first draft. At this stage, it is easy enough to add to, change, or otherwise modify the outline. But without any outline, there is only confusion.

Not forcing themselves to write something (which can be changed later) also means reporters delay until the last minute. This causes them to make other mistakes in stories, such as not having time to check for common errors, and not having time to rewrite.

The rewrite, as we will discuss, is not a penalty for having written something improperly the first time. It is a smoothing or improvement upon something that has already been done, and is a refinement of thoughts that have already been committed to paper or screen.

Procrastination

Stories are told of reporters who wait until the last minute to write. Granted, there is always enough to do in a newsroom—another phone call to make, another editor to talk to, other notes to check—so a reporter can always be doing something important.

What the reporter is really doing is putting off the inevitable. It is much like a student getting ready for a final exam, and doing everything imaginable other than studying. At the last minute, the student will get to the books, go over the material in the time left, and do as well as possible.

In the reporter's case, the problem may not be procrastination as much as it is uncertainty.

• The reporter is not quite sure which is the most important part of the story, and therefore is not sure of how or where to start.

- The reporter may be wondering which of several emphases he should take, and which emphasis he thinks the editor might take.
- There may be some confusion about the facts of the story, some uncertainty about just how the story is going to appear in final form.

And so the reporter, instead of putting thoughts on paper or writing a brief outline, thinks it through in her own mind. This may be helpful, but the same problems exist: she has not organized her thoughts or made any further commitment as to which way the story will be written.

Talking to an editor may be helpful at this point, and should be done wherever possible. But editors are often busy, and the reporter may not want the editor to know that she is not sure of which lead to use or how to proceed. It may not be easy to talk to an instructor about an assignment, but the same uncertainty and confusion that bothers the student in the classroom will be in the newsroom. Some steps must be taken to avoid the uncertainty.

- Ask an editor which of two or three approaches might be the best.
- Ask your instructor, when you have conferences about stories, which of two or three leads might be the best.

By talking it out with the editor or your instructor, the uncertainty is brought from the realm of the subconscious, inside your mind, to the "top of your mind" or out into the open, where something can be done with it. An editor or an instructor will appreciate that you have narrowed it down to one or two approaches, and will vote for one or ask you what you think. In either case, you are well ahead of where you were before.

Cramming the Lead

On occasion, the reporter will not focus on one or two important facts to be included in the lead, but will include everything in the lead.

As a result, the lead balloons to four or five typewritten lines, which would either be ten lines in a newspaper or too much to say without taking a breath on the air. In this case, the reporter may consider himself safe because everything of importance is in the lead, but the editor and readers are unhappy because they have to decide what is important.

The editor may not be able to change it because there is no time, and the reader will go on to something else rather than read something too long and confusing.

A Story to Tell

It becomes helpful in this case, and in many other writing situations, to think in terms of a story. A story, or even a joke with a good punch line, follows a regular form.

It has a beginning, a middle, and an end, or as writing coach Jack Hunter in Jacksonville says, "A beginning, a muddle and an end."

A story will have a setting, a message, and anecdotes or examples to help it along.

Granted, a news reporter changes the form of the story to put the most important things first. But that does not mean that she does not have a story to tell. Any news story, whether it is an obituary, a meeting, an announcement, or a feature story, does have a story to tell. Otherwise, it would not be included in the day's news.

But the problem of writing a story in structured form to meet the requirements of the media is that it forces the reporter to think in terms of the form, and not in terms of the story to be told. This is a serious mistake because not all stories follow the same form.

We will be emphasizing forms in certain stories in this book. In some cases using the form is simply a convenience. Remember that the reasons the media use obituaries, sports stories, or meeting stories is that there is a message in each of these stories. That message is very important, and the form of the story should not change or weaken the message. In fact, if the form is the one the audience usually expects, the form can enhance the message.

Rewrite

Most journalism students look at the rewrite as a penalty for not having done the story properly. The feeling is that anyone who did it right would not have to do it again.

Yet there are authors who look at the rewrite as the essence of the writing process. Former newsman, now book publisher and author William Zinsser says, "The essence of writing is rewriting. I've never thought of rewriting as an unfair burden—extra homework that I don't deserve. On the contrary, I think it is a privilege to be able to shape my writing until it's as clean and strong as I can make it" (Zinsser 1985: 210).

Speaking to Wisconsin Educational TV in 1986, Zinsser said, "I think a lot of people write the first thing that comes into their head and they do not rewrite. Nobody's sentences come out right the first time. Mine certainly don't. We have to write and reshape what you have written four, five, six, seven times, until you get it fairly near the way you want it.

"I think we all have an emotional equity in our first draft. We can't believe it wasn't born perfect. But the first draft is usually very bad. Mine certainly is."

Nationally syndicated columnist Ellen Goodman says: "What makes me happy is rewriting. In the first draft you get your ideas and your theme clear . . . and you certainly have to know where you are coming out. But the next time through it's like cleaning house, getting rid of all the junk, getting things in the right order, tightening things up. I like the process of making writing neat" (Goodman 1983: 115).

In media writing there is not always time for rewrite. However, there can be more time if the reporter organizes her time better, wants to rewrite, and understands that rewrite is an essential part of the writing process. No one expects the first draft to be finished or polished or perfect, so why settle for the first draft?

Not all news stories are the same. Some are short. Some follow formulas. Some are long and involved features. Some are long and involved governmental stories. And there are other formats as well.

The story is told of a college English professor who was serving as a writing coach one summer for a large daily newspaper. On his first tour of the newsroom, he was introduced to a reporter who was completing a story on deadline. The professor asked how long the story was and the reporter said it was perhaps 500 words. The professor next asked how long the reporter had to complete the story, and the reporter said something to the effect of, "Oh, I have a long time. I have at least an hour to complete this."

The professor, who wrote novels in addition to teaching, was taken aback. His face turned white, and he said "But I will often spend two weeks on one paragraph when I am doing a novel."

Neither the professor nor the reporter should have been astounded. An hour is perhaps about average for a reporter to do a medium-length story, one of several that person will be doing in a day. Novels take months and years to complete, and are far more complex and involved than most news stories. As the epigraph indicates in chapter 1, journalism is literature in a hurry.

The standards are high for both. The major difference is in length of story and type of coverage.

Reporters will learn the difference between long, complex

stories and short, three-to-six paragraph routine announcements. They will learn to pick and choose from types of stories. They will rewrite those stories that need rewriting, and write only once those formula stories that can be written quickly. Even then, the formula stories must be checked carefully for detail, accuracy, spelling, and grammar.

When you learn to budget your time, you will realize that a long Sunday feature is going to take several hours to write, while a short notice of an upcoming meeting can be done in a matter of minutes. But all stories will be done with all the care the reporter can muster.

Other Problems

While organizing and rewriting are generally problems for most reporters, they face a lot of other problems.

Some reporters will have problems others do not have.

Some will be impeccable in the use of grammar and in their spelling. Others will not.

Some will be able to choose the right word in an instant, others will take a lot longer.

Some will be able to interview easily, others will find it a chore.

The writing coach study found that reporters have the following problems, ranked right after the organizational problems discussed earlier in the chapter.

- Reporters don't have an ear for the language, so their copy lacks life.
- Reporters write too many procedural stories (government did this), and too few people stories (using people to illustrate what government stories are about).
- Reporters don't read enough, so they don't appreciate good writing (see Role Models, chapter 3).
- Reporters don't rewrite because they think they don't have enough time.
- Reporters don't rewrite because they don't think it will improve their copy.

Respect for the Reader

The American humorist Will Rogers once said, "You know everybody is ignorant, but on different subjects."

The reporter often becomes an expert in areas the public does not understand. The recent two hundred year anniversary of the Bill of Rights brought about some surveys that revealed most people didn't understand the First Amendment, much less that it was an amendment to the original Constitution.

It could be possible after covering the police beat for six months or a year to think the world is filled with criminals and drunks.

A reporter who covers the courthouse might become disenchanted with the legal system, or one who covers a presidential campaign might see unpleasant things during campaigns.

It can be easy to become cynical in the reporting business. It is important for the reporter to understand that he is a part of the public who reports to that public, and not a part of the governmental establishment or the crime scene or the legal profession.

As such, his professional role is that of an "explainer" to the part of society that does not understand or does not have the opportunity to learn what the reporter already knows.

In order for society to function smoothly, it must know what is happening in the rest of society. We should not expect that society knows everything we do, because we as reporters do not understand everything that other people in society understand. We are probably not too proficient in repairing computers, in drawing up a will, or in designing an automobile, for example.

We all have areas in which we have developed an expertise and in which we can help make society better in a small way. In our case, it is reporting on what the rest of society is doing that is important.

We should respect other members of society for what they know, and provide them with information on what else they need to know. It is easy to become cynical, but it is also easy to remember that we are all on this planet together, and a good reporter can make our lives together much more interesting and worthwhile.

Things to Remember

- Writing is a difficult and complicated process. Knowing how it works can help you to write news stories in a smoother and easier way.
- Most news reporters try to write stories without thinking through what they want to say first. As a result, they find it difficult to know what should be coming next in their story.
- A story should be considered as a logical unit, with a purpose the first thing to determine. Once that has been established, you will know better where you want to go with the facts you have.
- Understand that there is an important difference between

listing a given set of facts, and thinking through those facts to see what the story is. Every set of facts has a story within it.

- A rewrite is a part of the total concept of writing, not a penalty for having done something wrong. The first draft takes the idea from your mind to paper form, and the rewrite brightens and polishes it.

Exercise

1. Write down in two pages or less how you go about writing a college theme or essay for a non-journalism class.

    Do you put it off until the last minute? Do you worry about it before you gather any information? Do you expect it to be easy?

    Do you have a system in which you outline the material you have in some form before you start to write it?

    If not, how do you know the order in which you will present material if you have not thought it through first?

5
Understanding Process in Writing

"Writing is an exploration. You start from nothing and learn as you go."
—E. L. Doctorow

"[I] might become a writer, if God gave me five more years."
—Carl Sandburg, at age seventy-five

"A writer is someone for whom writing is more difficult."
—Thomas Mann

In This Chapter

Process theory breaks the act of writing into its component parts so the writer can understand which part, if any, needs more work to make a better story.

Writing is a disconnected process, seldom following one-two-three step order, and writers should realize this.

Writing a news story in many respects is like doing a scientific experiment—finding a question to answer, using reliable questioning methods, focusing on important answers, etc.

Why a great deal of thinking and analyzing needs to be done by a writer before he or she starts to write.

Why and how stories change as they are being written, and how new discoveries change the shape and form of the story.

WRITING is the easiest thing for some people to do and the most difficult thing for others. Students who say "I love to write" seldom say "I love to think," but the two are inseparable in newswriting.

The problems a person has in writing are often made easier by thinking through the various steps in writing. Instead of just sitting down to "write a story," it helps to analyze the steps that lead up to putting the final words on paper or the computer screen.

Writing as a Process

This has come to be known in English departments as "the process approach," and it is making its way into newsroom coaching and thinking.

Process is another way of thinking of writing, of breaking it down into its component parts, and of helping the writer avoid delays that develop when the writer tries to "do the entire story at once."

The "opposite" of process is product, or focusing only on what the writer produces.

In traditional English classes, the product approach included an instructor assigning a topic, and the student writing on it. The instruction focused on outlining and grammar. The paper, report, or product was given a grade, often without the student understanding what he or she had done right or wrong. The emphasis was on the final product and whether it met standards that were unclear to the student. How those standards were reached was also unclear.

The teacher was the person to be pleased; the student, in a sense, manufactured a product that would please the instructor.

Transferring this to a newsroom, we find a reporter in a hectic, tension-filled atmosphere, attempting to complete a story or product that meets traditional journalistic standards. He gets little feedback because time limits the number of comments an editor can make, or because the reporter does not ask for help, or because there is just too much to do in too little time. Very often, the reporter gets no feedback at all on a story he has spent hours doing. If the product was satisfactory, the editor was pleased, and sometimes even told the reporters he was pleased. Time is short. Who said life was fair?

This discussion on process, then, is not meant as an academic or historical review of two ways of teaching writing. It is designed to help the student writer understand that writing is made up of several distinct actions, some connected and some not. By understanding how the parts come together, the writer can see how the whole is produced. And by understanding the parts themselves, the writer can analyze his or her own writing to make it quicker or better.

Instead of producing a story on deadline and hoping for the best, understanding process helps the writer understand where the shortcomings may have been. Was the interview adequate? Was there enough planning before going out on the story? Did the questions lead to sufficient detail? Was there a central focus to the story, or did the reporter fail to find that important key? Was there a logical flow to the story, or just a collection of facts? Would the story have been improved by rewrite (they almost without exception are) or did the reporter fail to allow enough time to polish the first rough draft?

These and other questions will be discussed as we go through the idea of process.

The Background of Process Thinking

Jerome Zurek calls the introduction of process thinking to writing "the current revolution in composition instruction. What has occurred in composition instruction in the last two decades has been nothing less than the creation of an academic discipline. Journalism instructors will find some of these practices consistent with the best that occurs in newsrooms and journalism classrooms. Some ideas challenge common methods of teaching news writing" (Zurek 1986).

Instead of focusing on the final version of a student's piece of writing, attention is given to all aspects of the writing process: discovering what the writer wishes to write about, gathering information, making meaning, ordering ideas, revising, and editing.

Zurek suggests to journalists that the entire writing process should be taught; that discovery and exploration, developing a story and finding its focus, needs much more emphasis. He also states that not attended to in journalistic writing "are how a writer finds a subject to write about, the process by which a writer discovers and makes meaning while writing, and that the writer is active in the making of meaning and that the writer makes meaning in the act of writing" (Zurek 1986).

Linda Flower and J. R. Hayes (1981: 365) studied writers for five years and formulated a theory with four parts:

1. The process of writing is best understood as a set of distinctive thinking processes that writers orchestrate or organize during the act of composing.
2. These processes have a hierarchical (ranked order), highly embedded organization in which any given process can be embedded within any other.
3. The act of composing itself is a goal-directed thinking process, guided by the writer's own network of goals.
4. Writers create their goals in two key ways, by generating both high-level goals and supporting sub-goals that embody the writer's developing sense of purpose, and then, at times, by changing major goals or even establishing entirely new ones based on what has been learned in the act of writing.

In other words, nothing is clear and definite and finished when the reporter starts writing. It is important that young writers understand that they put the parts of a news story together and make meaning of it during that process.

Writers do not go out and "collect" completed news stories. News stories do not happen. Events happen, and the translation of those events is what becomes a news story.

Dealing with Confusion

A certain amount of uncertainty and confusion at the beginning of writing a news story is to be expected, not to be feared. How the reporter deals with that uncertainty is the key to a good story. Many of life's important events—dating, entering school, taking tests, and countless others—have a great deal of uncertainty to them. How well people succeed depends on how well they turn the uncertainty into something helpful, how well they use the process to their own benefit.

Maxine Hairston, who has studied the changes in the teaching of composition, says "most writers have only a partial notion of what they want to say when they begin to write, and their ideas develop in the process of writing." This is critical to the student's understanding of the writing process.

Hairston also points out, "the writing process is not linear, moving smoothly in one direction from start to finish. It is messy, complicated and uneven and repetitive. Writers write, plan, revise, anticipate and review throughout the writing process, moving back and forth among the different operations involved in writing without any apparent plan" (Hairston 1982).

Flower and Hayes point to important work done by Gordon Rohman in analyzing writing as *pre-writing* (before the words emerge on paper); *writing* (the stage at which a product is being produced); and *rewriting* (the final working of that product). Understanding that these are separate stages can be very important to a beginning writer. In the happily confused words of a student, quoted by Flower and Hayes "I don't know what I mean until I see what I say."

Lyle Olson (1992) points out that Zurek's concept of process thus means that writers and teachers should "pay attention to all aspects of the writing process: discovering what the writer wishes to write about, gathering information, making meaning, ordering ideas, revising, and editing."

Olson answers a common question about process, which asks how a person can write multiple drafts under pressure situations. Just as a student cannot write multiple drafts of an essay exam, "we have to explain to students that in some situations, such as a fast breaking news story, they will not have time to write more than one draft. On the other hand, we can encourage them to write multiple drafts of stories that are not as timely."

The focus of this book is on learning process as it applies to writing, and understanding that certain stories use process, and certain stories fall into formulas. Understanding a formula for one type of story does not mean that a reporter would use that same formula in another story. And where formulas do not apply, the student must understand process and focus to decide how to organize the material before the writing begins.

At about the same time that process thinking began to be discussed, a program to introduce writing into all aspects of the college curriculum also took hold. Called "Writing Across the Curriculum," it ties in nicely to the process concepts.

Among many concepts promoted in writing across the curriculum are the idea of clarifying what specific audience a message is intended for; looking at more than just the final draft of the story; the importance of thinking while writing and learning about the subject while you are putting words on paper; and getting involved with actual stories and issues to bring more realism and depth to the writing of stories.

Students usually find they learn much more about a subject when forced to write about it than when they do if they plan to take a multiple choice or true-false test. Making a presentation before a class makes them learn even more, because they must defend their points of view from those who would ask about the subject after their presentation (Zinsser 1988).

Writing news stories often brings a defense mechanism into play. Editors may ask for proof of statements made in the story. Readers will present their points of view in letters to the editor. The reporter is "on display" to thousands of persons at one time when stories appear in print or in the electronic media. This causes additional anxiety, which lessens with time.

College graduates often point to courses that involved more writing as being helpful to them when they are forced to write reports. Many journalism graduates who go to law school find that the thinking, organizing, and deadline skills they learned in journalism are important to their success in law schools. Having to sort through mounds of information to come up with a specific answer in a law case is much like sorting through information to find a focused lead for a reader.

The Scientific Process

The concept of process might be better understood if it is compared with the more familiar scientific research process. Students in the sciences are familiar with the scientific method, which starts with a problem statement and ends with a completed report. Elise Keolian Parsegian (1987) compared the reporting and writing process with the scientific process and found considerable similarity. Journalists start with a problem, determine what to ask, conduct research or gather data, analyze the data, draw conclusions, and make reports. All of these steps are parallel to those used by scientists in conducting research.

The difference, however, is that the reporters do not think of it as a scientific process. They think of it as some sort of mystique that they have learned in their own way, and not some organized, reliable, consistent method for solving problems.

And so, when they encounter a roadblock in writing a report

or doing research, they do not analyze to find what the next logical step is, they procrastinate or they think back to how they did it the last time, thus possibly repeating mistakes made previously.

There is a method to gathering information and writing it down, and it is not a mystery. The reporter needs to understand this.

How Reporters Write

There is a method to writing newspaper stories, and what little research has been done indicates that this method is weak at best.

Beverley Pitts (1982) is one of the few researchers to study how reporters write stories. She used a method tested in psychology, called protocol analysis. A small number of reporters were asked to talk aloud as they wrote their news stories, and their comments were then analyzed.

In Pitts' case studies, the reporters wrote the leads first, spending up to one-third of their time doing the lead. After the lead, they completed the stories using the lead as the "jumping off point," and they completed the stories by rereading and copy editing their stories. Stories were written a paragraph at a time, and each paragraph was directly related to the previous paragraph.

Pitts said the reporters did not have overall goals for each story, did not organize it in advance, and did not rank order the facts in order of importance. There was no evidence that they looked at their information as a story, only as a lead to focus the material and the rest of the story to complete the information report they had in mind.

Because the number of stories analyzed was small, Pitts warns against making conclusions about all reporters. However, this is the only research on how reporters write that has tried to get into reporters' thoughts as stories are being written.

It is clear in this sample that the lead, or the main thought of the story, was the heart of the organizing for the reporters. Little or no advance planning was done, and no rewriting was done. Editing and rechecking facts was done, but no consideration was made for using the first draft as an outline for a more full-blown story.

The thinking and organizing for the reporter was incorporated into the lead. The lead therefore became more than just the first few paragraphs, it became the heart of the story. It left the writer open to many of the faults that come with leads—too much information, stilted writing, too long sentences, etc.

The study is important because it gives beginning writers a

better understanding of how experienced writers write, and the habits they get into. The habits permit them to meet deadlines, but they also lead to problems in making stories understandable. We shall discuss these problems as we continue in this book.

Coaches and the Writing Process

Writing coaches are the people who direct the action on the front lines in newswriting. They are the ones who understand the problems writers have, and they are the ones who have to do something about these problems. What do they do when a reporter has trouble with time management or with organizing materials for a story?

First, let us understand that these are experienced people. They usually have degrees in either Journalism or English, and they have reported for an average of six years and edited for another 14 years.

Whenever possible, they sit down with reporters individually to discuss strengths and weaknesses of their writing. This is a time-consuming process, but necessary if the writer is to understand both problems and potential. Wolf and Thomason (1986) found that the number one teaching method used by coaches was the one-on-one conference, not usually available in newsrooms where there are no coaches or in classrooms where an instructor usually has a minimum of 15 students at a time.

Wolf and Thomason said that the 42 coaches in their study used the following methods when teaching organization:

- Teach outlining.
- Have the reporters commit to paper what the idea of the story is before they start to write.
- Tell reporters not to begin writing until they ask the question, "What am I trying to say, to whom and why?"
- Tell reporters to write their story without notes, then check their notebooks to get quotes and check details. This is considered a major help in putting the collection of facts into a story, as the reporter is concerned only with telling the most important parts of the story at this stage.
- Tell reporters to suggest headlines for their stories before they submit them, to formulate a controlling idea for the story.
- Provide examples of good writing to help reporters with organization, clarity, and conciseness.
- Use editing and rewriting in personal conferences with the reporter.

As in the earlier writing coach research, organization was the number one problem, followed by clarity and conciseness (a variation of wordiness found in the author's study). But Wolf and Thomason pointed out that organization was not only a problem for veteran writers, it was also the main problem for beginning reporters coming from smaller papers and for reporters coming out of college onto newspapers.

Organizing material is a problem that affects reporters of all ages, and should be addressed at the beginning stages of learning writing in college so that a reporter will know what to do about it.

Tina Lesher, a reporter who became a college professor, sees a direct link between the process instructional approach being proclaimed in classes and the writing coach movement with its process-oriented techniques.

She sees elements of process writing such as brainstorming for new ideas as similar to the newsroom practice of story generating at staff meetings. Revision and response as taught by Prof. Nancy Sommers are similar to rewriting and editing so familiar in newsrooms, to the extent that rewriting actually means an extensive rewrite and not merely editing (Lesher 1987: 8).

Sommers has shown that revision, as it is carried out by skilled writers, "is not an end-of-the-line repair process," but is a constant process of "re-vision," or re-seeing that goes on while the writer is composing.

Newswriters Writing about Process

Only a few persons cross the line between the classroom and the newsroom. Even fewer feel comfortable when going from an English classroom to a major newsroom.

One of the few to do this is Donald Murray, now a retired English professor from the University of New Hampshire and one-time editor at *The Boston Globe*. Much of what is new in newswriting can be attributed to Don Murray and people he has influenced.

Small wonder then that he was one of the first to outline what process means in writing news. In *Writing for Your Readers* (1983), he says that newswriting has three major parts:

- *Collecting information.* That which is new, including impressions, quotations and details.
- *Ordering.* Finding a pattern or context in information that will inform the reader.
- *Clarifying.* The writer "seeks to become invisible" by refining,

reordering, and getting down to the essentials of the information the reader needs.

Murray, serving as a writing coach, and Christopher Scanlan (1983), outline the components of process as follows:

- *Assignment*. Either the reporter or editor gets the original idea for the story.
- *Collecting information*. Usually more than can ever be used in a story, to be cut down as needed later while writing.
- *Focus*. Finding the (usually one) important thing the reader needs to know, the purpose for writing the story in the first place.
- *Ordering the material*. Defining some parts as more important than others, sometimes outlining to be sure to include all the key points.
- *Develop*. Taking further steps with the information to make it into a powerful story, complete with examples, details, and whatever specifics help tell the story.
- *Clarify*. Changing the prose to make it more powerful, eliminate confusion, or strengthen the main point of the story. The focus becomes clearer and the story is restructured to make the point as powerfully as possible.

Depending on the type of story and the deadline involved, you may take the time to rewrite entirely or to refine as well as you can within the time you have. And the process is not a straight 1-2-3-4 process. The writer will go back and forth, finding additional facts when he is in the clarifying stage, or ordering parts of the story as he is clarifying.

Critical to all discussions of process is the concept of discovery—finding something you did not know existed. The nature of news is to talk to people who know what you need to know, and to get them to tell you what your reader needs to know.

Much of this is new—information you did not know, had not thought about, or had expected would be in some other form. It is important that you not have expectations. A good reporter is able to roll with the surprises, and to expect that everything will not go smoothly. Life is like that.

Think about how close the professional's model of process is to that suggested earlier by Zurek (1986): Instead of focusing on the final version of a student's piece of writing, teachers pay attention to all aspects of the writing process—discovering what the writer wishes to write about, gathering information, making meaning, ordering ideas, revising, and editing.

These ideas are also close to those put forth in Writing Across the Curriculum: The idea of clarifying what specific audience a message is intended for; looking at more than just the final draft of the story; the importance of thinking while writing and learning about the subject and while putting words on paper; and getting involved with actual stories and issues to bring more realism and depth to the writing of stories.

Coaching for Magazines

Writing longer stories may call for more process thinking. Longer stories require more interviewing, which brings more detail and requires more organization. In surveying people who teach magazine and feature writing courses, Ann Schierhorn found that they analyze stories heavily and therefore do more process thinking.

She said coaching writers at this level shows reporters "new ways of assessing ideas, reporting, focusing and organizing a story in a manner that builds the writer's confidence" (Journalism Educator, Summer, 1991).

Don Fry calls the steps in process news writing Idea, Report, Organize, Draft, and Revise (Clark and Fry 1992: 63). It has also been described as idea, discovery, collect, focus, refine, rewrite.

Whatever the terminology, it is important for media writing students to understand that writing is a somewhat circular process. Students can come into it at several different points, and they are never really finished. You cannot gather too much information, you cannot rewrite it often enough, and it is never going to be perfect.

It is a process, and like perfection, it is never finished. Only time decides when you are finished. And if the student manages his time, he generally will have enough to make revisions and changes, which makes a better story. In more than 20 years of teaching, I have yet to see a second draft that was not better than the first.

As much as anything, understanding process permits the student writer to understand that she should not expect a perfect draft the first time. Putting words on paper for the first time is, in effect, an outline of the writer's thoughts and a commitment to organize in this fashion. The second and third and further drafts improve materials considerably each time because much of the uncertainty is gone and the writer knows the direction the story is going to take.

Process also helps the student to understand other important factors:

- A story is more than a listing of details. It has a purpose for being and therefore has an introduction, a body of detail, and a conclusion; or a beginning, a middle, and an end.
- Ideas change as they are written down. As thoughts are put on paper they trigger other thoughts. The mind cross checks for accuracy, consistency, and specifics. Other ideas come to mind, and the focus of the story becomes clearer.
- Leaving a detail out of a story at one stage is not a critical loss, because it can be put back in at another stage in the writing. It is key to know that the details can be added, but the story line should be committed to paper first. Tell the reader what the main features of the story are. Commit an outline as such, and then go back and fill in the details. If it is a story, it tells best without interruptions. Process permits the writer to go back into the story and add and clarify and modify.
- The more outlining or thinking done before the writer starts writing, the less uncertainty he or she will have while writing. If you know where you are going to go with your story, you have more confidence in what you are going to say and your story shows more confidence and more power.
- All writers have problems in putting thoughts onto paper. Knowing that others suffer and squirm when they sit down to write should permit you to get to the main tasks of gathering information and organizing it.

Warning: Process is a relatively new term in journalistic writing. It covers a thought process, and is not designed to be a cure-all for writing problems. Process is background thinking. If used properly, it will help you think through the way you write. It can eliminate mental blocks, slowdowns, and problems caused by the confusion of "What do I do next?"

However, process must be used differently in different situations. No two writing situations are the same because of different timing and different facts.

Process thinking should be used as a background to formula writing. Formulas are guides for writing some kinds of stories, such as obituaries or accidents, which have key parts similar to other obituary or accident stories. When writing formula stories, however, you should still be prepared to discover something new about each story that should be highlighted in the first paragraph of that story.

Newsrooms live and die on deadlines. Process writing, by its nature, takes more analysis than product writing. However, process writing can be faster because the time normally spent in confusion can be saved if the process is thought through carefully.

Persons who normally dawdle until deadlines can think their stories through more quickly and start writing sooner. If they understand revision properly, they can do a second or third draft in the time they normally allocate to one draft.

So, please understand the process concepts, but also understand that this is a somewhat new concept for journalistic writing. And like anything new, it may have some surprises. We think the benefits outweigh the shortcomings by a great deal.

Things to Remember

- Understand that many steps go into writing even a straightforward story. Know what these steps are and how each one adds to the final product.
- Understand that writers should not be expected to sit down and immediately turn out fine, readable prose. A story needs to be worked on steadily and carefully just as any other project until it develops into something worth talking about.
- Much of the work in writing news stories needs to be done before you start to type the first words of the story. This involves thinking, outlining, deciding the main points, etc.
- A story may change several times from the first idea to the final rewritten product. It changes with new information, with new insights from rewriting, and as you decide that your first focus may not have been the most important after all.

6

Gathering News: Reporting and Writing Go Hand-in-Hand

"The best writing I encounter is the work of writers who have trained themselves to look intently, to listen carefully and to read voraciously. By 'looking intently,' I have in mind the kind of looking described by the little girl in Lee Smith's beautiful first novel. She proposed 'to look very carefully at a thing,' so it would stay in mind forever."—James J. Kilpatrick

In This Chapter

Why you can't write good stories without good information.

Why developing story ideas may be more important than the actual writing.

Specific things reporters watch for—quotes, details, numbers, and specifics.

How to ask people for information, and how to write down what they give you.

Why you should always get more information than you need for a story.

The incredibly close ties between reporting and writing.

W E HAVE to start somewhere in this process of writing news for the reader. For better or for worse, we sometime start with materials handed out in class. "This is a fact sheet, now apply the story form we just talked about to this set of facts." This probably works with beginning stories, and as we said, you have to start somewhere.

But you cannot ask questions of a fact sheet. As soon as possible, you ought to be doing "live" stories.

This gives you practice in talking with sources. It lets you get back to them if you forgot to ask something, and it gives you details and quotes—the variety and spice of newswriting. Without them, the story is as exciting as day-old bread.

Reporters soon begin to realize that they cannot separate reporting and writing into two categories. They are parts of the same process, and they depend on each other. The better the interviewing, the better the story.

Beginners must understand that livelier stories come from livelier interviews, and livelier interviews come from reporters who have prepared properly for the interview. On rare occasions, reporters may have to go "cold" into an interview, but not often.

As reporters and writers gain experience, they soon realize that they cannot make an interesting story out of incomplete or dull information. If you do not get that information during the interview, you will not be able to use it in the story. Soon, you start going out to interviews as well prepared as possible, because you understand the relationship between reporting and writing—if one has a cold, the other will sneeze. If one is deficient, the other will suffer. You cannot write a good story unless you have conducted a good interview.

If you apply process to what we are talking about here, it makes it even more clear. You cannot polish or refine the story if you do not have details, quotes, or good information. You cannot find the focus to the story if you are not sure of your information. You cannot develop a lead if you are not certain you have all the information. You can't make an interesting story out of a dull idea.

And you cannot write a story unless you have translated the terms of the story, such as in taxes, into words and terms the reader can understand. If you have not converted mills into dollars in taxes, for example, you have not done enough interviewing or asked enough questions to make the story readable and worthwhile.

So, interviewing and other parts of reporting are so closely connected that they have to be considered equal partners in the newswriting process.

This chapter will be about the process of gathering news, starting with who to talk with and how to talk with them to get the best story information. It will also include what to specifically prepare for in an interview, how to be as accurate and objective as possible (not take the side of the source or be unfairly negative), and how to handle direct quotes. We will also discuss the most common errors reporters make in interviewing and how to avoid them.

Developing Ideas for Stories

Before talking to sources about information for stories, reporters need to think about what information or news the reader or viewer wants. This is where we refer to the discussion of the nature of news (chapter 1) and readers' habits (chapter 3).

Story ideas are everywhere, but they are not obvious unless reporters understand their readers or audience. Stories in the media are about the life and times of the people being served. No one story is going to interest everyone, but the more interesting stories will interest larger numbers of people.

It is one thing to want to have stories that interest the reader, yet quite another thing to develop them. Where do you go for story ideas?

There are a number of sources. At any given time, several of these sources may provide story ideas for that day, and on other days, they may all turn up dry.

Some will be stories the public needs to know about, while others will be stories the public may not need to know about in order to live, but they might be interested enough to stop and read or watch. News is a combination of what the reader needs to know and what the reader wants to know.

The reporter needs to know that the "discussion is as important as the decision in a democracy." Regardless of what the decision is, the public needs to know how it was reached so that they can assess the performance of elected officials. Let the readers know what their officials are thinking.

On the other hand, stories having to do with major winter blizzards, taxes, or new governmental policies may have a direct effect on our standard of living. In cases of fires, accidents, or weather calamities, this information might be so valuable as to help a person continue living.

A reporter must understand that news comes in different forms, and needs to be analyzed for underlying issues that relate to the readers. At first, a story may not seem significant. As time goes by, you will better understand what it is the public likes to read about—and what it needs to read about.

As a student taking other courses in addition to this reporting course, ask yourself what story ideas there are in your other courses. Are there examples or principles in the courses you are taking that could lead to stories of interest to a lot of readers? Sometimes the obvious doesn't come to us until later, but there are story ideas and experts in many fields, and they can benefit us all. The particular lecture you heard today may not relate to a subject of "hot" or dominating interest. But that doesn't mean the person who gave the lecture might not be a good source now or later.

One more thing. Just because the public needs to read about stories—taxes, governmental decisions, or the formation of new policies—doesn't mean these stories do not have to be interesting. Your job is to make them as personal and as interesting as you can within the limits of the law and good taste. More about that as we go along.

Story Ideas: Beats

Most media outlets have times when they get together and discuss what should be in the next issue, the next day's newscast, or the magazine to come out in six or eight weeks. These are based on brainstorming principles, in which one person's idea feeds on another's, and "two heads are better than one."

Most media outlets also watch the competition very closely. The newspapers will watch the television news and listen to some radio news broadcasts so that they will not be "scooped," i.e., find out that someone else has gotten to a story first. Television news broadcasts, which are limited by time, may not have as much space to include all of the information found in a newspaper, but they read the papers carefully to see what is being covered and which trends are developing. Magazines, which may have a month or more between issues, must also keep up with daily news reports to see what the public is thinking about. Media are quite free in borrowing ideas from each other, but they do not use the exact words or ideas others use for fear of legal retribution.

If the media watch each other for story ideas, where do the ideas themselves originate from? Someone has to have an idea first. But when several people cover the same beat, there is a good chance that experienced reporters on the same beat may have the same ideas at the same time.

A lot of ideas come from governmental units because almost everyone pays taxes and large numbers of people vote, so the media try to keep them informed. This develops into the concept of "beats," or regular offices or activities that a reporter is scheduled to cover, such as police, city hall, or various courts. If there are several reporters on a big city police beat, for example, they will all try to "scoop" the other reporters, or at least to avoid being scooped by them.

The critical question in beat coverage is whether the stories are being covered because they are of interest to the readers or to avoid being scooped by other media. At any rate, the public is served by knowing more about government and its activities. Whether they will read all of these stories is doubtful.

But any activity happening on a beat that the public should know about usually gets covered. This includes such things as accidents, break-ins, robberies, appointments to new jobs, meetings to set new policies, rapes, fires, juveniles caught breaking the law, murders, and increases in dog license fees. If the public has a valid interest in knowing about something to protect its own situation, it should be covered.

The concept of beats is changing as media change their coverage patterns. While the routine "beat areas," such as city hall, school boards, and courts, are still covered, specialists are covering wider areas such as health, law enforcement, education, government, shopping malls, and entertainment.

Reporters refer to these as vertical and horizontal beats. Vertical beats are the buildings, such as the city government offices, the court house, or the school district offices where traditional reporting has been done.

Horizontal beats are the wider emphasis areas, such as government, law enforcement, education, and health, which cover many buildings in different areas.

The modern horizontal beat reporter gets information on issues through computer networks, runs spreadsheets to analyze tax statements, and covers a much broader issue-oriented area. Neither

75

beat is dominant, but expect more emphasis on horizontal beats and wider coverage as the media and society focus in on issues and problems that need to be discussed and solved.

Story Ideas: Away from Beats

Most beat stories have happened within the last news cycle, usually twenty-four hours, but this time frame varies according to the medium involved. A lot of what the public needs to know happens over a longer period of time, say weeks or months or years.

There are *trend* stories. The crime rate is up or down in a community, or more students are applying to the local college for admission, or more people are coming down with a particular kind of disease. These must be covered by interviewing officials or persons involved to get the proper perspective, but generally will require that the reporter spend more time in research before going out to do the story than if he or she were covering a regular story on a beat. Many of these stories will relate to a beat, in which case the reporter will do the story in addition to covering the normal activities of the beat.

There are *people* stories. Someone is celebrating her 110th birthday, or a noted national television weatherman or sports star is in town for a promotional tour, or the manager of the local chamber of commerce retires after 27 years. There are as many stories as there are people to write about. In recent years, many newspapers have taken to selecting one death of an "ordinary" citizen during the day at random and interviewing survivors to tell the story of that person's life. Other papers run question and answer features with local citizens who are not prominent or elected but nonetheless well known. Average persons often have more interesting stories to tell than prominent persons or elected officials.

The trend stories and people stories are part of what is known as feature stories. Anything not happening within a given news cycle can be handled in a feature fashion. Does the reader need to know about a trend developing in the sheriff's office? Write a feature showing how it has developed and what it might mean.

Is the downtown section suffering from the new mall on the edge of town? Use whatever figures can be obtained, but don't expect the downtown merchants to give you an unbiased opinion.

Does a sports team have an unusual player or an unusual need that does not show in the box scores or game stories? A feature might be in order.

A lot of beats do not fit well into the once-every-24 hours

structure. Financial indicators may show how good today's business was, but the real story may be an increase in the market for the product a town is well known for. Travel stories may be appropriate if rates go up because the price of oil is going up, but new destinations or interesting side trips become known over a long period of time. And with the increase in numbers of senior citizens in this country, such things as retirement stories, pension programs, and even historical reviews of eras 30 and 40 years ago become of interest to large numbers of readers or viewers.

The mark of good reporters is that they always have more ideas for stories than they have time to do. Generally, they will get the best stories done first and the ideas that were not as good or as well-formed will not develop into stories. But without more ideas than you can use at one time, the only ones you have may not be very good. But you will use them because they are the only ones you have.

Sources of Features

Former Yankee baseball catcher and manager Yogi Berra once said, "A great deal of observing can be done by simply watching." A number of features can be developed just by watching people, programs, or events. Note what is happening in the supermarket, on the playground, or when people gather for social or business activities. What do they talk about before the meeting starts? What is the animated conversation about at the office before work starts in the morning? What is the chatter about at cocktail parties, before school, after church, or wherever groups of people gather?

Often, nothing newsworthy will come out of ordinary conversations. People talk for many different reasons, including letting others know they are in good health and things are normal. But in many cases people talk about the things that are the most important to them, and by listening carefully you can hear about their concerns.

Will there be a flu epidemic? Are schools good enough to provide the education youngsters will need for the next 50 years? Are appliances and furniture more expensive now, or better quality, or both? Is sexual harassment in the workplace very common, or do people just talk about it a lot? Are drugs a concern in your community, or does your community have to worry, but not as much as others?

With any of these ideas, reporters have to decide if the subject is important or interesting enough to be written about, and then find someone to talk about it. The people found are the sources of the story.

Developing Sources of Information for Stories

The principles of developing sources for news, of getting information from people, are the same in very small markets as they are in major metro markets. If you learn how to deal with sources while working for a rural weekly on an internship, you will know how to interview heads of state when you are working for internationally known newspapers.

There are two kinds of sources—the experts in a given field, and the people who are concerned with the type of story being written. Reporters interview the experts to find out the truth of the matter, to get quotes on whether there will be a flu epidemic or whether sexual harassment or drugs are more serious in one community than in others. These people are experts because they have experience in the field. They may administer programs in the subject area, teach the subject field, or deal with drugs in this community and others.

The experts can be found by systematic tracing of offices in your community. Find the subject area, see which offices deal with this topic, and then contact people with expertise to offer. Since these people are usually professionals, they have many other responsibilities and are very busy. It may be difficult to get them to stop what they are doing to answer questions.

But somewhere in your community is someone who has some light to shed on almost every topic you want to do a story on. All of us are not as fortunate as those in Washington, D.C., or New York, which have larger populations and more experts, but people can be found. A veteran journalist once told a class, "Washington, D.C., is the greatest news town in the world. Someone in that town knows something about any possible story you would want to write about. All you have to do is find them and get them to talk to you."

Considering that Washington has government agencies, foreign embassies, trade associations, lobbying groups, think tanks, national political party offices, museums, publishers, veterans' groups and countless other sources for information, the journalist was probably right.

Your community may not have as many people, but you can find someone to discuss any issue intelligently with you.

The statements from the experts in the field are not enough by themselves. They will undoubtedly be accurate, and they may be long. But they might read like a textbook unless examples from real life are used to bring the story to life. When you have time and or space to do a longer story, you need to talk to people whose lives have been affected by drugs or sexual harassment or the price of furniture or the nature of education. Some of these people are easy to find, others are not.

The same experts you talked with might give you tips on finding people involved in this subject. Some of them may not wish to have their names used, in which case you and your editor have to make a decision about whether to use the story or not.

Often there are members of support groups for diseases or problems who would be pleased to talk with you about what their groups are doing. By sharing their information, they might prevent others from having the same problem. By using the phone book and other directories, you should be able to find these people.

How to Interview

Good interviewing principles are based on knowledge and respect. The more knowledge you have about the subject before you start to interview, the better information you are going to get. If the source thinks you know as much about the subject as he does, he will treat you with respect, and you will get good information. If you come to an interview unprepared, the source does not have to give you any information, although he may still give you more than you already know.

So you must spend whatever time you can with whatever sources you have to be prepared for an interview. Since you are probably doing this kind of story for the first time, there are no exact models to follow. You might read stories from the files, but that was then, this is now, and you need to update the information. Use your library as much as you can, then talk to anyone else in the newsroom or the community who might know something about the subject.

Newspapers have libraries of stories previously published in the paper, called morgues. Electronic media have files of stories as well, which may be accessible through the computer, as more and more information sources are becoming available on the personal computer.

There is no magic number of persons to talk to, just as there is no magic source of materials to read. Read as much background information and talk to as many people as there is time for (there is never all the time needed), and go on to the interview.

We now go on to the second part of the statement that said good interviews are based on knowledge and respect.

Reporters show respect for the source by being on time, dressing appropriately, and being as well informed as possible. If you were asked at the last minute to fill in for someone who couldn't make it, tell the source so that he or she will at least respect your honesty.

Reporters also show respect for the person and the time they are giving for the interview by sticking to the topic (after a few pleasant words to break the ice) and getting right down to business.

By letting the interviewee know what you know about the subject, you show respect and also narrow the focus of the interview down to those questions you need answered. There is no need to go over material you both know, but you have to explain what you know so the source can relate to your knowledge level.

Be sure to spell the person's name correctly. (Have you ever had yours spelled wrong in a news story? Most people have.)

By focusing your thoughts on the most important questions, you may not have to take a great deal of valuable time. This should also put the source at ease.

Interviewing is a part of the reporting-writing process. Some of what you need during this time is an update of the information that you already have, some specific insights that the expert has, and quotes that will make the story more interesting.

You also need to be sure you are on the right track, so ask some general questions that will permit the source to make some general comments. For example, if you have read in a national magazine or seen on national television that the flu bug may be coming to your area, you might interview a doctor at the local hospital. You can ask specific questions about the symptoms or about how it will affect elderly people, but be sure to ask general questions as well.

For example, you might ask, "Is it safe to assume that there will be a flu outbreak in this community?" You might have assumed that from what you read, but there may be good and sufficient reasons why this is not so. And unless you ask the doctor this question specifically, you may leave the interview with the wrong assumption.

A major part of the story, such as the assumption that there will be a flu outbreak, must be stated in the interview so that it can be tested. A classic warning in the news business is never to assume anything.

In addition, remember that you are the reporter making a report about what someone else says. You are not the expert in the field, your job is to find that expert and have that person tell your readers whether or not there is going to be a flu epidemic. The reader wants to know what the expert says, not what you say.

Of course, choosing this story means that you think it is

important. But the fact remains, you are the person who carries the news, not makes the news.

Talking to people who might be influenced by the flu, or who have had experiences with the flu, or who know people who have had the flu will complete the story. A pharmacist could tell you if people are stocking up on medicine. Someone at a nursing home could tell you if precautions are being taken there. A school nurse or the university health center could give you examples, details, and cases that will make the story more interesting to read.

Remember, you are telling a story. The story is about whether there will be a flu scare or not, and the story needs a beginning, a middle, and an end.

The beginning would be the conclusion, based on interviews, as to whether there will be an epidemic. The middle would be quotes and statements from people involved, and the ending will vary, based on whether this is a straight news story or a feature story.

A straight news story would report what you have to say and then stop. A feature story would use an anecdote or an example or bring back a statement used in the story to give a more complete and satisfying ending. More will be discussed on these styles when we cover straight news stories and feature stories. For now, it is important to know that a news story is a story with a message, not merely a listing of what six or seven different people said.

This is the section of process that could be called clarifying. Even if readers do not think a flu epidemic is coming, they would take notice if the pharmacist says hundreds of people are buying medicine or if the nursing home says it is taking every precaution. Specific statements from people they know bring the story home to them.

How many interviews do you conduct? How many people do you talk with? There is no one answer.

If you find one doctor who says there will be no epidemic, and a pharmacist who says people are stocking up on medicine, then you need to talk to more people. More is always better, within the limits of time.

If you talk to three experts in a small community and they all say the same thing, then you are probably pretty safe. In a larger city this may not hold, and you may have to find someone in a medical association or someone who by virtue of her job is in contact with a large number of doctors. This opinion carries more weight because that person has already done what you would like to do—talk to more and more doctors.

Developing a Shorthand for Interviewing

You have probably noticed that people speak a lot faster than you can write. Some people speak even faster when they are nervous. As a beginning reporter, you may think you have to take everything down, word for word. That is impossible, and in fact, it is not even desirable.

There are several short cuts to take notes while you interview. The most obvious is a pocket tape recorder, wound to the proper spot on the tape, with fresh batteries. You courteously ask if you may use your tape recorder "to be sure that I am accurate" and you are golden. Right?

Not really.

Tape recorders do malfunction, but not enough times to cause anyone trouble anymore. But the presence of tape recorders may cause problems for the source and for the reporter. If you have someone handling sound in your crew, then this is probably not a problem.

The source may or may not have been recorded before, and so perhaps may be nervous. If it is a touchy subject (some are but not always), the source may prefer not to be recorded. Younger people (reporters) may be far more used to the new technology than older people (many of whom are sources).

So are you in trouble if your recorder doesn't work or if the source doesn't want to have it used? Not really. You may be better off. And here's why.

Knowing that there is a small chance that the tape recorder won't work, you need some backup. And the backup ties right into the process of reporting and writing. If you have done some research, you know what the probable questions are going to be. If you don't know probable questions, go back and do more research into the subject.

Write the questions out on a lined notepad, leaving several lines between questions. After you ask the question, you then have a space to write the answer.

Develop your own shorthand. Write your notes double spaced. If your community is Springfield, use an S whenever the name comes up. If the mayor is talking about City Council, use CC. Use numbers and abbreviations whenever you can. Use the first letter of the last name of the source to identify her statements in your notes. Abbreviate committee and commission and related words. Use Y for yes and N for no. If you get a chance to take a shorthand course, so much the better. Many British reporters do, but it has not caught on in the United States.

As soon as the interview is over and you leave the room, find a chair. Sit down, go over your shorthand, fill in the blank spaces, write out the abbreviations in full, and fill in whatever you could not get done at the time. This is why you double spaced. You might even ask the source to repeat something to give you more time to get it all down.

Most lined sheets have a margin on the left hand side. Use this to put in notes to yourself. If you don't understand something, put in a "?" and come back to it before you leave the interview. If something the source said puzzles you, put a check mark in the margin to remind yourself to check this out before you are done.

By far the greatest help in getting down everything a person says is having your questions prepared in advance. You do not need to write out fully worded questions. If you want to ask whether a suspect has been arraigned or will be arraigned tomorrow, just jot down "arraign date." Or if the mayor is planning to appoint someone according to the scuttlebutt you get "on the street," just write down "appoint Smith" and you will remember to ask it.

What you are doing, in effect, is outlining your interview by writing down the questions. If this helps you make sense of the interview, it will probably help you make sense of the story as well. Any time your thoughts are organized you will be a step ahead of the game.

Please understand that some interviews go according to the questions you have outlined, but a lot of them do not. Be prepared to shift gears or react to something the source says. If you expected a "Yes" answer and the source says "No," that is not a signal for business as usual. You have to react, and ask, "Why did you say no," or "We would have expected yes," or something of that nature.

It is for this reason, and others, that reporters rely on the five Ws and an H. The Ws are who, what, where, when, and why and the H is how.

They come in handy when outlining notes before the interview, and are a quick (but not foolproof) way to see if any important parts of the story are missing. There are those who suggest there is another W, that being "So what?" which would help eliminate a lot of needless stories. "So what" refers to questions of why we are doing this story. Is there a lot of interest on the part of readers for this information? If not, perhaps we ought not to be doing it.

Remember, never rely too much on a tape recorder or on the five Ws and an H. Thinking through the story before an interview and anticipating the answers is the best way to get a story down pat. If the answers are not the same as you anticipated, then you need to ask yourself (and your source) why there is a difference between what you expected and what was said.

Watch for Specifics

All news stories are not created equal. And all parts of any one news story are not equal. Some stories are more important than others, some facts are more important than others.

So before an interview, anticipate what the most important questions and answers are going to be.

Then be sure you get them right. Ask again if you are the least little bit unsure. You cannot afford to be uncertain about anything in the story when you sit down to write it.

Be sure to get the proper spelling for print media, the right pronunciation for radio, and the right spelling *and* pronunciation for television.

Make sure all the numbers add up. If the fire chief tells you three people died in the fire, and you have four names, ask him about it. Right there. Don't go back to the office where you have to call him again, and may not be able to reach him.

When doing a story on an accident, get the proper address and the direction in which each car was going. Do not assume.

Watch for specifics. Never say several people were injured in the collapse of a building when you can ask and find out there were seven. Get the color of a car sought in a robbery. Ask for specifics on age, height, and color of jacket if someone is lost. In a criminal case, be sure you know specifically what a person is charged with. If a valedictorian is named, get the grade point average, the choice of college, and the field of study (if known). Details brighten up a story, and make it specific. Specific is always better than general.

Joseph Pulitzer, for whom the Pulitzer Prizes are named, once said that the three most important things in reporting are Accuracy, Accuracy and Accuracy. Reporters in the movies asking the same questions over again may be a stereotype, but there is a basis for it.

When we get to the discussion of legal problems of the press, we will find that a lot of legal problems stem from reporters not being careful at this stage of the writing process.

And if you are not sure about specifics or facts or numbers or names, you can't be sure when you write the story.

Objectivity and Verification

There is another argument that may be older than and about as theoretical as "If a tree fell in the woods and no one heard it, was there actually a sound?"

The argument is this: "Can a real live reporter, with feelings and opinions, be truly objective?"

The answer (to this one, I am still trying to figure out the first one) is no, reporters cannot be 100 percent impartial or objective. But they can try their very best, and can ask others what they think as well.

By the stories we write, by the sources we interview, and by the quotes we use, we make decisions as to how a story is going to shape itself. Being human, we cannot balance all opinions with other opinions. We can certainly try, however.

What the reporter does, which is every bit as important as trying to be objective, is this: quoting directly from experts, people in authority, or other sources; and double checking the source to make sure this indeed is what was said. Language and thoughts are very theoretical and "slippery," so a good reporter double checks statements, facts, spellings, and any assumptions.

Verifying is asking someone else who is an expert in the field if this is also his or her opinion.

If an accountant said Company B is bankrupt, try to get another opinion from another accountant, if possible.

If the police statement says the man was charged with first degree homicide, and you are for any reason at all uncertain, ask again. Police have been known to make mistakes on official reports.

If someone calls your sports department and says the local college football coach is going to go to a much larger school as an assistant, call the coach. Call the larger school. Call the coach's assistants here in town. Call anyone you can. If it is not true, you're much better off not running anything than running an unsubstantiated rumor.

Verifying goes so far as to have editors who do obituaries call funeral homes to verify that it was the funeral home who just called ten minutes ago with the Smith obituary. Many people in this country have called in false obituaries just to embarrass people who have jilted them, beat them in a business deal, or otherwise humiliated them. One phone call to verify that this is accurate information may not be needed in 99 cases out of 100. But in that one case out of 100 you will be very glad you made the call.

Human beings are not perfect. They cannot be completely objective. But they can be very careful, and have respect for the dignity of individuals who might be hurt and for the integrity of the media.

Gathering More Information than You Need

Certain short specific stories need X amount of information and that is it. The five Ws and an H may cover break-ins, robberies, fires, and many standard kinds of stories.

On longer feature stories, including personality profiles, background stories, and a series, a good rule of thumb is to gather as much information as possible. Reporters may not think they need some specific details or some quote at the moment, but it may be better than anything else they have.

All details, quotes, and facts are not equal. Some are more interesting than others. If a reporter stops interviewing too soon, he may miss something really good. In long interviews for personality features, people may relax at the end of the interview and give better quotes than at any time during the interview.

And when he goes to write, he never knows for sure which fact or detail might come to mind. Something someone said late in the interview may summarize much of what it is about. When looking for just the right quote or anecdote to conclude the feature, the reporter may come up with something he did not think he was going to use when writing it down.

That's why writing is a process and one surprise after another. If time is available and the source is willing, spend a few more minutes. You may get something better than anything else you had before.

Case Study: The *Kansas City Star* and the Department of Agriculture

Reporters, even those who have been working for several years, often do not recognize the incredible amount of work that goes into award-winning stories.

The *Kansas City Star* spent 16 months developing its Pulitzer Prize-winning series "Failing the Grade: Betrayals and Blunders at the Department of Agriculture." For this series, they won a Pulitzer Prize for national reporting, the Society of Professional Journalists Award for non-deadline writing, and the George Polk Award for National Reporting.

During the 16-month investigation, the *Star* team conducted 1,000 interviews in 22 states; went through 35,000 pages of documents, filed 70 Freedom of Information requests for classified documents; and analyzed 8.2 million computer records of 1990 payments to farmers in all 50 states, Puerto Rico, Guam, the Virgin Islands, and the Northern Mariana Islands.

Among their findings: thousands of U.S. Department of Agriculture labels are misleading or dead wrong; USDA county committees have helped ruin black farmers across the south, and even today exclude black farmers from loans; and a small percentage of the nation's largest farms gobble up most of the subsidies.

Following are some leads and excerpts from their series. Notice how detailed and specific these stories get, and imagine how much work went into getting each story together. Notice how the powerful facts all but speak for themselves. Remember, it took a great deal of work to get these facts.

WASHINGTON—In Room 0714-South of the US Dept of Agriculture, Harold Machias redefined America's pickle standards.

It took eight years. Machias visited picklepackers across the country. He did a market study. He talked repeatedly with the Vinegar Institute. The only visible revision: permitting "a bit more stem" on pickles.

Machias acknowledges you won't even notice it. "I think it took way too long," he said.

Down the street in a cramped room, Bud Kerr runs the office for Small-Scale Agriculture. In fact, Kerr *is* the office.

"There are 2.1 million farms in America, most of them small," he said. "More than one hundred and eighteen thousand federal employees working for the Agriculture Department, and you've got one man working on small farms. It doesn't make sense."

In fact, we commit as much to the Agriculture Department— nearly $78 billion in 1992—as the value of all the crops produced each year by U.S. farmers.

We do know this: The USDA has 8,383 typists and clerks, 423 auditors, 488 surveyors, 1,084 loan specialists, 73 dietitians, 84 outdoor-recreation planners, 418 criminal investigators, 159 mathematicians, 22 geographers, 13 zoologists, 10 psychologists, a museum curator, 11 masons, two roofers, a motion picture projector operator, five model makers, a cemetery caretaker, three tree trimmers, and 12 sailors.

[While] the number of farms has dropped steadily from 7 million in the 1930s to about 2 million today, the department maintains a 1930s-era bureaucracy that operates offices in nearly every county in the United States. A computer survey by the *Kansas City Star* revealed more than 400 offices that issued fewer than one check a day to farmers in their counties.

"When you walk into the ASCS office, you feel like you are breaking up their Avon party," grouses Owen Finley, a wheat farmer in Chelsea, S.D.

Edward R. Madigan, U.S. Secretary of Agriculture, "I told the GAO that when I came to the department everybody received me warmly, said how happy they were to have me here, and proceeded to ignore me. And the comptroller general said 'You have just summarized our report.'"

John McCutcheon of the department's meat inspection service: Lincoln needed 267 words for the Gettysburg Address. The Lord's Prayer has 56 words. But a federal USDA order dealing with the price of cabbage had 26,911 words.

Howard Tice, executive director of the Kansas Association of Wheat Growers, says the USDA is "full of regulations that nobody really understands fully—not the farmer, not the bureaucracy. We've pushed and pushed for regulations that we could understand. But you've got Congress writing laws they don't really understand. And then you have bureaucrats interpreting those laws that they in turn don't always understand."

Red Tape: Last year a USDA county office ruled that members of the Oneida Indian Nation were, for purposes of the government, one farmer. So when the reservation filed its application for farm payments, local bureaucrats at first ruled that 9,000 Indians had to sign it.

Five times in five weeks in 1989, computers at the Food Safety and Inspection Service sent meat inspectors to the same packing plant, not to go inside and inspect the meat, but to make sure its parking lot was still paved.

The USDA will spend $10 billion this year on programs that pay farmers to grow crops, and millions more to help farmers grow more on less land. This results in huge surpluses, so the USDA also spent $2 billion to take land out of production.

In Mandan, N.D., Agriculture Department social scientist Don Harris said he and another researcher spent years on a project that never saw light. "I spent four years trying to measure the effect of windbreaks on plant growth next to it," Harris said, despite the fact that he found the same research had already been done—and proved pointless.

Robert Bergland, agriculture secretary under President Carter, published new dietary guidelines warning people to cut down on fatty foods. "I just got my head blown off by egg people, by cow people, by pig people who didn't want us to talk about fat in the diet," Bergland said.

More than 40 percent of the USDA farm payments go to farmers whose average net worth exceeds $750,000. That money comes from Americans whose median household net worth is $52,000. Caps were originally intended to limit each farmer to $50,000 a year in income support payments. But last year nearly 8,000 farms exceeded $50,000 in payments, and nearly 1,300 collected $100,000 or more, some collecting more than a half million dollars.

Stevens County, Kansas, has exactly 300 farms, according to the US farm census. Last year the USDA sent checks to 1,342 farmers there.

Last year the USDA sent money to 118,000 Kansas farmers, the *Star*'s computer survey found. But there are only 68,500 farmers in Kansas.

Streamlined methods of inspecting meat from Canada have been introduced, so now border checks stop only 1 in 15 trucks of Canadian imports. Now certain cancer causing drugs banned in US animals are showing up in pork imported from Canada, which has not banned the drugs.

In suburban Virginia, Carl Telleen serves reporters a vegetarian dinner. After 30 years with the inspection service—including several years on an inspection review team—the retired veterinarian will not eat poultry and eats very little red meat. He doesn't trust the process.

"Meat inspection is about as fouled up as it can be." said Delmer Jones, head of the national union representing USDA inspectors, "and its getting worse— not better. If we continue down the road we're on, we're going to see mass numbers of people dying from food poisoning."

Things to Remember

- There is more to writing a news story than just writing. Getting good information first is the secret to writing better stories.
- There is an art to interviewing people and developing your own shorthand, and some people are better at that art than others.
- There are certain times and statements during an interview or during news gathering that are more important than others. A reporter learns to watch for and pounce on good quotes, specifics, and details.
- A reporter should always get more information than he or she thinks is necessary. It is easier to throw away some of what you have than it is to find something you should have asked for but didn't.

Exercises

1. Watch the national news weekly magazines carefully. Understand that they have less space than a newspaper, but notice how carefully they include important statistics, quotes, and items that make a story come alive.
2. Talk to a reporter. Ask how he or she prepares for an interview, or how much of that person's time is spent interviewing before the actual writing. Does this surprise you?

7
Libel and Privacy: Respect for the Individual

In This Chapter

Balancing the public's right to know with the individual's rights to protection of reputation and privacy.

The growing specter of libel (injury to reputation) as a force in the media.

Steps a reporter can take to minimize, but not eliminate, the threat of libel.

Understanding how truth and privilege (dealing with the public business) can be used as defense against libel.

SUPPOSE for the moment that you had come into class, and the friend at the next desk said "Sorry to hear about your problem."

"Which problem do you mean?" you say, having no idea what this is about.

"Oh, the one in the student paper. It says you have been arrested on suspicion of distributing cocaine. See, right here."

As the blood drains from your face, you look at the story. There it is: your name, your campus address, and a story saying you had been arrested at 6:00 P.M. the night before on the cocaine charge. You had been at home off-campus having supper with your parents at 6:00 P.M. the night before.

After class, you go to the student paper and ask the editor what this is all about. She talks to the student reporter. The reporter says he got the name from the police blotter, and checked it with the student directory for spelling and accuracy.

You go to the police station, and the arrest record indicates someone whose name is very close to yours, but one letter off. It is not your name.

Your life will probably not be the same. The university may call you in to talk about "your problem," and people in your apartment may watch you more closely. Certainly you will deny it, but then they expect you to deny it.

You might choose to get even for the wrongs inflicted on you by filing a lawsuit. You could ask for money to compensate for the wrongs you have been through. This is a civil suit, with money as the goal, not a criminal suit, in which someone would go to jail.

This is libel, by definition "a defamation of character by written or printed words or pictures." If it had been in spoken form, it would have been slander. The *Associated Press Stylebook and Libel Manual* defines libel as "injury to reputation."

It says "Words, pictures or cartoons that expose a person to public hatred, shame, disgrace or ridicule, or induce an ill opinion of a person are libelous." The terms hatred and ridicule are usually used in defining libel, and you can understand how strong these terms are if you were the one charged in your student paper with possession of cocaine with intent to distribute.

Libel is extremely complicated and constantly changing. Libel laws are state laws, and they vary somewhat from state to state. In recent years, this issue has become even more ominous in the newsroom. More people are suing for libel, and more people are winning.

The Role of the Reporter in Libel

But before we get into the discussion of libel and how to avoid it, let's examine the role of the reporter in understanding and doing something about libel.

The reporter must first understand that the First Amendment to the Constitution gives the press the right to report by saying that Congress shall make no law abridging the freedom of speech, or of the press, among other factors.

But nowhere does it say that reporters can say anything they wish. No one has the right to shout "Fire!" in a crowded theater. It says that Congress cannot abridge (diminish or curtail) freedom of speech or of the press.

The reporter is not a lawyer, nor are most editors. Both must rely on other experts if they are faced with libel. However, editors do have more experience in the field than reporters, and they may have been through libel situations previously.

Thus, it is important that the reporter understand several things about libel.

- No matter how much a reporter studies libel law, she probably will not have time to become an expert. While she is doing her reporting, libel law will change. While students are often required to take a mass media law course if they are majoring in journalism or a related field, what they learned in school may be out of date shortly thereafter.
- If a reporter is sued for libel, most likely his editor and publisher will also be sued. People seeking relief from libel go where the money is, and this is usually the publisher of the newspaper. They may include the reporter in the suit, but they will also include the people with the money.
- It stands to reason that if the editor and publisher are to be sued, they ought to be informed of any potential cases of libel. The beginning reporter must go to the editor whenever any suspicion of libel comes up in a story. The reporter must

understand libel well enough to know when a case may develop. Editors will usually spot this when they read copy, but it still means the reporter must know where the potential for a lawsuit is.

• The reporter must do all in his or her power to stay informed about libel. Read the trade magazines, such as *Editor and Publisher,* and the professional magazines, such as *American Journalism Review* and *Columbia Journalism Review* and the magazines of the professional groups, such as Society of Professional Journalists. The *Associated Press Stylebook and Libel Manual* has a 20-page section for quick reference, covering not only libel but also privacy, public officials and public figures, and other areas reporters need to be aware of. While this textbook is primarily focused on writing and reporting, it does include a brief discussion of libel. No one should think that understanding these few pages is going to be enough to protect a reporter for the rest of a lifetime in journalism.

• Above all, remember two things. The single most important thing a reporter can do to avoid libel is to be as careful and accurate as possible (more about this later). Secondly, while interviewing and writing are personal, self-centered, and introspective tasks, the potential for libel is something that must be discussed openly with the editor. The stakes are too high for a beginning reporter not to ask experienced advice in cases where there is a potential for libel.

The State of Libel Litigation

The Libel Defense Resource Center in New York City, supported by the media, conducts a study on the state of libel suits every other year. Its most recent study showed that damage awards against the media in the last two years have averaged 10 times the judgments in the previous two years. The average libel award in 1990-91 was $1.5 million, as compared with the average for 1987-88 of $432,000 (*Editor and Publisher* 1992).

At the same time, the actual number of cases of libel is dropping. The center found only 30 cases in the United States over the past two years, as opposed to 60 the previous two years.

And when the libel awards from 1980 through 1990 had gone through appeal, only 28.7 percent of the cases were successful. Original verdicts averaging $2 million were reduced on appeal to an average of $259,000.

But even then, this is not good news. The "chilling effect" of libel is here to stay. Reporters and editors, especially on smaller papers, fear (and often avoid) doing investigative stories. The cost of going to court is simply too much. Columnist Jack Anderson, who has been sued many times but at one point had lost only one very minor case, has been seeking a law that would make the losers in libel cases pay the costs. Even if a newspaper wins the case, it becomes very expensive in terms of lawyers' fees and hours of preparation for trial.

For example, a sixteen-year case against a suburban paper ended with the paper paying "a tad over $100,000" in settlement in a case that went to the U.S. Supreme Court. The legal costs of pursuing the case were estimated at $500,000.

Why are libel awards increasing?

Americans are more adept at protecting themselves and more willing to sue when they think their rights have been trampled on.

In Nebraska recently, Robert L. McCune won $23,350 when the Nebraska Supreme Court ruled he had been slandered by a woman in the little town (population 780) in which he grew up. The woman, the trial indicated, told several people that McCune had the AIDS virus. McCune became nervous, was shunned by his former friends, was forced to quit his job, and suffered injury to his reputation.

In recent years, our country has increasingly focused on the rights of the individual in such things as sexual harassment, employment rights, police brutality, etc., so the individual understands his or her rights better than before. Juries may reflect the general population's feeling that the media are not as credible as before. The public does not trust many of its institutions—government, police, doctors, savings and loans—as much as before, and the media gets some of that mistrust.

Newspapers are not the only groups involved in libel cases. In recent years, libel cases have been filed against advertising agencies; against employees at an automotive firm for putting up a sign that ridiculed their boss; against a magazine for altering quotes that the magazine said did not change the meaning of the story; against public relations firms that sent out truthful though incomplete news releases; against a major national retail chain that posted signs at its cash register wrongly stating that a customer had been switching price tags; over letters to the editor in a medical journal about using animals for medical research; and against inaccuracies in headlines that were followed by correct stories.

And this is not new. Phil Reisman points out that in 1903, a police reporter interviewed a woman in a Chicago jail who claimed to be the legendary sharpshooter Annie Oakley. The woman said she was Annie Oakley, and told some stories that sounded true. The reporter filed the story with his paper, which then put it on two wire services. The real Annie Oakley, living at the time in Nutley, N.J., filed libel cases against 46 newspapers that ran the story and, so to speak, hit the bullseye on 44 of them.

The Concept of Malice

The word "malice" in general usage means a desire to inflict injury or suffering on another, especially when based on deep-seated meanness. In a legal sense, it means evil intent on the part of one who commits a wrongful act injurious to others (*Webster's Encyclopedia Unabridged Dictionary of the English Language*).

In media usage, the concept means that the courts have said it is important to get full and complete discussion of issues so the public can make up its mind. One item not protected, however, is the reporter who writes something he or she knows in advance to be false, or in reckless disregard of the truth. The power of the press does not include the power to say something about your enemies which you know to be wrong. A reporter cannot use the press to "get" someone who has been victorious over him in some other competition.

In general, as Deckle McLean (1989) said: "where there is evidence of a sincere effort in good faith by a media libel defendant, there is no clear and convincing proof of actual malice. If genuine effort is not evident, the courts may zero in on inadequacy of investigation, unreliability of sources or even common-law malice as convincingly clear proof of actual malice."

Not All Doom and Gloom

Let us try to put libel into perspective, without minimizing its importance one bit. Many reporters go through life without being sued at all. Some get threats of being sued, which they wisely report to their editors. There are far more threats than there are lawsuits, which are expensive for the person suing as well. And, as mentioned, many of the cases are not successful.

It is important to realize that some kinds of stories are more likely to cause people harm and injury to reputation than others. Stories relating to arrests, child abuse, or contagious diseases, for example, are more likely to upset someone than a feature about the time they met Elvis after a concert. Libel develops from sloppy reporting in arrest stories perhaps as much as any other because an arrest can damage a reputation. Misspellings, incorrectly reported addresses, improperly reported charges, and a lack of thorough understanding of the judicial process can lead to problems. The reporter on a police beat must understand everything that happens on that beat, or ask for guidance from her editor or other reporters.

Respect for the individual is critical here. Each person in a story must be reported as if he or she were a member of the reporter's family, because those persons are members of someone's family. The judicial system gives every person the right to defend themselves, but an inaccurate reporting of the case may mean the person feels as though he has been convicted in the public press before going to trial, if a trial is held.

Certain investigative stories depend on the use of unnamed sources to provide information a reporter cannot get in any other way. A reporter and the editor involved must understand the situation and the source well. An unscrupulous source could use the press to accomplish something he could not do through the courts. The source must be reliable, and should be willing to sign a statement verifying what he said so that this statement can be used if a trial becomes necessary.

On-the-record comments made in public meetings by elected or appointed officials may be reported. Off-the-record statements made by elected officials outside of official meetings, such as informal conversations at cocktail parties, do not have the same standing in law.

The reporter must separate facts from opinion. Facts can be verified, and should be verified by the reporter before writing a story. Opinions are expressions of the reporter's thoughts, and do not belong in a story. Opinions in columns no longer have the protection they once did because of the $500,000 Lake County Case previously discussed.

The Supreme Court said the opinion expressed in this case of a wrestling coach and a sports writer was not protected under law, and that the law "had not been intended to create a wholesale exemption for anything that might be labeled opinion."

News stories are not the only parts of a paper or a broadcast that can be held libelous. Letters to the editor or to a television station are not protected from libel. Just because the reporter did not originate the statement is no protection; the fact that the station or paper published or spread the statement is what counts. Letters must be as accurate as any news story.

Reporters must be careful about trying to rush a story into print at the last minute without adequate time to check all angles. Rushing for deadline causes errors in accuracy, failure to double check, or both.

Many small town papers with large percentages of senior citizens in their communities often run "Yesterday" columns reporting news from 10, 15, or 25 years ago on the week of publication.

Reporters are advised not to mention any arrests or convictions 25 years ago, since in all likelihood the person has paid the debt to society and should not have the transgression brought up again for no good reason.

However, if a person was charged with embezzlement in years past and is now running for treasurer of the city government, the tie between the two cases is very clear and the public should be informed.

The Three Criteria for Libel

In order for a statement to be libelous, it must have three elements:

It must be *published*. In Alton, Ill., a letter from a reporter to the FBI was considered published, and the newspaper lost a major case because of it. The posting of signs in a store saying someone had changed price tags was ruled libelous. The key factor is that the material must be seen by a third person and interpreted by that person to be defamatory.

It must *defame*. Generally, this means injury to reputation.

And, third, the person must be *identifiable*. The defamation must apply to a specific person, not a group. Someone other than the person suing or being sued must reasonably infer that the reference is to the person in question.

Defenses against Libel

The media have a role to play in informing society. In many of its stories, someone is not likely to be happy with the way she or her thoughts are portrayed. The reporter keeps this in mind while making assessments of what is important for the public to know. There will be many judgment calls, most of which are done in cooperation with the editor.

Truth

The primary defense against libel is that the story was the truth. However, since libel cases go before juries, the truth must be provable in a court of law. A reporter cannot simply state that he knows it to be true. He must have persons who will testify to the truth, or will sign statements that they know something to be true.

Once again, the concept of double checking sources, being sure all facts are accurate, and asking as many questions as need to be asked plays an important role. Failure to do any of these will lessen the chances the story will be true.

Privilege

Statements by and about elected or other public officials during the course of their public business may be reported as they were said. Therefore, if the mayor in an official city council meeting says, "The Director of trash and recycling is a crook," this can be reported just as it was said.

The public needs to know that this was said and to be able to determine (1) if it is true, or (2) if the mayor was wrong and why. If the mayor was correct, steps should be taken to remove the person from his job. If not, the public needs to know this about the mayor if he runs for office again.

As far as libel is concerned, the mayor cannot be sued because he said it in the conduct of official business. If you made a thorough and accurate report of what he said, and what was said in response, and you made every effort to do a professional reporting job, you would have qualified privilege and would probably not be sued.

This is the public's business, and the courts have encouraged full and free discussion of public business during public meetings. This is not to say that all officials in all meetings can be quoted, and state laws may vary. The mayor is probably qualified under privilege, the director of trash and recycling may not be.

The privilege statutes are not 100 percent pro-press. Reporters need to look at the local laws to see who is privileged and who is not and to check closely with their editors at all times.

What public officials say outside of official meetings or official reports is probably not privileged. It should be reported only after a thorough search into all of the facts.

Is a preliminary investigation that has not been put into a formal report privileged? It may not be in many areas.

Is a statement the mayor gave while he and the reporter were both pumping gas at the local self-service station privileged? I doubt it. Pumping gas does not constitute public business.

Why Libel Cases Develop

Reporters are human. Police are human. Sources are human.

What a reporter thinks is a fact may have been a mistake by a police officer. When a reporter sees 2448 Hamilton Way on the police report as the site of a drug bust, but writes 2248 Hamilton Way (or if the police list the address incorrectly on the police record or "blotter"), he is almost certain to hear from those at 2248, and perhaps their lawyer as well. Double check all numbers, figures, addresses, etc. Reporters get tired or distracted, but in reporting criminal activities, the risk for libel is so high reporters must be very careful.

The reporter who checks a name only once runs the risk of two people with the same name. This is not uncommon in any large community. But two people with the same name at the same address is uncommon, unless they are parent and child. Check the name and spelling against other records to be sure that the name and address coincide.

A student reporter took a man's name from the police blotter, checked and found a similar name in the student directory, and assumed the person in the student directory was the one on the police blotter. He was not. He was from another community.

Only a charitable father (who turned out to be a lawyer) and two retractions in succeeding issues prevented a lawsuit.

You as a reporter must respect the rights of any individual listed in a criminal docket or charged with some crime. Act as if it were your parent's or your name on the blotter. Give every person the same respect you would expect to get.

Other Legal Concepts of Importance

Public Figures

Persons who have not been elected to office but who are involved in public controversy are considered public figures. They are persons who have thrust themselves into a public issue, such as a citizen suing the city for damages during a storm.

However, the Supreme Court has ruled that the wife of a major industrial figure is not a public figure, because she has not thrust herself into the limelight to resolve a public issue. A person with only a minor involvement in a public cause is also not a public figure. The public figure rules are as confusing as those about public officials, so do not automatically assume that the person being written about is a public figure.

Fair Comment

Reporters covering sports, art shows, plays, movies, etc., can stay out of trouble by discussing the actual subject being reviewed and not the artist involved. Reporters must comment on the performance and give facts upon which they base their opinions. The principle behind this is that people who seek the public's support—and money—should be held up to public scrutiny. Reviews of restaurants, automobiles, and other products are allowed if these businesses seek to sell to the public.

A classic fair comment story is about the time a metro newspaper described a person as "the world's worst actor." The man sued and lost because the court said the company charged for its tickets and the review was not of the person but of his acting. When the actor came to town again some time later, the paper reviewed his work again and said the actor "did not live up to his usual standards."

Privacy

This may become the issue of the 1990s and beyond. The late actress Greta Garbo said, "I want to be alone." Many people would rather not be quoted or interviewed in the media. The courts have ruled that if a person is involved in an event of public interest, such as a public meeting or a fire or gas explosion, and is photographed, that person's privacy is in effect overridden by the public's need to know.

Newsworthiness is a defense, and once again, laws vary. Respect the rights of the individual while you are attempting to handle matters of interest to the public.

Another defense is similar to that in fair comment. If a person such as an actor, a ballplayer, or a politician courts the public's favor and support, that person loses some of his or her privacy. This is an emerging area of law, highlighted by such things as the Italian paparazzi's incessant shadowing of celebrities and the Gary Hart case in which he dared the media to prove he was not what he said he was.

Free Press and Fair Trial

Lawyers and public officials are much more wary about giving reporters information than they were many years ago. Lawyers have asked for postponements or change of venue because of heavy publicity. The individual has a right to a fair trial, and providing information before the trial may harm that right. But the public has a right to know if a dangerous person has been taken off the streets, so the courts and the media are balancing several important rights at the same time.

Judges have been known to close courtrooms, especially for pretrial hearings, and the media feel this prevents them from getting details and discussion on issues presented by the cases. Many media outlets have equipped their reporters with standard statements to be read before the court if the judge announces he or she will close the session. Such a statement is printed in the *AP Stylebook*.

Brand Names

A paper ran a story on students from the local college who had been elected to a group known as Who's Who in American Colleges and Universities. There are many recognition groups for people in all lines of endeavor. A one-column headline said Area Students/Honored/By Who's Who. Within three days the editor had a registered letter from New York from Marquis Who's Who, asking for a retraction in the headline. There are several organizations with the words "Who's Who" as a part of their title. The retraction was granted.

Trade magazines now run special sections each year protecting brand names, which have developed over the years into valuable commercial properties. If the names fall into public use, the commercial value will be lost. Reporters should use generic words such as soda instead of Pepsi, or tissue instead of Kleenex or earth movers instead of Caterpillars.

Among the many specific brand names that should be avoided are Realtor, Tabasco, American Express, Xerox, Weight Watchers, Gore Tex fabric, Frigidaire, Jockey, and even Little League, which is a trade marked name. If a city's youth baseball program is locally organized, call it youth baseball.

Things to Remember

- The rights of individuals must not be trampled upon while the media explain problems in society to their audiences.
- While libel laws are changing, a reporter can protect the media's interests by being scrupulously careful in reporting names, numbers, addresses, and other details, and by checking closely with editors whenever a possible libel situation comes up.
- Public officials conducting public business can be quoted, because courts have held the public has a right to know about how their business is conducted. However, comments by public officials outside of regular meetings do not have that same privilege in many cases.
- Libel laws change and vary in different states, so the reporter must keep informed as much as possible through publications, seminars, meetings, etc.
- The reporter must be aware that private citizens have protections public officials do not. Comments about theater and sports performances, for example, may be made, but comments about private activities do not have the same protection.

Exercise

1. Check the Libel Manual section of the *Associated Press Stylebook and Libel Manual*. Know what it contains and refer to it whenever you need it.

8

Developing Your Own Philosophy of Newswriting

"The best part of one's life is the working part, the creative part. Believe me, I love to succeed. However, the real spiritual and emotional excitement is in the doing."—Garson Kanin

"No tears in the writer, no tears in the reader."—Robert Frost

"Less is more, in prose as in architecture."—Donald Hall

In This Chapter

The student/writer needs to understand why he or she is writing before starting to write. Knowing the purpose of a story makes all the difference in putting it together smoothly.

Every story in every newscast or newspaper is not important to everyone. But the reporter must act as if every routine story is the most important story he or she has ever done.

Why writing is more difficult than many other professions, and how to make it easier.

THE STUDENT may be asking "Isn't he ever going to get to some actual writing?" Yes, in the next chapter.

There is a reason we have spent all this time establishing the groundwork for writing. Unless you know *why* you are writing something, you will tend to wander aimlessly. Your stories will have no focus and your readers will turn to something else very quickly.

It is critically important that news writers understand they are not writing for themselves. It is fine and acceptable for students to get into this field because they enjoy writing, because the joy of writing and a desire to write are both important.

But the purpose of newswriting is to inform others of what is important to them. Writing for creativity or personal expression can be channeled into journalism, but writing for the sake of writing is something that belongs in another field, perhaps English, creative writing, or poetry.

The joy of newswriting is in being at the center of the action, and in being able to interpret for readers and viewers things they need to know about. News can be something new and different that perhaps they did not know before or that they did not think of in that way.

News in this sense helps the audience adjust to what is new in society. Are there trends they need to know about? Are there dangerous criminals who must be handled with due process? Are there activities, people, or anniversaries that help bring more meaning to their lives?

Students need to develop a philosophy of writing, which in turn will make the writing more meaningful and purposeful. Writers can make the world a little better place to live by explaining things people need to know but do not have time to discover.

In a very real sense, the help and information people get from what reporters write can be as satisfying to the reporter as any creative thoughts put on paper.

But this means, as we discussed before, that the reporter must understand the story before he can tell it to the audience. And he must keep the reader/viewer's interests foremost in his mind before writing. A story written to please the reporter must be secondary to a story written to inform the reader.

Stories usually take place and are reported within one news cycle, such as one day or one week, depending on the medium being used. This means the writer has little time to finish the story, and it also means the reader has little time to read the story.

The reader may want to spend more time reading, watching, or listening to the news. In today's American society, there are so many things a person can do and wants to do that all of them do not get done. So the fact that the reader may spend 15 to 20 minutes with a newspaper or watch the evening news while reading the paper is not the fault of the journalist. It is a factor of society that he or she must live with and adjust to.

It means that in the time the audience devotes to the news, it wants to know right away what is important. As soon as people detect stories that are of little interest to their personal lives, they will go on to something else. The media are in a constant battle to gain the attention of the audience, and they must do everything within proper and legal means to tell the audience why the story is important.

It also means the reporter must come directly to the point in most stories. On feature stories or longer series, which are properly advertised or read on Sunday when people have more free time, a clever or indirect or story-telling lead might be appropriate. For the bulk of news stories, reporters have to cut to the heart of the matter as soon as possible to retain the interest of the audience. The writer has to adjust to the audience needs, not the audience to the writer.

The writer has to treat every story as being important to someone. If it is not, why is it being used? And if it is important, it must get every bit of the writer's attention during the time it is being written. There is no more important thing to think about at that moment. This means getting it right, getting it accurate, and seeing that there are no legal problems in the stories that are most likely to cause legal troubles. Understanding that each member of the audience gets the same respect as each member of your family will help in this regard.

The reporter and the reader want the same thing in news stories—something new, something they did not know before, and proper care taken in seeing that all information is accurate. Just because the reader doesn't spend the time to read every story does not mean that every story is not important—to someone.

The audience is made up of many groups of individuals with

special needs and interests. Not all stories appeal to all audiences, and only those really interested in the person or the subject are likely to read the story all the way through. These are also the people who are most likely to be concerned if mistakes are made.

The actual interviewing and writing are usually private, sometimes lonely, often scary processes. Beginning reporters tend to take things ᴏn their own shoulders, often afraid to ask questions. They fear the instructor or the editor will find out that the student doesn't know everything about the story or about the writing process.

Little do they realize that (1) the instructor and the editor have both been down the same road, experienced the same feelings and emotions, and wish to help the student through the process; and (2) no one understands everything there is to know about every story or about the writing process.

Putting thoughts on paper to reflect people or events as they actually happened is a very complex process. Consider how long a trial might take when all aspects of a crime are considered by a judge, jury, and both sides in a case. Then realize that the reporter is being asked to put together a news story about an event like this in a matter of an hour or two and make sense of very complex issues in a very short time. It can be done, but it is not for the faint of heart. The reporter must realize that help is available.

Talking the story over with someone else helps straighten it out in your mind. Asking an editor for the focus he or she would like helps to find the focus.

Showing enthusiasm and asking questions in a college writing class is to be encouraged. Students often think they should be passive, or not get involved. Each writing course is important, because you will probably have no writing classes (and precious little writing instruction of any kind) after you leave college.

Students should do everything they can to get as much as possible out of each class. Badger the instructor with writing problems that bother you at the time they bother you. This is the time to learn everything possible about writing for the media. Employers expect, perhaps unrealistically, that students will magically transform into polished writers by putting on the graduation cap. Learning writing is as much a process as the writing itself.

Writers should understand that "holes" (missing facts or statements) will appear from time to time in stories. Knowing this and understanding process theory gives the writer the chance to look at the process and find out where to get the needed information.

Writing has its very definite highs and lows. Christopher Scanlan of the *St. Petersburg Times* said:

...writing has always seemed like a roller coaster ride: dizzying heights of excitement and dips into valleys of despair.

Let's take a point, arbitrarily, right after I've published a story. Let's say it was a good story and people have said they liked it. I'm elated. That lasts a few seconds, replaced immediately by despair.

"The story was a fluke," a little voice whispers. "Just a lucky break. You'll never be able to match it again. In fact, you'll probably never get another story idea again and your bosses will realize you were just a flash in the pan."

It's helpful to know that it's normal to feel anxious after a story's published because people are going to read it and judge it and there's a lot at stake because we put ourselves on the line every day and we do care. We care if they read it all the way through. We care that it's right, from the spelling of the names to the central conclusions (Scanlan 1988).

Scanlan says it takes tenacity, humility, conceit, curiosity, empathy, the ability to lower standards, the ability to learn from others, persistence, and courage.

A tall order—for any profession.

Thoughts about not measuring up to your own standards are normal. Good writers probably have them more often than beginning writers, or writers who settle for a story just good enough to be printed. Writing coaches say they work more with their good writers than they do with the poorer ones. The good ones care more, want to improve, and want to learn more and more about writing. All of this is good.

It is natural at the beginning of any important undertaking to feel a little nervous. You were probably nervous the first time you went on a date, came to college, or took your first exam. It goes away, but a certain amount of nervous tension means you are alive and thinking and realize that what you are doing is important.

You will develop confidence as you write more and more, but some of the nervousness never goes away. You will be nervous when you start your first job or cover your first council meeting or write your first page one story.

It helps a lot if you expect writing to be hard work and don't expect to do things quickly and easily.

Expect stories to be difficult. Expect that there will be deadline pressures and go to work right now to get your work done on time. Worrying about pressures does not make them go away. Writing at least a first draft will help to resolve some of the tension. Then your focus moves from worrying about something to improving what you have. It is a lot easier the second time through a story.

No two lines of work are the same. Doctors, dentists, and

lawyers face pressures, deadlines, and tension. That is why they have internships and continuing education programs, and why they work so hard to understand their profession. All of this applies as well to newswriting.

Doctors on internships and lawyers in mock court practice cases also learn from others in their field. You should be doing the same.

Watch the television news reporters. Read the big city and small town newspapers. Listen to newscasts whenever you can. Notice what these people are doing and how it applies to what you are doing. You can't be a success in this business without being curious and wanting to share information. Almost all of them have been through a formal writing program at one time or another. Learn from them.

Things to Remember

- Newswriting is writing with a purpose. The purpose is to inform others, not to show how well you write. The two elements are not mutually exclusive, but informing is the first purpose.
- The student must know that little writing instruction is done on the job because of the time pressures in journalism, and so every writing course in college is very important.
- Every story must have something that is new, and it must be developed in an accurate setting. Other factors are less important than newness and accuracy.
- Writing is a lonely, private business, but writers can share their difficulties with instructors, editors, and friends to make it easier. Writers can also watch what other writers are doing so as to improve their own work.

PART II

MEDIA WRITING

9

Building Blocks: The Elements of Newswriting—Proper Words, Sentences, and Paragraphs

"Vigorous writing is concise. A sentence should contain no unnecessary words, a paragraph no unnecessary sentences, for the same reason that a drawing should have no unnecessary lines and a machine no unnecessary parts."—William Strunk

Donlee

In This Chapter

The overarching importance of accuracy.

Starting out "on the right foot"—understanding cliches, grammar problems, redundancies, and other "gremlins" that show up in copy.

Knowing when to keep writing, and when to stop to look something up.

Putting thoughts together in straightforward sentences—without qualifiers that "water down" thoughts and weaken sentences.

WE HAVE discussed the philosophy of newswriting—to tell the important stories in our society to the rest of society so that it can adjust to what is going on.

We have discussed the pressures, problems, and philosophy a reporter must work under. We've talked deadlines, pressures, and developing your own writing philosophy.

We have tried to set the stage for you so that when you sit down to write a story you will know why it is being written that way and what part one story plays in the entire role of the media.

We now need to set up the building blocks of which a story is made, so that you can put them together in the following chapters.

Accuracy

Regardless of anything else discussed here, accuracy is the first consideration. It is more important than style. It is more important than literary flourish. It is more important than anything else. Period.

A misspelled name tells the reader that the reporter didn't care enough to check or have enough respect for the individual to take the extra few seconds needed to look up the person's name.

A wrong address could lead to a libel case, as the reporter might identify the wrong person as the one arrested for murder, rape, or possession of a drug with intent to distribute.

The wrong time on a meeting could cause many people to show up at a time other than when the meeting is scheduled, to miss the meeting, and to think ill of the reporter for not checking.

Being accurate takes time, takes patience and means the reporter must have compassion for the individuals named in the story. It comes before anything else we discuss now.

Finding the Right Words

Avoiding Abstractions

There are those who are convinced reporters can talk about anything—including nuclear physics and relativity—if they use terms people can understand. It is up to the reporter to find the terms people need, not up to the reader or the source to understand what the reporter writes or what the city accountant says.

One of the most common problems is in financing. Government officials speak glibly of 4.7 mills, but how much is a mill? A mill is an abstract term. "Abstract" means apart from concrete realities, specific objects, or actual instances (Webster's Encyclopedic Unabridged).

A mill is a unit of measurement equal to one tenth of a cent. When used in taxes, it is one-tenth of one cent assessed against property value.

Knowing that is not helpful, until the reporter can relate a mill to "concrete realities, specific objects or actual instances." One-tenth of a cent may mean something, but not really.

Translating mills into actual dollars of taxes means working with a government official to tell how much the average homeowner would pay if his or her taxes went up 4.7 mills. It might mean $4 a month, it might mean $23 a year, depending on the local situation. But $4 a month or $23 a year is something concrete that a reader can relate to, and it means that the reporter has avoided abstractions.

Translating this is not easy, and far fewer newspersons or broadcasters do it than should do it. Reporters do the reader a disservice when they say the village is considering putting a 4.7 mill issue on the ballot without telling them what 4.7 mills is equal to in cold, hard, concrete cash.

Other abstractions:

Zoning is setting parts of a community aside for special purposes. Some areas will be residential, others will be factories, still others will be commercial and/or industrial. But B1 business or R3 residential mean nothing unless they are explained, and the reasons for zoning also need to be explained.

Arraignment is a common legal term that all lawyers know. Some readers know it means to be brought before a court to answer a charge police have filed against you. Many readers skip right over it. Wouldn't it be better to say XXX was brought before a judge this morning to answer police charges in the murder of YYY. Yes, it is longer, but isn't it clearer as well?

Change of venue is legal terminology for moving the trial to another city, probably because it is a heinous crime that has gotten a lot of publicity locally. Go ahead, use change of venue, but explain what it means right after you use the term.

The moral of this section is that a lot of legal terms are not understood by the average reader. Readers are not dumb, they just have not had occasion to face these terms before. Reporters have faced them before and understand them, so they should explain them.

The law is not the only field with specialized or abstract terms. How about *myocardial infarction* in medicine, *freedom of the press* in journalism, *juvenile delinquency* in sociology, *relativity* in physics, or hundreds of others? You may know these because you have had courses in them or have been exposed to them, but what about the person who has never seen the term before? A reporter's job is to explain that term, so you have to be sure you understand it first.

Finding the Exact Word for the Situation

We grew up separating the good guys from the bad guys. Bad guys include burglars, crooks, robbers, and thieves. But there are specific definitions for each of these words, and using them improperly is not uncommon.

A *burglar* breaks into someone else's house at night with the intent to commit a felony, or major crime.

A *crook* is slang for a dishonest person, usually a swindler or a thief.

A *robber* takes something by force or threat, usually but not always including a gun.

A *thief* is a person who steals secretly and without force. The targets may not even know the thief was there, and certainly a gun was not used in committing a crime.

It makes a great deal of difference which type of charge police file, and the reporter must be careful to get it right when interviewing the police.

And be sure not to call *anyone* a burglar, crook, robber, or thief until he or she has been convicted in a court of law with due process (another abstraction). Until a person is convicted, if convicted, the person is a suspect, nothing more.

A number of fields have similar distinctions between terms.

A *doctor* is a person licensed to practice medicine or dentistry, or a person who has been awarded a doctoral degree in an academic field, such as history, political science, or psychology.

A *physician* is a person who is legally licensed to practice medicine, a doctor of medicine, but is in general practice rather than surgery. Note that this excludes dentists and academic doctors.

A *surgeon* is a physician who specializes in surgery; i.e., operations. This excludes dentists, academic doctorates, and general practitioners in medicine. With each term we get more specialized.

A *lawyer* conducts lawsuits in a court of law or does legal business outside the court system.

An *attorney* is usually, but not always, a lawyer. An attorney may be someone legally empowered to act for someone else and in this case would not be a lawyer.

Counselor is a term used by lawyers and others, and in a legal sense means a person who conducts a case in court, but does not have to be a lawyer.

A *solicitor* in the usual sense is a lawyer working for a governmental unit; i.e., the city's lawyer.

In sports, a *manager* is the person who makes the decision on a professional baseball team, and a *coach* carries out his orders. In other sports, a coach makes the decisions, and a manager may be little more than a person who brings out the equipment.

If you are not sure of titles or proper terms to use, ask.

Common Mistakes in Grammar

There are a lot of terms used improperly in grammar, one of which is "alot." In spoken English, no one can tell the difference between alot and a lot. In written English, there is a lot of difference. A lot is two words when used correctly. This is similar to all right, which is incorrect when spelled as "alright." Use two words in both cases.

Please understand at the outset that none of us, instructors included, knows every rule of grammar. Very few human beings go through life without consulting a dictionary. The student should know that we all have different weaknesses, and that we need to be aware of them. It is not a sign of weakness to carry a pocket dictionary or a grammar reference with you when you write. It is expected. Know that you don't know it all, and be prepared to look it up quickly and as often as needed.

Perhaps the most common error in student papers is *it's* versus *its*. In conversation, there is no difference. In written English and media writing, there is a difference.

It's (with apostrophe) means it is. It's time to go to class.

Its (no apostrophe) is the possessive form, as in the team lost its lead.

Students generally should stop each time they use its or it's, and decide which is the proper usage. It doesn't take much time, but it's vitally important that the writer check its application each time.

Hopefully wins the prize at the moment for the most troublesome word. It has caught on in conversation like a wildfire in a California canyon. Hopefully is "in," it is "sincere," and everyone uses it—but it is usually used improperly.

Hopefully means something is done in a hopeful manner, as he talked to his ailing mother hopefully. To be used in "Hopefully, there will be no more war" is wrong. What is correct is "I hope there will be no more war."

Among other common mistakes (we can't cover them all here) are *different from* and *different than*. You would say he differs from his brother, so you should say he is different from his brother, not different than his brother.

Lay and *lie* also cause problems. You lay something down on a desk. Lay requires an object; you have to have something with it. The past tense is *laid,* as in she laid the book on the desk.

Lie does not have a direct object, does not have to have something with it, and means lying down. The body will *lie* in state. Its past tense is *lay,* (yes, it is confusing, especially in the past tense) as in he got sunburned as he *lay* on the beach, or while he was *lying* on the beach.

Over and *more than* are widely misused, even in the commercials on national television networks. Over means above, as in the plane flew over the city. More than means more than, as in he sold automobiles for more than 50 years. Do not say over 50 years, although many, many advertisers do.

Another set of problem words is *fewer* and *less*, also often confused with each other. Fewer means individual items, as he had fewer friends than she did, or her team had fewer base hits. If you can count them individually, it is fewer.

Less is for amount, quantities, or non-individual things. Florida has less cold weather than New York, but Florida has fewer cold days (you can count days, you can't count weather). His company employed less people is wrong, it should be fewer people. He had less help is correct, because you cannot count help in units.

That and *which* are two of the most troublesome words. These are both somewhat abstract words, and since they refer to other persons or items it is even more difficult to remember which one to use.

In grammar, *that* and *which* are used with restrictive and nonrestrictive clauses. A clause is a part of a sentence with its own subject and verb. The Associated Press style book uses the terms essential clauses (for restrictive) and nonessential clauses (for nonrestrictive.)

The essential or restrictive clause is one that must follow the *that* or *which* in order for the sentence to make sense. The nonrestrictive or nonessential clause is one that adds information about the topic, but could be eliminated and the sentence would still make sense.

The house that police were watching was on a dead-end street. That police were watching is a restrictive or essential clause because the information in the clause (that police were watching) is necessary to the sentence. The sentence makes no sense without the clause. Essential clauses are not set off by commas.

The house, which had new shutters, was on a dead-end street. Which had new shutters adds information to the sentence, but this information is nonrestrictive or nonessential and the sentence could live without it. Nonessential clauses are set off by commas, indicating that they could be eliminated without changing the meaning of the sentence.

When mentioning people in a clause, use who or whom. The supervisor who won the award had just started at the company (essential clause). The supervisor, who has just returned from Mexico (nonessential clause), was new on the job.

When you talk about objects or animals, use *that* for essential clauses and *which* for nonessential clauses. The car that needed a tire repair was in the garage (essential clause). The car, which had a new paint job, was in the garage (nonessential clause).

Cliches

A cliche is a sentence or phrase, usually expressing a popular or common thought or idea, which has lost originality, ingenuity, or impact by long overuse, such as *sadder but wiser* or *strong as an ox* (*Webster's Encyclopedic Unabridged Dictionary*).

Cliches are a special problem with newswriting. Not only do they say something that is not new but also they often imply an opinion. And since cliches "abound" in conversation, it seems difficult not to use them since we are so familiar with them. The use of cliches is so common that I have seen at least three satirical student editorials over the years using nothing but cliches—to warn against using cliches.

For example, we might have "a host of close personal friends" come to us "in the nick of time" to "point with pride" about their "brilliant victory" in the "battle" against cliches "at long last," and ask that we "take the acid test" "at breakneck speed" "in deadly earnest" to make our writing "an enjoyable occasion" and help to "iron out" our "continuing problems" before we reach "a ripe old age."

In some areas of news, especially sports, it is difficult to avoid cliches. The nature of football, basketball, and baseball (avoid calling them the pigskin, the roundball, and the horsehide sports) is that each game can be very much like the last one. In order to make them sound different from each other, sports writers "reach into their bag of cliches" and come up with statements that make each game unique.

"They came from behind" or "he gave 110 percent" (which is physically impossible, if you think of it) or "it was another nailbiter in the closing seconds" are all cliches. So are headlines that talk about how one team "tipped, nipped or ripped" another.

How do you avoid cliches? First, recognize that they do exist, and if you are not conscious of them, they can "creep into" your writing. Second, write about what makes each story unique, using the facts and specifics on hand. Most stories have something different about them, which is one of the reasons they are news. Focus on that difference, and not on the similarity with other stories (which "goes without saying" if you analyze the nature of news).

Therefore, say that "Langford tipped in a rebound with his left hand with 2.4 seconds left on the clock." This is far superior to saying "It went down to the final seconds before the Cardinals pulled another one out of the fire." Use the specifics in the most interesting possible way.

Or, say that "Jameson had 25 points for the night, 14 more than his average." That is better than saying he played "inspired basketball, and gave 110 percent."

Or say the team "missed six consecutive free throws in the final minute." The coach won't like it, but if it is the truth it is much better than saying "The Jaguars came so close to victory last night before falling in the last minute."

Don't tell the readers that the council had "another long meeting Monday night," tell them the meeting adjourned at 1:15 A.M. after six hours of discussion, mainly about the police wanting to form a union.

Remember that if the reader has heard the term many times from other sources, he or she will not think it is original with you. For that reason, you should avoid the "hip" or "cool" slang of the moment that is sweeping television programs. It may be "OK" in conversation, but it is "the deadly enemy" of the newswriter.

CLICHES THAT CLING: SHOULD WE AVOID THEM LIKE THE PLAG...
by Bruce DeSilva, associate editor of writing
The Hartford Courant, Hartford, Conn.

Coaches' Corner, Dec. 1990

My name is Bruce and I am a clicheaholic.

(Shouts from the people sitting on metal folding chairs in the church basement. "Hi, Bruce! Nice to meet you, Bruce!")

I've been cliche-free since Thursday.

(Applause. Whistles. Shouts of encouragement.)

My story is probably a lot like yours. Once I had a beautiful home, a lovely wife. We had three great kids. Little Nel, Honest John and Fearless Fred.

(Gasps.)

You guessed it. I picked out the names.

My wife was understanding and loving, not the kind to leave a guy the first time he said "three sheets to the wind," but my God, what that woman endured.

Finally she put her foot dow...

Finally, she was at the end of her ro...

The last stra...

Uh.

She said I had to stop. Give up the cliches for good, she said, and stop hanging around with the bad crowd at *The Hartford Courant*.

OK, I said. I promise, I said. But of course, it was a lie.

I became a secret cliche abuser. I muttered banalities under my breath. I wrote cliche-ridden letters-to-the-editor under other people's names. I wrote horrible things with Magic Markers on men's room walls.

You know what comes next. What had to happen. What always happens. I was found out.

For me, it was the urine test at work.

I was fired. Disgraced. Lovely Rita, the meter maid (did I mention that?) left me and took Little Nel, Honest John and Fearless Fred with her.

I don't remember much about the next five years. Just snatches. Yelling "You can lead a horse to water but you can't make him drink" at pedestrians who hurried past and tried not to hear. Hanging around school yards and whispering "a penny for your thoughts" to little girls. Getting beaten by a cop after telling him to "hit the road, Jack."

Then I met Soozie.

She threw me a lifeli...

She held out a helping ha...

She pulled my fat from the fi...

She gave me a new lease on li...

Uh...

It was like the cavalry coming over the hi...

(The people in the folding chairs hold their breath.)

She was an angel of mer...

The answer to my pray...

Uh.

She helped a lot.

(Wild applause. Foot stomping.)

So now, when I feel a banality coming on, I give Soozie a call. And she talks me down.

I'd like to marry her someday. Settle down. Raise some kids. But the cliches made me sterile.

From now on, it won't be easy for me. I know that. I've been sick a long time.

But I'm on the road to recov...

I'm taking it one day at a ti...

The Importance of Picking the Right Verb

The simple, straightforward sentence is made up of a subject, a verb, and an object of that verb. In other words, someone or some group (subject) is doing something (verb) that needs clarification (object).

The subject is usually the name of a person or the name of a group or the name of something. It can be shortened (The Director of Foreign Studies for the Division of Higher Education for the Board of Education of the United Methodist Church can become "a Methodist spokesman" in a lead), but it is usually pretty clear who the subject is. Writers do not have a lot of choice, except to try to keep it short.

However, writers do have a choice in the use of a verb. Verbs express action; the more specific or the more appropriate the verb, the better the sentence. The verb is the heart of the sentence and the livelier the heart is, the more powerful the sentence is. Picking the exact verb from the hundreds available to you will brighten up the sentence, give it a specific meaning, and show you are a careful writer.

There are three kinds of verbs:

Transitive verbs do something to someone. The someone receives the action. The professor was awarded a medal (the words "the medal" complete the sense of the sentence).

Intransitive verbs have no action. Her mother had returned. No object is needed to complete the sentence.

Linking verbs tell of the subject's state of being. Henderson was ill after he caught the flu bug. Is, are, looked (healthy), seemed (interested), grew (taller) are all linking verbs. Verbs of this type do not add action to the sentence, and so are often frowned upon. However, there are times when they must be used.

Picking specific verbs often means thinking through the sentence before writing. Writers have to know what they want to say, and have to want to say it as clearly and powerfully as possible.

For example, there is a clear difference between "an explosion *shattered* a building" and "an explosion *hit* a building." Shattered gives you a better picture of what happened.

A house *gutted* by fire and a house *burned* are two different stories, because a house gutted cannot be repaired, while a house burned can.

A piece of legislation *tabled* is more definite than that same legislation being *discussed*.

A person *pinned* under a car gives a stronger picture than someone *caught* when a car fell on her, or a statement saying she "was under the car when the emergency squad arrived."

Verb is from the Latin *verbum* for word, and it is clearly the most important word in the sentence. Choose carefully when deciding which word or words will tell the story best.

Verb abuse

Verbs can be misused as well. Student writers often make the following kinds of mistakes:

Turning a noun into a verb

It may seem chic in the business world to say, "Our company is headquartered in Rhode Island," but straightforward journalistic writing calls for saying, "Our company has headquarters in Rhode Island."

Likewise, it becomes fashionable to say someone *authored* a book rather than wrote it; or a plan was *finalized* rather than completed. (Editors have been known to all but fly into a rage when "finalize" or other words ending in -ize, such as prioritize or utilize, popped up in stories.)

Dictionaries and lawyers will have words such as *decasualize* (to reduce or eliminate the employment of casual labor) or *delegalize* (to revoke the legal status of), but that does not mean reporters have to use them. These words not only combine verb forms with noun bases, but also they add to our jargon. Lawyers may use the terms while talking to other lawyers, and since they both understand them, conversation goes on smoothly. But persons who have not heard or seen the words before will stop reading when they come to terms they do not know.

Subject-verb agreement

Students will have problems with certain kinds of noun-verb agreement. The rule is that a singular subject will have a singular verb (She did) and a plural subject will have a plural verb (They do).

The problem in journalism writing comes from nouns that seem to be plural, but are actually singular, called collective nouns. Many of these nouns are used in media writing, including council, team, majority, media, and statistics, among others.

When the collective noun is used as a group, it is singular. The council met its deadline, not their deadline, because there is only one council. The team met its goal, not their goal, because there is only one team.

When thinking of the group as individual members, use the plural. The council could not make up their minds, if there is a divided vote.

Similarly, the team lost its poise (one team), but the team would be going to their homes after the season (individual members).

Media is plural, the singular is medium. Newspapers are a medium, but newspapers, radio, television, and magazines are members of the mass media. Saying the media is in agreement on something is incorrect. The media are in agreement on a position is correct.

Statistics can have two meanings. It can mean a collection of data or it can mean a class in which that subject is taught. So you can say "Statistics is a difficult subject" and be correct, or you can say that the statistics (numbers) indicate (plural verb) and also be correct. It depends on the usage.

Active, not Passive, Verbs

Active verbs are those in which the subject does something: "He smashed his fist when he ran into the wall chasing a fly ball."

Passive verbs let the action happen to the subject. "His fist was smashed when he ran into the wall."

Active verbs are better because they show action, take fewer words, and come directly to the point.

"The House today passed higher unemployment benefits" is active.

"A package that would extend unemployment payments to those whose package has run out is" passive. Sentences using the passive verb are usually longer, seem a lot duller to read, and also seem more complicated. Often, when a writer is not confident of what she is going to write, it comes out as a passive sentence.

You should write the sentence, not let the sentence be written by you. Active verbs have power; passive verbs slow the sentence down. If you do not try to write a strong sentence, it will not be strong.

Specifics, Not Generalities

Reporters who do not ask for specific bits of information do not have them when they start to write. Including details is the difference between an average or dull story and a bright, interesting one that readers will enjoy.

A writer uses specifics as an artist uses a paintbrush. Details bring out the highlights of a painting, and they also bring out the highlights of a story.

A generality is that a woman celebrated her 110th birthday. A valuable and telling detail is saying that she "broke her hip the first time at 103 and the second time at 107."

A generality is that the 110-year-old Florida woman's two daughters care for her alternately every four months. A specific is that one comes from Kansas and the other from Oregon to stay four months at a time.

A generality is saying that a car was stolen from behind an all-night diner. A valuable detail is telling that the BMW 535i was stolen at 4:30 A.M. on Sunday when a motorist left the motor running as he went in for matches. A generality is saying that flood waters almost went over the top of the dam. A valuable detail is saying the water got to within an inch and one half of the top.

A generality is saying rents are increasing in your community. A specific is that the average rent for a two-bedroom apartment has gone up $75 a month in the last year, according to a survey of the 12 largest apartment complexes in town.

A generality is saying the school district will ask for 4.7 mills. A valuable detail is that the 4.7 mills will cost a person with a $50,000 home $240 a year in new taxes.

A valuable detail is not saying that a new ordinance passed, but that it passed 5-4 after three hours of often loud debate.

Unfortunately, beginning reporters often overlook details. They don't think that a comment or a fact or a number of a detail will make a difference. They may have laughed at a joke, but they won't include it in their story. They may have marveled at how many details a source has, but they won't include them because they think no one really cares. If it interested you, it will probably interest others.

Put it in your story, an editor can take it out later. But chances are pretty good that he or she will also like the specifics and the details.

If you think of media writing as news reports with specific details, you will remember to record those details when you take notes. Then include them as needed when you write the story. Anything specific and concrete is likely to make your story more believable—and more interesting.

Adjectives and Modifiers

Mark Twain, who had a lot of interesting things to say about writing, once said: "Whenever you see an adjective or an adverb, kill it on the spot." His point was that many of them, if not most, were unnecessary. They added opinion to the statement and not fact, and could be general, rather than specific.

Don't say someone was very tall, say he was 6 feet, 10 inches.

Don't say the patient had a weight problem, say he was 5 feet, five inches and weighed 310 pounds before the operation.

Don't say something "finally" happened, as many adverbs such as this are judgment terms. Who is to say that whatever "finally" happened did not take a long time for good reasons. "Finally" is a word reporters use to add opinion to a story when that opinion may not be justified.

Watch your adjectives and adverbs carefully. Are they really necessary or can you "finally" get rid of many of them?

Redundancies

A redundancy is saying the same thing over again twice in a row once right after the other in repetition. Just kidding. A redundancy is excessive repetition or overlapping, especially of words.

Redundancies occur all of the time in conversation because we do not edit or correct our words as we speak. But in media writing, writers must be specific on the meaning and cut out the redundancies.

One of the most common is to talk of a fire and to say "the home was completely destroyed." Watch for news reports—I am certain that during this semester you will see or hear of a home "completely destroyed by fire." To destroy means to reduce to useless fragments, so "completely destroyed" is a redundancy because something is either destroyed or it is not.

Another misused term is gutted, as in "the home was completely gutted by fire." To gut means to destroy the interior of a building, so again there is excessive wordage.

Think carefully about all words as you use them. There are literally hundreds of redundancies. Easter Sunday (Easter is always on a Sunday); Jewish rabbi (no other religion has rabbis); 4 P.M. in the afternoon (4:00 P.M. is always in the afternoon); foreign imports; incumbent sheriff (incumbent means he holds the office, if he was not in office he would not be the sheriff, or he might be a candidate for sheriff); the building will close *down* (or close *up* for that matter); currently busy or currently anything, currently is not needed; first annual (if it is the first, it has not been held annually); funeral services (a funeral is a service); consensus of opinion; true facts; somewhat unique; visible to the eye; regular meeting; final conclusions; proposed plan; basic fundamentals. The list goes on.

One Word for Many

Because time and space are valuable in the media, writers use one word instead of two or three. Instead of the words on the left, use the word on the right. (You can think of many more examples.)

In the vicinity of—near
At the present time—now
Able to convince—convinced
In the amount of—for
The majority of—most
The committee held a meeting—the committee met
In my way of thinking—I think
Was the honored recipient of—won
A distance of 40 miles—40 miles
In the event that—if
Make an adjustment to—adjust

While these and many other examples can be shortened, remember that the editing is best done in the editing or rewrite phase of writing. If you know what the main point is for a story, write the story as quickly and clearly as possible. This will mean that

127

you do not forget parts or the main point as you construct the story.

Once the first draft is done, *then* go through and cut two words or three words down to one. This is a valuable part of understanding process. You can put together your story first, and then adjust, clarify, and refine later.

Just don't lose the enthusiasm and the drive needed to put the story together by stopping at every other sentence to correct redundancies, wordiness, or other errors. Do correct them, but remember that the most important thing is to tell a clear and complete story. So write first, and edit after you get the story down on paper or the computer screen.

If this leads you to think that you have to understand the story as well as you can before you start writing, then we are making progress. Very important progress.

Keeping It Short

Since the readers have little time, writers have to organize their thoughts in a fashion that makes it easy for readers to follow. This means short sentences. There is no magic average, but if you type two lines without a period, you have probably gone too far. The newspaper needs short sentences to give a non-gray look. The broadcaster needs short sentences to be able to pause for breath.

But even more importantly, the audience needs short sentences to be able to understand the story. By adding qualifying statements or phrases that bring in side issues, by making the sentences too complex, or by "weaseling" a sentence by adding qualifiers (which is what we are doing in this very sentence), the reader loses the meaning.

Unfortunately, writing short sentences is more difficult than writing long sentences. The writer has to think it through to decide what the main point is and eliminate unnecessary material before writing the sentence. This is what takes time.

Just as unfortunately, most news stories are written under deadline, and writers often do not have the time to think them through as much as they would like.

When this subject comes up, students often say they are afraid of having sentences that are too short. They are afraid their writing will sound like a nursery rhyme. How long is too long, how short is too short?

Since we started this section with the heading *Keeping It Short*, we have had 14 sentences with a total of 235 words, or an average sentence length of 14 words. Notice that one was 42 words (the one about the long dependent clauses), and another was 29 words (the one about writers not having time). But there were also sentences with four, six, and ten words in them.

Use sentences of varying length, depending on what you want to say in each sentence. If you think and write naturally, you will write sentences of varying lengths.

A number of important studies have been done to describe how long sentences should be. This research has been going on since the 1940s, though there is little evidence that it has made major headway.

So, how do you write short in news style?

1. Decide what you have to say, and say it.
2. Avoid qualifying phrases before you get to the main point of the sentence. If the qualifiers are important, bring them in right after the main sentence.
3. Avoid complicated, many-syllable words. Long sentences combined with polysyllabics are too much for the mind to keep up with.
4. Use specifics rather than generals. Four is a specific, several is a general. 4:40 P.M. Tuesday is a specific, sometime late Tuesday afternoon is a general. The mind can picture a specific, but it has trouble handling several general statements in the same sentence.
5. Use familiar rather than unfamiliar words. A Senate committee is a familiar phrase, but the Senate Subcommittee on Military Affairs in South America is unfamiliar. Start with a Senate committee in the lead, and then use the full name of the committee. Police officer is a familiar phrase, campus safety and security officer is unfamiliar. The latter is the correct title and should be used, but when pressed for words in the beginning of the sentence, use "police officer."
6. Use short words. Even a 29-word sentence with short words can be understood, if it is presented normally. But a 29-word lead sentence that includes several qualifiers and polysyllabics can be hard to handle.

For example, using short words, you would say (Lead 1): "The West County school board is thinking about a new high school. They don't know yet where it will be built, or how much it will cost, but they agree it is necessary." (12 words first sentence, 21 words second sentence, average 16.5 words. Most complicated word is "necessary," which everyone understands.)

Now contrast this with the following (Lead 2): "The West County board of education, in a meeting that ran four hours Monday night, tabled two separate motions that would have specified the amount of millage and the proposed location of a new comprehensive senior high school." (38 words, with concepts such as tabled, millage, proposed, and comprehensive, some of which would need explanation.)

Again, please remember that Lead 1 took *more* time to think through and less time to write. Lead 2 took less time to think through and more time to write. But the reader would clearly understand Lead 1 and might have some difficulty (perhaps not that much) understanding Lead 2.

Simple Declarative Sentences

The letters S-V-O are sometimes used to remind the writer that each sentence should have a subject, a verb, and an object. The subject is who or what the sentence is about. The verb is what that person is doing (active voice) or what is happening to that person (passive voice). The object is the completion of the sentence, telling what the rest of the thought is.

The following are simple declarative sentences:

"John Greeley, 76, of 23327 Lorandy Avenue, died at his home today."

"The fable of the groundhog is predicting six more weeks of winter."

"A campus police officer has been arrested in the murder of a female student."

The following are long, complex sentences, taken from recent newspaper leads:

"Insufficient water pressure in the sprinkler system of the Retirement Manor nursing home on West Bloomfield Road and Cleveland Heights Boulevard could result in the home's fire insurance policy being increased or even canceled, according to a complaint registered with the city utilities division."

Simplify it to "A retirement home in the county says its water pressure is so low it could have big trouble if a fire broke out."

"Regional contribution agreements, spinoffs of state legislation that is designed to help urban communities rehabilitate their substandard housing, may be tested in Springfield Township under a proposal to be considered next week at the regional planning commission monthly meeting."

Simplify it to "Springfield Township may try a new plan to redo substandard housing. The township board is considering working together with other cities to get federal funds for rebuilding housing areas."

"Bucklett County will receive $25,000 from the fruits of crime, based on recent Supreme Court decisions that permit confiscation of personal and real property used in the commission of a felony, the county prosecutor said today."

Simplify to the following: "The state now permits counties to take homes, cars, and other items used in the commission of crimes, such as selling drugs. This year Bucklett County will get two Camaros, a Jeep wagon, four rifles and $10,000 (instead of a house) from people who were caught handling drugs. All will be used in anti-drug programs."

One Idea per Paragraph

The tendency in writing for English themes or other projects is to put several related thoughts into a paragraph. This makes sense when perhaps only one person is going to read what you write, and that person knows the subject very well.

In newswriting, many people will read what you write or hear what you say over the air. Some will be paying attention, some will understand it, some will take the time to read or listen carefully— and others will not.

Therefore, when writing to a wide and general audience, you need to be as specific as possible. You need to break your thoughts down clearly, and state them clearly. This is better accomplished by using one idea per paragraph and not combining two or three ideas into one graph. It makes the story easier to follow.

Therefore, when you write for the media, you should first outline your thoughts. This can be done either with a word outline or a longer outline.

Then use short sentences and short paragraphs. If you need a "magic number," try to limit yourself to four typed lines per paragraph. This would become eight lines in a newspaper story, and that is as long as you want to go.

Transition Between Paragraphs

Putting an outline together permits the writer to think about how to get from one main point to another. In writing terms, moving smoothly from one topic to the next is called transition.

A writer cannot move smoothly from one paragraph to the next unless he thinks it through first. When writing a news story as a story, there is a logical reason for organizing it a certain way. Think this through first and then proceed.

Unfortunately, reporters usually write the lead first and then go on to whatever else comes next. What little research there is on how news writers actually write indicates that there is very little organization or thinking about the entire story before they start writing. Beginning students who force themselves to think through the story first will have an enormous edge on those who write in the normal, "do-the-lead-first" approach.

The traditional method of writing news stories as shown in Pitts' (1982) research is to think about the lead first. The next step is to answer the questions the lead does not answer. The rest of the story follows in this pattern, all derived from the lead.

If the reporter thinks the entire story through first, he or she will know what has to come next, and the story will appear as a unit, as a story, not as a jam-packed lead with sentences that follow.

Focusing on the lead, the late Harry Stapler showed, makes the lead much longer than other sentences in the story. His study of 12 major papers showed the lead to average 28 words per sentence, and the rest of the story to average 21 words. It makes the lead too crowded, and confuses the reader (Stapler 1985).

We bring this up now so that you can try to make your sentences uniform and write a lead sentence that is not too long, but summarizes what is going on.

Writing short, concise sentences is more a matter of thinking than it is of writing. If you know the purpose of your story, you can do it in reasonably short sentences. If you are not sure what you are going to say when you start to write, your lead sentences, and all others as well, will show that indecision. They will be long, complex, full of modifiers and phrases, and as difficult to read as this sentence is. Do not do this!

Putting a Story Together

Most writers know how to develop a reasonably good lead, and they know when to stop writing, but organizing what is between the lead and the ending is a problem.

The confusion comes from relying too much on the lead and not knowing what to do after writing it. This can be corrected by "thinking *story*," which means understanding how the parts go together. This is a major aspect of writing, and is discussed with the styles and formulas.

There are times when a story is so good or is so well told that "it tells itself." These times are rare, but when they occur the reporter should let the source tell the story directly to the reader through the use of quotes, examples, and the source's actual words.

There are also major police, weather, or announcement stories that are so newsworthy that you write them very easily. But be aware that major stories tell themselves very rarely, and you ought to plan to organize most of the stories you write.

Choosing the right word and putting short sentences together are the basics of any story. If you know what you are doing with the story when you start, you will be able to put it together much more easily.

Copy Preparation

Students need to learn the symbols that editors use to mark copy. Instructors use them as well. In the day of the computer, students need to understand both the computer symbols and the paper symbols. Much class work will be done on the computer, but many reports or stories will even now be typed onto paper. Also, free lance articles may be submitted on paper, although electronic transfer is becoming more common.

So, the student needs to understand both sets of symbols. See table 3.1 for a review of copy editing functions.

Associated Press Style

Sometime during the writing process, the reporter needs to understand Associated Press or AP style.

The *AP Stylebook,* organized like a dictionary, makes decisions in cases where there are choices in spelling, numbers, capitalization, punctuation, and abbreviation. New editions are issued from time to time by a group of Associated Press editors who do an enormous amount of work, and then get together at conventions to provide a standard, uniform guide to writing copy.

For example, a dictionary may have two spellings for a word. The *AP Stylebook* will choose one, making it easier for editors to handle wire copy and to submit copy to the wire services.

Numbers, such as those on streets, could be either 18th street or Eighteenth Street. Certain words can be capitalized or not, other words ought to be capitalized all the time. Some words can be abbreviated or spelled out. AP style provides you with the rules to follow in making these decisions.

AP style will be covered in the Rewrite section of this book, in chapter 20. Your instructor might decide to work on it at this time.

It is in the Rewrite section because of the concern for keeping story ideas together. It is easier to write the story all the way through, and then correct for AP style after the writing is completed. Stopping several times in a story to make style corrections ruins the thought process.

Make no mistake. AP style must be followed. The only question is at which point in the process does the writer apply the style rules.

Students will find they can go anywhere in the United States and find AP style the dominant style system. Local variations will be present in most cases, but the heart of the style will be what writers are accustomed to. Once you learn it, it will follow you. If you don't learn it, it will haunt you. A fuller discussion of AP style is found in chapter 20.

Things to Remember

- Journalistic writing is precise and short. This puts a double burden on the writer to be accurate and brief. Understand that this is not easy, but it can be developed.
- Using specifics and information geared to the reader can make the material easier to read, but it takes extra care and extra steps to prepare. Expect that higher demands on news stories make them harder to write than many themes or term papers, even though they are shorter.
- The audience, in its haste to keep up with everything, wants things short. But the audience also jumps on grammatical, spelling, and style errors as a sign of weakness in the media. Reporters must do all they can to avoid common mistakes.
- Try to organize your writing into one main thought per paragraph, and one main thought per sentence. The thinking will take more time, but the reader will appreciate it.
- There is a time for writing and a time for checking grammar and errors. Write first, as completely as possible, and with the sense of doing a complete story. Correct for mistakes after the entire piece is written.
- Understand the importance of Associated Press style in making writing across the country uniform in certain factors. But do not attempt to stop after each sentence to check for AP style or you may lose your train of thought.

Exercises

1. Take the largest circulation newspaper in your city. Check one to three pages, reading each story all the way through. Watch

for all of the kinds of problems—errors, cliches, redundancies, generalities, etc.—mentioned in this chapter.

2. Do not assume that just because it is a large newspaper it is free of all errors or mistakes. Deadlines may place greater pressures on large papers than they do on small papers, which have problems with smaller and less experienced staffs.

3. Watch this newspaper or others for some of the basics of AP style—use of titles, capitals, abbreviations, and numbers. Is there a pattern and a consistency in how these items are used?

4. Take two or three stories of major news events that appear in this paper. Compare them with stories covering the same topic in the same day's USA Today. Notice the differences in how the stories are written. Is there a difference in the way the information is given to the reader in the two papers? Do you get more information on one story from one paper or the other? Is one more complete, and is this good or bad? Is there a major difference in the way the sentences and paragraphs are written, and is this good or bad? Which paper has more stories? Is it more important to have more stories or to have some stories written longer and more completely?

5. Which stories were harder to write—those in USA Today or those in the large circulation paper from your area?

10
Organizing Straightforward News Stories: The Inverted Pyramid and Related Systems

"You don't write because you want to say something; you write because you've got something to say."—F. Scott Fitzgerald

In This Chapter

Why you can't separate the form of the story from the purpose of the story.

Knowing how a "formula" can help with many routine news stories.

"Walking through" several forms of a single-event news story.

Using the journalist's five Ws and an H to good advantage.

Understanding the inverted pyramid and its limitations.

AFTER all of the discussion on writing, we are about to write. Do not think of what we have just been through as a discussion, lecture, or something theoretical and apart from actual writing. We have tried to set the stage, to have you understand the component parts of a story before you write actual stories.

Keep the things we have talked about in the back of your mind as you prepare to write stories. It may not be easy, but remember those principles as you begin to apply what you have learned about newswriting.

We will define *formula stories* or *single-incident* stories as those that follow the same pattern each time you write them, but with different sets of facts.

Most automobile accidents, robberies, and many fires can be written in the same form.

Each time a company promotes someone, the form is not the important thing—the name of the person is. When a person dies, the form of the story is not as important as identifying that person and telling about their life, family, and accomplishments.

We will use formula or single-event stories as the first pattern to learn, to be followed by a chapter on each of these types of stories:

- *More complex*, longer single-event stories.
- *Multiple-event* stories with several things happening at once, such as meetings, speeches, or press conferences.
- *Feature stories*, the more informal, personalized background stories about people or issues, which use many familiar literary writing techniques.
- *Broadcast writing*, written for the eye and the ear.
- *Public relations writing*, designed to explain a position, event, or activity.
- *Rewriting*, the refining, polishing part of the process that applies to all types of writing.

The Single-Event, Inverted Pyramid Story

This type of story applies to much of what is routine in media writing. It covers one item, one event, or one happening. The name "inverted pyramid" refers to the structure: an upside down pyramid, heavy on the top and getting thinner toward the bottom.

The brief history of the inverted pyramid, is as follows:

During the Civil War, reporters went to the scattered battlefields to cover the bloody battles of the war. They would file, or send, their stories back to their newspapers by telegraph.

At first, they would send chronological stories back, reporting the battle from the very first shot fired to the final victory. This took a great deal of time and expense on the telegraph system. This system worked reasonably well only if there were only one or two reporters at each battle. But when many reporters tried to file stories at the same time, and there was only one telegraph station, there was confusion. The telegraph services decided the only fair way was for each reporter to send one paragraph and then let the other reporters all send one paragraph until each reporter had sent at least one paragraph. Then the other reporters would be permitted to send another paragraph, in order, until everyone had "filed" their stories.

The reporters, anxious to get as much information as they could into that one paragraph and knowing it might be hours before they could file again, made sure they said who won, how many casualties there were, what the significance of the battle was, and whatever else they could get into the paragraph.

In terms of the five Ws and an H discussed before (Who, What, Where, When, Why, and How), they would cram as many as they could into the lead.

At the time, this was the right way to send stories. The competition was heavy, and the lines were few, and people had a full 24 hours to read their papers before another paper came out.

Now, advance the clock to the 1990s. Conditions are utterly different. Reporters can file directly from anywhere instantly. The audience can receive information in many different ways—newspaper, radio, television, satellite, computer-generated systems, microwave, maybe even wrist radio. Competition for the reader's attention is intense. But the inverted pyramid still remains an important part of journalism.

Many will tell you it is too much a part of journalism. Why many leads should be jam-packed with information when the audience has already seen or heard the story many times over is a real problem. Leads should reflect the audience's needs as well as the media's practices.

Having said this, you must remember two things: (1) many stories still use the inverted pyramid form; and (2) many stories are told better in some other form, such as narrative (story form) or feature style, or perhaps in a listing, not even a story form.

Any media writer, therefore, needs to understand the inverted pyramid form but, just as important, needs to know when another form of writing will tell the story better. We will discuss this as we go along.

The Inverted Pyramid Story

Let us assume you have just gotten the following facts over the phone: You get a call from James Madison University in Harrisonburg, Va. The person calling is the public relations officer. She says she has a story about one of the students from your hometown, and is calling because it is close to deadline, and she thinks it is important enough to run today.

The name of the student is Harlan Jefferson. He is a graduate of St. Francis High School in your town, where he was valedictorian of his class. He is also a varsity basketball player and the son of Mr. and Mrs. William Jefferson of 2424 W. Bend Avenue.

The reason for the call is that he has been elected president of the student government at James Madison. He will take office at the end of the month and won over four other candidates. He is a liberal studies major, a junior, and is planning to go to law school after he graduates from James Madison.

How do you start the story?

This is where you go back to the things we talked about previously:

- What is the most important fact in this story for the reader?
- What is the first thing the reader needs to know? Which of the five Ws and an H are important here?
- How can we write this in the fewest words so the reader can decide whether to read the rest of the story?

It all boils down to what is the most important part of this story. Ask yourself to say, in your own words, why this story is important. The answer is that a local person has been named to head the student government at a university in Virginia.

Do we write it like that? If we use those exact words, the reader will have to go on to the next sentence to find out who that person is. They may or may not do this.

The suggestion then would be to say "Harlan Jefferson (the

who part), a graduate of St. Francis High School, (further identification), has been elected president of the student government (what) at James Madison University" (where). This is 21 words, about right for a lead sentence.

Notice this sentence gives you the name, the local tie-in, and what the person has done to be in the news. The reader by this time can decide whether to read the rest of the story.

The second paragraph is somewhat of a problem for many writers. The tendency is to "go chronological," or to say something like "Jefferson is the son of Mr. and Mrs. William Jefferson, 2424 W. Bend Avenue, and was valedictorian of his graduating class at St. Francis." This is all true, but it is out of place.

Remember that you are telling a story, not listing the facts of this person's life. The story is that this person was elected president of student government, so facts relating to that election will continue the story in a logical fashion.

Say something like, "Jefferson was elected from a field of four candidates and will take office at the end of this month. He is a liberal studies major, and plans to enter law school after graduation." This tells you something about him as a person, and what his plans are.

After this, you might mention that he is the son of Mr. and Mrs. William Jefferson and is also a member of the varsity basketball team at James Madison. Both of these facts are important, but they are not as important to the story you are telling as the fact that he won the election over four candidates and takes office early next month.

The inverted pyramid is designed to do two things. First, it has the most important facts first. We start out directly with the name of the accomplishment.

We do not "tease" by stating that "A local person has won an important office," we come directly to the point. (And we would not use the word "important" either. It is one of those adjectives that we can get along without.)

We also do not start out by saying "James Madison University today announced that Harlan Jefferson has been elected president, etc." James Madison is an important part of this story, but not as important as the name of the person we know in the story. This is known as "backing in," or not coming directly to the point of the lead in the first few words.

The second important thing about the construction of the inverted pyramid is that it ends in a quiet and straightforward manner. After you mention the name of the parents and the fact that the young man plays basketball, there is very little left to say. The facts have been given out. You may add something about the enrollment, and the nature and location of James Madison, but that would be it.

You do not add a paragraph that says, "This is an excellent accomplishment for Jefferson and indicates he will do well in the future." This is known as a "cheerleading" ending and is entirely your opinion. If you wish to mention this on your editorial page, where the opinions are located, that would be fine.

But a normal inverted pyramid story stops dead in its tracks when it runs out of information. There is nothing more to say, so stop.

The fact that you have put the most important facts first, and stopped when you are done, also permits the editors to cut the story from the bottom first. If you run out of space in a newspaper, or time in a broadcast news situation, you can simply stop. By knowing that the most important part is first, you can have confidence that you can cut from the end of the story and still make the main point. This is important when you have little space or time to play with, and it is a standard practice in the media.

Now, let's try another inverted pyramid story. The facts are completely different, but the thinking process and the form of the story should be the same.

You get a call from the sheriff's department. Because of the heavy rains and flooding over the last three days, two bridges have been washed out. They are both along U.S. Highway 55 between Springfield and Jamestown. This means that the trip, which is normally about 12 miles and 25 minutes, is now going to take longer. Detours have been established along County Road 651, which has no bridges out, but the trip will now take 30 miles and probably 45 minutes or more.

The sheriff's office has no idea how long it is going to take to repair the bridges. That estimate will have to be made by the county engineer's office and they are out in the field surveying the damage and cannot be reached by phone.

Think it through. What is the most important part of this story? How can you say it directly and without wasting words? What does the reader need to know? What are the first few words you are going to start with?

The inverted pyramid seems difficult at first because it is not in the "logical" order we normally write or talk in. But it has been developed for a specific reason, and you can learn it with a little bit of practice.

Much of what is written for the news is done with an inverted pyramid lead, also known as single-incident lead or a summary lead. Some of the stories the media do have become so routine that formulas have been developed.

By understanding these formulas, you can save time on these routine stories and spend more time on the longer background, feature, and investigative stories we will discuss later.

Formula: Announcement Stories

The first story we discussed, the election of Harlan Jefferson to the student government presidency, is a type of an announcement story. The media regularly announce that someone has been elected to a board of trustees, named new director of an organization, appointed to West Point, or named the new basketball coach at a school.

These are "who" stories, because the name of the person is the big news. They should almost invariably start with the name of the person and conclude the first sentence with the name of the position.

> "Darnell Coleman is the new basketball coach at Slippery Elm High School."
> "William Farnsworth, president of Farnsworth Investors, has been named to the board of directors of the United Fund."
> "Jamie McLellan, 18, an honor graduate of Springfield High School, has been appointed to the United States Military Academy."

After the lead, you normally would go into the background of the person *as it pertains to the appointment*. Do not list the accomplishments of the person in chronological order, as what they did in college, in their first job, in their next job, etc.

For example, what has Darnell Coleman done to make him the choice for new coach over the dozens who applied for the job? This should go in the second sentence. Watch for sources who would have you write stories that say "So-and-so announced today that a decision has been reached on a new basketball coach." Readers do not want to know that a decision has been reached, they want to know who the person is and why they got the job over the other candidates.

After listing the accomplishments, you will at some point list such things as honors, graduation dates, and special accomplishments. These should be first reviewed for items that pertain to the appointment, and then listed in a reasonable order. At some point, you must list these items, but in doing a story you need to focus first on those items that pertain directly to the reason for the story.

Once again, the least important items can be cut from the end or bottom of the story if time or space become a problem.

Formula: Police Reports

Some people think the media report too much "bad" news. They think the listing of persons arrested for drunken driving, possession of marijuana, speeding, etc. is an invasion of privacy. Yet, this kind of news is an important help to the community in identifying those who should be watched for the safety of society.

It is important to note that not everything that makes the police blotter, or record, deserves to be news. Persons who are fined for parking over the allotted time on a meter are not really newsworthy because this is a minor offense. Youths under 16 years of age generally are not named, unless the crime is extremely offensive, because the courts feel they have the right to lead normal lives after paying for their mistakes.

Yet, many newspapers still list persons who were involved in minor traffic accidents, or who have been arrested for misdemeanors. The editors feel the readers need to be warned about potential troublemakers.

The formula for police stories can vary, depending on whether the person committing the crime is the important factor or whether the unusual nature of the crime is more important.

For example, if a businessperson or elected official were arrested for speeding, you might choose to start with the person's name, especially if that person was well known. One speeding offense is not unusual, but for it to happen to a well-known person in the community makes it more newsworthy. If the person is not well known in the community, you probably would either not use the story or list the person's name along with all of the others arrested on the same charge.

However, let us say someone was caught speeding three times in one month. That is a serious enough offense that the public should be aware of this person, whether he or she is prominent in the community or not.

And so your formula for a story such as this would be either one of the following:

"Mayor Henry Hatcher was arrested by his own police this week for speeding 55 miles an hour in a 35 mile per hour zone. The mayor had no comment as he paid his fine."
"A resident of Springfield Township has been arrested three times this month for exceeding the speed limit."

"Police say John Smith, of 343 Reading Highway, has picked up six points for these violations and one more conviction would put him in jail."

Determine first of all whether the main item of interest is the individual or the offense against society and build the story on this.

Remember, crime stories are among the leaders in problems leading to libel cases. Check names and spellings as carefully as possible, and if a story seems unusual in any way, talk it over with an editor before sending it to be printed.

Formula: Fire Stories

Fires are among the more tragic stories reporters cover. People are killed, buildings are destroyed, and fires often occur in the coldest months of the year.

It is important for the beginning reporter to understand that the value of a human life is much greater than the value of any building destroyed in a fire. Buildings can be rebuilt, people cannot. This is called the principle of people over property.

Therefore, the reporter's first consideration is for the safety and welfare of any residents of buildings that catch fire.

The lead can state such things as "No lives were lost in a spectacular fire that destroyed a home in the Ridgeville Heights section last night," or "Two persons died in a million-dollar fire and explosion at the Rabideau Chemicals warehouse in the Forest City Industrial Park last night."

Remember that you are telling a story of the fire. The first sentence tells what happens, though the names of the victims are usually not used in the first sentence unless they are very well known. Including names may also make the sentence too long.

The second sentence then goes on to give the names. "The victims were Mary Ellen Green, 41, of 1410 Westminster, Lot 4, and her daughter, Mary Alice, 14, a student at West Side Junior High School."

The next sentence tells of how firemen tried to get the victims out and give circumstances of the fire. Include information about how many fire companies went to the fire and what time the alarm was sounded, but put these in at the appropriate time. Do not start the first sentence after the lead by saying "Firemen were called at 3:40 A.M." Use such information wherever it fits into the story.

Formula: Accident Stories

Accident stories are similar to fire stories in that human life is worth more than any automobile or truck involved in an accident. Focus on the people, not the property.

Unfortunately, automobile accidents have become commonplace in our society. They are no longer the news they were in the early days of the automobile, or even the news they were as little as 20 years ago. Sad to say, people have almost become used to them.

Minor accidents are not even reported by most media, unless there are people involved whom everyone knows.

And in the case of major accidents, your first concern is for the condition of the people involved in auto crashes, bus crashes, plane crashes, etc.

Many newspapers now run lists of accidents under the heading "Accidents Occurred," and many will report accidents and crime news without using the names of the victims so as to avoid legal problems. Those who do this say it is more important for the reader to know that a certain type of crime occurred at a certain location at a certain time than it is to say who was involved. Other editors insist that there is no story without the name of the person involved.

The standard lead on an accident story then would say "Two persons were killed (or injured) at 3:00 P.M. Monday in a two-car crash on Middlebury Pike." The next sentence or paragraph would give the names of the persons injured and an up-to-date hospital report on their condition.

The next sentence or graph would discuss how the accident occurred, using statements given by police who covered the accident or persons who saw it happen. It is important that attribution be used properly so that the reader knows who is giving an account of the accident, whether it be police, bystanders, or the persons involved in the accident.

Formula: Government Stories

A great deal of what happens in government takes place at regular meetings of city and village councils, boards of education, judicial bodies, etc. These activities will be covered when we discuss meetings in chapter 12.

However, there are a lot of routine stories that need to be reported on from governmental agencies. These include dates for registering to vote, schedules for picking up garbage, appointments to governing boards, candidates announcing they will run for office, and many more.

The process is the same for these types of formula stories as for others, but the subjects vary so widely it is not easy to establish a formula. The writer has to determine the main subject of the story, and develop each story on that basis. The candidate running for office is a "who" story, much like an announcement story. The date to register to vote is a "when" story, the deadline date being the key item in the story. The schedule for garbage collection in your neighborhood is also a "when" story, and so on.

Formula: Obituaries

The obituary, or death notice, is misunderstood by most college students. Many do not understand why they have to write such stories, and students have been known to shy away from newspaper work because they have been told they may have to write obituaries.

The obituary is a formula story, but it is also a story that shows respect for the individual human being. Accuracy is seldom as important as in an obituary, and the reporter will gain a greater understanding of why it is so important that every name and every fact be double checked.

Most obituaries are clipped from the paper by the families involved and placed in personal files or scrapbooks. A mistake made in an obituary may be carried on for many, many years in this form.

The concern for the dignity of the individual, which is a central point in the democratic system, is also shown in the writing of obituaries. Every fact and every obituary itself, is double checked. While it is not common, there have been hoaxes in which persons attempted to "get even" with someone else by announcing that person's obituary in the media.

Therefore, the reporter should call back to the funeral director calling in an obituary to verify that it was indeed that funeral director, and not some stranger bent on revenge, who called in the obituary.

Papers with large circulations in metro areas often do not run standard obituaries, because they do not have the space to run each one. They run paid obituaries prepared by the funeral homes, which include flowery phrases not seen in regular obituaries, such as "loving father of" and "devoted husband to" among others. These are adjectives that are not used in standard obituaries.

Interest in obituaries varies according to the size of the community. In smaller communities, everyone knows everyone else (or at least some of their relatives), and obituaries may be the best read part of the newspaper. This is yet another reason for taking such great care in getting every fact correct. In larger metro areas, everyone does not know everyone else, but the interest is still high.

When writing an obituary, the writer should write it as carefully as if she were writing about a member of her own family. This kind of care should carry over into every story a person writes, because every story is important to someone. As many callers to newspapers have said, if we can't trust you to write an obituary accurately, why should we think you are accurate with all of the other stories in the newspaper?

Before we get into the writing form for obituaries, a word on the cause of death. Be sure to understand the policy of your newspaper or station before listing the cause of death as "cancer" or "AIDS." This is a decision the reporter cannot and should not make; it is a decision based on the company's policy.

For years, people who died of cancer were listed as having died of "a long illness." If anything, obituaries would suggest that persons could make a contribution to the local chapter of the American Cancer Society.

Medical science has made great strides in the treatment of cancer, and the problem has shifted to how to report the death of a person who had an AIDS-related illness. The wire services will include this fact in the obituaries of nationally prominent people. On the local level, the wishes of the individual and his or her family are generally adhered to. If the family asks that the word AIDS not be used, most papers will agree. However, there are many papers who feel that not mentioning this fact does not reflect society as it is, and they will mention AIDS if it has been verified by reliable sources.

A similar problem exists with persons who commit suicide. The persons close to the deceased will know that the death was a suicide, but unless a medical authority officially proclaims the death as suicide, it should not be listed as such.

Even if a medical authority says it was suicide, there are other factors to consider. What are the wishes of the family? What is the policy of the newspaper? These are decisions that must be made together with editors, not by the reporter alone.

The Form of the Obituary Story

Since the obituary is a "who" story, it starts with the name of the person who has died. Each paragraph includes the following materials:

Lead paragraph. Name of deceased, age, address, distinction (why the reader would know this person), and usually the place of death.

For example, "Virgil Eusebio, 88, of 232 S. Main St, who came to the United States at age 4 and later served 20 years as county prosecutor, died in his sleep at his home Monday morning."

Distinctions. Continue with distinctions, or reasons the reader knows this person. Continue as long as is warranted. This includes major political offices, community honors, and other distinctions for which he was known in the community.

For example, "Mr. Eusebio was a familiar figure in county politics, serving as chairman of the county Republican committee for 30 years. He had attended six national presidential nominating conventions, and was a partner in the firm of Eusebio, Brown and Stechowicz for 40 years."

Personal information, the next grouping, includes such things as schools and colleges from which he graduated, civic and social memberships, military service, and related activities. Note that this is not listed immediately after the lead paragraph, because the reader would like to know more about the person's accomplishments or distinctions before reading of his personal history.

Family information is next. This includes wife or husband, sons and daughters (with names and city locations of each), as well as number of grandchildren and great-grandchildren. Persons who do not know the deceased may know some of his direct family members. You may get into unfamiliar names of persons or cities, so check these names as carefully as the names of family members. (Can you spell Tucumcari, N.M., Atascadero, Cal., or Pataskala, O., without checking an atlas?)

Funeral arrangements is the next section. Be aware that different religious groups have different titles for leaders of their congregations, and check the AP style book to see who is a minister, a priest, a reverend, etc. Double check to see that you have all of the right times for services (and remember that a funeral is a service, so a funeral service is a redundancy). This material is usually provided by the family or the funeral director. Names of pallbearers are often included. Remember, this is the only public record of the funeral that will be made available to most people.

Special notices, often having to do with donations, are usually the last item mentioned in an obituary report. The family may ask that donations be made to a church, hospital, or charity that was important to the deceased. For some time, newspapers would say, "In lieu of flowers, friends may make contributions to (name of group)." This can upset those who sell flowers, and can be avoided by not using the phrase "In lieu of flowers."

Feature obituaries are becoming more popular, especially with newspapers in larger areas. These papers try to focus on the life of an average person and her contributions to the community. The idea is that all persons make contributions in their own way, and despite the fact that the media do not have enough time or space to feature everyone, they can feature one person a day.

This usually means a company policy has been set. Be aware of how these feature obituaries are chosen, and be prepared to learn a great deal when you do one. A very valuable lesson can be learned by talking to grieving family members. If you present yourself properly and sympathetically, they will discuss the person's life with you.

This will become a very valuable skill on the rare occasions when you have to talk to grieving family members who have just been through an accident, a violent crime, or something traumatic. They all have stories to tell, and the public needs to know some of the information they have to offer. It can help the audience to put the event into perspective and adjust to the world as it is.

And so, if you are assigned an obituary, learn from it. Learn respect for human dignity, the value of accuracy, and that every reader has a story. Unfortunately, we cannot run all of the stories, but this understanding will serve you well when you get to features, personal profiles, and other kinds of writing.

A New Look at Writing Obituaries

In recent years, Jim Nicholson of the *Philadelphia Daily News* has brought national attention to the writing of obituaries. Among other awards, he won a Knight-Ridder Newspapers Editorial Excellence award in 1991 and the Distinguished Writing Award of the American Society of Newspaper Editors in 1987. Before he turned to obits, he had five nominations for Pulitzers, a Sigma Delta Chi award for stories on corruption in the building of Veterans' Stadium, and a Scripps Howard award for stories on outlaw motorcycle gangs.

Normally, awards are not given for writing obituaries, but Nicholson has elevated this aspect of newswriting to a new level. He writes richly detailed, colorful obituaries of ordinary Philadelphians, as we shall see shortly.

His motivation, after many years in the newspaper business, is unusual. He feels the obituary exalts the common man, so he takes ordinary lives of ordinary people, examines details and subtleties, and writes about it in inspired prose. He has elevated obituary writing to an art form, and has changed the way newspaper people think about obituaries.

"The real heroes are among the common man—the guy who keeps your water running, the guy who does your dry cleaning, operates the street cars, keeps the traffic moving. Who would you miss more if you went on a six-week vacation—the secretary of state or your trashman?" he asks (Caughey 1988).

After 25 years as a street reporter, Nicholson had put 150 people in jail with investigative stories.

> Before I finished my career as an investigator, a lot of them were out of prison and doing better than I was. This is the greatest, most satisfying job I have ever had. Any one of my obits will outlive any investigative thing I have ever done. People make 200 to 300 copies of them and hand them out at funerals. People laminate my obits and give them to friends.
>
> I've had (newspaper) people tell me, well, somebody has to do it. It carries minus prestige and authority. And then there is the subject: death. I thought I would have limited tolerance for it.
>
> Now I know we're not talking about death; we're talking about life. If you take out the words "died" and "funeral services" you would have a feature, not an obit. There are no uninteresting obits, only uninteresting questions asked by the reporter.
>
> I have learned a tremendous amount over the years I have been doing this. Dignity, honor and courage that I never saw on the street in 25 years. In the people's homes in the most intimate moment of grief, I see courage and nobility. Talk about restoring your faith in mankind.

Leads from some of Jim Nicholson's obits follow. Please note these are only the leads or summaries of the obituaries, many of which run 30 paragraphs or more. Note the dignity and caring with which each obit is handled, and keep in mind that Nicholson gets his information by talking with relatives.

> Annette Quigley, who believed that the gift of love would perish unless it was passed on to others, died Sunday. She was 85 and lived in Havertown, Delaware County.
>
> Once a woman and her seven year old daughter stood in the rain at a bus stop in front of the Quigley's home on the Jersey shore. Annette gave the woman a glass of water and learned that she was running away from an abusive husband. Annette took them in for the summer. This was in addition to caring for her eight children and her husband. They all left in better shape than when they arrived.
>
> That Annette could have been in a position to help anyone defied all odds. Her early life seemed locked into a foreboding destiny that promised no gifts of love and happiness. Her parents' marriage was arranged, her father died when she

was very young, and her mother died in an influenza epidemic. Her step-father was cruel and at age 12 "my childhood was over," she said.

Joseph J. 'Pop' Ferry Jr., a strong man whose life's blood coursed throughout the community he loved, died Tuesday. He was 78 and lived in Gloucester City, N.J.

He was a big Irishman who kept a broad shoulder pushed against the wheel all his life, pushing to make a living for his large family or pushing to start a boys club or a volunteer fire company. He pushed to the last.

The first impression anyone got when introduced to Pop was of his hands. They were big enough to sit in. They were hams that years ago had taken wiseguys out in one lick, but for much of his adult life were cupped around the shoulders of young kids Pop wanted to grow up straight.

Pop got into other people's business if he thought they were going wrong with a marriage or liquor or whatever. "Hey, I wanna talk to you..." he'd say. His son said "If he knew you were in trouble, he would have you either crying or have your head down low. He'd put you in your place, straighten you out. He'd go out of his way to straighten somebody out."

Margaret E. Davis, a private housekeeper and active church member who made friends everywhere she went, died Saturday. She was 80 and lived in the city's West Oak Lane section.

She was a woman who thought it was the friendly thing to do to strike up a conversation with anyone who was standing next to her in a store or sitting in the adjoining seat on a bus. Often she and her new acquaintance exchanged phone numbers, which were followed by friendly chats and many times resulted in her new friend visiting her church.

For more than 60 years, Davis was a member and active worker at Wesley AME Zion Church.

Julia Mae Hamilton, who told her six children that she wanted to see six high school diplomas in her hand before they went out into the world, died Wednesday. She was 59 and lived in South Philadelphia.

All the kids got their diplomas. "If you never do nothing else in your life, please bring me that piece of paper," Hamilton told each of her children. And she kept those diplomas, the yearbooks, the pictures and other memorabilia, which she said would be theirs to have someday.

"She was the center brick, the keystone of the arch," her daughter said. "Move that, and the whole house would have come down. She was the tiny voice that was always whispering in tiny ears, 'You can do it.'"

Francis J. "Frank" Lenny, an editor who knew what made good news stories and how to handle the people who wrote them, died Wednesday. He was 52 and lived in Westville, N.J.

Frank Lenny drove hard for more than 30 years in a business that often caps the careers of its hard-driving with pacemakers and bleeding ulcers. He spent most of his career prodding prima donna reporters, penciling copy and pushing stories up a pneumatic tube while running on a high octane diet of vending machine snacks, nicotine and alcohol.

He had undergone an operation to implant a defibrillator to regulate his heartbeat and died about eight hours later.

Formula: Sports Event Stories

Covering sports is a specialty unto itself. Many reporters enter the field specifically to cover sports, and resent having to cover "straight news." Others cover the regular news beats, and would have little idea of how to cover a sports event.

This is not good. Many outstanding writers in American history have started in sports and gone on to write fiction, novels, books, and other major literary contributions.

Many beginning news reporters will find an opportunity for overtime pay or additional assignments if they can cover sports. Public relations work often involves covering sports teams, and on smaller broadcast and television stations reporters are expected to cover sports as well.

And, if you know how to cover sports, it will help you to cover other news items as well.

Think about it. You go to a basketball game and your roommate stays home studying. You get back from the game and the roommate says, "Who won?" As soon as you say who won, the next question is, "Was it a good game?"

This is what sports reporters have to do. They have to tell the audience who won and what the highlights of the game were. And they have to do it in the first paragraph.

Your roommate didn't ask you to give a play-by-play, or a quarter-by-quarter wrap up. Yet, this is what beginning reporters will do. They will tell who won, they will tell the score, and then they will go into a quarter-by-quarter wrap-up, as much as space or time will permit.

Telling who won and what kind of game it was can also be applied to other kinds of news stories.

If you went to a governmental meeting, you would not tell your roommate each item on the agenda. You would be more likely to tell the person the most important thing that went on, such as, "You are going to have to pay $5 a year more for your auto license tags next year."

If it is an announcement story, you would describe who has been appointed to what, not the fact that a press conference was held and the president of the company started out by reviewing the company's history for the past five years.

So, tell the reader who won, what the score was, and what kind of a game it was. This might mean sitting through a three-hour baseball game and writing ten paragraphs about three hours of action, but so be it. The reader is not concerned that you had to sit there for three hours, he or she wants to know who won and what kind of game it was.

One of the main problems sports reporters have to deal with is cliches. There are generally 10 to 12 football games per season, perhaps 25 to 30 basketball games, and another 15 to 20 baseball games in the spring for most non-professional teams. Not all the games can be exciting. Some will be poorly played, some will not. Some will have importance in the standings, some will not.

So in the three hours the reporter sits watching the game, he or she has to determine why this game is important in the standings or for some individuals, how this game was different from all the others, or is there something else important about this game. For example, has someone set a record? By the time you cover 50 events in one season, it becomes difficult to find something interesting about each game.

Good reporters will find that difference. They will know who is approaching a team or school record, they will know why Team A cannot beat Team B, they will show how a coach's decision led to a victory. They watch for the things that make a story worth reading.

The weak reporters will not look for the differences in the games. They will resort to cliches, such as "an exciting game," "a last-minute nail biter," or "the best game of the last five years." And they will tell you who won (in the sixth paragraph) and immediately lapse into a minute-by-minute account of the game.

By the time the story has come out, the audience already knows who won. They want to know what kind of a game it was.

And so a good lead might be "West Central defeated Morrison, 55–45, last night, holding Morrison to one point in the fourth quarter."

Or, "Jason Petrenka didn't plan on a hat trick last night, but he did get three goals anyway in a 9–3 Millersville rout over Canfield." Personalizing sports stories makes them much more interesting, but involves more work. You have to talk to the players after the game to get their thoughts about what went on.

Examples of Inverted Pyramid Stories

Remember this: just because an inverted pyramid follows a certain formula does not mean that it is routine. Some of the most exciting and interesting stories are cast in an inverted pyramid form. All the form means is that the information is rank-ordered, that the most important comes first, and that the least interesting is at the end.

What follows are five stories, two of them with sidebars (accompanying stories) about exciting, important, and complicated events. What they have in common is that they summarize the story in the first paragraph or two.

The first story, for example, is about a seven-hour siege by a deranged man (described in the sidebar) in a bar and grill in Berkeley, Cal. Notice how you can read the first few paragraphs of the story, which are reprinted here, and tell almost everything you need to know about the story. If you want to know more about the individual from people who knew him, you would read the sidebar ("Gunman was man of extremes"). Note how many specifics are included in the first few paragraphs without making the lead difficult to read.

The story is headlined "Deadly siege near UC; Two dead, 9 wounded in assault" and written by William Brand of the *Oakland Tribune*. It ran Sept. 28, 1990.

A deranged Berkeley man with a briefcase arsenal of rapid-fire weapons was gunned down on the floor of Henry's Publick House and Grill in the Durant Hotel yesterday morning—seven hours after he killed a UC-Berkeley student, wounded nine others and took 33 hostages.

During those hours between

GUNMAN WAS MAN OF EXTREMES
by Kelly Gust

BERKELEY—People who knew him described Mehrdad Dashti as a quiet man, a religious man, and a "nerd" who just didn't seem the type to kill.

But police reports, observations from his probation officer and letters that fill Dashti's cramped Berkeley apartment paint a picture of the initial outburst of shooting at 12:15 A.M. and 7:25 A.M. when a Berkeley police hostage squad burst into the bar with weapons flaming, the hostages were terrified by 29-year-old, Iranian born Mehrdad Dashti.

In a series of rambling discourses during the night, he told his hostages American women were the cause of the downfall of civilization...

a tortured man who heard voices, a paranoid schizophrenic.

Dashti, the man who killed one student and terrorized 33 others yesterday, was convinced the government was using his brain for secret telepathic experiments.

"For the past three years I have been the victim of some kind of an experiment that is going on around here...This is some kind of mental communication power by which people can basically talk to each other not using their mouth and by means of brain waves only," Dashti, 29, said in a letter to authorities last year.

"I am used as a combination message center, loudspeaker...The problem is that as a result of this experiment I am not able to lead a normal human life," he said.

He had sent the letters to President Bush, Chief Justice Rehnquist, San Francisco mayor Art Agnos, the FBI, and others.

One of the most-honored series of stories in recent years was produced by *The Greenville News* in Greenville, S.C. and resulted in the resignation of the president of the University of South Carolina. Most of the stories as they broke were single-incident, inverted pyramid stories.

The *News* staff bulldozed a landfill to discover 30 boxes of missing records that revealed questionable spending of millions of dollars in public funds. Their series won the largest monetary prize offered in journalism, the $25,000 Selden Ring award, administered by the University of Southern California.

Southern Cal says the series disclosed "abusive extravagance" by then-university president James B. Holderman, including using foundation funds for family vacations, limousine services, university staff bonuses, and a low interest home loan. The state of South Carolina started its own investigation, and most of the officials involved, including the president, resigned. The appropriate policies were restructured so similar problems cannot recur.

Among the findings: the cost of the three-week Hawaiian vacation for the former president and his family was almost $30,000; the university foundation gave the president $25,000 and paid off a $17,000 lease on his car one month after he resigned; the foundation paid the former president, school officials, and football coaches about $800,000 in salary supplements and bonuses.

Members of the investigative team were executive editor John

Pittman, managing editor Tom Hutchison, assistant managing editor Chris Weston, and reporters William Fox and Tim Smith.

The series won top honors in National Headliner Awards investigative reporting over 1,500 entries; was a finalist in the investigative reporting category for the Pulitzer Prize; won first place in the Investigative Reporters and Editors contest for investigative reporting; and won the Public Service award given by the Associated Press Managing Editors' Association.

Several of the leads in the series were as follows:

"The South Carolina Supreme Court unanimously ruled Monday that the University of South Carolina's Research and Development Foundation is a public body and must open its records to the public."

"Another three boxes of records for years sought by *The Greenville News* in its lawsuit against a University of South Carolina Foundation were dug up by the newspaper Sunday in the Columbia landfill."

"Former University of South Carolina President James B. Holderman was indicted Friday on charges of using his public office for personal gain and receiving extra compensation.

The charges stem from $25,000 Holderman received for introducing lawyers from the firms of former Gov. Bob McNair to the Dominican Republic president in a bid to free a Puerto Rico businessman on cocaine charges."

"James B. Holderman was sentenced Tuesday to five years probation and 500 hours of community service work after pleading no contest to felony tax evasion and guilty to an ethics charge."

One of the typical problems a beginning reporter has is writing a chronological lead; that is, he writes the story in the time order the events happened in the story (first this happened, then this, then this). In 99 cases out of 100, this is the wrong way to write a lead. In the following case, a story about a trial, it is the right way to do the story.

We use this example to show you that all rules have exceptions. Understand that you do not write things in the order in which they occur, but then if a rare case develops, disregard the rule. But do not disregard the rules all of the time.

The story was written by Matt O'Connor of the *Chicago Tribune* and published on July 14, 1992.

'YOU'VE GOT 10 SECONDS, THEN I FIRE'

The robber was waving a gun in his right hand and holding a police scanner in his left hand as he purposefully walked into the small suburban bank.

"Get in the vault and get me $30,000," he ordered the head teller. "You've got 10 seconds and then I am going to start shooting."

The teller ran to the vault and nervously fumbled with the combination as he heard the bandit begin to count backward from 10.

As the robber neared the end of his count, the teller flung open the vault door. He reached in, grabbed as much cash as he physically could, then ran back to the counter and threw the money toward the robber.

The bandit, trying to hide his features behind a fake beard, sunglasses and a cap, stuffed the cash in a bag and fled.

Thus went the fifth of eight holdups pulled off by a serial bandit who became known as the "bearded bank robber" and netted almost $180,000 over two years, Assistant U.S. Atty. Victoria Peters told a federal jury Monday.

At the start of what is expected to be a two-week trial in U.S. District Court, Peters identified the suspect as defendant Jeffrey Erickson, 34, a one-time Hoffman Estates police trainee and the owner of a used-book store.

In opening remarks, Peters disclosed that 11 bank employees and one customer have identified Erickson as the disguised robber they saw hold up seven northwest and north suburban banks and one South Side bank.

The witnesses picked out Erickson as he and five other men stood in lineups wearing disguises used by the bandit: usually a false beard, a baseball cap, sunglasses and driving gloves.

Another witness identified Erickson in a lineup as the man she saw shooting and wounding a Palatine police officer after a routine traffic stop near her home, Peters said.

The FBI also has determined from shell casings found at the shooting scene that a gun later found in Erickson's Hanover Park home was the one used to shoot the Palatine police officer.

But Erickson's lawyer, Richard Mottweiler, warned jurors

that Erickson and the others in the lineup wore prison jumpsuits, not the clothes seen on the robber. And, Mottweiler said, the Palatine witness saw only the profile of the gunman as she looked on from her house and was "only fairly sure" that it was Erickson.

The government's first witness, Jackie Santiago, a former teller at the First Nationwide Bank in Wilmette, identified Erickson as the bearded robber who held her up at gunpoint in the first of the eight robberies, on Jan. 9, 1990.

In court, Erickson could have been mistaken for a bespectacled accountant, dressed conservatively in a dark blue suit and maroon tie, his hair much shorter than at the time of his arrest last December.

During the holdup, Santiago was calm enough to activate the bank alarm and to include marked bills and a pack that explodes red dye on the bandit in the bag with the cash.

But at the police lineup, two years later, Santiago said, "I was really scared."

"When I saw one of them, it made my heart beat fast," she said under questioning by Assistant U.S. Atty. Lisa Osofsky. "Even though it had been a long time I had that feeling inside me that I knew him."

She picked Erickson in the lineup, testimony indicated.

After that first bank robbery, authorities found red dye all over the inside of a stolen car abandoned near the bank, Peters said.

After that, the bearded bank robber was careful to instruct tellers not to give him any "funny money" or "exploding money," Peters told jurors.

Later, Peters said, Erickson "perfected a sort of blueprint" for bank robberies: entering the bank waving a gun in his right hand and holding a police scanner in his left hand so he would know instantly if police learned of the bank robbery.

In a loud, demanding voice, a disguised Erickson profanely threatened to blow tellers' heads off if they didn't have more than specific amounts of money, Peters said.

Erickson always used stolen cars to make his getaway, having left the foreign-made compact cars near the bank earlier with paper or other material to hide the missing ignition he removed, Peters said.

That eventually led to his arrest, she said. The FBI staked out two stolen Mazdas and arrested Erickson moments after he got into one and reached for a screwdriver to start it up, Peters said.

Erickson's wife, Jill, who was shot and killed after she led agents on a wild chase following her husband's arrest, was charged as an unindicted co-conspirator. Authorities believe she was the second robber in the last of Erickson's eight holdups and helped him move stolen cars close to the banks the night before the robberies.

Matt O'Connor has fine-tuned the single-incident lead as well. Notice how much information he puts into this complex, involved, 250-word story, which appeared in the *Chicago Tribune*, May 9, 1992, p. 5.

A veteran Chicago police officer was convicted Friday by a federal jury on charges she aided her son's large-scale heroin operation.

Prosecutors had accused Gloria Steele, 43, of laundering drug proceeds by investing in real estate, allowing underlings to mix and package heroin in her flat and supplying her son with police intelligence to evade arrest.

The jury also convicted her son, Thomas Wesson, 24, of being the leader of a South Side heroin business that one top aide said earned $50,000 a day at its peak.

Wesson faces a mandatory sentence of life in prison, according to Assistant U.S. atty. Ronald Safer.

The jury found Steele, Wesson and a third defendant, Lisa Harris, 23, guilty on all charges.

Authorities said Wesson ran a sophisticated operation that included telephone operators, such as Harris, who let customers know up-to-the-minute whereabouts of street sellers who frequently changed their locations to evade police.

Steele, a 16-year police veteran who worked the front desk at the Wentworth District station when she was arrested in February, was accused of tipping her son to "hot" areas where police were concentrating their drug-fighting efforts.

Prosecutors also documented that Steele had invested hundreds of thousands of dollars in real estate to prove that she had laundered drug money for her son's heroin business.

Twenty-two defendants had pleaded guilty to narcotics and other charges before the trial, and many of them testified against Steele and Wesson.

Sometimes humorous angles develop in serious stories. The following story was written by Jeff Lipton for *The Virginia Gazette*, Williamsburg, Va., on June 6, 1992.

The inverted pyramid still holds, but the facts are funny enough to add a little interest to the story.

BANK ROBBER BETRAYED BY LOYAL DOG

YORK, Va.—A bank robber should have left his dog home Thursday before holding up the Crestar Branch at the Grafton Shopping Center of $1,900.

He entered the bank shortly after 3 P.M. and passed a note to a teller saying he was armed with a gun, pulling back a safari jacket to show the weapon in the holster. He grabbed the money bag and fled to a car driven by a woman companion.

When he jumped inside, the red dye-pack exploded. He bolted from the car and ran across Route 17, followed by Twinkie, a small mixed-breed female dog belonging to the couple and along for the ride.

After he climbed a fence, he noticed the dog had followed him and was trying to scale it, and he went back to help her over. Sheriff Press Williams picks up the story.

"He couldn't pull her over the fence and realized it was taking too much time, so he left her there."

Deputies arrived within 10 minutes and grabbed the dog. Twinkie's dog tag led investigators to identify the suspect as Phillip Walter Schanck of Brettwood Court in Williamsburg. He disappeared into a wooded area, and efforts to find him with police dogs and helicopters were unsuccessful.

Schanck was arrested 24 hours later on a tip that he was cashing his paycheck at Almost A Bank in Denbigh. He was charged with robbery, entering a bank with a firearm, and using a firearm in commission of a felony. He's in the county jail without bond.

All but $20 of the bank money was recovered on the shoulder of Oriana Road. The dog was taken to the shelter and then returned to Schanck's companion.

"Twinkie was our star witness," Williams said. "She helped us crack the case."

Things to Remember

- Know that all news stories are not similar in purpose and therefore not similar in form.
- Understand that some stories are really similar to previous stories, but the names and details have changed. Once the

purpose and the form are understood, the news writer can use the same formula again—adapted to current facts.

• Know that the inverted pyramid form is useful for many basic news stories, but it is far from the only style the journalist should use. It is only one of many types of stories. The inverted pyramid has a rich history, but may not be adapted to the news needs of society as society changes.

Exercises

1. Read your local newspaper or watch or listen to a news broadcast. Can you determine whether formula or inverted pyramid stories are being used?
2. Do you notice how the most important information is in the first paragraph, contrary to writing you will do for other classes on campus?
3. Compare obituaries from two different newspapers. Is the form the same? Should it be? Does either paper write obituaries in feature form, or are they all in formula?

Practice

Write news stories based on the following sets of facts. Reread the chapter to determine which form should be used. Discuss with your instructor how you are going to write these stories after you have thought them through.

Fact Set 1

In May of 1993, City Manager Elden Sprelaw of Mound City retired after 30 years running the city. He was 75 years old.

Since his retirement, the city has been run by members of council who are looking for a new city manager.

At 11:00 A.M. this morning a press conference was held and the new city manager is Luella Montoya, 46, who has been in city management for ten years.

She is a graduate of the University of Arizona in public administration and has a master's from Columbia University in urban planning. She has worked for four different cities in her career, the most recent being as assistant city manager of Lompoc, Calif.

She is married and her husband is in the insurance business. The family has two sons, Luis and Loren, ages nine and four.

Fact Set 2

Germantown High School played North Wing City in football Friday night. It was the last game before the state playoffs next week.

In the first quarter, Germantown scored on a field goal.

In the second quarter, North Wing City scored a touchdown on a 77-yard punt return by Abner Amos. The extra point was good.

In the third quarter, Germantown kicked two field goals. Jason Manson thus had three field goals for the game.

There was no scoring in the final period. Germantown won, 9–7.

Germantown qualified for the playoffs and will meet Achilles next Friday. Germantown finished unbeaten at 11–0 for the season. It was the first win over North Wing City in 22 years.

Fact Set 3

This is the Hansen-Jensen Funeral Home calling. I would like to give you the facts of the obituary of Richard Wilhemener. (You are writing for the McKeesport paper.)

He was born in Chautauqua, N.Y., on Dec. 31, 1940. His parents were Charles and Mary Jones Wilhemener. The family later moved to Buffalo and then to Pittsburgh, where Richard Wilhemener was born.

He graduated from Lewis Tech high school in 1958 and from the University of Illinois in 1962 as an electrical engineer. He had been employed since graduation from college by Westinghouse in Pittsburgh and lived in McKeesport, Pa., since 1965. His address was 978 Garden Road.

He is survived by his wife Angeline, twin sons Marty and Mark, age 19, and daughter Marianne, age 16.

He was a member of Christ the King Lutheran Church, the Pittsburgh Opera Association, and the Salvation Army Board of Directors.

Services will be conducted Tuesday at the church, with visitation at the funeral home on Monday evening from 5:00 P.M. to 9:00 P.M.

Reality Check

The following is information in note form for three separate stories. Some of it is useful, some of it is not. You must first discard the extraneous material, then put what is worthwhile into a news story.

Fire Story

Write one story from the following. You read the following information from the fire department reports. Emergency call at 12:01 A.M. to the Spotted Zebra Bar, 1108 Western Road. Report of heart attack. When crew arrived, no one knew of any heart attack. Returned to station.

2:15 A.M. car fire in brand new Corvette at 24-Hour Mart, the convenience store at 924 Haskins. Fire put out within 30 seconds. Tow truck called to remove car. Driver named Henry Nehemiah, 21, of 417 S. Suffolk, said he has been trying to start the car when it flooded and fire started on the hot engine. Car was a total loss, crew chief said.

4:10 A.M. Fire Department got a call from man working third shift at General Motors Plant on Industrial Parkway. Said he passed a house in flames in the 200 block of South Dexter. Fire truck dispatched, Chief Henry Wonkler said. Fire was at 202 S. Wonkler, Apt. B upstairs. Assistant Chief Lew Ayres said firemen could not get in upstairs because of flames, but the two retired persons who lived downstairs were helped out of the building and taken to the fire station to stay warm. It was 12 degrees above zero at the time of the fire. The elderly couple said a young man, probably about 21 years old, was upstairs but firemen could not find him or get him out. Fire was confined to the upstairs, after two other fire crews were called to the scene. Traffic was stopped at both ends of Dexter and no one was permitted into the area. At about 6:15 A.M., firemen found the body of the young man, identified by Chief Wonkler as Rafael Quirene, age 22, who was a computer programmer at The OneTwoThree Software Development Corporation. He had come to the city from New York two years ago, and was engaged to be married in three months, the chief said. Cause of fire was still being investigated, but the chief said he was reasonably sure a cigarette probably burned the sofa in which the victim was found, and death was due to smoke inhalation. Names of retired persons were Hilda and August Gormanov, both 78. He retired from the Atlas Foundry 13 years ago. She was a homemaker. They are both fine, and living with family now.

11
Organizing a Complex Single-Event Story

"Easy writing makes hard reading."—Ernest Hemingway

In This Chapter

What to do when the single-event story is considerably longer than average.

Going through a complex single-event story step by step.

How to rank order elements in a story to help organize that story.

What to do after writing the lead.

Why writing the first draft sets up an even better second draft.

THERE are several ways to write a news story, depending on the facts in the story. Assume we have collected our information, and it is time to write a story.

And assume that the story is *not* a straightforward news item that can be handled in the single-event lead format discussed in the previous chapter.

Many stories can be handled with a single announcement, such as a report on one accident, or a story on one basketball game. Others are more complicated.

This part of the process is called *Focus*, where we organize and put together a longer news story.

The preliminary steps remain the same. We must understand what the reader wants in a news story, we must understand the importance of accuracy, and we must know how to interview and gather the news so that we have all the information we need, among other things.

This can be a difficult time. In a more complicated story, we may not know where to start. It is not at all unusual for student writers to procrastinate when they get to this point.

It might be helpful at this time to "walk through" a complex news story.

Let's start with a set of facts that could have been gathered at a news conference held by the police department to announce the arrest of two men for bank robbery. While bank robbery may not be common, it is certainly not unusual and it is newsworthy. Everyone has a stake in the banking system and they want to know about abuses of the banking system. Bank robbery requires a certain perverted courage and bravado that makes it challenging, and we need to know if our bank was the victim of this kind of act.

Here are the facts. All of the information is directly from the police spokesman, Capt. Hanford Williams.

The First National Bank and Trust company has four branches and a main office in Springfield. The branch at the corner of West Avenue and 14th Streets was the scene of a robbery this morning.

At 9:03 A.M., three minutes after the branch opened, two men walked into the bank. As they came through the front door they pulled their ski caps down over their faces, using them as masks. The eyes and mouth places on the caps were open.

One man opened a briefcase and pulled out a revolver. He said in a calm voice, "This is a holdup. We want all your money, nothing smaller than five dollar bills."

The other man went behind the counter with a grocery bag. Two clerks, whose names were not released by the police, were behind the counter. They handed money to the man, and silently tripped the alarm, which went off in the police station.

One of the clerks also dropped a false packet into the bag, a packet which looked like a stack of $20 bills, but was actually a canister of red dye with a timing device set to go off in four minutes.

While this was starting, the manager of the branch, Harry Kenniston, was in his office in back of the bank. He saw the robbery in progress, and slipped out the back door. He went to his car, which had a CB radio in it.

The two men left the bank within a minute after the robbery started. They took an undisclosed amount of money. (Banks generally will not give out the amount taken so as not to encourage additional robberies.) They took off their stocking caps and got into a small red pickup truck.

It was now about 9:05. Mr. Kenniston was on the CB radio to the police, trying not to be obvious to the two men, who did not notice him. Kenniston told police that the men were getting into the pickup, and gave the license number. Police told him to follow the pickup, but not to get too close. They were on their way, alerted by the silent alarm.

The pickup headed east on West Avenue, but went only two blocks before it pulled into a parking lot at the City View Shopping Center. The men got out, and got into a compact sports car in a lime green color. Kenniston advised police what was happening.

It was now 9:09. Police surrounded the lime green car as it attempted to leave the shopping parking lot, a mile from Interstate 111.

Captain Williams continued:

"Police vehicles were at the front and rear of the suspect car. A policeman approached the car and ordered the men out. Both men got out of the car with their hands up, and the arrest was made without incident. A .38 caliber revolver and a briefcase with money were recovered.

"The passenger in the automobile was observed with red dye on his hands. The pick-up truck abandoned in the lot was found to be covered with red dye inside the truck.

"The two men being held at the city corrections facility pending arraignment are Walter Thomas Wallace, 34, of 2407-14th Street and Albert James Wellington, 23, same address. Their apartment is three blocks from the scene of the robbery. The men made no statements to the police, and they will be arraigned before Common Pleas Court Judge Donald P. Exeter tomorrow at 9:00 A.M."

Dividing a Set of Facts into Parts

Where do you start? What do you do first? This is a fast-paced, interesting, and complex story.

This is the stage at which you have to decide which framework and type of lead to use. Since this is an actual event that happened within a news cycle, it falls into the category of straight news story. It is not, for example, a feature story, which focuses on a personality or may develop over a longer period of time.

And since it has several parts to it, and gets somewhat complicated at times, it is not a straightforward formula story. You cannot apply a pre-set formula to it, add names and addresses, and follow the form you would use in an obituary, an accident story, or an announcement story. It is more complex than that.

It falls into the category of inverted pyramid lead, or complex lead, which requires more thought before beginning to write. You must summarize the important things in the first few words, and then complete the story in a meaningful way.

Let us analyze this story, step-by-step, and see how it is to be written. This gets to be complicated, so stay with us.

The story includes several parts, which should be examined in terms of which is the most important, the most recent, and/or the most interesting.

These include:

The use of ski masks, the sounding of the silent alarm, the use of CB radio to call police, the switching of cars, the capture in the parking lot, the arrest and detention of two men, and the discovery of red dye on people and vehicles.

Clearly, there are a lot of things happening here. What are the rules for doing such a story?

This story falls under the category of single-incident stories.

Other categories, such as formula stories, feature stories, personality profiles, etc., will be discussed in following chapters. One thing happened—a bank was robbed. Several steps were taken during the robbery and the apprehension of suspects, but it is one event.

Finding the Reader's Interest

What does the reader want or need to know when hearing that a bank has been robbed? What would your roommate or your mother ask if you told her there had been a bank robbery at a branch near by?

The questions would include which bank, when did it happen, did anyone get hurt, and did they catch the people who did it?

The suspense of knowing whether or not the suspects were captured is important. If the suspects were not captured, readers would like to know who did it, what they look like, what they were wearing, etc., so that they might identify the suspects and help in their capture.

So you have to organize your story to tell the reader that a bank was robbed but that two suspects are in custody. Whenever possible, tell the reader what the conclusion of an event is, so that they can read the first sentence or first paragraph and know the most recent and the most important parts of the story.

Please understand that this was a *story*. It had a beginning, a middle, and an end. In this case, it had a robbery, a chase and two arrests. It had a problem (robbery), and a resolution (arrests). It has to be treated as a story, not a collection of related incidents, or the simple rewriting of notes from the press conference. It has to be written in a way that will bring accurate information in an interesting way, or the reader will not get the important information out of the story.

But saying that a bank was robbed and two men were captured does not tell the interesting parts of the story. You need to include something about how they were captured, and to tell some of the things that make this bank robbery different from others. These include switching cars, being tracked by a branch manager on CB radio, and the fact that red dye was found on the hands of some of the suspects. You need to include the necessary information (robbery, arrests) with the interesting information (chase, CB, switching cars, red dye).

It can be done. You can include the necessary with the interesting and make the story something worth reading.

Steps to Take Before You Write

- Make sure you have all the information. If there is something you don't understand, ask the police captain at the briefing, or call him back while writing the story. If you don't understand something about the story when you start to write, you will not understand it later in the writing process. Above all, the story must be accurate.
- At first, list a word or two for each of the major parts of your story on a small piece of paper, or type them into your computer. Include entry into bank, ski masks, canister of red dye, CB radio, chase, arrest.
- Now, decide which of these items is the most important for the reader to know. This is called "rank ordering," or giving a "1" for the most important, and others "2," "3," etc., down to the last number. Most important is first, and more recent information is favored over older information. Our judgments are based on news values, discussed in chapter 1.
- For this story, let us agree that "1" belongs to the arrest, "2" to the chase, "3" to the red dye, "4" to the CB radio, "5" to the ski masks, and "6" to the entry into the bank three minutes after it opened. You might not agree completely with this ranking, but in order to keep things moving, let's start with that.

Rank ordering is very important to putting things in focus for news stories. At first, you may wish to list these items on a sheet of paper with numbers alongside them. Later, when you have done more stories, you will do this mentally. And when you understand formula stories, you will get this sequence down once or twice and use it whenever you write a certain category of stories.

Without rank ordering, you do not know where to start. Equally as important, you do not know which items follow in logical sequence, so you do not know where your story is going. Unless you have thought it through in some fashion, you do not know how your story is going to end, so you do not know how to get from Point A to Point B to Point C and to the end of the story.

After we have gathered our information and rank ordered it, we are ready to begin writing.

Start with the Most Important Facts

If the most important thing is the arrests, start with it first.

"Two men were arrested today" should be your first words. In most news stories, the most important parts of the story are the first words typed.

Now, you could have started with one of the other five Ws or an H. You could have said, as many beginning news writers do, any of the following: "Police today announced that they had arrested . . ." But is the fact that police made an announcement important? Don't police make several announcements a day, or at least several a week?

Or, you might have started with the time element: "Shortly after 9:00 A.M. today, two men entered the First National Bank and Trust branch at West Avenue and 14th Street." This is known as the chronological lead, because it deals with the time and usually follows this with a step-by-step recitation of facts as they happened. But it is not what the reader wants to know, and should be avoided. The reader wants to know how something like this ended, not how it started.

You also could have used the Who part of this story, by saying: "Walter Thomas Wallace, 34, and Albert James Wellington, 23, both of 2407-14th Street, were arrested this morning in connection with the robbery at the First Federal Bank and Trust, at West and 14th, three blocks from where they lived." True? Certainly. Interesting. Yes. Easy to read? No.

Are these men well enough known that mentioning their names brings recognition by most readers? Are the names more important than the fact that two men were arrested in a strange and unusual chase after a bank robbery? No, probably not.

Another common false start is for a beginning reporter to say "A bank robbery took place this morning at . . ." This, again, is not the most interesting way to start a story. It sounds like an old story, or that all bank robberies are the same.

Writing the Lead

You must first organize each story in a thought process similar to the one just discussed. The facts will be different for each story, and the reader interest will be different in each case, but you must organize your material first. Only after you have thought through a story can you begin to write the lead.

Without organizing, you may jump in with something interesting or cute or clever, and use it for your lead. Despite the fact that it may interest you the most, or may have been the highlight of a long, dull meeting, it may not be what the reader needs to know first.

And, unless you have thought it through, you may write the lead and then be stuck for the rest of the story. The lead is perhaps one, two, or three paragraphs, and unless you have organized yourself, you will not know what to write after those paragraphs.

Experienced reporters who have written many stories can usually start without organizing their material in some fashion, because they have written several stories about bank robberies, government meetings, accidents, or whatever. They have a framework in mind for each kind of story.

But even these reporters will have trouble with longer, more complex stories or with types of stories they have not done before. Writing coaches say the number one problem reporters have in writing stories is that they do not organize before they write.

Before we start, remember that this is a story about an unsuccessful and somewhat unusual bank robbery in which two men have been arrested. The reader needs to know immediately what happened, and if the suspects were caught, and it must be done in a way that will make him or her want to read the rest of the story.

As we said earlier, "Two men were arrested today" would be a good way to start because it says in a very few words what the story is all about. This is not a complete sentence at the moment, and we will finish it shortly.

But notice (and this will help you with other stories) that we have started out with a subject for the sentence ("Two men") and a verb ("were arrested"). When you are starting most stories, you need to identify who or what the story is about (the subject) and what action that subject took or was subjected to (the verb).

In an obituary, you give the name and age of the deceased and who said that person died. In a sports story, you give the name of the winner and the score. In a weather story, you say "Rain blanketed the Midwest," or whatever is the case, and you use the subject and the verb to tell what was important. None of these examples is a complete thought, and we will handle that problem now.

If we say "Two men were arrested," what else does the reader need to know? Arrested for what? Are the police sure they are the ones? When did all this happen? Choose from your list of five Ws and an H.

Let's try "Two men were arrested this morning (when) within minutes (interesting fact) of a robbery (what) of the First National Bank and Trust branch at West Avenue and 14th Street (where)."

Does this tell the reader everything he needs to know to decide whether to read the rest of the story? Probably yes.

Does it tell you everything about the story? No, it is only the lead-in, the first paragraph or so.

Is it too long? It is 25 words (not counting the parenthetical material). This is a little above normal, but there are no complicated words of many syllables.

Is it interestingly written? It is straightforward and probably not too exciting, but we will work on improving it later. First, you have to get the facts into the story, get it all organized, write it once, and then get it bright and shiny.

What Happens After the Lead is Written?

Remember, the lead is just one part of the story. It may be the most difficult part, but please understand it is not the only concern.

Many experienced news writers tend to spend most of their energy on the lead without thinking of their work as a story, and have difficulty with the rest of the story. They are not sure what to do after they do the lead, so they just start listing sets of facts.

Many beginning writers lapse into chronological reporting after doing a lead like this. Their (wrong) tendency is to say in the second paragraph:

"The incident started at 9:03 when two men wearing ski masks walked into the bank and demanded money." There comes a time in a story when you have to tell things in the order that they happened, but not yet.

You need to answer the questions a reader might have after reading the first paragraph. What would you want to know after you had read "Two men were arrested this morning within minutes after a robbery of the First Federal Bank and Trust at West Avenue and 14th Street?"

If you were normally curious, you would want to know who the two men were. You might also want to know how they were captured within minutes of the robbery. By putting these two parts into the sentence, you have signalled the reader that something else in more depth will follow.

This is called *foreshadowing*. It helps to tell a story. It keeps the lead short. And it makes a logical transition into the rest of the story. It lets you start the next paragraph by answering the questions that were left in the first paragraph.

If you have organized your thoughts before starting to write, the lead will be followed logically by the parts that make the story. While we are not storytellers in the sense of "Once upon a time," neither are we people who repeat minute by minute the comments made at a press conference.

If you were to use the names you might start the second graph with: "The men are Walter Thomas Wallace, 34, and Albert James

Wellington, 23, both of 2407-14th Street, who live about three blocks from the branch they are accused of entering."

If you were to go with the "within minutes" angle, you might say: "Police said use of a CB radio by the branch manager enabled them to follow the two men, and make the arrest within five minutes of when it happened."

You could then give the names of the suspects. Please note that they are still suspects, even though the evidence is strong against them, until they are convicted. They are not robbers until they have been convicted in a court of law, which could take months or years. Use of the proper word is critical here.

Completing the Story

You know the principles involved in writing the lead and the following paragraph. You can now use them to complete the story. If you have thought it through and organized it in some fashion before you started writing, this will be a lot easier.

The next paragraph, if you used the "within minutes" angle, would go on to tell the details of the arrest, the fact that they are now in jail, and concluding statements, such as the police would not divulge the amount of money taken, the name of the judge, and the time of arraignment (which means being taken before the judge to enter a plea).

If the second graph used the names of the suspects, you could then go on to details about the chase.

Concluding the Story

When do you stop writing? In a single-event story such as this, and in most single-event stories, you stop writing when you run out of fresh information.

In feature stories, which we will discuss later, you come to a more formal or a more "bang-bang" ending. You save a good anecdote or a catchy saying for the end, and try to give the reader a bonus for reading through the entire story. You make a conscious effort to improve the story by providing a strong ending. Many editors suggest that you think about the ending when structuring the story, right after you organize and think about your lead. In this kind of a story, then, you know where you are going to end before you start writing.

But in the kind of story we are doing here, you continue until there is no more worthwhile information to tell. The least important information goes in the last paragraph.

In pre-computer times, this was done so that the person putting the type in the page could remove the last paragraph if the story was a little too long. It was difficult to get exact type measures when copy was set by hand or on typesetting machines.

Today, most computers used in newsrooms can predict down to the tenth of an inch how long a story will be. If there is enough time, the editor can either add space for the story or ask you to cut the story down to the proper length. But even here, you need to have the least important information at the end to be sure the most important is included.

In the bank robbery story, what the least important part of the story is becomes a matter of debate. It depends on how you organize the story, but since you have the names, the arrest, the arraignment, and details of the chase early in the story, you would probably conclude with details of the chase leading up to the arrest.

Rewriting and Polishing the Lead

Writing this story has been a difficult and time-consuming process. It can get to be exhausting if you do several of these stories during the course of a news day, although you are not likely to do two bank robberies in the same day. If this happened, you would put the two together into another form of story, discussed in this book under Roundup.

If you are like most reporters, you probably would heave a sigh of relief, turn in your story, and go on to something else.

So why would you want to rewrite the story?

In my 20-plus years of teaching journalism, I have yet to see a story that is not better after a rewrite than it was originally.

The process (starting with an idea, gathering information, finding a focus, and writing the story) is actually a form of organizing your ideas and materials. When you put it down on paper or on the computer screen, you have completed your organization—for the moment.

Writers in other fields rewrite their material time and time again. The news media do not have days to work with individual paragraphs of novels. But any writing can be improved with additional work.

Reporters who are used to waiting until the last minute to turn in copy often find themselves in difficulty because they do not allow enough time or they must rush at the last minute. If they would write them early in the deadline period and rewrite them when time permits, they would have better and more readable stories.

Something happens when you complete the writing of the first draft that is difficult to explain. It is as though you have thought the story through as completely as you can, but as soon as it is complete, you begin to think about it again. It is as if the brain finally gets to see the entire product, and it becomes defensive, saying "I could have done better than that."

Doing better then becomes the purpose of the rewrite. The mind is cleared of the responsibility of picking the best material and organizing all the notes, quotes, and other details in the story. It sees the complete picture, and looks at this new unit as something that can be improved upon.

Looking back at this story, is there something that makes this robbery stand out from other bank robberies? The fact that the men lived within three blocks of the bank is one thing. The fact that the entire event took only five minutes from start to finish is unusual. And the fact that the men had the red dye on their hands when they were caught sets this apart from other robberies. Dye canisters are not a new device, and in some cases robbers have been known to throw out the canisters as soon as they leave the bank.

While we are rewriting, we want to make this something a little livelier and more interesting than a routine robbery report, as long as we work within the facts and do not make anything up.

As you go through your facts again, the words "red-handed" may come to mind. As you rewrite the story, the next version might come out like this:

Two Springfield men were literally caught red-handed within five minutes of a robbery this morning at the First Federal Bank and Trust, three blocks from where the men lived.

Police were assisted in their chase by the manager of the bank, who followed the getaway car and reported on its progress with a Citizen's Band radio.

Police identified the men as _____ and _____.

They will be arraigned Tuesday morning on charges of _____.

Police arrested the men at a shopping center parking lot _____.

Two men had entered the bank at 9:03 A.M. _____.

Can you see how the rewrite is better and more lively than the first story?

More importantly, can you see how it could have been difficult to write the second lead *unless you had written the story once before*, or unless you had written many similar stories?

Understanding that writing even a "straight" news story involves a complex process is the first step to wisdom in writing news stories. There are many other steps to follow, but this is the first step.

What seems so easy on first reading is actually the end of a rather complicated thought process that is, and should be, difficult at first. After you have done many of them, it will (naturally) become easier.

But until then, follow the same instructions as the tourist looking for Carnegie Hall in New York. When he asked a young musician carrying a trombone case how to get to Carnegie Hall, he replied without hesitation:

"Practice, man, practice."

Review: Things I Would Not Do

Do not start writing until you have all of the details firmly in your mind, and you have outlined it in some fashion. Experienced writers might do this, but it presents problems for beginners.

Do not start without some form of rank ordering, in which you tell yourself what the most important parts of the story are.

Do not start with the first facts of the case and go through the steps as reported in the press conference. This is called the chronological approach, and does not tell the reader the most important thing—that two men were captured—until too late in the story. The reader may have stopped reading by that time.

Do not develop a lead, and then in the next paragraph, lapse into the chronological reporting of an event.

Do not start with "A bank was robbed this morning" because that does not include the last minute items and it is not as important as other facts.

Do not start writing unless you know what the subject, verb, and object of your lead are going to be. Who is the story about? What did they do? What else is needed to make the thought complete?

And do think of the set of facts you have as a story, with a beginning, a middle, and an end. Organize it in a form that will answer the reader's most important questions first.

Comparing the Single-Event Story with the More Complex Single-Event Story

Let us compare the bank robbery story we have just been through with a simpler story, such as the election of Harlan Jefferson to the presidency of the student government at James Madison University (presented in chapter 10).

Both are single events—a bank robbery and an election.

176

Both require a similar organization, putting the most important fact in the first few words.

Both require the writer to think through the entire story before doing the lead and the second paragraph.

Both work on the principle that there is a story here, with a beginning (lead), a transition to other details, and an ending to the story.

And both would probably be improved if the writer allowed time for a rewrite. Adequate time is not always available, but if the reporter knows rewrite is important, she might take more time to include it in her planning.

The main similarity is that news writers have to think through each story before they write. The Civil War-era styles of telling a story in the sequence in which it happened, or setting the stage with an elaborate preamble such as "An exciting and potentially dangerous situation unfolded today at the First National Bank and Trust company" do not apply in all cases. A lead-in might be appropriate in some broadcast stories, but not in print media stories. More on this as we discuss broadcast styles of writing.

The main difference between the two stories is that the robbery is much more complex and involved. Several "mini-events" are happening one after the other, and you have to decide which is most important for the reader to know. But you have to wait until all of the facts are in, which may be hours after the event, or until the last possible minute, before beginning to write. You must constantly revise as this is a changing story, not a static, straightforward announcement story that is "cut and dried" and very unlikely to change.

The writing is secondary to the thinking. You have to plan what to say based on the latest bank robbery information, and to realize that you may have to change it again until the deadline shuts the door.

This is a continuing story, and one that will change the next day as new information comes in. We will discuss this aspect when we get to "second day stories" under Advanced Writing Developments in chapter 21.

Now, let's look at actual samples of several complicated single-event stories, including gun battles in the streets, dangerous chemicals being produced by factories, and the effect of the savings and loan scandals on individual investors.

Notice how summaries are developed and how the facts of each case are borne out by the leads. Then think about the cooperation and the steps that went into putting together extended stories of this type.

The first story does not bear a headline; rather the "slug" is "Agents Shot" by the Associated Press. (Local papers do the actual headlines.) The story is by Eva Parziale, now chief of bureau with AP in Portland, Ore., but at that time on the staff of AP in Miami.

Parziale went to the scene of the shootout at 10:00 A.M. and remained on the scene until 6:00 P.M., dictating stories to the Miami office from the scene. Material from Washington, D.C., FBI headquarters, and from a hospital press conference was added to the story by the AP desk crew in Miami. Parziale also was involved in doing a Question and Answer series on the shootout for AP (Radio) Network News and helped the AP graphics department in New York create a visual of the scene, describing such things as the distance from body to body.

In the first story, pay close attention to the amount of specifics and detail and the number of quotes gathered in a relatively short period of time under considerable stress.

MIAMI—A blazing gun battle erupted when the FBI closed in on heavily armed suspected bank robbers Friday, leaving two agents and two suspects dead, five agents wounded and battered cars and spent ammunition littering a busy suburban intersection.

The hail of bullets and shotgun blasts went "on and on and on," said one witness in Kendall, an unincorporated area south of Miami that is home to more than 100,000 people.

"I thought it was a drug deal that went bad, because that is what everyone does down here," said Duane Parker, 24, who said he saw the entire battle.

"Then I thought it was a 'Miami Vice' episode, but then I saw the blood and the dead guys and thought: 'No way.'"

The slain agents were identified in an FBI release as Benjamin T. Grogan, 53, a 25-year veteran and Jerry Dove, 30, an agent since 1982. The hometowns were not included in the release. It was the first time since 1979 that two FBI agents were killed in a single incident.

After agents spotted the car they were looking for during surveillance, they radioed for backup, said Joseph V. Corless, special agent in charge of the Miami FBI.

"Apparently when they believed they had sufficient assistance, an attempt was made to pull this vehicle over. At that point, a confrontation ensued, shots were fired," Corless said.

Witnesses said the agents interrupted their gunfire when

motorists, unaware of what was happening, drove down the street.

"Those idiots kept going on through," said spectator Billie Holloway. "But the agents knew they were civilians and halted their fire."

FBI Director William H. Webster identified the slain suspects as Michael Platt, 32, and William R. Matix, whose age was not given. Speaking at a Washington, D.C., news conference, Webster said the men "were particularly violent individuals" and were heavily armed.

"It appears they were armed with at least one automatic weapon capable of firing at least 30 rounds in a single container and one shotgun that appears to have been modified to carry additional shells," he said.

The FBI agents used handguns and one shotgun, Webster said.

Asked about other incidents involving the suspects, Webster said: "A number of people have been shot," adding that the owner of a car used in a robbery had disappeared and was believed dead.

Corless, wearing dark glasses, was somber when he gave a terse statement at the scene. He refused to answer questions.

Behind him were four wrecked FBI cars that were involved in the fatal operation. One had slammed into a building, another smashed into a tree alongside the suspects' car, and two cars apparently hit each other. One of them had five holes, possibly from shotgun blasts.

Blood stained the street in two places where victims had fallen.

Dozens of agents and police swarmed to the middle class neighborhood of shops and duplex homes after the gun battle at the busy intersection shortly after 9:30 A.M.

The FBI would not say whether any suspects got away, and Metro-Dade police officers at the scene said they did not know whether any other suspects were involved.

"All I heard was the shots. There must have been 100 rounds fired. They were shooting for 10 minutes," said Mario Tejeiro, who was unloading a truck at an office complex near the scene.

"It went on and on," said Charlie Davis, who lives nearby.

Agents Gordon McNeill, 43, a 19-year veteran, and John Hanlon, 47, with the FBI since 1963, were listed in serious but stable condition with gunshot wounds at Baptist Hospital, Corless said. Edmundo Mireles, 33, an agent since 1979, was listed in serious condition at South Miami Hospital, he said.

Two other agents, Richard Manauzzi, 43, and Gilbert Orrantia, 27, were treated for minor injuries at Jackson Memorial Hospital and released.

Eight FBI agents were at the scene when the shooting erupted, Corless said at a briefing at Baptist Hospital.

"This is just a devastating day for the FBI in Miami," he said, adding there was no evidence that any other suspects were involved in the shootout.

Since 1908, 27 FBI agents have been killed on duty, Corless said.

The last time two agents were killed in a single incident was in August 1979 when a man broke into the FBI office in El Centro, Calif., and began shooting, FBI spokesman Jack French said in Washington. The man killed himself after being wounded by a dying agent.

Agents Friday morning were doing surveillance when they spotted a stolen black Monte Carlo with a license plate matching the number of one they suspected of being used in recent Miami-area holdups, officials said.

"The FBI received information from previous investigations that this area would be the most logical place for the next bank robbery," said Al Carballosa, Metro-Dade police spokesman.

He said he recalled at least three other armored car robberies and at least two bank robberies in southwestern Dade County during the last year.

"In the holdups, the group would wait for the guards and just shoot them. They were ruthless," Carballosa said.

The next example took five months to investigate and won a National Headliner award for outstanding news reporting in a news feature or series. It was entitled "CFCs: DuPont's Safety White Wash."

Merrit Wallick, environment reporter for the *Wilmington (Del.) News-Journal*, conducted a coast-to-coast investigation, examining internal memos at DuPont and thousands of pages of records, questioning DuPont officials for more than 20 hours, and conducting more than 100 other interviews.

The entire series ran almost 12 full-sized newspaper pages over four days, including art, charts, time lines, and side bar stories.

The introductory information on the special reprint starts out as follows:

The Dupont Co. has long portrayed itself as a company that places the highest value on protecting human health and the environment.

In March, the *News Journal* uncovered evidence calling that reputation into question. As we dug deeper, more evidence emerged challenging that carefully cultivated image.

DuPont's conduct in testing and promoting its Freon Chlorofluorocarbons became a touchstone for testing DuPont's actions against its claims.

For 50 years, DuPont sold the chemicals on the basis of their safety. Those chemicals have killed scores and sickened others. They also have precipitated a global environmental crisis—depletion of earth's protective ozone layer.

Did DuPont place profit over public welfare?

When Standard Manufacturing Co. contacted the DuPont Co. in 1986 on behalf of an employee who routinely breathed solvent Freon 113 on the job, it was assured by DuPont officials the woman had nothing to fear.

DuPont never told anyone at the Dallas plant that its own expert believed DuPont's study on Freon 113 was flawed.

Fielding a 1979 inquiry from the automobile industry, DuPont kept silent on test results linking Freon 113 to cancer. For years DuPont made a habit of saying as little as possible on the dangers of Freon 113.

Indeed for 50 years DuPont has assured a world hungry for Freon 113 that the prized chemical was safe—nearly as harmless as water.

A five month investigation by the *News Journal* has revealed that DuPont never has had sufficient evidence to justify the safety claims it widely made about the popular solvent, today used primarily in the electronics industry. But it had ample evidence of the chemical's dangers.

Research cited by the company as proof of the chemical's safety was frequently inadequate and shoddy by scientific standards, a conclusion sometimes reached by DuPont scientists but not shared with the public. Moreover, outside studies suggest that longtime exposure to the fumes of Freon 113 may cause cancer and other diseases.

The long-term health effects of Freon 113 matter to more than the tens of thousands of people who work with it. The chemical—650 million pounds were produced in 1987 alone—is found virtually everywhere on earth. In 1980, when concentrations of it in the air were lower than they are now, one study found

Freon 113 in every sample of the milk randomly selected from nursing mothers.

Nobody—including DuPont—knows the long-term health effects of Freon 113.

The immediate dangers—that breathing too much Freon 113 causes immediate deaths—have been clear for 20 years. Although more than 100 people have died suddenly after breathing Freon 113 and other Freons, DuPont downplayed that danger for decades.

Freon 113 is a solvent used primarily for cleaning printed circuit boards. In the late 1970s and 1980s it became the fastest growing and most profitable Freon in DuPont's lineup of chlorofluorocarbons, constituting 28 per cent of the world production of CFCs by 1988. (CFCs, with an atmospheric lifetime of up to 400 years, cause 60 percent of ozone depletion. The ozone is a naturally occurring concentration of gas about 25 miles above the surface of the earth, which filters out harmful ultraviolet rays.)

Scott McCartney, southwest regional reporter for AP in Dallas, handled a complex story by using people to illustrate the main points he wants to make. He won the 1991 Stanley Walker award from the Texas Institute of Letters for "S&Ls on Main Street, effect of S&L crisis on homeowners, investors and vacationers."

Notice the personalizing, and how he closes with figures which give you a much better idea of how great the impact of the savings and loan scandal can be.

Jean Shoults was careful to pick a stable neighborhood with solid home values when she moved her family to Arlington, Texas, two years ago. But a single government decision may cost her $25,000 in home equity.

"You think you're buying the American dream and it turns into a nightmare.

Mrs. Shoults says, "We are savings and loan victims." (The government is attempting to sell the land in her subdivision to contractors who would put up less expensive homes than the one Mrs. Shoults owns, thus dropping her home in value.)

More and more people are finding they, too, are S&L victims. Small businesses can't find loans. Subcontractors don't get paid for work they have already done. Real estate markets are in ruins, neighborhoods tied up in government red tape.

Homeowners like Judy and Dave Crenshaw in Colorado

Springs battle through three mortgage companies, and lose out on one home, before finally getting a deal approved.

Joan Leff gets teary thinking about her future. She, too, is a victim, but she's more of a victim of risk-taking of high-flying S&L executives unleashed by deregulation of their industry.

Mrs. Leff took all the money she had—$90,000 from a divorce settlement—to Lincoln Savings and Loan to buy a certificate of deposit that would give her monthly interest to help pay her rent.

Instead a salesman talked her into a bond that paid slightly higher interest. She thought the bond was safe and sure, like a CD.

It wasn't.

Unable to pay her rent, Mrs. Leff moved into a cheap one-bedroom apartment, where she still lives.

"The loss was almost worse than the loss of my marriage."

Michael Kay seemed even farther removed from the thrift scandal. He sells jewelry at a strip shopping center in north Phoenix, and until recently, business was good.

But his shopping center fell into the hands of government regulators and lost most of its tenants. No tenants, no traffic.

Kay had to move a mile down the street, which cost his business $50,000.

Capitalize on this, the memo began and went on to list a dozen selling points for bond salesmen at Lincoln Savings and Loan branches. It ended with this:

And always remember, the weak, meek and ignorant are always good targets.

Some customers who came into the federally insured Lincoln Savings to buy a certificate of deposit or put large sums in savings accounts were steered to the now worthless junk bonds with the promise they were just as safe as CDs, but paid more.

"It was an elderly scam," said Jeri Mallon, a retired hospital administrator who invested $40,000 in the bonds. "They told me the bonds were as good as gold. It's a shame when you realize people aren't truthful, or honest. It hurts."

"They told me the government would have to go under before this would," said John Brunner, a Hollywood puppeteer who invested $76,000. "You feel like we were just really swindled."

U.S. Rep. Jim Leach, R-Iowa, a member of the House Banking Committee figures the S&L scandal will cost the average American family $20 a month for the next 30 years.

It would cost $147 billion to $203 billion to set everything right if a check could be written today, according to various estimates. The latest government estimate is $160 billion, plus another $340 billion in interest to pay it off over 30 years.

(This) $500 billion is enough to give $2,000 to every man, woman and child in the United States—or $100 to every human on the planet.

With the $160 billion in principal, the U.S. could pay for the next 53 years of AIDS research, education and care. It could also just about wipe out the federal budget deficit, estimated at $169 billion for 1991.

For just $1 billion, Donald Trump could afford 40 failed marriages at $25 million each. Or he could buy a $40,000 Cadillac every day for the next 872 years.

That is just $1 billion of the $500 billion estimated bill for the S&L scandal.

Things to Remember

- Longer stories based on one event require more organizing time. You should not start writing until you have outlined in some form the events you wish to write about.
- When organizing, think in terms of what the reader or audience would like to know first.
- Rank order the elements in terms of which is most important as a way of organizing the material.
- Only after writing the story the first time will things come to mind that will help you improve the story with a second draft.

Practice

Write stories based on the following information.

Fact Set 1: Clean Air

The World Health Organization and the United Nations Environmental Programs group have released a report concerned about worldwide air pollution. The report indicates that as more and more people move to the cities to find jobs, the air over cities around the world is getting worse. Unfortunately, these underdeveloped countries cannot provide enough jobs in rural areas where the air is clean. The report says persons moving to major cities will have increasing threats of damage to heart, lungs, and brain from this pollution. The report also ranks several of the world's largest cities in terms of clean air. Los Angeles has the worst ozone problem in the world, the report says. Mexico City has the dirtiest air. London, Tokyo, and New York were rated as having among the cleanest air of the major cities in the world.

Fact Set 2: Mayor

During the political campaign that ended last month, Mayor Ron Bonten of Shelter Valley was accused of requesting $100,000 from contractors for approving highway construction in the city. His opponent also claimed the mayor had not paid income taxes for the last three years. Bonten won re-election to a two-year term starting in three weeks by 55 to 45 percent. Three days ago formal charges were filed against the mayor by the county prosecuting attorney for failure to pay income taxes and for accepting gifts from contractors. Today the mayor resigned from office, effective immediately. He said he was not guilty, but that he needed the time to prepare a defense and to be ready for trial. "Let the people and the courts decide," he said.

Fact Set 3: Accident

Stefan Bellaw was 16 years old four days ago. He took the written test for his driver's license and passed it this morning. He is permitted to drive an automobile on a learner's permit, which he has, as long as an adult is riding with him in the front seat. His mother was with him. Bellaw got in his mother's car after he completed the driving test, and pulled out into West Side Highway. He failed to notice the car pulling onto the same road from his right, and Bellaw drove right into the side of the second car. The driver of the second car was Carl Johnson, 34, a traffic control officer for the city police department. No one was hurt, but the police car was a total loss. Bellaw was cited for failure to yield the right of way.

Fact Set 4: Fraud

The last two administrations have been making an effort to get the government out of many businesses, and have been attempting to subcontract businesses to private firms and individuals. Many efforts have been made to "privatize" business as a cost-cutting and efficiency measure. Today, the Office of Management and Budget, White House auditors, and a 12-agency task force released a report. They contend that there is widespread fraud in private contracting. They say contractors are buying group tickets to sporting events and charging them to the contract, buying cruises for persons who approve contracts, and using money from the contracts to increase salaries of company officials. They say a report to this effect is being sent to the Congress. The task force says it is unable to pinpoint the exact cause of this, but estimates the fraud to be "in the millions of dollars."

Fact Set 5: Hole in One

Jack Rentel is retired. He worked 40 years at Central Chemical in the purchasing department. He started playing golf when he was 50, and has a handicap of 18. On the 17th of August, he was playing with his two friends, John Coloney and Eric DeRosier, when he made a hole in one on the 17th hole of Colonial City Country Club. The hole is 153 yards long and he used a four iron. On the 17th of September, on the same hole, playing with the same friends, and using the same club, he shot another hole in one.

Fact Set 6: Principal

Eldred Longberry, 46, has been a principal at Midway Elementary school for 12 years. He has won numerous awards for creative curriculum development and for his students' high levels of achievement. Last year he took over and developed a drug prevention program that was recognized as a model throughout the district. Yesterday at 8:00 A.M., an hour before school started, he was arrested in the parking lot of the school. Police say he sold a packet of "speed" to an undercover agent for $100, and also accepted $800 for previous sales to the same agent. He will be brought before a judge this afternoon and faces 10 years in jail if convicted.

Reality Check

Make one story from the following information, discarding that which is not needed to tell the story. Charles Karafall is 35 and an automobile salesman. He lives in the Willshire Brook Condominiums on South Chelsea Avenue. He sells Saturns at a dealership on the north edge of town. He travels a lot and has been to Hawaii four times for winning prizes in auto sales contests. He returned from Hawaii for the fourth time this week. He had been gone for ten days.

Karafall told police two days ago that while he was gone someone entered his condo and took two of his gold credit cards. They left the rest of the cards, and did not take anything else in the house. He told police he thinks the person may have read a story in the paper saying Karafall had won Salesman of the Year for his district and would be on Maui playing golf for 10 days.

He also had 12 calls on his answering machine from merchants wanting to check whether he had given his son permission to use his credit card. Karafall is not married, has never been married, and has no children. The person had charged more than $2,000 worth of merchandise in 10 days from six merchants, including 14 videos, eight cartons of cigarettes, an Armani sports jacket worth $400, an $800 stereo system, and other items police did not disclose. Other calls from merchants are being checked to see if more merchandise was charged, police said.

Police Chief Howard Hentsen said two detectives worked all day on the case. By talking to the merchants, they were able to draw a profile of the person who had charged the merchandise. Merchants said he was about 18, said it was his father's card, that the father would approve the purchases, and that he had enough cash to pay for it if they wanted cash instead. All of the stores were in the same mall, the Cambridge Corners Mall on Rt. 252, one mile west of town.

By finding fingerprints in Karafall home, police say they can identify a person if a suspect is found. A police drawing of the suspect shows a young white male with dark curly hair and a mustache, about 5 feet, 8 inches and 135 pounds.

Police believe the man may still be in town and are giving the media the police drawing so that they can identify the person.

As you are writing the story, you get a call from police chief Hentsen's office. They have arrested Howard Spottswood, 18, of 324 West Maple, a recently laid-off carpenter. Police say his fingerprints match those at the scene. Mr. Karafall told police the man had installed a new railing on his stairway about three months prior to the incident, and never returned the key. Spottswood will be arraigned tomorrow in Municipal Court at 1:00 P.M. If he cannot afford a lawyer, one will be appointed for him.

12

Meetings, Speeches, and Roundup Stories: When It All Happens at Once

"I know so much I don't know where to begin."
—College professor giving a commencement
speech as portrayed in a cartoon.

In This Chapter

> Stories in which several things happen at one time or during
> one meeting, and the reporter is required to write it all in
> one story.
>
> The job of the reporter is to understand everything as clearly as
> possible before beginning to write. That takes some doing in
> more complicated stories.
>
> The reporter must understand the nature of the event, or the
> procedures of the meeting, and gather as much detail and
> information as possible.

THE STORY forms we are learning are getting more complicated.
This is the multiple-incident lead, probably the most complicated of all, in which the reporter tries to summarize what has happened over several hours of discussion, or several days of activity such as blizzards or rainstorms, or a series of accidents or disasters.

Ideally, a news story should cover only one event, which is easier to understand and simpler to report. Many media try to break a major story into its elements, doing one story on each element. This is to be preferred, if it can be done, but in many cases the reporter is expected to do one story to cover an entire meeting, press conference, or other activity.

But life is not that easy or straightforward.

Governmental units meet regularly, but not every day, and several items must be discussed at one meeting. Out of a three or four hour meeting, writers have to produce one story that reports on the discussion that went on as well as the decisions that were made, because the audience needs to know why decisions were made.

A press conference is held to announce a position on an issue, and opponents show up to make their statements. Your story must include both points of view.

A politician or a celebrity comes in to give a speech, but the public wants to know something the speaker may not wish to talk about. So you cover the speech but you also make every effort to ask the questions the politician may not wish to answer but that the public wants to know about. And you have to combine both items—the speech and the questions—into one story.

After a blizzard or a crippling snowstorm, it may be better to write about the impact of the storm on several communities, not just your own. The same multiple-incident approach is needed when covering tournament basketball, for example, where there are many games at many sites in one night.

A rare use of a multiple-incident story is a report on action during a war. Action is going on at several fronts at the same time, and the reporter or wire service must pull the main points together into one story to tell the audience what happened during the past 24-hour period.

Perhaps the classic multiple-incident story is an election. Literally hundreds of contests from coast to coast are decided on one night, and the night when the presidential race is decided is the most frantic of all. Newsrooms work through the night on election nights, bringing in extra reporters, calling sources at 3:00 A.M. to get missing results, and putting national, state, regional and local results together by the earliest possible time. Newspapers, radio, and television stations and national networks plan for weeks in advance so that they can project winners as soon as possible.

Election coverage may call for a national roundup, a state roundup, and a local roundup, among others. An election is something every newsroom both dreads and looks forward to, because it is the time when the democratic system is at its most exciting.

The Multiple-Incident Process

Regardless of how many results are decided on election night, or how many towns are snowed in by a blizzard, or how many decisions are made in a city council meeting on one night, the reader has the same question he has with single incident stories: "What does this mean to me?"

Therefore, the writer must think through the story as if it were a single-incident story, and tell the reader what is important. It may be that the Democrats or the Republicans made major strides in this election, or that schools will be closed for at least three more days because of the storm, or that police and firemen have asked the city council for a 7 percent raise.

The writer must think through several events in a multiple-incident story as if she were thinking through several elements of a single-incident story. Just as she thought through the bank robbery story and picked one or two elements as the most recent and most important, she must think through a blizzard story and decide which communities were worst hit or what the most important impact of the storm is.

Lead Focusing on One Incident

The lead can be one incident, if it is clearly more important than others, or several incidents together in one sentence, if they are of equal importance or value.

For example, "A tornado roared through Greene County Sunday night, killing four persons in a trailer park just west of Central City."

The key part of a multiple-incident lead is the second paragraph. The audience has been told what the writer thinks the most important thing is by what she uses in the lead.

If a single element is used in the lead, all other major elements should be outlined in the next paragraph. This means the reader or listener would have to go only to the second paragraph to find out what is important.

If you were to continue the tornado story, a second paragraph could be: "The storm also destroyed at least six homes, damaged two school buildings, and disrupted electrical power to 10 communities."

Lead Focusing on Several Incidents

If several elements are linked together equally in the lead, the second paragraph should be used to list any other items that are also important. Again, the reader should not have to go to the very end of the story to find the item that he is especially interested in.

For example, if no one had been killed in the tornado, the several-element lead could be, "A tornado roared through Greene County Sunday night, destroying six homes, damaging two school buildings, and disrupting electrical power to 10 communities."

The lead and the second paragraph may actually be one or more paragraphs in each case.

But once the lead and the second graph are complete, the writer should then amplify on each of the incidents in the order in which they were presented in the first two graphs.

In the tornado story with fatalities, this would mean discussing the circumstances of the four deaths first, followed by the homes destroyed, the school buildings damaged, and the power disrupted.

In the tornado story without fatalities, it would mean starting with the homes, then discussing the school buildings and the electrical power. Always list the detailed reports on each incident in the same order in which they appeared in the first reference. It is assumed that writers place the most important items first in each case.

If the major story in the election was a hotly contested race for sheriff, the lead would focus on this race. The second paragraph, or set of paragraphs, would then talk about the election of other officials, such as commissioners, county auditor, and county treasurer, for example.

After this paragraph or paragraphs, the story would return to a discussion of the sheriff's race, taking as many paragraphs as are necessary to tell the story of that race fully.

After this is completed, the races for commissioners, auditor, and treasurer would be discussed in as much detail as needed, and in the same order as presented in the first listing. The story might conclude with some comments about uncontested races or some other less significant element of this group of races.

Remember, this is a more complicated story. More time is required to think it through before you start to write. Ask yourself what the reader wants to know and go through each event or each different item to see which is most important. You cannot start writing until you have organized it, and with multiple-incident stories, the organizing is much more difficult.

After you have had experience doing these stories, you will learn to organize material while gathering it. You will decide what is important as you report the stories, and when you start to write you will already have a good idea of how to organize the story. At first, however, you will have to think it through and perhaps outline the material on paper before starting to write.

Multiple Incident: Meeting Stories

Covering meetings is a staple of the news business. Reporters very often give up their Monday and/or Tuesday nights one or more times a month to cover meetings. All official business of governmental units must be conducted in open public meetings, although some officials would like to hold meetings without the press "interfering."

A reporter who has never covered a meeting before may think that everything happens at once and people speak at all different times. But there is a clearly developed routine under which meetings are conducted, and after a few times the reporter begins to understand the method in what seemed like madness the first time.

Not all meetings are exciting and interesting. In fact, most meetings are routine, and the number of times when large crowds gather at a public meeting is low. Often reporters and elected or appointed officials will be the only persons on hand for a meeting.

Meetings also have a particular jargon of their own, which varies from state to state. Legal procedures must be followed, votes must be taken on many matters, and a regular system must be followed, generally that outlined in Robert's Rules of Order to determine who gets to speak when.

Terms that are familiar to the elected officials will not be to the reporter. Some items will be voted on, some will be tabled, and a vote on others cannot be taken at the same meeting. However, if the elected group declares the matter an "emergency" (and votes on that), some matters can be voted on at once. Much of what is discussed is routine transfer of funds or procedural material of interest only to the council, and in all likelihood will not be used in news stories.

Add to this the fact that the first-time reporter may not know the officials or the issues, and confusion may set in.

Advance preparation is the key to eliminating the confusion. The reporter should be able to obtain an agenda, either at the meeting or before, by talking to the clerk or other appropriate officials. By talking to reporters who have previously covered the beat, he will get an idea of who the officials are and what the politics may be in any situation. Only then will he be able to begin making sense of a meeting like this. Some officials can usually be counted on to talk about the items after the meeting, but others, for their own reasons, may not be as outgoing as the reporter would like.

By doing "homework" before the meeting, the reporter can anticipate what the issues will be. By getting an agenda, the reporter will know what is to be discussed. And by talking to officials after the meeting, he can fill in the details on anything he may not have been clear about.

All of this work before and after a meeting is important if the reporter is to write a clear story about the meeting. Unless the reporter understands everything *before* starting to write, the story will not be clear or accurate.

Now, after having said all of this, let us make a very important point. The meeting is not the news, the actions and discussion at the meeting are the news.

Too many beginning writers will start by saying, "The Bayview council met in regular session Monday night." The fact that the meeting was held is not news. Most councils will meet perhaps 26 times a year.

It would be better to say, "The Bayview council Monday night voted to join a six-city group that is trying to lower utility rates."

And by the principle of rewrite, it would be even better to say, "Citizen complaints about rapidly escalating electric rates in Bayview have resulted in some action.

The city has decided to join with six others to find ways to lower rates."

It is always better to phrase a story with the interest of the readers first, and the interests of the council second. There is a major difference between "Citizen complaints about rapidly escalating rates" and "The council Monday night voted to . . ."

For one thing, the first few words of the first lead get right to the point while the second lead is concerned more with procedures than with people or issues. The reporter could start all 26 meeting stories with "The Bayview council Monday night voted to (and fill in the blanks)" because the council will almost always vote on something every meeting. That is not the news—the issues are the news.

What does this have to do with multiple-incident stories? Take that same process of deciding what is in the lead on the escalating rates and multiply it by perhaps six or seven major items at some meetings, perhaps three or four at others.

For, in addition to escalating rates, the council may make decisions on firefighters' grievances, what to do about new state recycling laws, whether to have fireworks on July 4 (insurance rates are going up), and whether to change the charter under which the city operates.

In recent years, more and more newspapers might consider making each of these individual items into a small story, each with its own subhead. Readers could then choose the ones they are interested in, and not have to plow through a multiple-incident lead.

However, at the same time, advertising revenues are down for almost all media in times of recession, and this means the amount of space to run a story may be cut as well. If the space is cut, the editor will likely ask the reporter to write one story, which is back to the multiple-incident lead situation again.

So, instead of deciding which elements within a story should be the most important and be placed in the lead, the reporter decides which stories (out of several) are the most important. Each of these stories might make an individual story, but when combined into a multi-incident story, must be judged against all other stories in the meeting to determine which is the most important.

After this, the procedure used in the multiple-incident process is again used. Either focus on one story as the lead, or list two or more stories that were discussed and build an equivalent type lead.

For the most part, school board meetings will follow the same general rules and principles as city council meetings. The same goes for planning commissions, park and recreation boards, chamber of commerce meetings, and similar types of activities.

Multiple Incident: Speech Stories

In some ways, speeches are the least predictable of multiple-incident stories. While some politicians give out advance copies and then read their speeches word for word, this is not always the case.

A lot of persons speaking before civic groups or on campuses do not have a copy of "the speech," as politicians refer to the one speech repeated at each campaign stop. Instead, these non-politicians make up a special speech for each occasion, or else will follow a brief outline and ad lib at the end.

Just as with meeting stories, the reporter is encouraged to get further information either before the speech (by reading up on the speaker or going to the files to see what else he or she has done or said lately), after the speech, or both.

A reporter once covered a speech by the president of the largest university in the state. At the time the community he was speaking to was campaigning for a two-year campus. The speech did not mention the campus, but a couple of questions about it were asked during the question and answer period. The president's comments about the branch campus made page one. The speech was played inside.

Often politicians will be embroiled in issues they wish they had not been involved in, including extramarital affairs, avoidance of the draft, campaign contributions from political action committees, etc. They will not discuss these in the prepared speech, and so it is up to the reporter to ask about them at any opportunity. Politicians and many other elected and appointed officials would rather avoid questions in many instances, which is why reporters seem so "pushy" at news conferences. The reporter feels the public has a right to know about some things and will ask questions at any opportunity.

When writing a speech story, the reporter must begin by remembering, as with meeting stories, that the fact that a speech was given is not the story, unless it is the President himself making a campaign stop in a community. The audience wants to know what is said, not the fact that a speech was given.

And keep in mind that if nothing new is said at a speech, the media are under no obligation to report it. The media cover what is new, not what has been said before.

In most cases, the writer will have to summarize the main point or points made during the speech. Seldom does a speaker summarize the speech in his own words in a bright and interesting way. Therefore, the quote lead is very rarely used, but quotes are used throughout the story.

Use the speaker's words when they are more interesting than the paraphrase, or the reporter's words.

Having said all this, we now return to the principles of multiple-incident leads. Analyze all that the speaker said, find that which is new and interesting and valuable to the readers, and incorporate this into the speech story. Often, there will be more than one issue of interest, even though speakers are taught to limit the main points they try to make in a speech.

If there is one main point, use a single-incident lead and then mention the other important items in the next paragraph.

Somewhere in the first three or four paragraphs, give the speaker's background. The reader wants to know who is saying this and what their qualifications are. This paragraph should also mention the local tie, the group before whom the speech was given.

Multiple Incident: Press Conferences

Actually, press conference is an out-of-date phrase. It was coined when newspapers were the primary information medium. More recently, they have come to be called news or media conferences.

They occur when someone calls the media together in one location to make an announcement of something they consider to be of news value. Once again, the reporter is not obligated to write about it, and the fact that a news conference was held is not the news itself.

Since the conference is called by the source, the source is in charge. The source can cut off the conference immediately after reading a prepared statement and thus avoid any questions. I once helped arrange a press conference for Mrs. Rose Kennedy at Detroit Metro Airport to speak about the Special Olympics program, which Mrs. Kennedy was in the area to promote. As soon as her prepared statement was over, reporters asked her about her family and about presidential politics. She said, in all innocence, 'Oh, I didn't come here to discuss politics," and left the room.

It is often difficult for one reporter to get a meaningful story or a good quote because of the atmosphere at a media conference. Television lights, broadcast mikes, and hordes of hangers-on make the press conference a spectacle of one-way information rather than an opportunity to get meaningful news.

All of the rules that apply to writing multiple-incident leads also apply to media conferences, which will more often focus on a single issue.

Multiple Incident: Roundup Stories

Next to an election, nothing is more hectic than a weather emergency in a newsroom. Imagine trying to report on how difficult the traffic is during a blizzard when many of the reporters cannot make it into the newsroom because of the snow. On occasion, papers have been put out by the reporters who were unable to leave the building because they were snowed in. Imagine the frustration of a reporter who works extremely hard on a weather roundup only to find out the delivery trucks cannot get the paper out.

Radio stations are frustrated during weather emergencies when they are trying to receive calls from schools being closed down, and students calling in jam the phone lines. Or consider the case of the media in California or Tokyo or other earthquake zones in trying to report on the story when their own personal safety is in danger.

Natural disasters like floods and tornadoes are also difficult to cover. Everything is happening at once, and trying to keep in touch with officials is difficult because they are on the scene and phone lines are jammed for the most part.

Normal weather is assigned to a small box on page one or to its own routine spot in the press, or to regularly scheduled but brief reports on radio. Only on television had weather developed into an important part of the newscast until *USA Today* began running its color weather maps.

Yet weather has an effect on every reader, and should be covered fully. Weather disasters have extremely high audience interest.

In a tornado, blizzard, or other weather disasters, the area with the most damage, the most snow, or the most injuries would get the most attention. The second graph would list those places with lesser damage, and the story would be organized as outlined above.

All of the principles discussed in multiple-incident stories apply here as well. In stories of this nature, specific details are what people want to read about. When interviewing persons for information for these stories, be sure to ask for examples.

Two excellent examples of roundup stories both come from the same city: Oakland, California. The first deals with a destructive wildfire which raced through the hills east of Oakland, the second with the start of the Gulf War. Both stories were covered extensively by the *Oakland Tribune*, which published special editions after each one.

The *Tribune* on December 2, 1991, published "FIRESTORM: The week the hills burned," a 76-page tabloid section of stories about the fire that started Oct. 20, 1991. Here is how Managing Editor Eric Newton described the disaster:

> The most destructive wildfire in California history rose on a hot windy Sunday from the embers of a brush fire that had not been fully doused the day before. A spark raged into a 2,000 degree inferno that flew over reservoirs and incinerated entire neighborhoods. It burned for three days over three square miles, killing 25 people and gutting more than 3,000 homes, leaving 5,000 homeless. It caused $1.68 billion in damage.

In the first week, the *Tribune* published 500 stories, columns, and photographs on more than 100 pages. Because of the wide-ranging nature of the fire, the roundup story was used widely during the week. These are some of the leads that were recorded in the 64 pages of FIRESTORM.

DAY 1. EASTBAY BLAZE DESTROYS HUNDREDS OF HILLSIDE HOMES
by Craig Staats and Carolyn Newbergh, *Tribune* staff writers

---

A ferocious, out-of-control brush fire, whipped by hot, dry 30-mile per hour winds, roared through the Oakland-Berkeley Hills yesterday, leaving a path of death and destruction behind.

The fire—slowing in its advance late last night—claimed a sobering toll, authorities said.

At least 10 people were killed, including an Oakland police officer, and nine people were reported missing.

At least 250 structures had burned to the ground and the fire, which kept changing directions, blackened 1,500 acres.

Frightened hill residents fled for their lives, taking whatever valuables they could grab—clothes, pets and family photographs.

"It's the most terrifying experience I've been through," said Tralee Dobson, who lives on Oakland's Caldwell Road. "It sounded like there were bombers overhead. That's how loud the roar of the fire was. We could hear the electrical transformers explode."

"The fire exploded all around us," said attorney Curtis Karplus, who jumped off his home's six-foot balcony to escape.

"I thought it was all over."

Volunteers Open Hearts and Wallets

A steady stream of cars lined the streets along Webster and Sixth Streets last night as people donated food and drinks at the Salvation Army Adult Rehabilitation Center.

By 9 P.M., about 1,500 people had brought goods to the center, ranging from home-baked cookies to 7,000 pounds of spaghetti and sauce from the Spaghetti Factory in Oakland.

More than 100 volunteers worked in a chaotic frenzy, unloading cars, sorting foods and making 5,000 sandwiches that were sent into the hills along with cold drinks and cots for the firefighters.

Representatives of the Salvation Army said goods can be

delivered to any Salvation Army Adult Rehabilitation Center in the Bay Area.

Other relief efforts include a special fund to meet the needs of fire victims that was set up jointly by the United Way of the Bay Area and the Red Cross. The organizations initiated the fund with $25,000. To contribute call 772-HELP, or send a check payable to the Eastbay Fire Emergency Fund at 410 Bush St., San Francisco, CA 94108.

SMOKING RUINS DASH MOST HOPES
But a handful of homeowners find a miracle
by Kevin Fagan

As he trudged slowly up the hill past an eerie moonscape of smoking piles, blackened car shells and splayed power lines, Greg Haines kept hoping.

He kept that hope right up to the second he rounded the corner of his Upper Rockridge neighborhood—the very corner where he spent 12 happy years building the $700,000 home of his dreams. Then the hope died.

"My God," he cried, sinking to his knees, and covering his face with his hands. "My God. It's gone."

Before Haines lay a smoldering heap of coals and one skinny chimney where his house used to be...

At least a half dozen cars sat virtually untouched in front of cement stubs that used to be their garages. One Cadillac had a full tank of gas and an unburned parking ticket on its windshield.

RUINS LOOK LIKE HILLS WERE
UNDER AERIAL BOMBING
by Paul Grabowicz and Bill Snyder

Entire blocks have been reduced to smoldering stretches of rubble. Streets are littered with the burned-out hulks of cars and telephone wires dangle like spaghetti from blackened telephone poles.

...On Sherwick Drive, 10 burned and abandoned cars are crammed together—the result of a traffic jam when panic-stricken residents tried to flee.

The heat in the subdivision was so intense that the chrome on cars has melted into small puddles and all that remains of their rubber tires is a tangle of steel belting.

199

... The fire left bizarre calling cards. At 412 Hiller Drive a "sold" sign remains weirdly untouched in front of a home that has been burned to the foundation.

"It looks like the aftermath of a napalm attack," said Oakland police motorcycle patrolman Steven Allen as he stopped to survey the scene.

MANY SUBURBS VULNERABLE TO FIRE
by Marina Gottschalk

Orinda or Hayward, El Cerrito or Castro Valley—the devastating firestorm that destroyed much of the Oakland Hills could easily have happened in other Eastbay communities.

Fire officials in several Alameda and Contra Costa county communities face many of the same circumstances—an abundance of dry overgrowth, homes with wooden shake roofs, steep terrains—that, coupled with last weekend's hot, dry winds and low humidity, could produce the same catastrophe.

"Now everybody is so aware of the fire danger," said Fire Chief Samuel Treece of Kensington, a community perched above Berkeley and Albany that could have been wiped from the map if the 1,900-acre fire had occurred there.

Interestingly, several communities began taking some disaster preparedness steps after the 1989 Loma Prieta earthquake that, officials now realize, could pay off in the event of a major fire.

[The story then includes reports from officials in El Cerrito, Richmond, Hayward, Castro Valley and Fremont.]

Some of the stories show how devastating the fire can be. Here are two. The first deals with what the fire did to expensive automobiles that were caught in the fire.

LUXURY CARS MELT DOWN
ABOUT 2,000 CARS DAMAGED;
Wrecks fetch $50 as scrap
by Brett Mahoney

Fire gutted Mercedes, BMWs, Saabs and Ferraris—cars once worth tens of thousands of dollars each—now are worth about $50 apiece, according to local car wrecking companies.

Expensive, gleaming cars were anything but uncommon

in the Oakland-Berkeley Hills. But in one brief, fiery sweep, these dream machines have become nightmarish heaps of blackened scrap metal often worth no more than a single B.F. Goodrich tire.

The fire department estimates there were approximately 2,000 cars that were damaged in the blaze.

And State Farm Insurance alone has received nearly 300 auto claims. Lisa Ormond of State Farm says 75 percent of those claims were for total losses.

Another major story that shows the impact of the fire is by Monte Poole, and relates the tragedy of former major league baseball player Reggie Jackson.

Jackson, who played in Oakland, New York and other cities, had his *third* home destroyed by fire during the 1991 firestorm. Here is Poole's story headlined "Three strikes fired at Jackson." Notice the detail and the care that went into putting this story together.

Scores of his former neighbors vehemently insist on reviewing the charred remains of their homes, but not Reggie Jackson. He sits 400 miles away. And he insists he will not go back. Ever.

"No, no, no," Jackson says. "I'm beaten up. I'm done. I give up."

If any living soul has a reason to hold a deep aversion to the effects of a disastrous fire, it is Jackson, who began his storied baseball career as a member of the Oakland A's and has maintained a home in the Oakland Hills for the past 18 years.

"I really have not seen it," he says of the remains of what used to be his home on Yankee Hill Road in Hiller Highlands. "I don't need to go. I've already been through two catastrophic fires. And I know what the remnants are: there are none."

"There will be coins, and bent, contorted metal. But if anything that was in that kind of heat—anything not fireproof, will be melted, if it's plastic or metal. If it's paper, even inside metal, it will turn to ash. I've experienced that twice already."

"I don't need to go back."

Three years have passed since flames last licked at Jackson's possessions. He lost 34 cars and motorcycles from his prized collection when "spontaneous combustion" caused a blaze in a Berkeley warehouse in August 1988. The case remains in litigation.

Twelve years earlier, Jackson lost a home on the same Yankee Hill Road property. He had moved into the home in

1973, his fifth season with the A's, and three years later it was destroyed.

"I had it rebuilt and they did a beautiful job," Jackson said.

Now it is gone again, taking with it a wealth of baseball history.

"There were a couple of World Series trophies," Jackson says. "About six Joe DiMaggio balls. A lot of Mickey Mantle stuff. I had a Babe Ruth bat and a Lou Gehrig."

Jackson also had bats used by Mays and Hank Aaron and Roberto Clemente and Ernie Banks and Dick Allen.

Several old baseball uniforms were lost, as was a huge trophy encasing the bat and ball used for Jackson's 2,000th hit. There were All-Star rings and World Series rings.

Two Rolex watches, one of which was given to Jackson by a group that voted him "Player of the Decade" of the 1970s.

Also lost were collections of guns and model cars and cowboy hats, along with two cars—one of which was a customized Mercedes Benz, which Jackson says was worth about $200,000.

Jackson, 45, was in a hotel room in New Jersey when he heard about the fire. He became riveted to the TV. He was worried about his two sisters in Oakland, but it didn't take too long to discover the fate of his home.

"It was about 10 P.M. California time and I was watching a news helicopter over the area," Jackson says. "The guy said, 'I'm now over Hiller Highlands and Hiller Highlands looks as if a bomb has hit it...The only thing that remains of all the beautiful hillside homes are burning charcoals.'"

"When he said that, I had dry tears. I really couldn't cry. And I got cold and started shaking. I put on a couple of sweatshirts and a jacket and a pair of pants and just sat in the room."

(He flew back to California) and rode to within three miles of his home with Everett Moss, a friend and business associate. They were just down the hill. That was close enough. Jackson knows all too well what fire does.

"I understand people going back to get a sense of something final," Jackson said, "but I've seen two of these. I don't need to go back."

The *Tribune* also produced a 64-page booklet put together shortly after war broke out in Kuwait. Entitled "The Bay Area At War," it was edited by Eric Newton and Roger Rapoport, and co-published by the *Tribune* and Heyday Books. It covers comments and quotes from persons who remembered the exact instant they knew that the U.S. was going to war with Iraq over Kuwait.

While it is not a traditional roundup story, samples are included so that you can see how quotes and interviews can give new perspectives to a story. Note the variety and range, and the good insights offered in these quotes.

"Even though I wasn't surprised, I was still shocked by it," said El Cerrito artist Steve McMillan. "I almost cried."

McMillan was so struck that he wrote the word "WAR" on his etching notes at exactly 3:38 P.M.

It was still possible to imagine that peace could prevail. Even veterans of combat who knew better, like Oakland's Henry Texeira, a helicopter pilot in Vietnam, held their breath. "I kept hoping that there was going to be some sort of last-minute resolution of it—we kept waiting for the blinking."

"You look down at that airplane and find live missiles loaded," said a wondering Captain Mike Miller, 28, an F-15 pilot from Kingsport, Tenn. "We never thought we'd be in a major war, what with the Berlin Wall coming down and all."

As the news spread in the first hour, pockets of ignorance remained. Sitting on a BART train as it pulled into Oakland's 12th street station, Lola Allen, who had recently completed a military tour of duty, worried about her friends serving in the Gulf. "Nobody knows," she thought, as fellow passengers did their crossword puzzles and read novels. "I'm unraveling, and nobody knows."

Namjir Elnajim, who became an American citizen 19 years ago, had just returned from visiting family in Iraq. He traveled to Iraq on January 7 to donate five footlockers of medicine for children. Ten minutes after he arrived at the San Francisco airport, the war started. America's lightning air attack meant just one thing to him—concern for the 200 relatives he had left behind in his old homeland.

"This is the saddest day of my life. It should not be this way," Elnajim said. "Never did I think that anything like this would happen.

"Iraq is my homeland. America is my homeland." With one homeland bombing the other, Elnajim likens his anguish to "watching your father beating your mother."

San Leandro proclaimed itself a "Yellow Ribbon City." In Pleasanton, a few hundred residents put out ribbons for the weekend after the war began. By the following weekend, there were thousands. And a week later, Fremont joined with a sea of yellow ribbons.

"When I drove through town and I saw all those yellow ribbons, I thought 'The silent majority has spoken out at last,'" said Pleasanton realtor Chris Miller. A helicopter pilot in Vietnam in 1962–64, Miller remembers coming home to an indifferent nation, feeling strongly that the job he had been sent to do wasn't done.

"This is a lot different than Vietnam," he said. "This time people really are supporting the troops."

"The peace protests created an impression that anti-war sentiment is deeper than it really is," claimed Jean Meredith, a Contra Costa Republican party official. "I think generally people see the protesters as the same old group. I think we get obscured in the Bay Area because of the protests and the media attention that they get."

Around the Bay area, support for the troops and the war effort became more visible. Blood banks reported the ranks of donors jumped dramatically. When Frank Cappella, a Pleasanton plumbing contractor, started his program to guarantee jobs for returning Gulf War veterans, in a flash, he received $20,000 in cash donations and promises of dozens of jobs.

In Antioch, a shopping center marketing manager printed thousands of blank postcards addressed to servicemen and women in the gulf. Not a single merchant declined a request to give out the cards. Once they reached store counters, they were scooped up by an appreciative public.

The most requested song on KSAN and KNEW, the country stations, was Lee Greenwood's sabre-rattling, patriotic "God Bless the U.S.A." On pop music stations, Bette Midler's version of "From A Distance" was a constant request. Another big request—Whitney Houston's rendition of "The Star Spangled Banner," which she sung at Super Bowl XXV.

Things to Remember

- There are times when several events of importance happen at one time, including meetings, elections, natural disasters, speeches and other occasions. These call for special understanding on the part of the reporter.
- The reporter can either choose a single-incident lead, followed

by a second paragraph that rounds up other major items, or can choose a lead that includes several major items. The remainder of the story depends on which of these two leads is chosen.

- In many cases, the reporting is more difficult than the writing in a multiple-incident story. The greatest effort comes in straightening out complicated, confusing events before sitting down to write.

Practice

Write stories based on the following information.

Fact Set 1: Snowstorm

You are working in a northern state when a major snowstorm hits. Your area includes six counties, which we will call Alpha, Bravo, Charlie, Delta, Echo and Foxtrot.

In Alpha County all six school districts are closed, and some of them may be closed for more than a week. Snow Bunny Mountain reports 12 inches of new snow. In the village of Castroville, six families at the end of the gas line were moved to Castro High School due to a gas line failure.

Bravo and Charlie counties report lighter snow, perhaps four to six inches maximum, school delays of up to two hours, but no postponements or other problems.

The roof of the largest grocery store in Charlie County, the Solomon Brothers Superette, collapsed under the weight of up to 18 inches of snow. One person was trapped in the building, but was rescued by emergency units and was not injured. The store is a total loss, with insurance estimates at $500,000.

One person was killed in Echo county when her car went off the road in the snowstorm and fell 200 feet down an embankment. She was identified as Ella Lester, 65, of Huminga, who was returning from her job in the cafeteria at Echo County High School when the school was closed due to the continuing snow. Police in Echo County estimate they have had 12 to 14 inches of snow in the past 24 hours.

Sheriff's deputies, firemen, and police in Foxtrot County report no unusual problems and only a light snow of one to three inches.

Note: Just as you begin to write this, you get a phone call saying all five schools in Charlie County have been closed for the next two days. Further announcements will be made as appropriate.

Fact Set 2: Air Crashes

The wire services provide you with information on three separate air crashes. Combine them into one story. All crashes happened within three hours today.

1. A business jet slid off the runway in a rainstorm in Salt Lake City. The pilot and one passenger were killed when the plane crashed into a storage building at the airport. The plane was owned by a computer printer company from San Francisco, and was en route to Salt Lake City.

   Dead are the pilot and one passenger. One other passenger was taken to Memorial Hospital but no condition report is available. Names are not available at this time, but the crash victims were from San Francisco.

2. Two planes collided in the sky over Minot, N.D. They were both Air Force cargo jets. Air Force officials said the planes were going through refueling training. One plane has refueling equipment and three others fly in formation under that plane. They each go to the refueling boom in turn. No one is sure what happened.

   Six men from one plane and seven from another died when the planes crashed to the ground. An investigation was started at once.

3. One person was killed when a sightseeing plane that flies in the Grand Canyon area crashed shortly after takeoff. The plane was not flying in the Grand Canyon at the time. Airport officials in Flagstaff, Arizona, said the plane's engine had just been repaired and the pilot was testing it when it failed. The pilot's name was not released but his home is in Phoenix.

Fact Set 3: Fire Chief

Each time the Rawleigh Island City Council meets, all department heads give reports to the council. Fire Chief William Baylor, who is the head of a 27-member fire department, gives his report each time. He has been chief for 15 years, and was a fireman 25 years before that. This week during the regular council meeting, he stated: "Well, I am going to take this opportunity to announce to everyone in city government that I am going to retire as of the end of this month. I have not announced this to anyone, and I have discussed it only with my wife. We feel the time has come for me to relax, do some fishing, and get to know my grandchildren. There are several good people who are eligible to be chief, and I will work with anyone you select. Thank you for all you have done for me, and I guess that is about it." The council did not respond immediately, somewhat in disbelief. Mayor Charles Camero said, "I am as dumfounded as anyone. This man is an institution in this town and respected throughout the state. We can't afford to lose him, but from what he said there is no way he is going to change his mind." Later, the mayor said to you that he felt the city's financial problems led to this, that the chief was "simply tired of trying to give the city a department it could be proud of on a budget that is a joke." The chief left after the meeting and declined an opportunity to talk to the press. "I've said enough, and it sticks," he said.

Fact Set 4: Teacher Strike

Things have come to a head in the three-week long Metro District teacher strike. The opening of school has been delayed for 10 days while the teachers and the school board, with a new superintendent, try to come to agreement on a new contract. The last contract, which was three years long, ended the day before school started. Students have picketed the schools to get them started, and the parents' organization says it is going to court next week to force the teachers back to school. This morning Circuit Court Judge Alfred L. Lombardo ordered the Springbrook Teachers' Federation leadership to go back to work. SFT president Marietta Hendershot read a statement to the 500 teachers at a meeting in the Springbrook Senior High auditorium. In a flat, emotionless voice she read, "Judge Lombardo has ordered me to order you to go back to your classrooms as of . . ." Before she could complete the reading of the written statement, the teachers stood up as a group and shouted "No, No, we won't go!" and walked out of the auditorium, into their cars and left the school. Hendershot told the press she had complied with the judge's order, and hoped the teachers would reconsider." The next step is up to the judge, not me," she said. Superintendent Mary Ancill said the school board would be back in court this afternoon seeking another order to get the teachers back in class in two days. The teachers have been offered a 3.25 percent raise; they are asking for a 3 percent retroactive raise for the last two years and arbitration for a 6 percent increase for each of the next two years.

Reality Check

Read the following information. Then, (1) rank order the items from most important to least important; and (2) write a news story based on that rank ordering. Remember to consider what is in the interest of your readers first. Use only the newsworthy information.

Reality Check 1: Athena City Council

Item 1. Call of the roll by clerk of the council. All council members answered present, except Henry Wildinger, attending the funeral of a brother in Chicago.

Item 2. Report from the Mayor. Mayor Henry Morgan reported the Chamber of Commerce has agreed to split the cost on a new set of Christmas lights for downtown. He also said he had attended a meeting last week of 14 regional mayors planning a combined self-insurance program for all cities, but it is too early to say whether it will work out or not.

Item 3. City utilities director William Francine gave his report. He said leaf pickup is a week behind because two members of the crew have been hospitalized. All leaves should be picked up this week.

Item 4. City tax administrator Hoover Wilson said the city is losing $400,000 a year in income because people who work out of town do not pay income tax in Athena. He suggested council consider reducing the credit people get for paying out-of-town taxes, and charge income tax for everyone who lives in the city, regardless of where they work. He suggested the city reduce by one-half the allowance they give for people working out of town, and add a one-half percent rate for everyone living in town and working out of town. He said this would raise $500,000 a year. The mayor said he felt this was a sound idea, that the city needed new fire equipment and this was one way to do it. Council referred the matter to the budget committee, with a request that a report be made to the full council in one month.

Item 5. Fire Chief Will Duett said he was completing a request for a $230,000 pumper that was badly needed for the new Executive House high-rise apartment buildings going up near the football stadium. Council Budget Committee chair Phyllis Renner said the city was aware of the request, but that it preferred to pay cash and did not have the cash available at this time.

Item 6. Police Chief Woody Ashenbrenner said he had nothing new to report this week. The expected problems at last week's crosstown high school football rivalry between Central and South did not materialize and everything went smoothly despite the unexpectedly large crowd of 20,000 persons.

Item 7. Council discussed new legislation, but did not place any items on first reading. (Three public readings of all legislation are required so that the public will have a chance to speak their feelings about any legislation.)

Item 8. Public comment. This is time set aside for any member of the community to discuss any topic with council. No one was present to talk to council at this meeting.

Meeting adjourned.

Reality Check 2: Tornado

OKLAHOMA CITY—The state of Oklahoma was hit by seven different tornadoes Monday morning while most of its residents slept. National Weather Service officials said the tornadoes hit in four different communities between 1:10 A.M. and 3:10 A.M. The communities were Claremore, Chelsea, Vinita, and Miami. Claremore is the home of the Will Rogers Memorial. All communities are in northeast Oklahoma on or very near Interstate 44, the road known earlier in American history as Route 66. From one end of the tornado area to the other is 60 miles long. In Claremore, there was no damage to the Will Rogers Memorial, honoring the famous American humorist. However, more than $100,000 damage was incurred when a bowling establishment was flattened, and mobile homes worth another $200,000 were completely destroyed. No injuries. In Chelsea, population 1,750, six persons living in a home for the elderly died when power was cut off and a roof collapsed. A Chevrolet dealership was destroyed and early estimates are that the damage was more than $200,000. Schools will be closed all day today and probably longer in Chelsea. In Vinita, 15 miles northwest of Chelsea, eight midnight shift workers on an oilfield rig died when the rig collapsed. Emergency crews could not get to them for three hours because of downed trees blocking roads. The worst hit of all was Miami, a town located seven miles from Kansas and 12 miles from Missouri. A three-mile long train was stopped by debris on the tracks and two separate incidents occurred where cars and pickups ran into the side of the stopped train in the dark. Four persons were killed, two in each incident. Two were in an emergency vehicle attempting to rescue drivers pinned under trees and two others were police department volunteers called in to patrol downtown Miami where dozens of businesses had broken windows. The governor has declared an emergency and the president is asking the federal government to do all it can to provide low cost loans. Hospitals in the area report more than 100 persons brought in for injuries during the first hour and the total may reach 400 hospitalized, according to the state police patrol. In addition to the damages already reported, it is expected another $500,000 minimum will be incurred in Vinita and Miami.

13
Feature Stories: Looking at News from a Different Angle

In This Chapter

Feature writing is a longer, more complex, more conversational type of writing. It can be used to tell about people, to personalize issues, or to explain dramatic trends in people terms.

While the structure is less formal than the inverted pyramid or formula stories, the feature is not easier to write. The reporter must find a focus, develop an interesting lead, and dig up enough anecdotes and examples to make a good story.

The feature lead is designed not to give the news, but to get the person interested in reading the rest of the story. The "hook," or "catchy" lead, often takes time to develop.

The feature ending is not like the ending of other news stories. It is a reward to the reader for having read the entire story, and generally has a "bang" of its own. Feature writers save incidents, anecdotes, or examples to use as endings.

Above all, a feature is a story, an example of a person or incident that needs to be retold so society can understand what is happening in other parts of society.

FEATURE stories highlight a person, idea, or issue. They are opposite from an inverted pyramid story in form and style. They are longer, looser, less structured—and a lot more difficult to write than most students think.

This is the type of writing students think of when they say, "I love to write." This is what they may have done in high school when they got good reactions from students whose accomplishments were recognized.

But contrary to widespread thought, features are not easier to write. Having many forms to choose from makes them more difficult to write, because they are all different. Every new feature is new ground to break, and you can't just plug in the information.

Features go way back in American journalism. Ben Day of the New York "penny press era" in the 1830s was one of the first to feature individuals in human interest stories. He was trying to develop a democratic press, a press for everyone, and so he wrote about the common people. This was a major departure for his time, because the focus in newspapers until then had been on government and business.

Ben Day's stories were among the first to show human interest as opposed to governmental or business emphasis. Over the years, features have developed into a specialty form to bring depth into the news, to explain people and issues behind the news, to show the human side. They are the "people stories," the ones the audience can relate to, the ones that tell "the story behind the story."

When a national television network starts out a report on a proposed cut in veterans' benefits by showing what it will mean to one individual, it is personalizing a serious issue story. It is much easier to show the impact of proposed legislation by describing what it will mean to one person.

A story about cutting veterans' benefits to those on welfare is a governmental story, a procedural story. Taking away all of the income that John Jones, a Vietnam war vet, gets every month is featurizing what the impact of the program will be. The reader, who may know someone who is a vet or may be a vet himself, can relate to the personal example much better.

There are many types of features, but all must have a purpose. There is nothing wrong with running a story about someone just because they are interesting, and many papers do that. But if what that person does or knows can help clarify an issue, trend, or historical event, so much the better.

Beginning students are well advised to find features that mean something, rather than random ideas that can be used at any time. Too many features are about interesting people and do not illustrate a point about which society is concerned at the moment.

Finding random features, such as the couple married 75 years or the National Merit finalist at your high school, is easy—for the first one or two features. After that, your "luck" runs out and finding feature ideas on a regular basis becomes difficult.

At this point, you need to do the search for features "backwards." Find an important principle to write about first, and then find someone who is knowledgeable about the subject. Find a problem in the community, and find someone who has answers to that problem. Find a holiday that needs to be publicized, and then find someone with special memories about that holiday. Find out if drugs are a problem in the community by talking to people who deal with the problem every day. They can give you examples and illustrations to make an ordinary topic into an extraordinary story.

It is difficult for students who do not read or watch or listen to news regularly to come up with feature ideas. Unless you know what the issues are and which ones need clarification, you will be groping in the dark for feature ideas.

Students are well-advised at this stage of their writing careers to read two or more newspapers a day, watch the evening news on national television, and listen to at least the morning news on radio. Go to your college library for newspapers and magazines. There is no way to develop story ideas without paying attention to what is going on in the media.

This is a change in pattern for some students, who have not focused on their life's work yet and do not understand why they have to pay attention to news they do not think is of interest to them. Students may not agree that what they are hearing or reading is the most important news people need to know. Good, this is a fine place to start thinking about what news is.

Please understand that keeping up with what the media are reporting is only a basic minimum. To be better than the competition in your medium, you have to come up with ideas that other people do not have. You cannot settle for doing just what they do if you expect to be creative or more valuable to your readers, in other words, a leader in your field.

You must localize national issues in a way they do not. You have to work harder to find the human angle to stories. You have to find sources who can illustrate what the impact of a school tax or an income tax will be.

The media are extremely competitive, and unless you do something other media do not do, the audience will think you are the one who is following the leader. In fact, you could have the news first but other media transmit news faster (radio gets out much sooner than newspapers or television). Therefore, you have to develop new ideas about how to play stories, and this usually means developing new feature angles.

Features and Process Writing

The feature is a classic example of process in writing.

Feature stories are usually longer, more complicated, and more detailed. More complicated means more organization before sitting down to write. In fact, it means thinking about which of several angles to take before asking questions.

Finding the focus of a feature can be frustrating, and can lead to a lot of wasted time when you have much more information than you need. On the other hand, you must be able to change your story in mid-stream if the news changes or if you find a more interesting angle, so you have to keep asking questions.

Writing a longer story means finding themes and sub-themes, principle and example, or anecdotes to keep the story lively. You cannot simply list the items gathered in an interview, you have to put them together into a story. Organizing is so much more important than in a short story because you have so many more parts to put together into one cohesive story. You need to outline, at least in your mind, so as to know where the story is going. A feature has so many more possible forms than a straight news story that "getting a handle" on what you want to say is not at all easy.

Writing extra drafts of a feature story is not a luxury, it is a necessity. The first draft helps think it through, and in a long story this is a complicated thought process.

More time spent on organizing a feature will mean less time spent on writing. A longer story may mean more gaps in the information, so you may have to interview again. The interplay between collect and focus and refine, as discussed in the section on process writing, comes into play here as well. Just when you think you have the story "down cold," you realize there is something else you need to ask.

This is one of the reasons features are not done at one sitting but over several days. Ideas will get a focus after you think about them for a day or two. The mind will prompt you with questions you didn't even think of at the time of the interview. Questions you need answered to complete the story will pop into your mind after you have thought of it for a day or two. Sounds strange, I know, but the mind works while you sleep and do other things, and having enough time to think through a feature is an important part of its success.

Analyzing a Feature Story

The following is one of my favorite feature stories. It talks about people, about good and bad times, about individual discipline, and it is fun to read. Read it all the way through first, and then we will analyze it. While you read it notice the conversational, story-telling tone. No big words, just plain folks, fun to read: some of the hallmarks of feature writing.

LESSON'S DIVIDEND: $100,000
Custodian's estate goes to seminary
by David E. Kepple
Staff Writer, *Dayton Daily News*
Saturday, Dec. 3, 1988

Lonnie Porter's mother taught him to sew, to cook and to save money. Porter learned well, and United Theological Seminary has become the beneficiary of those lessons.

Porter, a former custodian at the seminary who died in January at the age of 93, willed his entire estate—worth slightly more than $100,000—to the United Methodist school.

Porter, who salted most of his money away in a savings account over the years, attached no strings to its use.

In responding to the gift, however, the UTS board of trustees voted Oct. 28 to establish the Lonnie C. Porter Endowment Fund, earmarking the money to support the seminary's Black Ministry Studies program, still in its infancy.

The bequest did not come as a surprise to seminary officials.

Porter, who lived simply in a house on Frizzell Avenue in West Dayton until his death, had discussed his plans with the Rev. Henry W. Brooks, UTS vice president. Brooks and Porter were long-time friends, dating back to 1955 when Porter came to work at the seminary and Brooks enrolled there as a student.

"I asked him one time, 'Lonnie, how did you get started saving money?'" Brooks recalled. "He said, 'Well, my mama taught me three things. She taught me how to sew, she taught me how to cook and she taught me how to save money.'"

Porter's wife, Mattie, died in the late 1960s. The couple didn't have any children and Porter had no close living relatives. "The seminary community was kind of his family," Brooks said. "He knew everyone on a first-name basis."

Porter and his wife moved to Dayton from Lexington, Ky., in 1955 and he went to work at the seminary as a member of the maintenance staff. Fout Hall was his longtime responsibility. The building, largest dormitory on campus with about 70 units, also includes dining room facilities for the school.

Rather small in stature but kind of wiry, "he just never quit," Brooks recalled. "He was just always over there working— took great pride in his work."

For a number of years after his retirement in 1972, Porter would frequently stop back at the school to visit with Brooks and old cronies from the maintenance crew, until a number of them retired also.

Some years back, Brooks learned of Porter's substantial savings when he was helping him get established at a new bank office downtown after a branch of the old Winters National Bank closed.

"He was really quite upset because he didn't understand the difference between a bank savings book and the computer printouts that were becoming in vogue," Brooks said. "It was at that point that he showed me the (savings) book that he had,

215

and I about fell out of my chair. He had something like $70,000."

Brooks said at that time Porter's money was all in a low-interest bearing account. Brooks and the bank manager convinced him that if he allowed the money to be placed into a higher-yield savings plan, he could dramatically increase his income.

Porter, who received money from Social Security and a small pension, continued his frugal habits until the time of his death, by which time his savings account had mounted to about $95,000, Brooks said.

After all Porter's medical bills, funeral expenses and other administrative costs were taken care of, his estate netted out to slightly more than $100,000.

The vice president said he once asked Porter why he would leave all his money to the seminary.

"And he said, 'Well, that's the best place I ever worked.... They treated me like a human being.'"

Now, let's analyze this story. Let's look at each part and see how it fits into the total picture.

Lead: "Lonnie Porter's mother taught him to sew, to cook and to save money. Porter learned well, and United Theological Seminary has become the beneficiary of those lessons."

This is obviously not an inverted pyramid or single incident lead. It sounds a little like a puzzle. It is designed not to tell the story, but to show you why you ought to read the rest of the story.

Notice the tight, no-words-wasted writing. The first words are Lonnie Porter. The first sentence is a tersely worded moral to the story. No age, address, or other details are given, not even a mention of how much the seminary will benefit. The writer then brings in the "Nut graph" or the reason the story is being told:

Porter, a former custodian at the seminary who died in January at the age of 93, willed his entire estate—worth slightly more than $100,000—to the United Methodist school.

Porter, who salted most of his money away in a savings account over the years, attached no strings to its use.

In responding to the gift, however, the UTS board of trustees voted Oct. 28 to establish the Lonnie C. Porter Endowment Fund, earmarking the money to support the seminary's Black Ministry Studies program, still in its infancy.

These graphs give the "hard news," or what would pass for a single incident lead if the media decided to play it that way. They give you an idea of who Lonnie Porter was, how much the will was for, and what it will be used for.

By this time, we have "hooked" readers into the story by whetting their appetites and we have given the important details.

But a feature story is more than this. Once you have set up the story, you have to deliver what you have promised. This means providing details, satisfying the reader's curiosity, and giving the reader a reward for sticking with the story.

If you have read the story this far, you might be asking questions such as: Was this a surprise? Who is this person? Why did he give this to a seminary?

The writer will spend most of the rest of the story answering these questions.

But the writer himself will not answer them. He will let the source of the story answer them. This is show, not tell. Let the source speak.

This is also the time to include principle and example, showing that Lonnie loved where he worked (principle) by saying he came back to visit often after he had retired (example).

On the first draft, use what you think is interesting. Chances are good that if it is interesting to you it will also be interesting to others. You can always rewrite or cut it down to size later.

The use of direct quotes is a must in feature stories. The reader would like to hear things directly from the mouth of the source, if possible. The writer's job is to find the quotes that are said better by the source than they are by the writer.

For example, Rev. Brooks, the vice president, recounts: "I asked him one time, 'Lonnie, how did you get started saving money?'" Brooks recalled. "He said, 'Well, my mama taught me three things. She taught me how to sew, she taught me how to cook and she taught me how to save money.'"

There is no way a reporter can improve on that. It is direct, it is powerful, and it is folksy. It makes a wonderful quote. The reporter after a few interviews will begin to look for the good quotes. Not all sources give good quotes, so be delighted to get them when you do.

Often, a reporter has to ask sources for specifics, for things they remember about someone, or for examples. In explaining why Porter was so close to the seminary, Brooks says: "The seminary community was kind of his family. He knew everyone on a first-name basis." The vice president continues: "He just never quit. He was just always over there working—took great pride in his work."

In describing how he got involved with Lonnie's finances, he says: "He [Lonnie] was really quite upset because he didn't understand the difference between a bank savings book and the computer printouts that were becoming in vogue. It was at that point that he showed me the (savings) book that he had, and I about fell out of my chair. He had something like $70,000."

It doesn't get much more descriptive and interesting than "I about fell out of my chair."

You generally will use what you have in terms of good quotes, and fill the space assigned to you. Eventually, you will run out of material and will have to stop. But don't just stop, as you would in an inverted pyramid story.

The ending is something a reporter takes special pride in. He wants the reader to get a reward for having read all the way through the story, so he saves something special for the last graph. Try to save something similar to a "punch line" (some places call it a "walk off," as in dropping a good punch line and walking off) for the ending. The reporter wants the reader to leave the story with a good feeling, and to have her say, "Boy, you ought to read this. This was a good story."

Therefore, the Lonnie Porter story ends with a quote, but one that answers a question the reader might have had throughout this story: why did he leave his money to the seminary? It is not only a powerful ending, but also closes with an appropriate moral to the story:

> The vice president said he once asked Porter why he would leave all his money to the seminary.
>
> "And he said, 'Well, that's the best place I ever worked . . . They treated me like a human being.'"

What Makes Features Different from Hard News Stories?

A feature is everything a single incident or formula story is not. It is longer, more detailed, and more fun to read and write. A feature is not event- or news-cycle oriented. A feature can offer a different look at the same things, a fresh perspective. It can help readers understand the background of an event or it can focus on the individuals involved in the news. It provides details, word pictures, and insights not available in inverted pyramid or breaking news.

A feature has a different structure, very loosely any form that gets the job done. If it is the right approach, take the reader through a drug bust chronologically. Or use a narrative story lead, such as might be found in a novel. Find an example or anecdote that typifies the person or issue and then start with it.

This is often described as direct lead versus delayed lead. A direct lead is one in an inverted pyramid or single-incident story, where the first few words explain what the important information is. A delayed lead is using the nut graph, in which writers wait three or four paragraphs to tell the reader what the important information is, which leads the reader into the story.

When you read, watch how other authors start their stories. Not *if* you read but *when* you read. Avid readers make good writers, and those who do not like to read for pleasure will not like to write for pleasure.

A Feature Lead Is Different

The lead is designed to catch the reader's interest, and the writer tries to find the most captivating or interesting material she can find to start with. No summaries, paraphrases, or formulas. Just be sure that what you write makes the reader want to read more.

Telling you that there are many types of feature leads or that writers don't have to follow the inverted pyramid or formula leads doesn't provide specific help. What is permissible in a lead? Anything that fits the facts of the feature and is interesting.

- You could use a quote, if it is interesting.
- You could use an anecdote that tells readers something about the person or the situation.
- You could start with a question, although that form is often overdone.
- You could start out telling a story, the familiar narrative form so well known in books.
- You could paint a word picture by showing a setting in which the story takes place, but don't go too far astray from the main point of the feature.

A Feature's Ending Is Different

Save something special for the ending in a feature. Do not let it die with a whimper as you would in a straight news story. It is important that the writer watch for quotes, anecdotes, examples, or other illustrations as she gathers her information. Save one of the good ones as an ending.

One thing beginning writers often do is called a cheerleading ending such as "Jones is sure to be a success and a credit to his high school" or "Since Mooney has done this much at such a young age, he is sure to be heard from in the future."

This is an opinion. Readers want to make up their own minds about whether these people will be successful. The fact that you are doing a story on them implies that you assume they are out of the ordinary. But let readers decide whether this person will be a credit to his school, or whether he will be heard from.

Writers provide the facts, readers provide the opinion. Writers show, not tell. And use an anecdote, a cute story, or a good quote to end the feature.

A Feature's Production Schedule Is Different

Hard news stories are written immediately, within minutes after the information is available. Features are done over several days or perhaps a week.

It is usually much better to do features on a schedule like this: if a story is due to the editor on a Friday, do the interviewing as early as possible, say, on a Monday. Let the information you gathered "perk" in your mind Tuesday and maybe Wednesday and then write on Wednesday or Thursday. On Tuesday and maybe Wednesday, while you are doing other assignments, you will think of things you missed in the interview, or you will think of things to focus on in the story. Don't ask how (this is not a psych class), but most feature writers will tell you this is true. The mind has a way of bringing up something you missed, or something you didn't think of at the time will pop up later.

If you try to write the story the same day you gather the information, this cognitive process will not happen. There are times you have to do this, but if you can afford some time between gathering and writing, you will get a better story.

A Feature Has a Nut Graph

A nut graph is also known as the "ooh-aah" graph. Somewhere in the first four to six graphs, you have to tell why you are writing the story. You have to indicate to the reader why this person is newsworthy, or explain the reason for the story. Once you have hooked the reader with your feature lead, the reader deserves to be told what the story is about.

A Feature Is Often a Focus on the Person

Features often focus on the person rather than the event or the issue. Focus on the human interest in the story. Play up things that are interesting, but with messages underlying them. Explain a complicated issue by showing the role of the individual. Personality profiles are good, but they should be on someone in the news, unless you are running a regular feature about average readers (which is very popular in many areas). You ought to have a news reason for the story, rather than just doing stories because you happened to meet someone interesting.

A Feature Is Difficult to Research

Often, a feature is more difficult to research than a straight news story. You want it to be unique, something not everyone else has. The facts must be specific to the story, so a wire service or other story lead can be used only as a tie-in; you have to do your own legwork.

If you use a subject or a story that is not new, as in a background piece, then you have to find a new angle. Since a feature is not breaking news, it has to be more interesting than the breaking news to take its place. Be sure you know what your paper, station, or magazine has already run, and find a new angle from that point forward. Nothing is more embarrassing than to suggest a story that has already been run.

Focus on the Angle

Once you find the angle, you have to focus. The tendency of beginning writers is to go on and on, to collect more information than is needed and then try to run it all.

You should collect more information than needed, but do not expect to use it all. Use only that which pertains to the story. Find the facts, details, and anecdotes that illustrate the principle you are trying to make. You may have to leave out a cute anecdote if it is not pertinent to the story. It may hurt, but you can't use everything.

Types of Features

Background Features

Background features illustrate key points about breaking news stories or trends. When the Soviet bloc was breaking up, the hard news was about what Gorbachev and Yeltsin were doing, and how the coup ran its course.

But the stories about the former Soviet Union and Eastern Europe included countless features: why the Russian soldiers were not being sent home; how the citizens were coping with higher prices and shortages; what the individual republics thought of each other, and the problems this posed; and how and whether Western investments would be brought in to save the different economies.

These are called backgrounders, or hard features, or behind the news stories.

Personality Profiles

Depending on the size of your community, personality profiles can cover candidates for office, new schoolteachers, or citizen of the year. They do not have to be elected or public officials or business people. They can be ordinary people who have done extraordinary things. Many papers are now featuring different individuals each week who have not been in the news or elected to office or founded a new company. The theory is that average citizens like to read about average citizens, that personality profiles are more relevant to average readers when they are about average readers.

Profiles must include details that indicate specifically what this person has done. They ought to include that person's words. Let the reader hear directly from this person. Check with other sources to verify the facts of the story or the nature of the person. Talk to secretaries, friends, enemies, political rivals, business rivals; draw a word picture of that person's home or office or whatever surroundings they are in.

Dig twice as hard for personal anecdotes or remembrances. People will not want to give them sometimes, but they do tell you a great deal about the person.

Despite the fact that this is about a person, it also should have a central theme. Why is that person being interviewed? What subject do you want to know about? How can you tie the central theme in with the different subjects you want to bring up? How can you paint a picture of the personality of the person while still bringing in the issues or subjects the reader needs to know about this person?

Anniversary Features

These features can include the fiftieth or one hundredth anniversary of a famous event or happening. They appeal to older readers who remember the event, and who make up an important part of the readership. Regular historical features, 10, 25, and 50 years ago, bring back memories to older readers and tell younger readers something they may not have known.

Seasonal Features

Columbus Day, Thanksgiving, Christmas, New Year's—there are dozens of such events during the year. A seasonal feature can be very ho hum, and it is often difficult to find a new angle on something that has been discussed every year.

How is this holiday being celebrated differently? What are the new toys? How does the economy affect this celebration? How much of this observance is religious in nature, and what is being done in that area? It takes much more research and observation to do a new and good seasonal story than almost any other, because everyone knows about spring, Easter, and Memorial Day.

I once spent two full days trying to find an ideal person to interview for Memorial Day, and finally was told about a 94-year-old man who was on his way across the Atlantic to France when World War I ended. He still had his uniform and it still fit, 76 years after he had worn it the last time.

Examples of Features

The best way to understand features is to read them. What follows is a series of features from newspapers and magazines, from all parts of the country, covering topics serious and not-so-serious.

Remember that the feature story can cover virtually any topic. This becomes a problem for beginning writers, who at first want to write about everything, and then later find it difficult to find good story ideas. One way of solving this dilemma is to think about problems in society and new ways to discuss them, ways that will inform and educate.

The first two stories are about drugs, one about the introduction of crack cocaine into the Greater Buffalo area and what has happened since, and the second about young "mad scientist" chemistry students in Upper Michigan developing an even stronger, more deadly drug in backwoods sheds and garages.

Read these stories with an eye to their structure, whether their leads "grab" you or not, and how the authors build their stories. Watch for how the endings are handled, and how the quotes are used.

Enter Crack Cocaine

Mike Kurilovitch of the *Niagara (N.Y.) Gazette* wrote the first story on crack cocaine in the Niagara-Buffalo area. Crack at that time was something new and unusual, but it was clear it was going to become a powerful force. Excerpts from the story which appeared on May 28, 1989, follow.

CRACK: DRUG TIGHTENS GRIP ON COUNTY

The nightmare became reality for local police on Dec. 5, 1985, when a Niagara Falls drug dealer was arrested at the Greater Buffalo International Airport. Hidden in his bag were $50,000 worth of heroin, some PCP, and a sampling of a new drug he referred to as "smokable cocaine."

It came in crumbly, tan-colored chunks packaged in tiny plastic vials. Police hadn't seen it before. Even the dealer bringing it in didn't know its name.

His New York City connections had furnished him with samples of the drug "to see if it would catch on in the area," a County Drug Task Force agent said. "We were kind of puzzled. We couldn't figure out what the hell it could be," the agent recalled. "We'd seen freebase cocaine before, but never already manufactured in the smokable form like that."

Analysis at the county lab determined the substance to be a purified form of cocaine.

A year later the dealer had been convicted of fourth degree criminal possession of a controlled substance, and is serving a 7½ to 15 year sentence.

The city's first crack dealer had been put away, but the nightmare was just beginning.

Since that time:

- Crack now accounts for 85 percent of all drug arrests in the county, and those arrests were up 50 percent in the first four months of this year compared to last year;
- The Niagara County Department of Social Services has reported an alarming increase in the rate of child abuse cases directly linked to crack abuse.
- About 10 percent of all emergency room cases at Niagara Falls Memorial Medical Center are linked to crack abuse, resident physician Dr. Paul Rohart estimated. An average of four people a week are admitted to the Center's substance abuse program.
- More than a third of the murders in Niagara Falls in the past three years—five of 14—were drug-related, police say.
- Property crimes in Niagara Falls are up 15 percent over last year, directly related to persons trying to support their habits by stealing property. Assaults were up 20 percent, car thefts 31 percent.

- Law enforcement agencies have seized nearly $5 million in property and assets from drug traffickers in Niagara County.
- County Coroner James Joyce attributed 25 deaths in Niagara Falls in the last year to cocaine intoxication. Most of the victims were under 30, he said.

Crack goes far beyond that, however. Many residents live in fear in drug-dealing neighborhoods. Some move out, if they can. And users say that nothing— stealing, robbing your mother, selling your body—is beyond someone who needs a fix.

Crack reaches nerve centers in the brain within eight seconds of ingestion, about 12 times faster than inhaled cocaine, researchers say. But the effects generally vanish within 10 to 15 minutes and are replaced by a period known as a "crash." To alleviate that sensation, users must smoke again.

"You'd be surprised at the guys copping (buying drugs) on their lunch hours in business trucks," an agent said. "We see guys in coats and ties driving Lincoln Continentals, and we see kids riding up on bikes buying the stuff."

The first few days of the month are prime times, Niagara Falls police detective John Chella pointed out, because that is when welfare checks arrive in the mail. He said it is not uncommon for users to spend their welfare checks and food stamps on crack. One user and dealer told the *Gazette* that dealers usually give clients 75 cents credit for a dollar's worth of food stamps.

A Dangerous New Home-Made Drug

Now notice a 1992 variation on the same theme, which describes how Detroit police were worried about a new, synthetic drug manufactured in garages and sheds 600 miles away in Upper Michigan. Made by chemistry majors in remote national forest areas, it gave users a six-day high.

These are background features, stories that go behind the headlines to explain why the headline stories are happening. Scott Bowles of the *Detroit News* wrote this story for the Sept. 27 edition in 1992, headlined "Scary 'cat': New drug creeps in from the U.P."

Bowles is the 1992 winner of the Al Nakkula Award for Police Reporting, sponsored by the Rocky Mountain News, the Denver Press Club, and the University of Colorado School of Journalism and Mass Communications. His award recognized his "crisp writing, well researched and well developed breaking stories, and longer pieces that showed he recognized patterns in crime and used sources other than the police."

It began last year as a chemical experiment in rural pockets of the western Upper Peninsula, an attempt by college students to duplicate the modest high of a chewable narcotic leaf known as khat.

But what emerged from their makeshift labs is a powdered drug so potent it dwarfs crack cocaine and heroin in its addictive punch, authorities say.

And it may be headed to Metro Detroit.

Narcotics agents with the Detroit Police and Wayne County Sheriff's Department have been put on the alert for Methcatinone—or "cat," as it was dubbed by the students who created it.

The synthetic stimulant, which was recently placed on the U.S. Drug Enforcement Agency's list of controlled substances, can generate a high that lasts up to six days, agents say.

Some samples of the narcotic confiscated in the Upper Peninsula were so potent that a user would almost certainly become addicted, authorities said.

"If you tried the purest stuff for the first time, there's a 99 percent chance you'd do it again, and again, until you're hooked," said Wayne County Sheriff Robert Ficano. "It's about as powerful as you can get."

Since May, Michigan State Police have raided 10 cat operations in the Upper Peninsula, primarily in Iron County, where woods cloak the fumes from production labs set up in sheds and garages.

Narcotics officers found some of the lab workers surviving solely off the white powder, which creates a burst of energy and a euphoric rush—going without food or sleep for 72 hours . . .

Cat marks the latest salvo from a new generation of drug dealers who are avoiding the risk of smuggling narcotics by producing their own. In addition to cat, college and street level chemists have also produced a synthetic version of heroin, police say.

"There seems to be a lot of young, bright chemists who are getting into the business," Ficano said. "They've got no concern for what they are producing, and this time, I don't think they have any idea they're playing with fire."

A volatile elixir of pharmaceuticals and household cleansers, cat usually contains small doses of Drano or battery acid, which

226

acts as a catalyst. The drug reportedly produces a "stimulant" high, creating feelings of exhilaration, heightened awareness and invincibility. Cat sells for about $100 a gram, and is typically inhaled, though some users melt and inject it...

Cat's creators were trying to clone a relatively mild narcotic. The khat leaf, used for centuries in the Mideast, has been sold over the counter in some Metro Detroit stores because it has gotten by U.S. Customs officers who don't realize it is a controlled substance...

And while the drug has not yet resulted in any reported deaths, Ficano fears a spread to metropolitan areas will result in fatal overdoses and "10 times worse birth defects than anything we're seeing right now."

Synthetic drugs pose an unusual threat to police, who are trained to fight dope dealers, not manufacturers. "They're becoming one of our biggest problems," said Detroit Police Commander Rudy Thomas, head of the department's narcotic division. "If we could solve the crack and heroin problem tomorrow, we'd still have to deal with the chemists. They're like mad scientists."

Those scientists have recently developed Fentanyl, a synthetic form of heroin that is 20 to 30 times more potent than its predecessor.

Thomas said the manufacturers tested Fentanyl by giving free samples to drug addicts, and monitoring the effects. If the addict suffered harmful effects—or died—the drug went back to the lab for revisions.

"They're smart enough not to take the stuff themselves," Thomas said. "So they're treating people like guinea pigs."

Ironically, cat's potency may become its commercial weakness. Thomas said he expects the drug's reputation for addiction to spread quickly on the street.

"Even a junkie has his limits," Thomas said. They don't mess with something they know is going to kill them.

"I'm afraid a few of them are going to learn it too late."

Mixing Religion with Alcohol

Other ideas are more subtle, developing more slowly as a reporter gets to know a beat. A comment made by someone on a beat to beginning reporters might slip by them, but more experienced reporters can see patterns developing.

Judy Tarjanyi, *The Toledo Blade*'s religion editor, developed a story on clergy and alcohol and what happens when the two mix too

freely. It was one of three entries in a set that won the Ohio
Newspaper Women's Association's triple entry award for large
newspapers in 1991.

Follow as she describes not only the problems but also solutions.

ALCOHOLIC PRIEST EVIDENCE OF TOLERANT CHURCH ATTITUDE

The beer that flows at many parish fund-raising festivals is one
example of the Roman Catholic Church's tolerant attitude
toward alcohol, but its priests provide ample testimony, as well.

Although some other Christian denominations expect their
clergy—and in many cases, their members—to abstain from
alcohol or, at least, to use it discreetly, the Catholic church still
allows a priest with a drink in hand to fit nicely into the social
landscape.

Parishioners may even smile and pour for their priests,
happy that "Father" can relax and enjoy a few after a long week
of hospital visits, masses, and crisis calls.

The smiles fade, however, for priests who are believed to
have exceeded their limit.

A priest in the Toledo Diocese recently was accused in a
lawsuit of striking a woman parishioner while he was allegedly
under the influence of alcohol.

The woman and her husband are charging that their
former pastor is an alcoholic. They have sued the priest, the
Toledo Diocese and the bishop, saying that he is dangerous,
and that the bishop ignored past episodes involving the priest.

The priest remained at the parish for more than a year
after the incident cited in the lawsuit. He was transferred in July,
1990, to a parish in Toledo, and has been on health leave since
Jan. 30.

The diocese declines to say where he is.

The alleged incident raises questions about priests and
alcohol, and what a church that allows them to drink does when
social drinking leads to alcoholism.

Priests in the Toledo Diocese who have had problems
with alcohol have been quietly sent away for extended treatment,
often returning successfully to ministry in the church. In the
interest of remaining sober, many also obtain permission to
substitute grape juice for wine when celebrating Mass.

One such priest, who asked for anonymity in keeping with
the principles of Alcoholics Anonymous, said he agreed to seek

228

treatment for his own alcoholism after the bishop told him he was concerned about the priest's heavy drinking.

"There were instances when people knew I consumed too much alcohol," the priest said. "My behavior wasn't erratic and I didn't violate the law, (but) people who cared about me called the bishop or wrote to him."

The priest completed a treatment program at Guest House, a center for alcoholic priests and now is working in a parish and attending AA meetings several times a week.

The fact that Guest House exists suggests that there are enough alcoholic priests to justify its continued operation, but administrators there say the disease is no more prevalent in priests than it is in the general population, where alcoholism occurs at a rate of about 10 percent.

The Rev. Edward Maher, a staff member of Guest House, said the faculty has treated more than 4,000 priests, religious brothers, and seminarians in centers like Lake Orion, Mich., and Rochester, Minn., since 1956. Both locations average about 150 patients a year, down from a peak of 200 when there were more priests in the church.

When priests come to Guest House, Father Maher said, "a lot come kicking and screaming. Some choose to come. Some are sent by their bishops or religious superiors. Some come more or less willingly."

Father Maher and others say it is primarily genetic factors and not job stress or the loneliness of the celibate life that send most priests into the downward spiral of alcoholic drinking.

...However, priests who have a genetic capacity for alcoholism may have enhanced opportunities to become alcoholics, according to the recovering alcoholic priest who requests anonymity.

"There are lots of people who protect us. Because they treasure their priests, they tolerate a lot of unacceptable behavior," he said.

Furthermore, the priest said, there is no question, the priest's job is emotionally stressful.

"You're dealing with people's lives and extremes of emotion. There is tremendous joy at the birth of a new child...and traumatic experiences like death, severe illness and the aging process. Our work lives and personal lives are filled with intense emotions. This means there is greater occasion for potential alcoholism to surface," he said.

But priests who drink to alleviate loneliness, he said, quickly find that drinking causes loneliness. "It's the exact opposite of what people perceive. The further it progresses along the chain of addictive, dependent drinking, the more the person isolates himself because of the effect of the chemical..."

Catholic clergy do not consider their church's tolerant attitude toward alcohol to be a factor in encouraging alcoholism because they say the church encourages moderation, not drunkenness. They also point out that alcoholism occurs even among religious groups that forbid drinking.

However, the Southern Baptist denomination, which preaches abstinence, claims to have a low incidence of alcoholism among clergy. "When it has occurred, it's so infrequent that usually the ministers drop out of the clergy," says Dr. Brooks Faulkner, senior manager for church staff support with the denomination's Sunday School Board.

What's Really in a Landfill?

Imagine analyzing a garbage dump to develop a national award-winning story! University of Arizona anthropology professor William Rathje did. In fact, he dug into seven of them, and in so doing found several nuggets of truth about recycling. His article in *The Atlantic Monthly*, December 1989, p. 102, is an outstanding debunking of "old wives' tales" about what causes our landfills to fill up so quickly. See if you don't learn something from this.

RUBBISH!

The physical reality inside a landfill is considerably different from what you might suppose. I spent some time with The Garbage Project's team over the past two years digging into seven landfills: two outside Chicago, two in the San Francisco Bay area, two in Tucson, and one in Phoenix. (The Garbage Project is a program of the University of Arizona which has been going since the 1970s and which has generated insights into what is in landfills.)

We exhumed 16,000 pounds of garbage, weighing every item we found and sorting them all into 27 basic categories and then into 162 subgroupings. In those eight tons of garbage and dirt cover, there were fewer than sixteen pounds of fast-food packaging; in other words, only about a tenth of one percent of the landfill's contents by weight consisted of fast-food packaging. Less than one percent of the contents by weight was disposable diapers. The entire category of things made from plastic accounted for less than five percent of the landfills' content by weight, 12 percent by volume.

The real culprit in every landfill is plain old paper—non fast-food paper, and mostly paper that isn't for packaging. Paper accounts for 40 to 50 percent of everything we throw away, both by weight and by volume.

If fast-food packaging is the Emperor's New Clothes of garbage, then a number of categories of paper goods collectively deserve the role of Invisible Man. In all the hand-wringing over the garbage crisis, has a single voice been raised against the proliferation of telephone books?

Each two-volume set of Yellow Pages distributed in Phoenix last year—to be thrown out this year—weighed 8.63 pounds, for a total of 6,000 tons of wastepaper. And competitors of the Yellow Pages have appeared virtually everywhere. Dig a trench through a landfill and you will see layers of phone books, like geological strata, or layers of cake.

Just as conspicuous as telephone books are newspapers, which make up 10 to 18 percent of the contents of a typical municipal landfill by volume. Even after several years they are usually well preserved. During a recent landfill dig in Phoenix, I found newspapers dating back to 1952 that looked so fresh you might read it over breakfast. Deep within landfills, copies of the *New York Times* editorial about fast-food containers will remain legible until well into the next century.

... In terms of landfill volume, plastic's share has remained unchanged since 1970. And plastic, being inert, doesn't introduce toxic chemicals into the environment.

Only about ten percent of old newspapers go on to be recycled into newspapers. What newspapers are really good for is making cereal and other boxes (if it's gray on the inside, it's from recycled stock), the insides of automobiles (the average car contains about sixty pounds of recycled newsprint), wallboard and insulation.

Also ... people don't recycle as much as they say they do (but they recycle just about as much as they say their neighbors do).

Second, household patterns of recycling vary over time; recycling is not yet a consistent habit.

Third, high income and education and even a measure of environmental concern do not predict household recycling rates. The only reliable predictor is the price paid for the commodity at buyback centers. When prices rose, say, for newsprint, the number of newspapers found in the local garbage suddenly declined.

A rough consensus has emerged among specialists as to how America can at least manage its garbage, if not make it pretty or go away. Safely sited and designed landfills should be employed in the three quarters of the country where there is still room for them. Incinerators with appropriate safety devices and trained workers can be carefully sited anywhere but make the most sense in the Northeast.

And states and municipalities need to cut deals with wastepaper and scrap dealers on splitting the money to be made from recycling. This is a minimum. Several additional steps could be taken to rescue the biggest component of garbage: paper. Freight rates could be revised to make the transport of paper for recycling cheaper than the transport of wood for pulp. Also, many things could be done to increase the demand for recycled paper. For example, the federal government, which uses more paper by far than any institution in America, could insist that most federal paperwork can be done on recycled paper. Beyond confronting the biggest-ticket item head-on, most garbage specialists would recommend a highly selective attack on a few kinds of plastic: not because plastic doesn't degrade or is ugly or bulky but because recycling certain plastics in household garbage would yield high-grade costly resins for new plastics and make incineration easier for the furnace grates, and perhaps safer.

Finally, we need to expand our knowledge base. At present, we have more reliable information about Neptune than we do about this country's solid waste stream.

"The Tears Were Everywhere"

Many feature stories are human-interest stories that tug at our hearts, that show the personal plights of individuals in ways that really touch the readers.

Ellen Robinson-Haynes, *The Sacramento Bee*'s award-winning medical writer, wrote a thoughtful, compassionate human interest series on a young boy with leukemia. The story won a feature writing award from the Society of Professional Journalists and first place in the national awards competition of the Leukemia Society of America.

Notice in these excerpts how she uses direct quotes from

youngsters, short but powerful sentences, and a sense of being there, producing a solid writing job.

ADAM RHODES AND HIS BATTLE WITH LEUKEMIA

Adam Rhodes will never forget when it started.

The pain came suddenly at a Kings' game in December.

"Like a needle through my leg," the 9-year-old remembers.

In the third quarter, his father carried him screaming to the car.

Three weeks later, deep into a heated Nintendo battle with his friend Ben, the pain came again...

In February the pain came again. This time in his arm. The next night, it was in his ankles...

In the pediatrician's office, late one afternoon, Barbara Rhodes noticed tiny red pinpoints on Adam's legs and chest.

Out in the hall, Barbara Rhodes waylaid the pediatrician.

"Maybe I'm a panicked mother," she remembers saying, "but do you think it's leukemia?"

It's possible, she heard.

It was 8 P.M. when the phone rang.

"Barbara," the pediatrician said, "you were right. Adam tested positive for leukemia. You need to get him into the hospital now."

[Notice how the emotion comes through in this excerpt:]

The Rhodeses faced a choice between two aggressive and toxic treatments that had to begin the next day.

Both treatments mixed and matched drugs with impossibly long names and potentially deadly side effects. One was a standard recipe. The other was a new recipe that might improve Adam's 50-65 percent survival rate. They chose the new recipe.

"At that point I was angry because Delane and I had to make that decision," Barbara Rhodes remembers. "I felt like we were playing God with his life, and I didn't want to do that."

The tears were everywhere.

"And all I could think of was that my child has leukemia and this isn't fair," she says. "Why isn't there a cure for it? Why do I have to make this decision? I sat there wishing he didn't have this, wishing so bad for a normal life."

[Discussions with other youngsters often show true feelings better than any words writers can use. Show, don't tell.]

A couple of days after Adam left the hospital, his friend

Ben came to visit. Barbara Rhodes stood in the hallway and watched her vulnerable son greet his friend.

"They were walking back to his room, and Adam said, 'I haven't seen you in a long time.' Then he said, 'I have cancer.' That was it, they went into his room and played Nintendo."

Some days later . . .

The questions stung.

"Are you going to die, Adam?" the boy asked.

"No," the 9-year-old responded.

"If you do," the neighbor boy persisted, "can I have your Nintendo games?"

Adam left the room. As he pedaled away on his scooter, he said "Gee, you're real supportive. Thanks a lot."

[Despite the fact this is a complicated medical story, notice how Robinson-Haynes avoids technical terms.]

Immediately facing Adam are some dreadful prospects. Nosebleeds that can last hours, stubborn widespread infections, anemias, vomiting, relentless fatigue—all side effects of an immune system bombarded by toxic drugs that kill healthy cells along with leukemia cells.

Adam's solid sense of himself is helping him cope with all this, according to Lynn Moore, pediatric social worker at the University Medical Center. A couple of weeks ago, Adam said to his mother, "You know what, Mom? God must have really wanted me to be with you and Daddy. You could never get pregnant but after you adopted me, God let you get pregnant with Tyler and Lanae.

"I'm so glad God gave me to you instead of someone who wouldn't have known that I had leukemia."

[And in the final story of the series:]

Day-Glo jump ropes dot the playground at Lake Forest Elementary School.

Dozens of eager children are gathered around the nearby flag, barely containing their impatience to get on with the impending Valentine jump-a-thon.

Then—with the Beach Boy's hit "Be True to Your School" shattering the crisp foothill air, the kids grab the rope and go for it.

Right away it is clear—Adam Rhodes is one hot-shot rope jumper.

To these El Dorado Hills youngsters, the 10-year-old is also something of a hero. Just a year ago, they saw him stricken with acute lymphocytic leukemia, a dreaded childhood cancer that claims three or four of every 10 of its victims.

Halfway into the fourth grade and a year through treatment at the pediatric cancer center at UC Davis Medical Center, however, Adam is back in full swing.

The Scouts Are Watching Tony

There are hundreds of features in sports, a category that lends ˙self to personalizing and writing human interest stories. Dave Seigerman of the *Jackson (Tenn.) Sun* knew a good feature when he saw it shooting "rainbows" from 30 feet and watched the college scouts coming to every game. He won a Best of Gannett award for his story in 1991. His story turned out to be about the recruiting as much as the player or the scouts.

BASKETBALL STAR MAINTAINS
POISE UNDER PRESSURE

From his oversized hands flow beautiful, arching rainbows—basketball shots that look effortless from as far away as 30 feet.

At the end of each one is a legion of salesmen dressed in college sweatshirts, waiting with a pot of gold and a smile.

Crowds roar with every Tony Delk shot that finds its mark, which is almost one out of every two attempts. Teammates offer high-fives; scouts in the stands scribble notations excitedly on their pads; opposing coaches shake their heads in frustration and awe.

Delk, the state's leading scorer with an average of 37.3 points per game, just trots back to play defense for Haywood High's Tomcats, unaffected by the commotion he has caused. He is aware of the limelight, the mounting pressure from the recruiters. But he managed to take it in stride.

"Honestly, I can't really notice all the pressure. I just don't let it go to my head," said Delk, the youngest of Lester and Florence Delk's 10 children.

Only 16 years old, the junior guard has already received enough correspondence from major colleges to overflow the eight-gallon cooler where he stuffs his mail. Street and Smith's magazine fingered him as an honorable mention All-American in its pre-season issue, and he is already being regarded as one of the nation's top recruits from the class of 1992.

The spotlight had fallen so directly on Delk after less than two full seasons of varsity basketball that there is no longer margin for error. He has the kind of talent that makes college basketball coaches travel hundreds of miles to drool over his performances in person. Someone from a major university is likely to be in the stands every time he plays. He cannot afford to be disappointing on any night...

Scouts from Vanderbilt and Mississippi saw him play against North Side last month. The next day, a representative from Tennessee called Haywood Coach Rick Sullivan's office, and a visitor from Mississippi State came to watch Delk practice.

"With the early signing periods, we're forced to intensify our recruiting of an athlete at an earlier age," said Mississippi State assistant coach Rick Stansbury. "If you wait to go out after a high-profile kid until he's a senior, it's too late."

Sullivan never tells Delk about the scouts until after the game. That helps Delk stay focused on the action.

"Coach Sullivan tells us all to go out and do our very best every game because you never know who's there watching."

Or who will be calling the next day. Sullivan handles all of Delk's correspondence initially, sorting through mail and phone calls before passing the information along. Delk's recruitment has become so much a part of Sullivan's everyday job that he had to get an answering machine for his basketball office telephone.

Somehow, Delk maintains perspective, a Herculean task considering that his future goes along for the ride every time he launches a three-point try.

[Editor's note: Delk enrolled at the University of Kentucky.]

Two Graduations, One Afternoon

Some stories are just plain fun to start with, and they get better. Take the one about the identical twins graduating on the same day from colleges 35 miles apart, and their parents resigned to each seeing one daughter graduate. Then the registrar at one college hears about it, and...

Jill Riepenhoff of the *Columbus Dispatch* tells about it in "Parents hustle to see twins graduate" in the Monday, May 11, 1992 issue of her paper.

Watch the hook lead, and the quotes from everyone involved. It's a fun story.

To their parents' delight, Leslie Plowman yesterday graduated near the top of her class, and her twin sister, Allison, was next to last—but academics didn't factor into their placements.

It was arranged that way so Mary and Norvell Plowman could watch both their 22-year-old daughters, identical twins, receive their diplomas.

Leslie graduated yesterday afternoon from Denison University and Allison graduated from Ohio Wesleyan University.

Only 35 miles, 20 traffic lights (seven of which were red) and two "Sunday drivers" were between the two schools.

Leslie was third in her class of 500 to get her diploma. Allison was 479th in her class of 480. The commencements began 30 minutes apart.

"We were just going to divide up," Mr. Plowman said, but Denison registrar Larry Murdock heard about the predicament two weeks ago.

He contacted Wesleyan's registrar, and between them, they placed the twins at the beginning and end of their ceremonies in hopes of giving the family enough time to drive from Granville to Delaware.

"It's absolutely delightful," Mr. Plowman said. "They (the colleges) did it all on their own initiative. It was very thoughtful."

The Plowmans, of Little Rock, Ark., bid their farewells to Leslie before the start of her commencement.

Mr. Plowman snapped a few photographs as she received her diploma, then Leslie's parents ran to the car for the 40-minute drive.

"It's going to be nice to sit on the place for a couple of hours," Mrs. Plowman said once the family arrived at Wesleyan with plenty of time to watch Allison cross the stage. "It's been like this all weekend."

On Saturday, the Plowmans had lunch with Allison and then went to a party at Leslie's house.

Saturday night, Mr. Plowman and his eldest daughter, Melanie, went to dinner with Leslie while Mrs. Plowman and their youngest child, Jason, ate with Allison.

Yesterday, the family started at Wesleyan for breakfast; then went to Denison for lunch.

"I was so nervous they weren't going to make it," Allison said. "You can videotape it, but it's not the same. I'm disappointed I did not get to see Leslie graduate."

Allison said it is a coincidence they ended up at colleges 40 miles apart.

"At first we were mad we were going to be so close," she said. "We were always dead set on different schools.

"For four years, we've been driving back and forth to see each other. It's funny it ends like this."

"Hey, Darlin', Let Me Write This"

Beth Macy of the *Roanoke Times & World-News* won first place in general feature writing in a national competition of the American Association of Sunday and Feature Writers with this personality feature.

See if you don't think you know Mudcat by the time you are finished reading these selections from his personality feature. Note the nut graph starting the second section, which gives you an entirely different perspective on the subject. (Capital letters indicate loud voices.)

MUDCAT THE MAVERICK

If Dave Saunders is anything, he is talk.

It's talk that allows him to make cold calls on potential real-estate investors and charm his way into their bank accounts—no business cards, no briefcases, no notes necessary.

He's talking when he is in his car, a Ford Explorer with Eddie Bauer seat covers and a Cellular One on the floor.

He's talking—effusively—when he walks you through the Marketplace Center, the downtown redevelopment project he's putting together with his best friend, Richard Wells.

And he's talking, really loudly, when he calls you up on his car phone to discuss this story:

"HEY DARLIN', You should let ME write this article; I'm a DAMN GOOD WRITER . . . Have you talked to DOUG WILDER (governor of Virginia) yet? You should call DON BEYER (lieutenant governor). . . . You talked to WARNER DALHOUSE? (President of the Dominion Bank) WHAT DID HE SAY?"

Developer Dave Saunders speaks loudly and carries a big shtick. He says outrageous things, really, things that sane people don't generally tell reporters. There's no question he won't answer. The phrase "no comment" never enters his mind.

Dave, are you a millionaire?

"Uh, YES."

Dave, do you have an addictive personality? "ABSOLUTELY. WITHOUT QUESTION."

Dave, are you all talk? Grinning: "THERE'S NOTHING BULL----ABOUT ME, DARLIN'."

Now 42, with silver hair, Italian shoes and a BMW for a second car, Saunders is still unpredictable and still telling stories.

Like the time he was 15, and took over the pulpit at his church during Youth Sunday...and saved two souls.

Dave Saunders is a high-powered salesman and a drunk, he says, "nothing more, nothing less."

"January 3, 1983, was the day I stopped," he says (right after he thought about killing himself). "I still have to work at not drinking—every day."

Saunders then sought emotional help and went about trying to undo the damage his heavy drinking had caused. "For 18 months I cried myself to sleep over losing my family. I was such an emotional wreck, selling was all I had left, and I sold everything I could get my hands on." In three years he was the top salesman at his real estate firm.

A friend describes "Mudcat" Saunders this way. "He's only got two speeds—full speed and full speed." Naturally, that kind of attitude is going to rub some people the wrong way.

"Say What? Are You With Me on This?"

Each generation has its own way of telling itself it is special. Forms of speech change over the years and often are understood only by those who belong to the group. The patterns can vary from city to city, state to state. See how much of this story, which was difficult to report, is relevant to you.

TEENS SLING SLANG
You say "no way" can you interpret their lingo? Yes, way!
by Keith Alexander and Adrianne Flynn
***Dayton Daily News*, May 9, 1992, p. 1**

Words make the teen, not always the getup or hookup.
Word!
It's jumpin' to say slammin'.
In most public places it's friend to phlegm grits and definitely friend to perp with gats.
Sarcasm is sweet, but frontin' is not.
Confused?
No need to be. To learn to talk like this, all you have to do is kick it, and listen to the people around you.
Peace!
When most people think of a funky-fresh, slammin' city, they think of Dayton.
Not!

But young people here beg to differ. Dayton may not be on the "hip" list with such cities as New York or Los Angeles, but teen-agers here have developed their own slang that has left many adults in a fog.

They're called the hip-hop generation and thanks to rap music, Wayne's World characters from television and movies, and cable video channels such as MTV and Black Entertainment Television, teenagers have developed the slang of the 90s.

"It gets our expressions out. It's just like, a teen-ager thing to do," said 16-year-old Centreville Senior High School sophomore Jennifer Mazziotti.

It's definitely not a parent thing. Although some try.

"I like this 'not' that they use," said Pamela Osswald, 37, of Arcanum. But the mother of three said it's often difficult to understand the way teen-agers use certain words.

"You say it wrong and it's so hilarious," Osswald's daughter Erin, 12, interrupted, giggling. "She even says 'not' wrong."

When Osswald was a teen-ager, such words as "groovy," "far out" and "square" were hip. But things have changed.

Suburban Slang

A dictionary of suburban kids' slang:

Boomin'—sensational; "That Jaguar convertible is boomin'."
Getup—a set of clothing; especially one that matches perfectly. "Even your hat says LA Lakers. What a great get-up!"
Grits—cigarettes; "He got a pack of grits and his Mom doesn't know it."
Hook me up—find me a girlfriend/boyfriend; "You've got to hook me up. I've got to have someone to go to the dance with."
Jewel—a nice person or thing; "You're a jewel for copying your chemistry notes for me."
Mint—said by girls; an extremely good looking guy; "Luke Perry in Beverly Hills 90210 is mint."
Not—used at the end of a sentence to negate the preceeding; "I love my math teacher—NOT."
Phlegm—to smoke cigarettes; "I'm going out for lunch so I can phlegm some grits."
Schwing—From Wayne's World; the feeling a young man gets when he sees a good looking girl; "Schwing."
Slammin'—sensational; "That girl is slammin'."
Sweet—very, very good; "That girl (in a string bikini) is sweet!"

Urban Slang

A dictionary of urban kids' slang:

Digits—phone number; "Can I have your digits?"

Dis—disrespect, ignored; "Why didn't you call me back last night, you just dis'd me."

Fierce—Sharp, flawless; "She is beautiful, she's fierce."

Five-O—cops, police; "Watch out you guys, here comes Five-O."

Fried—crazy; "He's really fried."

Frontin'—trying to be something you're not.

Gat—gun; "Put that gat in its holster."

Giving drama—overreacting; "I wish you'd calm down and stop giving me all this drama."

Hook up—matching set of clothing; "That is a nice hook up."

J—jealous; "She saw her boyfriend with another girl, she got really j."

Kick it—relax, formerly "chill"; "Let's go to the park and kick it."

Peace—g'bye, take it easy, "Nice talking to you, peace."

Perp—perpetrating.

Straight—nice, cute; "He's all right, he's straight.

Tore up—ugly; "That boy is tore up."

How Many More Funerals?

A strong feature story will point out problems that are not obvious to everyone in the audience. While national studies show more students than ever are taking part in high school sports, in Washington, D.C., this is not true. *Washington Post* sports reporter Bill Brubaker dramatically shows what has happened to sports programs in the inner city in the first of a two-part series.

WHERE HAVE ALL THE ATHLETES GONE?
Bill Brubaker
Washington Post Staff Writer
Sunday, March 29, 1992

A decade ago, more than 100 boys filled the football locker room at Anacostia High School in Southeast Washington. "We had so many kids, we had to turn some of them away," said Willie Stewart, the school's football coach. "We didn't have enough equipment for everybody."

Last season only 37 boys suited up at Anacostia. "To get

that many kids, I had to post signs around the school," Stewart said. "And solicit for players in the English classes" that every student must take.

Where did all the athletes go? To the suburbs, to the streets, sometimes to the morgue.

"Over the last three years, I have attended eight funerals," Stewart said recently. "All were former players of mine. Most were shot because they were involved in selling drugs. Some were found handcuffed. Shot in the back of the head. Hands tied. Tape across their eyes and mouth. Gruesome stuff."

Over the last decade, as enrollment in the city's schools fell by about 20 percent, participation in Washington's high school and youth sports programs has declined by about 50 percent. This has forced tradition-proud schools and clubs to forfeit games and in some cases eliminate teams, according to coaches and sports administrators.

The kids in a city once renowned for the quality of its high school athletes are notably less sports-minded. "You just don't see the kids playing the way you used to," said John Thompson, Georgetown University's basketball coach and a product of Washington's playgrounds and Archbishop Carroll High School.

The drug culture is one reason for the decline of participation in sports, but there are others. The city's schools now require students to maintain a 2.0, or C, average to play sports, a standard that has driven many of them off organized teams, according to coaches and school administrators. School athletic facilities are often dilapidated, another negative influence. School superintendent Franklin L. Smith says the quality of coaches is too often substandard.

Demographics also help explain what has happened. The population in the city and its schools has been shrinking. From 1980 to 1990 the number of children 17 years old and younger declined 23 percent in the District. Enrollment in D.C. public high schools has fallen nearly 20 percent since the 1981-82 school year.

At Anacostia High, while the number of football players fell from more than 100 to 37 over the past decade, enrollment fell from 1,033 to 701 during the same period. Middle class black families, once effectively barred from the suburbs by housing discrimination, have moved out of the city in large numbers. More of them now live in the suburbs than in the city.

Coaches from the D.C. public high schools as well as the Metropolitan Police Boys and Girls Club complain that many parents are not supporting their child's after-school activities.

"We have a lot of kids from one-parent homes," Stewart said one afternoon this winter, watching students file into the Anacostia cafeteria. "Usually, they're being raised by a grandmother or an aunt. Mom and dad—for whatever reason— are off in the sunset. So the kids aren't getting that encouragement."

"In football, we have 44 of these young 75-pounders out for a game on a Saturday morning, and you're lucky to see 10 or 12 parents at the game," said Fred Thomas, the boys and girls club's executive vice president. "There's no interest."

Thomas said the club's long-standing mandate—to serve children aged 6 to 18—has been jolted by changing values and priorities. "We have for the most part abandoned the 6 to 18-year-old age group," he said. "These young adults say 'I don't need the Boys Club. I don't need the school. What I need, I get from the street.'"

As Washington's murder rate surged to an all-time record last year—489 people were killed—city officials vowed to focus new attention on after-school programs.

"Funeral homes actually are replacing playgrounds as a gathering place for our children...who could imagine?" Mayor Sharon Pratt Kelly said in late November as she announced plans to increase youth activities as part of a multimillion-dollar anti-crime package.

A week later the D.C school board convened an Athletics Council to study the school's interscholastic programs. "With high dropout rates, violence and drugs and endemic poverty assailing our community, the essential role of athletics is perhaps more important than ever," D.C. School Superintendent Franklin L. Smith and school board member Jay Silberman wrote in a letter to community leaders.

Some kids, said Allen Chin, acting athletic director for the District's school system, "can't tangibly see the benefits from athletics now. Besides wearing a uniform, what do you get? You get a trophy or a medal. But if you go out with a gang, what do you get? You get hard cash. You get a car. You get something you can see."

Some public schools have produced outstanding individual teams. In spite of its declining enrollment, Anacostia won division championships in football and basketball this year. But private high schools such as Carroll, Gonzaga and St. Johns also have strong programs that attract District youngsters. So do some suburban schools, such as perennial basketball power DeMatha in Hyattsville.

Police Boys and Girls Club and D.C. recreation department

programs still serve as training grounds for high school athletes, as they have for decades. And there's no shortage of elementary school-age children competing in club and recreation center leagues.

The dropoff begins when these children become teenagers. In the 13 Washington public high schools that offer interscholastic sports, participation is off by about half in the last decade, according to Chin. Between 800 and 1,000 of the District's 12,500 high school students will have competed by the end of this school year, Chin said. Nationally, participation in high school sports has not changed significantly in a decade.

"A lot of kids don't play sports because they're lazy," said Monique Holman, 18, a senior at Anacostia. "I'm not on the track team this year because I was too lazy to get a physical exam. I didn't feel like taking the long bus ride downtown."

"I have friends who have tremendous basketball skills, but they're out there on the wrong track," said Chris Rhames, 16, a basketball player at Ballou High in Southeast Washington. "I'll say to them, 'Why don't you try out for the basketball team?' They'll say, 'I ain't trying to be about the basketball team now. I'm trying to make some money.'"

"It's the decline of the total morale of people," Chin said. "It's an overall attitude of society: We just don't care. We're going to watch out for No. 1. It's the 'I' syndrome: 'I'm taking care of me first. Everyone else can go to hell.'"

Chin said he first noticed a drop in participation in the mid-1980s when he was athletic director at Anacostia. "You started seeing kids say, 'I can't come to practice; I've got to work.'"

Many prospective athletes took legitimate after-school jobs, either to help their families or buy status-symbol clothes and sneakers, coaches said.

"I played football last fall, but I had to stop," said Clinton Avant, a 6-1, 234 pound junior at Anacostia. "I had a family crisis and we needed some money. So I delivered newspapers and gave my mother money for groceries."

"I know kids who dropped sports so they could go on their senior class trip," said Karnillus Finch, 17, a basketball player at Ballou. "Their parents didn't have the money so they had to earn it themselves."

Other students traded in opportunities to wear football or basketball uniforms—and earn college sports scholarships— for an activity that seems easier, or more lucrative.

"I've seen a lot of good athletes—my age and younger—start to miss games, slack off in school, and then get messed up with the people on the corner," said Xavier "Boo" Singletary, 13, a star Police Boys and Girls Club basketball player. "They'll work for the drug dealers for money or to get protection, so nobody will mess with them."

"The fast dollar is keeping a lot of kids out," said Darryl Burrows, 24, a former Boys and Girls Club athlete. "Kids are not fascinated by sports like they used to be. They are fascinated by guns and weapons. They think: Hey, I need to find a way to get me a gun and some bullets. That way, they feel powerful. They don't say: I need to find me a good gym where I can work out."

District coaches tell numerous stories of athletes they have lost to the streets. For example, Bruce Williams, athletic director at Springarn, recalled a track star in the mid '80s who began idolizing Rayful Edmond III, the Washington cocaine kingpin now serving a life-without-parole sentence.

"We used to have team talks, and Rayful's name would come up," said Williams, who coaches Springarn's boys' track team. "This athlete would say how smart and slick Rayful was, how Rayful was beating the system."

The athlete began selling drugs late in his senior year—"and we lost him," Williams said. "He hit the streets and had a new car every six months. He got locked up three or four times and he'd call me from jail."

Then there was the girls' track star who began skipping practices. "What the girl was doing every day was making a bank run for her boy friend who was a hustler," Williams said.

The 2.0 grade requirement has kept many athletes on the sidelines—and forced some onto the streets, coaches said. The D.C. Coaches Association has asked the Board of Education to soften the standard so a student with a 1.5 average (D-plus or C-minus, depending on teacher discretion) can compete on a probationary basis.

Supt. Smith said in a recent interview he generally supports a 1.5 minimum if students are given additional academic support. But Smith said he questions coaches' assertions that the 2.0 requirement is forcing athletes onto the streets.

"Maybe it's a valid, I'll say excuse—a valid excuse," he said. "But that's what our business is all about. We are in the education business. And to get a 2.0 only says that you are average. Going into the 21st century not too many people are going to be successful who are below average."

In many other school systems, such as New York City's, student-athletes are not required to maintain minimum averages. Rather, they must pass four subjects each grading period—a standard endorsed by the National Federation of State High School Associations.

Coaches note that the 2.0 requirement was instituted at a time (1986) when enrollments were shrinking in D.C. public high schools and opportunities for drug selling were increasing with the introduction of crack cocaine on the Washington streets.

At H. D. Woodson High, long-time coach Bob Headen recalled how a football player became a drug seller after he failed to maintain a 2.0 average. "He was a 6-3, 270 pound guard who had All-America potential. He ended up with a 1.9 average after his junior year so we couldn't hold on to him. Now he's in prison, serving 10 years."

Anacostia's Stewart ticked off names of former athletes who, he said, "were lost to the streets" after they failed to maintain 2.0 averages. Former track star William Lumpkin, for example, is serving 39 years to life in prison for shooting two D.C. Police undercover narcotics officers in 1987.

"As a tenth-grader, Lumpkin had one of the best times (in the 880-yard run) for a high school track guy in the country," Stewart said. "Every college in the country was recruiting him. Then he got into grade trouble and couldn't participate. Fortunately, he just got locked up. He wasn't blown away."

Supt. Smith, a coach and principal in the Petersburg, Va., system during the 1970s, said coaches must share the responsibility for the declining participation. "The quality of the people who are in the field coaching is just not there...I see coaches and it bothers me. I see coaches losing what we respected our coaches for."

Smith sighed. "I'm a former coach," he said. "Why, as coaches, are we allowing our athletes—to whom we're supposedly serving as second fathers or first fathers—to drop out of school or have poor grades in the first place?"

High school and youth sports administrators agree that too many coaches come into the profession to satisfy their egos rather than improve children's lives. "We have to screen coaches better," said Frank Parks, executive secretary of the D.C. Coaches Association.

Parks added that coaches' "enthusiasm would be greater" if they received better wages. One D.C. head football coach receives a $2,000 annual stipend on top of his teacher's salary—$2,616 less than his counterpart in Montgomery County.

In other respects, the city, after years of neglect, has come up with sufficient funds for school athletics. The budget for sports has grown from a woeful $500,000 a year to a respectable $3.5 million in 1991.

Outdated or non-existent facilities have contributed to the decline of participation at many schools. At Springarn High, once an athletic powerhouse that produced Basketball Hall of Famers Elgin Baylor and Dave Bing and a nationally recognized 31-0 team in 1984–85, officials attribute a decline in sports participation to poor facilities and an almost 50 percent drop in enrollment in the last decade.

"Kids seem to gravitate to schools that have new facilities," said Williams, Springarn's athletic director. "We don't have a swimming pool. We didn't have a wrestling mat until this year. Kids look at materialistic things, especially if they've never had anything."

Conditions are also bad at Bell Multi-Cultural High School, whose enrollment of 565 is more than half Hispanic. "We don't have a gym. We don't have fields. We don't have showers. We don't have a weight room. We don't have anything, basically," said Maria Tukeva, Bell's principal.

Supt. Smith called the school system's athletic facilities "poor" but said money has been appropriated to make improvements. Several gyms and fields have been upgraded in recent months.

Schools with higher enrollments, such as Eastern (1,996) and Wilson (1,485), and better facilities (Coolidge has a show-place gym, Eastern a much-envied football field) have attracted larger numbers of athletes.

At Wilson, situated in a middle income neighborhood in upper Northwest and drawing students from all over the city, 65 boys tried out for this season's basketball team. "We opened up our tryouts to the entire school," said Eddie Saah, a long-time D.C. basketball coach who took over Wilson's program last fall. "In the past, the team was basically selected during the summer leagues, before the school year began. This year, we got more kids involved."

But in the city's poorer neighborhoods, like Anacostia, coaches have struggled to get kids to participate. Stewart has coached football for 23 years in D.C. public schools, the last 13 at Anacostia. And as the District's crime rate has risen, so has the number of late-night phone calls to his home.

"The calls usually come from former players," Stewart

said. "They'll say 'Coach, so-and-so has been killed.' I've gone to eight funerals the last three years, and I have the same speech for each one I attended, 'Maybe if we could have gotten them involved in some things other than the streets, we wouldn't be here.'"

Stewart says he requires his present players to accompany him to the funeral homes.

"I take them to the wakes so they can see for themselves," he said. "I tell them that if they opt to follow that road, it could very well be them lying in that casket. I try to give them the shock treatment."

Yet in the evening, on his drive home from Anacostia High, Stewart says he often sees former athletes—and would-have-been athletes—standing on the corners of Southeast.

"I've talked to these kids, tried to get through to them," he said. "But not all of them listen. They'll swear on a stack of Bibles that they aren't selling. Then I'll see them drive away in a new (Ford) Bronco. It's sad."

"How many more funerals must we attend?"

Things to Remember

- Good feature stories are not easier to write than other kinds of stories. They require extensive reporting, finding a focus, developing a good ending, and sprinkling plenty of examples and anecdotes through the writing.
- Quotes and details are the heart of feature stories. Let readers or viewers see for themselves what kind of person or issue you are describing. Give readers an idea or a "feel" for the situation.
- The structure of the feature story is different from all other forms of media writing. The lead entices the reader to go into the story; the "nut graph" tells why you are writing the story; and the ending is as interesting and powerful as the lead. It is an entire package, which must be thought out before the writer starts.
- A good feature writer allows enough time for the mind to think about the story, and to help the writer. Good features can seldom be researched in one day and written the next. It takes time to think through everything you are writing about.

Practice

Write stories based on the following information.

Fact Set 1: Fax Machines

Fax machines are everywhere. You see them in businesses throughout the community, in universities, in industry, and increasingly in the home.

You call a local manufacturer who says, "We could not live without them. We get orders by fax, contracts by fax, and information from suppliers and salesmen by fax."

A local auto dealer not only gets prices and repair orders from Detroit on his fax, he sent out birthday notices when his son was born last week to friends and associates.

A lawyer in your city has been known to fax other lawyers jokes on his machine—but not lawyer jokes.

Motorcycle dealers fax their financing requests to banks and real estate agents fax official papers to the court house without leaving their office.

For some people, it is revolutionary. A woman closing a real estate deal in another state had a certified letter faxed to that state. Not familiar with the process, she asked as the paper went through the fax machine "How long will it take to get there?"

The operator of the fax machine said, "It is there already. It went over telephone lines."

The lady was amazed. "This must be something like my mother when she first watched a telephone operate," she said.

These are just some facts about fax. For your assignment, go to the library or ask people in your college what they use facsimile machines for. See how many anecdotes and incidents you can come up with to make a good story.

Fact Set 2: Coach

Your county has six high school teams. For many years, the Yellow Jackets of Alexander Hamilton High were the doormats of the league. They could not win for losing, and averaged two or three wins in a nine game season. Three years ago the former coach retired, and all 11 of the offensive players and eight of the defensive starters graduated at the same time the coach retired. The next year the team was 7-3 and the following two years the team has been 8-2 each season. This year for the first time in the history of the school, the team made the state playoffs. The coach who has been there during this period is Billy Jo Hardin, a graduate of Hamilton High 20 years ago, who had coached at three other high schools and at a major university as defensive coordinator before returning to Hamilton as head coach. Today he was named Coach of the Year in Division II in your state. When you interview him, he says the following: "I am as surprised as anyone about our success. I build a program on year-round conditioning, nothing extreme, but steady conditioning. . . . I was not expecting this much intensity out of our athletes, but it is there. All I had to do was tap it. . . .

"Football is dignity. You treat a young man with dignity, tell him what you expect, get him in the proper frame of mind and in good condition, and there is nothing to it. . . . Why did I come back to Hamilton from a major university? It was time to settle down and give my children a permanent home. Like Billy Jo, Jr., who will be in eighth grade next year and has been trying out at quarterback in junior high . . . We love it here, and this award is just too much. I like surprises, and I get them every year when we start practice. I was not prepared for this surprise, however."

Fact Set 3: Lube to Go

Dexter Pontius worked for eight years in a local automobile dealership as a mechanic and assistant service manager, dealing with new and used car maintenance. He noticed as a small shop went in down the street from the dealership that offered 10 minute oil changes, and he got an idea. Why not provide oil and lubrication services to people at their homes, so those who needed their car all day could have it done at home and lose the use of their car for only 15 minutes, not several hours. He started advertising in the classified section of the newspaper, and had metallic signs he could use on his pickup truck. At first he started with small metal ramps you can buy at a hardware store, but later got into fancier equipment. He now has a specially equipped pickup with a generator and an air compressor and carries his oil and lube stock with him as he travels. He now has contracts with commercial fleets, such as utility companies, ambulances and construction firms, among others. He does their cars, trucks, and pickups on the weekend so they do not lose the use of the vehicles during the week. His trailer has two ramps that extend out the back of the truck, and he has done lube service as early as 6:00 A.M. and as late at 11:00 P.M. Families going on vacation call him if they cannot get service before they leave on a trip. The price is $19.95.

Fact Set 4: Oh, Fudge!

Mark and Marion Mendella were both junior high teachers until two years ago. Then they needed to make fudge for the PTA sale at their daughter's school, and one thing led to another. The fudge was very popular, and parents placed additional orders (for money) right on the spot. At the County Fair that summer, the Mendellas set up an "Oh, Fudge" shop in a small trailer and sold out the first three days. By the end of the summer they had worked eight county fairs. In the fall, they set up their trailer at football games, flea markets, reunions, community activities, and wherever they were requested to go. This week, they announced that they will leave teaching at the end of this school year and start to franchise "Oh, Fudge!" Mark said they have 25 requests for franchises and are beginning training sessions in the winter months so that franchisees can go to fairs and summer activities. "This thing just really exploded. We never had any idea it would go beyond the PTA!" The couple got the idea from the fudge shops they saw on Mackinac Island, a popular summer tourist community in Lake Huron, just east of the Michigan Mackinac Bridge. "It just seems the time is right. We will probably expand into cookies this summer to see how that works. I don't think Debby Fields has anything to worry about—yet." Franchises cost $8,000 plus a percentage of the sales for the first three years.

Marion says there are no secret ingredients, but she is not about to tell anyone other than franchisees what the secret process is.

14
Writing for the Eye and Ear: Radio and Television

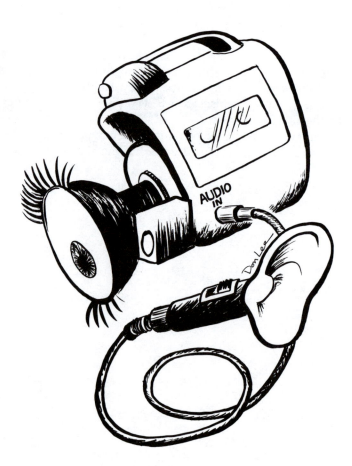

In This Chapter

Writing for the broadcast media presents different problems. The writer must be concerned with how words sound, or with how words go with the pictures on the screen.

Listener and viewer habits are such that they are *not* likely to be devoting 100 percent of their attention to the newscast. Know this when writing the news.

Since many times radio and television can be "live" at the scene of an event, immediacy is important in writing news for electronic media.

TODAY'S college students have grown up with radio and television as a part of their entire lives. Radio is more than 70 years old in the United States and mass television is almost 50 years old. While not as old as newspapers, they have at least as much power in providing news, and do things newspapers cannot do with sound or pictures.

There are a lot of radio and television stations. While there are 1,570 daily newspapers and 6,640 weeklies, there are 12,980 radio stations and more than 1,930 television stations. In 1993, almost 65 percent of the nation had cable, with 11,588 cable systems in 30,900 communities, each having more than 30 channels. While cable does not originate a great deal of programming, it does make news from neighboring states and countries available to places that could not get it without cable. This expands the reach of television news, much more than a newspaper circulating outside its home town.

While for the most part, radio and television news is very different in form, there are some similarities between news as we have been discussing it and news on the electronic media.

Similarities

Regardless of how it is presented, news is news. Print and broadcast reporters cover the same meetings, disasters, weather, and sports teams. Immediacy is more important in broadcast news, but it is not forgotten in the print media. Clear, straightforward language, written with accuracy and to avoid libel, is just as important in the electronic media as in print. Principles of clarity and good writing apply to all writing. You still have to understand the subject of the story before you sit down to write it, regardless of the medium.

But having said that, let there be no doubt that there are major differences between newspapers and the electronic media in the way they present news. Each has its purpose and none is significantly more important than the others, although those working in each medium take justifiable pride and become somewhat defensive about each one's importance. In recent years, when national economic problems have made advertising more difficult to obtain, these defensive positions have hardened somewhat.

Many persons have gone from newspaper work into television or from radio work into newspapers, etc. The initial adjustment from one medium to another can be difficult, but the basic understanding of what news is remains the same for all three.

As technology continues to advance and computers develop an even greater role in distributing news, the differences in form between the media are likely to lessen—and perhaps disappear. Reporters must know what each medium demands, but they must also know how to find the important facts and organize material so the audience can understand it.

Differences

The Impact of Each Medium

There are many differences between the print and electronic media, not only the way the news is transmitted, but also the time allotted to each, and the distance readers/viewers see between themselves and the newspaper or the television.

Television and radio news have a sense of being there, of involvement with the story, which newspapers cannot touch. Live news broadcasts, with sound and living color, of political conventions, war coverage, or sports events are much more dramatic than the next day report in the newspaper.

Yet studies show that large percentages of those who watch a broadcast also want to read about it the next day in the newspaper to verify their views of what happened. Newspapers offer a depth of detail and understanding that the electronic media cannot match because of time limits.

However, newspapers reach mostly local and sometimes regional audiences. There is a very limited number of national newspapers, and serious discussions on the evening news or other national news programs reach far more people than any one newspaper can.

This does not make the news that is transmitted electronically any less valuable, just more condensed. When major networks become a "town meeting of the air" to discuss national issues, especially elections and wars, they cannot be beaten for timely, in-depth presentations.

It has been said many times that all the news on a 30-minute telecast (about 20 minutes worth), if printed, would cover about two-thirds of one newspaper page. But radio and television news done well can have much more impact than a printed news story. If you see someone saying something on television or hear them saying it on radio, it is much easier to believe than reading a news report in someone else's words. Seeing the devastation done by a tornado in a news program on television cannot be matched by words in print.

Even a direct quote in print does not have the same power that a direct quote on television does, especially live television. There is no substitute for being there, and with live television the audience is there as things happen.

The Economics of the Media

Television and radio, with the exception of all-news stations, are primarily entertainment media and offer news as a secondary item. Even with the national networks, far more money is spent on regular programming than television newscasts.

This is not to paint a negative picture of national networks, but to point out that more money is made from the entertainment aspect of the electronic media than the news. Hour-long evening network newscasts have long been discussed, but an extra half hour of news would cut into the profitable 7:00 P.M. (EST) time slot, also know as "prime time access" because it comes just before the networks run their prime time shows. In many major markets, local television newscasts have gone to one hour or more, but few cut into the 7:00 P.M. slot.

Money the local stations and networks make from their prime time offerings, including sitcoms, game shows, and sports, help to pay for the cost of television news. In recent years, however, there is a growing trend toward making broadcast news pay for itself.

Newspapers make their money from selling ads to merchants who wish to reach people who read the news. Newspapers sell the importance of news to the advertiser, who in turn buys an audience for his or her products. About 80 percent of a newspaper's income comes from ads and another 20 percent from subscriptions and single copy sales. If newspapers wish to devote more space to news, they can do so, whereas radio and television are limited to the number of minutes in a day. They cannot expand time, and to offer live coverage of government hearings or non-paid programming cuts into their revenue. Many stations do break in to regular programming with breaking stories, however.

Because of the nature of the electronic media, most stations have fewer reporters than the local daily newspaper. Many small radio stations have one- or two-person news staffs, who often have other duties at the station as well. This severely limits the amount of time they can devote strictly to news work.

The Listener to Broadcast News

One of the beliefs of beginning news writers is that the reader or listener stops everything to listen to a newscast or read a news story. Studies have shown that this is not likely.

Newspaper readers can't do too much else while reading, yet they are likely to be watching television, riding a bus, or talking to the children at the same time as they read a newspaper. Life in the 1990s is hectic, and few readers stop everything to read a newspaper. If they do, it is late in the evening after the children's activities are over for the night and they have a few moments of quiet.

The listener to radio, during the most popular times for radio, is usually doing something else, like driving to work. The drive time, roughly 7:00 to 9:00 in the morning and 4:00 to 6:00 in the afternoon, is by far the best time for radio to reach its listeners. But their attention may be distracted by something on the freeway or by thoughts about what to do when they get to the office or back home. They may be talking to fellow carpoolers, or perhaps talking to someone on a car phone.

Geoff Haynes, assistant to the managing editor of the Associated Press in New York, suggests radio stories ought to be written "as though the listener is driving a '67 Volkswagen with the top rolled down. Be clear and concise and don't be afraid to repeat information at the end of an urgent story, as in 'And again, that downtown warehouse fire is still out of control and has claimed at least one life.'"

Granted, listeners are tuned to their favorite station, but they are certainly not listening to it to the exclusion of any other activity. It is critical that the reporter understand the nature of the audience, because it has a very clear impact on the way stories are written, which we will discuss shortly.

We should point out that the radio audience is not one audience but several audiences. Based on age and music interests, the audience could be high school students interested in rock music, people in their twenties and thirties interested in '70s music or soft rock, or older persons interested in classical music, public radio, or all news radio. The news presented on these different stations must be geared to the nature of the audience, and what is appropriate for news on a rock station may be out of the question on a light music format station. Even the news changes based on the nature of the audience.

The problem is no less severe in television. With 65 percent of the homes in America connected to cable, television news has another enemy—the remote control. In addition to all of the other distractions, the viewer has a choice of instantly switching to another channel. If a news report is dull or if a commercial comes on, off they go to cartoons, sports channels, movie channels, or something else. Again, television newscasters must be aware of the fickle nature of their audience. This is why among the most used words on television are "Stay tuned" or "We'll be right back."

News people have to work hard to get and keep the attention of the audience. There is no overwhelming interest in news that keeps the audience "glued" to any station or channel. If the broadcaster doesn't realize this is a competitive world, her listeners will go on to something else while she is satisfied to "read" the news on the air.

Limits on the Electronic Media

Because of smaller staffs and more deadlines, the electronic media have to be more selective about what they cover. A small staff cannot cover all events in person. And when reporters do cover an event, they will have to cut the story to the very essence because time is so limited. The writing in that sense becomes more difficult and more hectic than newspaper writing, and the time pressures are tougher as well. Deadlines can occur several times every hour, not just once a day.

How limited is the time available to radio news? A two-minute radio news story, which is extremely long, is about one page double spaced. A more usual, shorter, 30-second news story is perhaps 75 words total, or 3.5 times the length of a reasonable newspaper lead. The average radio story, then, must be done in what amounts to three and a half paragraphs of the typical news story in print. Public radio news reporters often are allowed to do longer, five- to seven-minute stories. Fifteen lines or 150 words equals one minute of news.

A writer should average perhaps 12 to 15 words a sentence, about half as long as many newspaper leads. The Associated Press suggests that if a reporter types two lines on a video screen without stopping, the sentence is too long.

The writer must understand all of this (and the following conditions) before beginning to write a radio or television news story. The exact number of words in a sentence or a story is not as important as this: there should be one clear thought per sentence. If the sentence is too long, the thought is not clear. Each thought should build on the previous one. Thoughts should be presented in such an order as to allow easy understanding. Short sentences permit the newscaster to stop for air naturally at the end of a sentence.

Writing News for the Electronic Media

When you sit down to write news for radio or television, take into account all of the items mentioned previously in this chapter. There is limited time to prepare copy because of recurring deadlines. There is limited time to present any given item. And writers need to know the nature of their audience to select news items for the report.

Smoothness

The news writer should have concern for anything that will make the newscaster stumble as he is reading news while getting ready to insert a cartridge and watching the clock at the same time. There should be no long sentences, no misspellings, and no long introductory phrases that might cause the newscaster to lose attention, to have to pause for a breath, or otherwise disrupt the reading of the news. Being able to read a sentence without worrying about it is a major plus for an announcer.

Emphasis

The writer should think through the five Ws and an H to determine which of them is the most important. In radio, since local news is important and radio is a timely medium, the "where" and "when" are usually emphasized the most often. The "why" is almost always something the listener wants to know. There is not enough time for all of the five Ws and an H in each story, so more editing has to be done than in newspaper writing.

Tone

Good newswriting uses conversational tone in news and prominently displays features, but not in formula or inverted pyramid forms. There is no inverted pyramid form in radio, and some feature forms (with the nut graph in the third or fourth paragraph) would simply be too long for radio.

The term *conversational* means short, familiar words, not rambling, as many conversations tend to be. Conversational in this sense means more of a relaxed directed dialogue, but without "journalese," government jargon, or inside baseball terms, among others.

Start out by mentioning what happened (an accident on the turnpike just north of downtown). The logical dialogue or question would be, "Was anyone hurt?" You would then answer that.

The next question, if you were telling a friend about the accident, would be, "Is it anyone we know?" And you might answer, "It was two college students from New York on their way to visit relatives."

How did it happen? "Police said the car slid on an icy patch." By this time you would probably have all of the information needed for the radio news story.

The conversational tone means you would write it as if you were conducting a conversation with a friend, not as if you were trying to put all of the important facts in the first sentence, as with an inverted pyramid lead.

Go Slow with Names

A newspaper report would say, "John Martoni, 36, of 2435 Lafayette, was injured in a one-car accident yesterday." Readers would know immediately if they knew that person or not, and could double check the name and address.

In radio, if you give the name first, listeners may have forgotten who it is by the time they found out what happened to him. So you would say something like "A man (or woman, or teenager) was seriously injured yesterday in a one-car accident," or "The owner of an art gallery at Port Charlotte was injured in a one-car accident yesterday." This, in effect, gives the audience a warning that you are going to give the name next and that an accident report is upcoming.

You must tell why the people are important before you give the name. "A Washington Township dentist was named to head the United Fund today," or "The winningest football coach in the state will speak at the football banquet tonight," or "A man sought by the FBI for delivering 300 pounds of marijuana was arrested today." Then go on to give the name in the next sentence.

Use the Present Tense

Before we go much further, we have to emphasize using the present tense. Radio is immediate, and radio writers try to point up the most recent element in their stories. While a newspaper story will say, "The Convenient Mart was burglarized last night," radio will say "Police are investigating a break-in at the Convenient Mart last night."

Because of its immediate nature, a radio station can say "school is being delayed" because it is at the time the statement is made.

Therefore, in the examples listed under "Go Slow with Names," radio's preferred style would be, "The owner of an art gallery is listed in good condition this morning" or "A Centerville dentist is the new president of the county United Fund." Try to make things as recent as possible to let the audience know you have updated the material.

Emphasize the now, up to the minute, as we speak, within the hour, ten minutes ago.

No Passive Voice

"The raid was conducted by the FBI" should be rewritten as "The FBI conducted the raid." Put the subject first, make a short clear sentence.

Titles Precede the Name

Credibility comes from the title, not the name, so the title comes first. And the attribution comes in the first part of the sentence so the audience knows right off who said it.

When the title is a long one, it may be helpful to have it follow the name, as in "John Anderson, who is a vice president of marketing for the Marathon Oil Corporation, said today..."

You don't want to give a sentence and make the listener wait until the end to find out who said it. If it is a long sentence, listeners will have forgotten it by the time they get to the part about who said it.

"Principal Richard Allen says two days will be added to the school calendar to make up for snow days." He is the authority, and tell the listener right off that this information comes from an authority.

Avoid the Use of Pronouns

Pronouns refer to the last person mentioned. In print, readers can check back to see who that was. In broadcast, the audience cannot. "The sheriff said Wilson was in jail at the moment. He will be arraigned tomorrow." Who will be arraigned, the sheriff or Wilson?

Numbers

Spell out numbers 11 and under (broadcast style differs from newspaper style here) so there is no confusion. Use figures for 12 through 999,999 and write out one million and on higher. Broadcasters use (M) before million as in "eight (M) million dollars." Many also suggest a hyphen between the number and the word, such as 600-million or 14-dozen, so as to tie the words together.

But be careful. "A million" can sound like "eight million," so say one million instead of a million.

Be Specific but Not to a Fault

If a truck containing 221 bushels of apples turned over, say there were "more than 200 bushels." Being too specific takes away from the flow of the story, so say the book costs about 25 dollars at most book stores.

Avoid Clauses to Set the Scene

Newspaper style, focusing on the who, could be, "The former head of the Kansas Education Association, John Hugoe, was named chairman of the Missouri Equal Rights Commission today."

In broadcast style, you would say, "The Missouri Equal Rights Commission has a new chairman today. He is John Hugoe (Hugo) who had been director of the Kansas Education Association."

Transitions

Transitions are needed to tell the audience that the newscaster is switching from one story to another. You could announce the switch by giving a new location, or a new category of news, such as "Checking the forecast," or "In sports."

Quotes

Quotes "come alive" on television because the person giving the quote is seen on the screen. Quotes are popular on radio because a "sound bite" gives you the actual voice of the speaker. If the newscasters do not have sound bites, they will usually paraphrase, or use their own words to say what the person would have said.

If something very important or very dramatic was said, the practice is as follows. The statement is introduced by "The president said, and we quote," or "The president said, in his words," and then give the quote.

Abbreviations

Abbreviations can be confusing. Spell out states, since so many start with A or M or N, and don't make the newscaster stop to figure out if ND is North Dakota or something else. He or she doesn't have time to stop.

Pronunciation Guides

This is a special problem for radio and television, one that does not concern newspapers. Pronouncing unfamiliar names can be a real problem when a newscaster is reading a story under deadline. Most stations have a pronunciation guide so that when newscasters see Menachem Begin, Ray Laakaniemi, or Moammar Gaddafi, they will not stop in mid-sentence. It would be done something like this: Menachem Begin (meh NOCK im BAY gin), Laakaniemi (lock a NEE mee), and Gaddafi (ka DOFF ee).

Certain cities spelled the same way will be pronounced differently. Lima, Peru, is LEE ma, but Lima, Ohio is LI-ma. An announcer loses credibility if she does not check the pronunciation in radio and the pronunciation and spelling on television.

Bessemer is BESS e mer in Alabama and BEZZ mer in Michigan; Worcester in Massachusetts is pronounced Wooster; Ypsilanti in Michigan is pronounced Ipsilanti not Yipsilanti. The Monongahela (Mo nong ga HEELA) river in Pennsylvania is not the same as Monongalia County in West Virginia, (pronounced Mo non GAYL ya). However, the Monongahela River flows from Monongalia County.

And this says nothing of the literally hundreds of cities across the nation with the same names, some of them named after earlier communities of the same name, such as Springfield, Greenville, Hillsdale, Westwood, Oakland, Jackson, Monroe, Jefferson, and Independence. Be sure you know the right state when you use a common city name. If you are new to a station, check pronunciations with the news director or producer.

Television Specifics

Pictures are to television as actualities are to radio, and actualities on radio are as quotes in a news story. Television adds color to make the story more credible and powerful.

Remember that the picture is an integral part of the story. Why use words to describe something if the picture shows it better? In the script, refer to the pictures on the screen ("write to the picture"), similar to cutlines under a photo. The photo is already there on TV, the reporter's job is to tie loose ends together. Tell why it is important, who the people are, why you are using this particular picture, etc.

Remember that we think of television as the visual medium, but radio is a visual medium, too. You must paint a picture in the listener's mind. Doing this involves crisp description of a scene and use of familiar metaphors.

The beginning reporter must reorganize to think visually, to get the best pictures possible, and thus to let the pictures do the talking as much as possible. After all, seeing is believing, and the job of the reporter is to build on the picture, to add information that is not readily visible in the picture.

Natural sound from an event is often the best way to capture the essence of an event. For a story on a tractor-pulling contest, why not run the sound of one of the belching behemoths under your voice-over report. Open with the sound of a tractor for four to five seconds and then begin the story with the sound fading under your voice. It is a sure way of taking the listener to the scene of the contest.

Broadcasters must remember to use a voice tone appropriate to the nature of the story. Don't sound perky while reading a story about three children dying in a house fire.

Types of Broadcast Leads

If you have been following this book carefully, you can almost predict what is going to happen here.

Come directly to the point, set the stage, don't waste words, and use short, clear sentences. One to two lines of your video screen is the limit. Get the reader's attention. That much is the same as print leads. In some cases, the form can be the same as in print. If the story is very important, you just go directly into it. For example, "The Dana Corporation is closing its transmission plant, eliminating 300 jobs."

Start with the source, go directly into the meat of the story, give the figures at the end to show how many are involved. No extra details, no involved sentences, just straight news.

This is for very important stories that need no embellishment.

Less important stories need to be set up. This is called the *throwaway lead* or the *second sentence lead*. It alerts the reader to what is coming.

"A California man has been named the new director of the local hospital."

"The Tigers had it going for a while this afternoon, then it got away."

"Wall Street had an interesting day, to say the least."

None of these tell you the specific news, but they let you know it is coming.

When on the air, newscasters often have to introduce someone who is going to give a report. This is called a *lead-in*.

"And now a report on the blizzard warning from meteorologist Carry Sands." (Notice how the lead-in does not summarize what weather is expected.)

Or it could say, "A tornado struck down early this morning in the Charity Lake section of Borento county." (Notice how the lead does not mention whether there were fatalities or how much the damage is.)

These lead-ins are in effect telling the listener, OK, listen up, we are going to talk about the tornado now. If you went directly into the story by saying, "Four persons were killed in a tornado" listeners might not be ready for this, and by the time they heard "tornado," they would already have missed the damage estimates and/or fatalities.

Or the lead could be a more elaborate "package," as in the following:

"Good evening. Our main story today is that three day old walkout at the Superior Casting and Foundry. Here is Tom Brewer on the east side with that report."

(Please note that this does not give away the storyline or the ending, it just introduces the person who is going to do the talking. That person then goes on to give the critical news elements.)

At the end of a taped or live report, the newscaster will usually come on and say "Thank you, Tom, for that report" or will add some information such as "Tom says the talks are expected to continue through the night."

These closing remarks not only add courtesies or additional information to the report but also have the effect of closing out the package of information. The newscaster led into it, and the newscaster leads out of it. He or she can then go on to a new item because the viewer has the sense that this item is complete. It has come full circle.

A *roundup lead*, similar to the roundup lead in print, is used when several things are happening.

"The tornado has hit in at least four towns in our viewing area. Here's a report from Joe Black in the mobile unit."

Handling the Wires

The following suggestions are from Geoff Haynes, of AP in New York. The Associated Press and United Press International are the two main providers of broadcast news wires. Their news is written to be read without rewriting, but you may need to localize a story or rewrite it to conform to your station's style.

Wire copy is meant to provide stations with national, international, state, and regional stories. The wire services often won't cover local stories unless they are of statewide interest.

Associated Press copy comes in the form of NewsMinutes (the hour's top stories written in two sentences each), NewsWatches (top stories in three or four sentences), and separates, which are longer, detailed stories on a single topic.

The wire services and several radio networks also provide audio services that are delivered by satellite. The audio services include regular newscasts, sportscasts, farm news, and business reports. The wire services and networks also will feed stations actualities (sound bites) of the day's major newsmakers. This can be edited and used in your newscast.

In the case of Associated Press, wire stories are generated by AP reporters and the members who subscribe to the service. Radio and television stations are expected to share their top stories with the AP for use by other stations around the state, country, and even the world. The Associated Press is a non-profit news cooperative owned by AP subscribers. Stations that share the news with the AP typically receive credit at the bottom of the story for originating the story. One way to show others in the business that you are an active newsperson is to contribute regularly to the wire services.

Watch the wire services for stories you can localize. The noise ordinance passed in a community across the state may be something local officials in your town have just heard about and are beginning to consider as well.

Stories out of the state capital or even the Congress can be localized by getting the reaction of your local lawmaker in a taped interview. International breaking stories can be localized, too. A story about the overthrow of a government in Latin America can be brought home by interviewing a professor from the local college who is an expert on the region.

Sample Broadcasts

Following are actual scripts from two major broadcast organizations, the Associated Press and America in the Morning on the Mutual

Broadcast Network. Note especially the phonetic pronunciations and the short sentences with one clear thought each.

Associated Press Michigan Newswatch 05-28-92
MICHIGAN MIDDAY NEWS SUMMARY

HERE'S THE LATEST MICHIGAN NEWS FROM THE
ASSOCIATED PRESS:

(WASHINGTON)—MICHIGAN CONGRESSMAN BOB TRAXLER
OF BAY CITY IS HOSPITALIZED TODAY AFTER BEING
MUGGED OVERNIGHT IN WASHINGTON, D-C. TRAXLER WAS
FOUND UNCONSCIOUS BY CAPITOL POLICE ABOUT 1:30
THIS MORNING NEAR THE CAPITOL BUILDING. POLICE SAY HE
WAS BEATEN AND ROBBED OF EIGHT DOLLARS AS HE
LEFT A WASHINGTON MOTEL. TRAXLER RECEIVED A NUMBER
OF STITCHES AND WAS ADMITTED TO WASHINGTON
HOSPITAL CENTER. HE'S IN STABLE CONDITION. POLICE SAY
NO ARRESTS HAVE BEEN MADE.

(DETROIT)—UNIONIZED HOTEL EMPLOYEES ARE FUMING THAT
THE UNITED AUTO WORKERS UNION HAS BOOKED ROOMS
IN NON-UNION HOTELS FOR ITS CONVENTION NEXT MONTH IN
SAN DIEGO. THOUSANDS OF DELEGATES FROM AROUND THE
COUNTRY WILL BE IN SAN DIEGO FOR THE MEETING JUNE
14TH-TO-THE-19TH. NANCY BROWNING, BUSINESS MANAGER
FOR LOCAL 30 OF THE HOTEL AND RESTAURANT EMPLOYEES
UNION IN SAN DIEGO, SAYS HER UNION THREE MONTHS
AGO SENT THE UAW A LIST OF HOTELS. SHE SAID SHE NEVER
GOT A RESPONSE. A UAW LEADER WHO ASKED NOT TO
BE IDENTIFIED SAYS THE NON-UNION ROOMS WERE BOOKED
BECAUSE ANOTHER CONVENTION BEAT THE UAW TO SAN
DIEGO'S UNION HOTELS.

(SEATTLE)—A FORMER NILES MAN PUT HIS JUNIOR HIGH
SCHOOL VIOLIN ON THE AUCTION BLOCK EXPECTING TO
GET 400 DOLLARS. HE GOT 17-THOUSAND INSTEAD. 36-YEAR-OLD
DAVE BARBER DECIDED TO UNLOAD THE VIOLIN THAT WAS
GATHERING DUST FOR MORE THAN 20 YEARS AFTER HIS PARENTS
BOUGHT IT FOR ABOUT ONE-THOUSAND DOLLARS WHEN
HE WAS A STUDENT IN NILES. BUT BIDDERS AT THE SEATTLE
FOLKLIFE FESTIVAL THIS WEEK KNEW SOMETHING THAT
BARBER DIDN'T. THE VIOLIN WAS A RELATIVELY OBSCURE
ITALIAN-MADE SCARAMPELLA MANUFACTURED IN THE EARLY

1900S. AUCTIONEERS SAID THE SEATTLE BUYER, WHO ASKED
TO REMAIN ANONYMOUS, PLANS TO RESELL THE
INSTRUMENT FOR UP TO 30-THOUSAND DOLLARS. BARBER SAYS
HE PLANS TO SHARE HIS WINDFALL WITH HIS PARENTS.

(EAST LANSING)—MICHIGAN STATE'S BOARD OF DIRECTORS
TODAY NAMED AN N-C-DOUBLE-A OFFICIAL AS THE
SCHOOL'S NEW ATHLETIC DIRECTOR. SHE IS MERRILY DEAN
BAKER. THE BOARD VOTED SIX-TO-TWO IN FAVOR OF
BAKER, WHO IS THE ASSISTANT EXECUTIVE DIRECTOR OF THE
N-C-DOUBLE-A. THE TWO TRUSTEES VOTING AGAINST WERE
JOEL FERGUSON AND PATRICK WEISS. HER FIVE-YEAR
APPOINTMENT THAT PAYS 118-THOUSAND DOLLARS A YEAR
BEGINS MAY 15TH. SHE REPLACES GEORGE PERLES, WHO
REMAINS AS FOOTBALL COACH.

(DETROIT)—DESPITE SOME ENCOURAGING SIGNS FROM THE
ECONOMY, MICHIGAN'S UNEMPLOYMENT ROSE IN MARCH.
THE JOBLESS RATE JUMPED THREE-TENTHS OF A PERCENTAGE
POINT AND NOW STANDS AT 9-POINT-3. THAT'S THE HIGHEST
JOBLESS RATE AMONG THE ELEVEN INDUSTRIAL STATES. THE
FEDERAL BUREAU OF LABOR STATISTICS SAYS THE NUMBER
OF UNEMPLOYED IN MICHIGAN GREW BY 17-THOUSAND PEOPLE
LAST MONTH. NATIONWIDE, THE UNEMPLOYMENT RATE WAS
UNCHANGED IN MARCH AT 7-POINT-3 PERCENT.

The following scripts are written by Jim Bohannon, host of
"America on the Morning" and the "Jim Bohannon Show" on the
Mutual Broadcasting System. They are reprinted here in the form
Bohannon uses them on the air.

The writing is considerably different from AP, and is styled to
fit Bohannon's delivery. It is featurelike, individual—and fun to
read.

Read the stories all the way through. The endings are special.

First is a report on April 8, 1991, on the Democratic primaries
held the previous day.
"bill still fits the bill. with mutual news, i'm jim bohannon.
4 more...states ...could be the clinton battle cry this
morning...as the democratic front runner swept primaries in
new york, wisconsin, kansas and minnesota...but...
circumstances could STILL cast a...paul...on the campaign:
(voice actuality here) (248...thought out) paul tsongas
former candidate paul tsongas will decide...in the next

day or 2 . . . if he'll slip his bandwagon back out of neutral . . .
after finishing ahead of THIS man in new york and kansas:
(25 . . . 08 . . . clucking here) jerry brown
for jerry brown . . . the cluck stops HERE . . . in FOURTH place
in delegates . . . after clinton . . . tsongas . . . and uncommitted.
next up . . . are the virginia caucuses . . . saturday . . . but
FIRST . . . clinton will find out how he plays on both sides
of peoria. That includes meeting with caterpillar tractor
management . . .

Next, some poetry to close out a newscast on June 17, 1991;
congratulations go to mona van dine
a st. louis poet who's feeling just fine
as the nation's poet laureate, a feminine first
an honor which leaves her ready to burst.
so best wishes to this marvelous muse.
i'm jim bohannon, mutual news.

Wednesday, October 2, 1991

sonny bono . . . formerly of the singing group . . . sonny and
cher . . . and currently mayor of palm springs, california . . . is
throwing his hat into a bigger ring. he's running as a republican
for the senate seat held by the retiring alan cranston. it
remains to be seen how many california voters turn out to be
pro bono.

Sept 27, 1991

philadelphia 76-ers basketball player charles barkley is blasting
fellow players who gripe about not making the u.s. olympic
team . . . saying he's not sure isiah thomas is good enough . . . and
that . . . had there been tryouts for the team . . . bill lambeer
wouldn't have even been invited. barkley also puts down the
76-ers new uniforms . . . saying they look like his daughter
got hold of some crayons. barkley made his comments while
accepting an award as the "athlete who has done the most
to reflect credit on philadelphia."

October 1, 1991

liza minnelli . . . star of stage, screen, tv, and recordings . . . is
now a star of concrete as well. she's gotten her own star

on the hollywood walk of fame...joining her mother, the late judy garland...who has THREE stars. talk about following in your mother's footsteps.

January 17, 1992

there's been a great train robbery in west hartford, connecticut; robbers broke into the home of gary clark...and stole some 450 model trains. what's more...they took the DIESELS...not the less valuable steam engines...leaving clark's net worth derailed...by 120,000 dollars.

November 12, 1991

helen garrett of los angeles has RECEIVED a check from her condo...after the condo association put a notice on its bulletin board...accusing her of prolonged smooching in the condominium parking lot...turns out it was a case of mistaken identity...and garrett sued...finally winning an undisclosed settlement in this...bussing controversy.

July 22, 1991

sterling distributors...a canadian underwear manufacturer...has begun selling skivvies in BOTTLES...under the name BUM-weiser. and yes, beer company anheuser busch is taking sterling to court—in hopes of—suing the shorts off of them.

Things to Remember

- The person writing broadcast news must understand the many differences between print and broadcast news—the different styles, audiences, and distractions.
- Radio and television listeners have so many choices literally at their fingertips that they can switch programs quickly. The writer must present his or her best performance to keep the audience tuned in.
- Broadcast news writers must be conversational, and must also be short, clear, and to the point. But they should let the audience know what is coming ahead of time so that the audience will be forewarned to listen for news of interest.

Practice

Take any of the following stories used earlier in this book, and write them in broadcast style:

Chapter 1—Judge not by name alone, or 11-year-old robber
Chapter 3—Kidnaper foiled
Chapter 11—Agents Shot
Chapter 12—Snow examples in Fact Sets at end of chapter
Chapter 13—Lonnie Porter feature.

15
The Business of Public Relations: Writing to Explain

In This Chapter

Defining what public relations is and what it does.
What kinds of writing are needed for public relations?
How do you change attitudes through the media?
How public relations and media people work together, and how they sometimes have different opinions about the same stories.

What is Public Relations?

The most difficult part about public relations is explaining what it is and what it does. Public relations is not writing per se; it is a management function designed to get people to understand what the company or organization is doing and why.

Much of public relations writing is designed to be used in newspapers or in the broadcast media, and so many aspects of public relations writing have already been discussed. We will discuss how the inverted pyramid, features, and roundup stories apply in writing for public relations.

There are also many other specialized kinds of writing, which we will discuss at the end of this chapter. These kinds of writing are reserved for other courses, not a beginning newswriting class.

The difference between newswriting and public relations writing is that public relations writing is done to support a viewpoint, or to get someone to support a group or a plan. The purpose of newswriting is to inform. The purpose of public relations writing is to persuade.

News reporters report on the facts as they see them, and so do public relations writers. But public relations writers attempt to represent the interest of the group in terms of how it relates to the general public. They work to let you know what their group or organization thinks about an issue.

This is not a bad thing. If we believe in the marketplace of ideas, where ideas compete and the best ones are accepted, public relations plays an important part. In the days of George Washington and Ben Franklin, everyone knew everyone else, and people made their own reputations. Today, in a complex, interrelated world, it is not easy to get the attention of everyone to make your own reputation. That is where public relations comes in.

And since there are so many groups that need public relations support, there are more public relations people in the United States than newspaper reporters, editors, or broadcasters.

Robert Kendall (1984) uses U.S. Census Bureau figures to say there were between 319,000 and 384,000 practicing public relations persons in the United States in 1980. "Add lobbyists, industrial relations, fund raisers, communications, promotions, and others and the number goes up to between 438,000 and 554,000."

With a growth rate of 36 to 57 percent between 1894 and 1990, Kendall in 1984 predicted there would be a million Americans involved in public relations in 1990.

One of the best known definitions of public relations comes from the sixth edition of Cutlip, Center, and Broom, a leading textbook in public relations education: "Public relations is the management function which evaluates public attitudes, identifies the policies and procedures of an individual or an organization with the public interest, and plans and executes a program of action to earn public understanding and acceptance" (Cutlip, Center, and Broom 1985: 3).

What Public Relations Does

Any individual, group, or organization needs public understanding or acceptance. When trying to attract students to a college campus, sell automobiles to the general public, or raise money for cancer research, an organization needs to have public support. And the larger an organization, the more it needs specialized people to help win that acceptance.

These people are public relations people. Some of them write news stories to be sent to the mass media. Others write speeches the president gives. Others do annual reports, alumni magazines, or newsletters for interested persons scattered all over the world. Some conduct research to find out what the public thinks of the group and its programs. All of them explain their group's status and point of view to people who can't be there in person to see it for themselves.

Public relations is a management function; that is, a deliberately planned effort to keep interested people aware of what goes on with the group. Without this effort, no one knows what groups are doing, and people without knowledge will probably not support their efforts.

A public in the sense of public relations is defined as a group of people with a common interest in a group or company. They may work for it, be a customer of it, have attended it, belong to the union, own stock in the firm, or in some way know who the group is and what it does.

Let's take the case of one of the big three American automobile makers. If the company decides to increase the price of its cars for next year, this will probably make the workers, the stockholders, the administration, and the dealers happy. But it will make customers and perhaps the media unhappy. The customers are but one of several publics that will be influenced by the actions of the company, and the company has to explain to the customers why an increase is necessary.

Or let us say that this same company is faced with a strike. The employees want more money; they say salaries have not kept up with the cost of inflation. In this case, the media want information about the potential strike, and all of the publics need to know what is going to happen. The stockholders will not be happy, nor will the dealers or management of the company. The public relations person has to communicate the intentions of the firm to all of the groups, whether he or she believes in the policy or not. The public relations person is often in the middle of differing points of view about a controversy.

The job of public relations is to increase that support by increasing the public's understanding of the nature and goals of the organization, thereby getting the public to support, contribute, help, or speak well of the organization to others.

Attitude Change

Getting people from where their attitudes are to where the sponsoring company or group would like them to be requires an attitude change. If you think changing an attitude is easy, just tell your parents they have been voting for the wrong political party for the last 20 years.

We develop attitudes over a long period of time, based on our personal history and interests. We don't like to give up our attitudes just because someone else has a different attitude. People like to keep the attitudes they have developed from their interaction with family, friends, churches, and memberships. It feels good to agree with people you live with and work with.

Attitude change is a very slow process, often compared to the ancient water torture test. Uncivilized folks would torture their enemy by exposing them to repeated drops of water. The first few drops made no impression, but once the skin became tender, each additional drop would sting and then burn painfully.

In the same way, one news item or news story or one brochure is not likely to change someone's mind, just as one discussion will not change someone's mind on an issue. Attitudes might change over long periods of time, one event or one news item at a time. But it takes persistent effort on the part of the person trying to change someone else's mind.

This means an extended program of attitude change, often

called a campaign, which uses all media and all types of communication to get the message to the public. The mass media may not be as effective as the interpersonal media, and so efforts will be made to get members, employees, stockholders, and other supporters to talk to their friends and others whose support is needed.

Any organization, in order to grow and prosper, needs to have more and more people supporting it. So public relations people try to impress them, explain the group's position, give them facts that make the organization look good, and admit it when a mistake has been made.

Reaching Scattered Publics

Since most people interested in your group may be scattered throughout the city, the state, the country, or the world, you have to keep them informed. One of the most economical ways is to get stories about your company in the newspaper or on radio and television. Even though face-to-face conversation may be more persuasive, it is very difficult to accomplish if 40,000 alumni or 300,000 stockholders need to be reached.

Beginning students who think they would like public relations because they work well with people should keep this in mind. It is important to like people, but it is even more important to keep them informed fully and quickly, and face-to-face communication is just not fast enough. Some form of a mail campaign or a mass media campaign must be undertaken to reach thousands of people at one time.

Getting your story into the mass media becomes one of several ways of getting your point across. The only trouble is that there are a lot of firms, groups, and individuals who would also like to get their viewpoints into the mass media every day, and a lot of them do not make it.

The public relations person considers his viewpoint to be news. The media person, who decides what news she thinks her audience wants to know about, does not always agree. In the vast majority of cases the media does not run the information it gets from public relations sources.

First of all, there is so much news and so many press releases each day that no paper or station could ever run them all. Second, the editors must decide what they think the public wants to know about, and so they have to choose. In so doing, they eliminate many stories and many press releases. Third, public relations people have many other ways to get information to the people they need to reach.

These other methods are classified as *internal communication*, with those who work for or are a part of the organization, and *external communication*, with those people who live and work outside the organization. The methods run from the simple to the complex, from letters, speeches, and company publications to grand marketing strategies that involve expensive research, extensive planning, and the commitment of the entire organization.

Overreliance on the Press Release

Students planning to enter public relations must know how to write press releases—but they must also know that few releases actually see print or air time because so many releases are sent out. By knowing how to write good press releases, they may find greater acceptance of their messages.

One of the ongoing controversies in the media is between the public relations person who feels he or she has legitimate news to offer, and the newspaper or broadcast editor who sees this news as publicity designed to make the publicist's firm look good.

In one sense, they are both right. Since news values are subjective, and since many public relations persons have worked in the media, the publicist's perception of what is news may be as valid as the editor's. But since newspeople feel they never have enough space (which is also true), they tend to look at a news release as something to benefit the client. This is true, but it could also be news at the same time.

Studies indicate that the media generally win the argument. Lillian Lodge Kopenhaver (1985) studied 47 papers in Florida, and found that almost half of the editors used fewer than 10 percent of the releases they received. Only six of the 47 papers used more than 25 percent of the releases they received. Editors said they did not use releases because the releases (in order of importance) lacked news value, lacked a local angle, had no information, were not timely, and had poor writing and mechanical or grammatical errors.

Linda Morton (1986) studied 408 news releases sent out from Oklahoma State University to 191 papers in Oklahoma. Of all the releases sent to them, dailies used 7.6 percent, weeklies used 9 percent, and twice-weekly papers used 21.6 percent.

Interestingly, Morton showed four categories of news that were used more extensively, and three categories used almost not at all. She said consumer information that could be used directly by the public was accepted 24 percent of the time; coming events, 15 percent; stories about research being done on the campus, 10 percent; and timely topics relating to issues in the news, 9 percent. In other words, news that the editor felt the reader could get direct value from were used, but at the highest rate, only one paper in four used them.

Categories that got almost no attention at all were the following: Past events, such as happenings on campus, were used by 4 percent of the papers; features, defined as all articles about people associated with the university, were used by 3 percent of the papers; and institutional news (activities, services, and accomplishments of the university) were used by only 1 percent of the papers.

If the purpose of the university is to inform its audience about what it is doing, there is a reasonable response by the press. However, news that the university deliberately sends out to "toot its own horn" gets almost no reception from the newspapers. When sending useful information, the university benefits. When tooting its own horn, it is ignored.

Media Relations: The Public Relations Viewpoint

It is difficult to explain the complexity of a simple situation such as a public relations person wanting to get a story in the mass media. What seems to be a straightforward, yes-or-no situation on the surface is actually very complex.

From the public relations person's point of view, her group or company has legitimate reasons for being included in the news of the day. The company is located in the community; its employees read the paper or watch or listen to local news broadcasts. Its employees should get the same recognition as employees of other firms, and the statements of a major employer may concern more people than many routine actions at a governmental meeting.

Many public relations writers may have worked for newspapers or broadcast outlets before they got into public relations. They know that a lot of what is used in news columns comes from other public relations people, especially on weekends when there is little governmental or routine news.

The good public relations writers check the newspaper's policies and style, and prepare professional copy that is accurate, clean, and free of errors. They check with the newspaper for deadlines, and send the material in well ahead of time.

Public relations people realize the story they are sending in will help their firm gain understanding or improve their "image," but see no problem in that since their firm or group is a part of the community.

And they know that many newspapers or broadcast outlets will not use a press release verbatim because it will sound as if that newspaper is using the same story as all other outlets. News writers want their story to be unlike everyone else's, and so they rewrite it to find a fresh angle.

Media Relations: The Media Viewpoint

While everything that has been said from the public relations viewpoint may be true, the media still use a very small percentage of the press releases they obtain. There are many reasons for this.

The media call information obtained from public relations people "handouts," a disparaging term meaning it was prepared from someone else's point of view and not the media's. The media generally understand that press releases are to help enhance the image of the sender, but they will use them if they consider them news. Too often they do not.

A part of this is because many public relations people send every release to many outlets without regard for whether this is news to the local media. A company with a branch office in one community sends that community a press release about an appointment in another community. A commercial firm serving the oil business sends all of its releases to any newspaper located in oil producing areas, whether there is a local tie or not. Companies on the New York Stock Exchange, which are required to publicize factors that may increase or decrease stock prices, send stories to hundreds of media outlets.

Many companies or groups issuing releases do not change their mailing lists for years, sometimes sending releases to persons who have left the firm or died some years before. Others do not prepare their releases professionally; they do not follow newswriting style, they allow misspellings to go uncaught, or they write about stories with no local ties.

Most newspapers start each day going over the wire service stories for the day, reporting on meetings or police news that happened the night before, and looking at features produced by the staff earlier in the week. Public relations items are generally the lowest priority of news for that day, and fall victim to a lack of space and/or a lack of time to get it in.

A lack of space is a major factor for excluding even local news about groups or institutions that are a part of the community. There simply is not enough space to run every story submitted.

Therefore, the media never encourage any public relations person to believe that their stories will be used. They know that even if the organization has a good reputation, there may not be room for the news on that day.

They also know that public relations persons work for an organization and must have loyalty to that organization. They know that a public relations person will not speak poorly about their organization, and the media respect that.

Developing Trust in Media Relations

In order for the public good to be served, newspersons and public relations persons must understand and be honest with each other.

Public relations people should not send releases to the media unless there is a good chance they will be used. When they do send releases, the media will have more time to assess them and will have respect for the public relations person for not flooding the media with stories on every possible item.

Public relations persons should realize that there may be other outlets—internal publications, magazines, newsletters—that might get the message out and not crowd the mass media. In effect, the PR person must know how his job includes not only mass media relations but many other facets as well.

Above all, the public relations person has to be honest with the media. The media will call when they have stories to check out, just as PR people will send stories out when they have a need. PR people should tell the reporter as much as they can, and then say "I cannot answer that" when company policy requires that stance. The reporter will respect this honesty, but will go to other sources to get the information, if possible.

There are several things a news media person should do to maintain good relations with public relations persons.

The media should make no promises about when something will be printed. If an editor overrules the reporter, she will be in a position of having misled the public relations person.

If a public relations person asks that a release be held until a certain time (embargo) so that all media will have an equal chance of running it, the media should honor that request. If a media cannot honor the embargo, it should tell the public relations person at the time the request is made.

When rewriting releases, media should keep them as accurate as possible.

Media should not paint all public relations people with the same brush. All public relations personnel do not have the same level of skills or commitment to accuracy.

Writing for Public Relations: The Similarities

Keep in mind that the public relations person will often have to write the same release in several forms, rewriting it to highlight the interests of the different publics receiving the information. For example, news about a potential strike (if it is indeed covered in a press release) would focus on different aspects of the strike for stockholders, community newspapers, the trade press, union membership, dealers, and other publics.

The forms of writing used in the media are the forms of writing used in public relations. Formula stories and feature stories, inverted pyramids and delayed leads—all of the writing techniques are the same. If you expect a newspaper or radio station to use your material, it must be in the form they want it in, not in the form you want it in.

Therefore, the standard forms of newswriting, such as formula stories, inverted pyramid, or feature stories, can all be used. The "who" or "why" aspect of each story might change depending on the angle the public wants to know about, but the form would remain the same.

Writing for Public Relations: The Differences

Press releases must fit into goals of an organization and have a purpose. Therefore, writers must know the goals of the organization before they write stories, lest they waste their time with pointless stories.

Since press releases are a part of organizational goals, they must be cleared by the persons who establish or try to reach those goals. This requires clearances, often with several people. Writers must understand that they need more time to do many press releases than they would to do a news story or a feature. In some cases, legal experts must be consulted, but in any case, the writer should know that he or she fits into a company structure and must work within that structure.

For the same reason, the same story may be written several times for different audiences. Those persons interested in your organization who do not live in the same community need to have newsletters or magazines or other ways of being informed.

Not all media are equal in value in public relations. External media (the mass media) may be effective in some cases, but internal media (company publications, newsletters, bulletin boards) may be more effective in getting out other messages. The public relations person must know, or learn, which are the most effective media in given circumstances.

Public relations also includes many other kinds of writing—advertising copy when needed; public service announcements on radio and television; audio visual and slide copy for visual presentations; special events scripts such as announcements at banquets, presentations of awards, progress totals at United Fund meetings; employee information on health, benefits, and cooperative programs; catalog and brochure copy for recruitment or sales materials; television scripts; speeches written for officials in the organization; annual reports of the business year; memos from one department to another; and other items too numerous to mention.

Every public relations office is different in terms of personnel and goals, and the types of writing required cannot be covered in a basic text such as this. Students should take as much writing as possible while undergraduates, and those in public relations should definitely take a special public relations writing course.

A person sending out press releases needs to do much more planning than a person writing news stories. The story must be checked for accuracy before it goes out; release dates and embargoes must be established as needed; and contact persons should be alerted.

The public relations person must know the goals and requirements of each of the media he or she deals with, and must keep in touch with new people coming into those media positions.

The public relations person must be in agreement with the aims of the group. If you do not believe in what the group stands for, you cannot represent it very well. If you have personal convictions that run strongly against the basic beliefs of your firm or organization, you cannot do a good job.

Things to Remember

- Public relations practices differ greatly according to the main purpose of the job involved. But most are involved in explaining to large groups of people the programs, policies, and problems of corporations, institutions, and other groups.
- Writing for public relations is based on writing for the media, but also includes many other specialized kinds of writing not covered in this course.
- Public relations people and media people do not always agree about the value of a given news story. Media could never use all of the stories supplied by public relations, because there are too many of them, many of which have not been properly targeted or prepared.
- Public relations people who are good at what they do work

closely with the media and understand the needs of the media. Media who appreciate getting all sides to stories understand that they can get good information from public relations people.

Exercises

1. Take a Monday issue of a local or regional newspaper. Go through each story, including the sports sections but avoiding the syndicated columns (Dear Abby, Mike Royko, etc.). What percentage of the stories indicate that a spokesperson, a public relations person, or a corporation had something to do with getting the story to the media? Is there a reason why a Monday paper might be different from other days of the week?
2. Ask your local newspaper to give you the press releases that they *did not* use on a given day. Look at these stories and see if you can determine how many of them were not properly prepared for the market in question. Are the mailing addresses up to date? Are the stories designed to inform the media or to promote the company, and should there be a difference? How many of the envelopes were not opened, and can the editor tell you why they were not opened?
3. Talk to the editor of your campus newspaper or the news director of your campus radio or television station. Ask them how many press releases they get each day, and how many they use. Ask them why they do not use them, if they do not.

Reality Check

While there is no one form for public relations writing, you can adapt formula, feature, or broadcast leads for public relations stories. Check the *Wall Street Journal* or *USA Today* for items that public relations people might have been involved with. Are they formula, feature, roundup, inverted pyramid, or other?

PART III

REWRITE—TURNING A GOOD STORY INTO AN EVEN BETTER ONE

16
After You Write: The Role of Rewrite

"There's never time to do it right, but there is always time to do it over."—One of Murphy's Laws

In This Chapter

Why rewriting is not actually rewriting.
Why the first draft should not be the final draft.

ONE OF my students this semester had two stories "eaten" by two different computers. The first happened on a deadline exercise, the second fell victim to a computer virus while she was printing a story she had worked on for three weeks.

Resigned to her fate, and working almost without notes, she found that the rewrite she was forced to do was easier to write than the first draft the computer had taken from her.

She focused on the main points of the story, and having written it once before found it easier to complete. She then went back to her notes for some specifics and details and not only had a better story, but one that took less time to write.

Most students like to rewrite their stories as much as they like root canal work or taking three finals in one day. Many beginning reporters feel that rewriting or revising a story is about as much fun as working overtime for no extra pay.

Whether you call it rewriting, revising, or doing another draft, the reaction is the same. Most students look at the assignment as if the instructor were saying "you failed, and you have to do it again."

Not so.

If we follow the process discussions we have had earlier, we understand that revising or rewriting is a natural progression into a smoother and more readable story.

Revising does not have to be like taking bitter medicine. If properly understood, it can add greatly to the enjoyment and satisfaction of writing.

Perhaps a better word than rewrite might be polishing the story. We will speak in a separate chapter about polishing the lead, but in this case let us think about the process of polishing.

You are probably going to become defensive about something that you have worked long and hard over. You may resent someone telling you there is a better way to do something. And yet by discussing that person's ideas, you get another mind or another pair of eyes on your story, which can only help.

Marilyn Moyer, writing coach at the *Arkansas Gazette*, says reporters look on her suggestions for revision as a

hate/love relationship. Hate comes first, then they like it. No one wants to be criticized, to be told they have to do their work over. I ask pointed questions, but at the same time every writer I have ever worked with wants to be edited, wants suggestions, wants their stories to be better.

The rewrites may not get easier. The reporters get a little less sure of themselves at first. Sometimes they overcompensate. But then sometimes they'll give me a story and it will be right on. And they're used to the process now.

Most have been through it once or twice and they know what to expect. And the best ones come back for more (Moyer 1991: 3).

Far from being a pain in the neck, coaching and revising stories with someone who has worked with hundreds of news stories turn out be a significant benefit for reporters.

Rick Zahler of the *Seattle Times* talks about his coaching technique: "My latest stage consists of intensive individual coaching of selected writers, with rigorous weekly schedules of looking at their work. I talk with them about it, about their relationships with editors. I am absolutely convinced that the way you get people to grow is to have that intense relationship with them" (Zahler 1986: 3).

Science fiction writer Ray Bradbury says:

The average young person you meet today seems to have the motto, "If at first you don't succeed, stop right there." They want to start at the top of their profession and not learn their art on the way up. That way they miss all the fun.

If you write a hundred short stories and they are all bad, that doesn't mean you've failed. You fail only if you stop writing.

I've written about 2,000 short stories. I've only published about 300 and I feel I am still learning. Any man who keeps writing is not a failure. He may not be a great writer, but if he applies the old-fashioned virtues of hard, constant labor, he'll eventually make some kind of career for himself as a writer (Bradbury 1991: 10).

Former *Boston Globe* writing coach Alan Richman (1989) talks about the reporters who "will gladly spend five days reporting a 1,200 word story, but won't spend five hours writing it. I'm shocked at how little time they spend, even when they are not on deadline. Writing is hard work. It's time grown men and women were told this."

How much time you spend writing, rewriting, and revising depends on how much time you have. In newspapers, radio, and television, the time is often a matter of minutes or hours, in a rare occasion a day or two or three. Magazines have more time, and books even more.

The point is that different media have different time limits. Feature stories that may take a week to complete may sit in the reporter's terminal for two or three days before they are revised or rewritten. Single-event stories may go directly from the reporter's notes into the computer and come out in a matter of minutes. No one in the media has the time book authors have, but novels bring additional types of writing pressures that the daily media do not have.

But for a student to think that the first draft of a story is the final, polished draft is as far from the truth as it to think we all have a week or two to revise a paragraph. The first draft is just the beginning, and students should keep this in mind as they plan to write the story.

It is all right to be not completely satisfied with the first draft of a story. It is permissible to feel a little ill at ease, to think that you could have done better if you had more time. Even after a couple of weeks on a paragraph, the professor may not feel it is just what he or she wants it to be.

To understand that each draft revision makes a better story is half of the battle. Writers need to organize their time to allow a few minutes for revising even the most straightforward formula story. The world of ideas is such that something will usually come up that needs to be clarified after the first draft.

The first draft, as we have said before, is simply putting onto paper the thoughts that had been "bouncing around" in your head. Once you have committed them to paper, you then have the chance to polish them, to correct them, to make them livelier and brighter, and to double check for all of the many changes that might be necessary.

Students have a tendency to heave a huge sigh of relief upon completing the first draft. It is a burden on their mind that may have been bothering them for several days or even an entire semester. The thought that a few more minutes working with the first draft might make it into something more interesting and exciting has not occurred to many of them.

But they are now so close to having a product of which they can be proud that they ought to take the additional steps to make it as good as it can possibly be.

These steps might include what is normally called editing, the checking of each word to be sure it is the right word and that it is properly spelled. Or these steps might include looking at the transition from one sentence and one paragraph to the next, to see if the story holds together as a story or if there is a better way to tell it.

They could also mean taking a look at the focus, or the main point of the story. Now that the writer has committed these words to paper, is that the main point they really wanted to make in the first place? In a formula story, this would mean focusing on the first graph or the main point of the story in the lead. In a feature story, it might mean focusing on the nut graph, the third, fourth, of fifth graph of the story that tells the reader what the story is all about.

The point is that there is still time at this stage of the writing process to make changes, update, refocus, polish, or enliven, if the writer takes the time. Once the story has been passed along to other eyes to read or edit, the story passes out of the control of the original writer.

The emphasis on writing coaches in newsrooms over the past decade has meant that an extra pair of eyes is focused on the story. That pair does not say "change this or that" as much as it says "how did you come to this conclusion?" or "Is this the main point you wanted to make?" In that sense, the coach is an extra reader for writers, a person whose job is to help them see the things they might have missed.

Rather than becoming a problem for the writer, the coach is there to help that person see the story in a different light, to bring his or her experience to bear on finding the focus or the new angle. An instructor is that same pair of eyes in the classroom.

In addition to helping the reporter or student improve that one story, the coach often can help improve thought patterns so the writer will not have to go through the same situation alone another time. Intervention at the proper time can help the writer see the story as others see it, and do something about it before the last possible minute.

Things to Remember

- Writing is a process. The first draft is the start at making a polished professional story, but it is not the end of the process.
- Few writers like to rewrite, but almost all writers can see that a second and third draft makes a better story. They need to organize their time, whenever possible, to write additional drafts.

Practice

Write stories based on the following short sets of facts, then rewrite the first drafts to see if the second draft isn't better and easier to write.

289

Fact Set 1: General Motors

A year ago, General Motors announced it would be "down-sizing," reducing the number of employees in the company to meet greater competition in the auto industry. At the time, it announced it would eventually lay off or give early retirement to 74,000 employees. In the long run, GM will produce 5.4 million cars and trucks a year, as opposed to 6.7 million in earlier years. Today, the company announced it was going to close plants in the following cities in the next two years: Wilmington, Del.; Flint, Kalamazoo, and Livonia, Mich.; Syracuse, N.Y.; Trenton, N.J., and the rear axle plant on Hemisphere Road in your city. The local plant employs 800 people, and will operate for two more years. The plant will then be offered for sale. Further announcements will be made in months to come, but no other information is available at this time, local officials tell you.

Fact Set 2: Hiring

This has been a slow business year. Department store sales are off 15 percent at Sigworth's, the city's largest locally owned department store, and are also down at the mall anchor stores. With the holiday season coming up, you have been asked to determine what the situation is for the Christmas hiring of part-time workers. You talk to the four major department store managers in town, and three say it will be "down a little" this year, one says she expects to hire 20 percent more than last year. All four predict Christmas will be a good business season. They all agree that part-timers will be hired later in the year, perhaps only for the last three weeks, and that more regular workers will get more overtime. This is because no one is sure just how busy they will be. This is going to be a "back to basics" Christmas, they say, and discount stores will probably do better than traditional department stores.

17
Refining Leads

In This Chapter

Why the inverted pyramid is only one way to write a lead.

Why you should think of the straight lead as a summary of the story and the feature lead as the first hint of what is to come.

How long should a lead be? There is no one answer.

Using your words in a lead versus using other people's words.

How to avoid the most common mistakes when writing straight news leads.

I N ALL of newswriting, there exists no greater confusion than that surrounding the lead. It is the beginning and the end, the bane and the boon, the highlight and the low light of the writer's task.

It is the most important part of the story, and it is the most misunderstood part of the writing. And as the news media change to meet changing reader needs, the lead must change as well. Things do not stay the same. The history and purpose of one type of lead, the inverted pyramid, was discussed in chapter 10.

The Purpose of a Lead

Webster's Encyclopedic Unabridged Dictionary has 54 definitions for the word "lead." Number 41 is "Journalism: a short summary serving as an introduction to a news story, article or other copy."

The lead summarizes what is important and lets readers decide if they want to read the rest of the story. In the case of a formula lead, if they know who died and when, for example, they may well not want to read any more because they did not know the person. The lead has therefore served the purpose of identifying who the story is about and what happened, and the reader has to spend no more than a few seconds with it.

In the case of a feature story, the lead itself may not be one or two paragraphs, but could be a half-dozen or more. However, somewhere in the first few paragraphs the readers need to be notified in a "nut graph" what this story is going to be about. Again, they can then make a decision as to whether or not they will read the rest of the story based on the introduction and the "nut graph," which summarizes the reasons for the story.

There are other lead types as well, covering types of stories discussed in a previous chapter. They include multiple-incident leads as opposed to single-incident leads; round-up leads that cover a single event with many facets, such as an election or a winter storm or a tornado; and speech stories, which cover not only the speech but questions before and after and other comments made by the speaker.

Organizing the Lead

If, as the dictionary says, a lead is a summary, you have to know what is in the story before you can summarize. You cannot summarize something you do not understand, and the more completely you understand it the better the summary.

Organizing a story is the single greatest problem news reporters have, according to a national study of writing coaches. Developing a lead is the most important part of organizing the story. This discussion is intended to help beginning writers understand the entire process of writing a lead and a story and to overcome that organizational "block" to better writing. *If you understand why you don't write the lead until at least midway through the process, you will be able to write with fewer hesitations.* Knowing what you are going through before you get into it makes the mystical and the difficult less of a problem.

Unlike themes for English class or other forms of writing, news stories do not start chronologically. A chronological report does not summarize, it goes step-by-step leading up to a grand finale. The finale should come first in a news story, especially a formula or inverted pyramid story. The readers do not want to know what happened first, they want the entire event summarized for them in a formula story, or to enjoy playing mind games with the writer if it is a feature story.

Therefore, the completion of the lead is not the first thing a writer does—it may be the last. And herein lies the confusion in writing leads.

A lot of time is wasted deciding whether to outline first or just start writing. Most reporters will just start writing on routine stories, and in my opinion, would be much better served if they were to spend just a few minutes outlining in a very brief form what they expect to write.

Not only does an outline help summarize for the writer, it helps organize. Knowing where you are going to go with your story helps you develop the lead and understand what you are going to do with the rest of the story. And when you have put even a few words of outline on paper, you have made a commitment to yourself. No longer are these aimless ideas bouncing around in your head, there are words on paper and it is somewhere to start.

The Inverted Pyramid: Strengths and Weaknesses

The inverted pyramid is only one of several kinds of leads that can be used for media writing. It has been the workhorse of journalism for more than 100 years, and it may be less important than before. But it is still very important to the beginning writer.

Strengths

The inverted pyramid forces the writer to think about the story in terms of reader interest. The writer must consciously decide between several facts to see which is of most importance to the reader.

This also means that the reader's interest is served. Without really understanding the inverted pyramid, readers know they want to spend as little time as possible with each story. They want to know what is in each story for them. If the obituary is of someone they do not know, then they will go on to something else.

The inverted pyramid story can be cut from the bottom. If the least important is the last part of the story, then an editor running short of space can cut from the bottom without having to read the story over again on deadline. With computers now able to measure stories by tenths of an inch, this is not as important, but it is still a factor.

Weaknesses

The inverted pyramid is not a natural form of writing, or of conversation. People do not try to put all five Ws or an H into their conversations. The public does not talk this way, nor do they understand why the media write this way, and they may have difficulties understanding leads written this way.

Simply put, the inverted pyramid can force writers into trying to put too much into a sentence. The writer has to be very careful about this aspect of the problem. Short, natural sentences with logical thought patterns are easier to follow. But they usually take one or more steps beyond the inverted pyramid to write.

The inverted pyramid also tends to dominate thinking about newswriting. Since it is tough to learn, reporters may remember it best and think all stories need this form. This is not true.

And, as mentioned previously, readers now need more background from their print news because they get the instant news from the electronic media. Too much reliance on the inverted pyramid can make the print media irrelevant because the electronic media get there first. The task of the print media is to develop more background stories to give reasons why the stories happen. These background stories, more often than not, will require feature leads.

The Beginning or the End of the Process?

A common misconception among beginning reporters is that "If I could just get this lead, I would have the entire story done." If you have all the facts, know what the purpose for the story is, and know how you will structure the story, *then* you can work on the lead and "have the entire story done." There is no mystery and there are no shortcuts to writing leads.

If the lead is to summarize the entire story, as it does in most governmental meetings or complex stories, how can it be written first? You have to at least outline the rest of the story in order to know what the summary statement is going to be, and so your lead comes at the end of this part of the process.

In a formula story such as an accident, an obit, or an appointment, you must read all of your information before attempting a lead. One angle, fact or unusual facet of the story may be the one you would like to write the lead about.

In a feature story, your lead must "catch" or "hook" readers into wanting to read the rest of the story. Unless you know the rest of the story, how can you decide what will hook the readers? You have to bake the cake before you can put on the frosting.

It could be said that writing the lead is the end of the process and not the beginning, yet beginning writers often assume that the lead should come to them right now and without any confusion. Not so.

And so if you sit down to do a news story and have trouble writing the lead (and most reporters do), try another approach. Outline the main parts of the story, ask yourself what you are trying to prove, and later (perhaps much later) do the lead after you know what will be done with the story.

Some experienced writers write all of their story first and then summarize what they have just written in the lead. While they are doing this, they think of a good ending for a feature story, which is just as important as the beginning in a feature.

During the calm before the storm, the time just before you start writing a news story, ask yourself, "What is the main point of this story, and what are several examples I will use to prove that point?" When you have done this, then you can start to write, and not before. Putting down at least a word outline will help you a great deal in knowing which topics to write about and in which order.

A publisher I grew to respect in Michigan, Bob Myers of the Lapeer County Press, had his reporters write their stories and then asked, "Why is this important to the reader?" Instead of some complicated procedural story, or some involved governmental think piece, the lead would then come out something like: "Your taxes are not likely to go up this year in Imlay City," or "The county says there is not enough money to fix the roads. The townships say 'don't look at us. We don't have any money, either.'"

How Long Should a Lead Be?

Beginning reporters will almost always ask "How long should the lead be?" Sorry, but there is no magic number.

Maybe the best answer would be "long enough." (See the Don Fry article following.)

The lead should be one clear, straightforward sentence covering the summary of the meeting or the main point of the story. Write it cleverly if you can, but be short and straight about it. If it goes beyond two lines on a typewriter page or computer screen, it has too many modifiers and qualifiers. Two lines typed is four lines in a newspaper. Two or three lines typed will make a broadcaster run out of breath. This paragraph is seven lines long, and you should be feeling uncomfortable about it already.

> *This lead is too long:* "After a loud, three-hour meeting Monday night in West Milton council chambers, council referred a controversial cat-leash ordinance back to subcommittee, and may vote on it in two weeks."
>
> *This is better:* "City council got in a 'cat fight' Monday night, and fought it to a draw. They may vote on a cat-leash ordinance in two weeks."

> *This is too long:* "The interest in property tax reassessments in Hunston Township resulted in 40 people protesting their taxes at Monday night's regular meeting of the township board, but Commissioner Pete Sentkowski said all petitioners would be heard, and all taxpayers would be treated fairly."
>
> *This is better:* "There were more than 40 people protesting their new tax assessments Monday night, so many that the Hunston Township trustees had to give people numbers. And even then, the meeting was not over until 1:00 A.M., and not everyone had been heard."

This is too long: "The chairman of the athletic advisory board at East Uppsala University has told reporters that a vote of confidence vote for Coach Harry Rickey was held, and that the coach failed to get a majority of the committee on his side."

This is better: "Harry Rickey may be out as coach at East Uppsala University. The advisory board failed to give him a vote of confidence."

Take one thought at a time, and break complex sentences into shorter parts so they can be understood better. The following story, published in *Coaches' Corner*, June 1980, p. 4., provides guidelines for writing leads:

LEAD WRITING BY THE NUMBERS
by Don Fry, head of the writing group at the Poynter Institute in St. Petersburg, Fla.

Journalists ask me one question more than any other: How long should the lead be? Reporters want the number of words they can get away with. Editors want a maximum they can turn into policy. I frustrate both of these groups by responding to their number question in words. Like this.

The leads need to be long enough to accomplish three tasks: grab the reader, tell the reader what the piece is about, and tip the reader what the piece will be like. In short: hook, table of contents and tone.

So, uh, how many words is that?

Not many.

Most editors deal with overlong leads by simply shortening them, usually by zapping "unnecessary" words. Easy, if that's the problem. Most overlong leads contain too many things, not too many words. And simply whacking out the clutter yourself teaches the writer nothing.

Some editors try to teach their reporters discipline by "bouncing back" overlong leads. Unfortunately, reporters may find nothing wrong with their precious babies. They sit and grumble about power-mad bosses.

An editor can educate a reporter by reading the mega-lead to the writer aloud sllooowwwlllllyyyyyy. The reporter wiggles and squirms and finally blurts out, "I guess that's the end of the lead." And the editor says, "If it feels long to you, imagine how it'll feel to your reader."

Yeah, but how many words would feel too long?
Too many.

Next the editor teaches the reporter not how to shorten that lead, but how to design and write a short one, something like this: "How can you get yourself and the story on the stage quickly?" or "How much info does the reader need in this first handshake?" or "Write a headline and then flesh it out."

Many reporters blend the "5Ws and the H" scheme with the unnatural gravity of the inverted pyramid, ending up with a lead containing all five Ws and the H and some long titles plus attribution. Editors can break their reporters from this "densepack" technique by telling them that they don't have to do it, no matter what their teachers told them.

Awright, awright, we got it. Now how many words are we talking about?

Well, stop as soon as you can.

Paraphrasing

An important difference in summarizing a story is between using the exact words of the speakers or your own words to explain what the speaker said.

The first has been referred to as stenography, because people's words are used verbatim. The second is reporting, because writers tell in their own words what happened. And when reporters use their own words, they can shorten the sentences and make the meaning more clear.

In complicated stories, paraphrasing can get to the heart of an issue more quickly. Imagine you are telling your mother, friend, or spouse what happened in your own words. You wouldn't say, "The interest in property tax reassessments in Hunston Township..." You are more likely to tell someone close to you, "Boy, those people are mad as hornets." That is a much better start.

Anticipation

There are reporters who can sit down at a typewriter and write a good story the first time through. Chances are they have been at this business for a long time, that they have written several similar stories before, and that they were thinking about their lead while they were listening to the meeting or interviewing the source. They *anticipated*.

In many stories, you have a pretty good idea what the story is going to be about before going out to gather the information. You can think about what the lead is when asking questions, a good way to verify that you are on the right track.

If your lead doesn't pan out because the facts change, then write the story the way it came out. But remember that you can be planning and thinking about the story while you are doing it. Ask questions that will either verify what you think or shoot it down, and be sure to get the information you need to answer all of the questions.

For those who insist on writing the lead first, write the lead several times, rather quickly. Do two or three leads, allowing a minute or so for each. Longer time is just procrastination.

Be sure your ideas are clear first, then get clever with the words next. You can be clever or cute (if it is appropriate) only after you are sure what your main point is going to be.

Common Mistakes

After teaching and editing for several years, I have come to the conclusion that beginning writers should be told right at the start what kinds of leads to *avoid*.

These are leads you *do not* want to write.

The Chronological Lead

Small newspapers and some college papers will start a meeting story by saying "The school tax bond committee met last night starting at 7:00 P.M."

There may be a reason to start a story like this, but I do not know it. This is stenography. This is not waiting to see what your story will be. This is not thinking through what your audience needs to know.

It would be better to say, "Riverview Heights voters will be asked to approve an additional 4 mills in November, an average of $45 a year for the average homeowner in the city." Write about what happened, not how it started.

Similarly, do not say "Billy Graham spoke in Roanoke Rapids last night." What he said is far more important than the fact that he was there to speak.

The Delayed Chronological Lead

This kind of structure gives you a good lead, but then lapses immediately into the chronological.

It gets us into the discussion of the body of the story, but relates so closely to the chronological lead that it must be discussed here.

An example would be the following:

"Two men have been arrested in an auto-theft scam that used 10-year-old boys as spotters or lookouts.

"Police started a search for the suspects after a condo owner reported his red Lincoln convertible stolen at 7:00 A.M. yesterday from a parking lot near a school bus stop in Marian.

"Police conducted a search throughout the day for the convertible and found it 12 miles away in what police said was 'a chop shop.'"

The inverted pyramid and summary leads require the writer to answer any questions left over from the first paragraph as soon as possible, preferably in the next paragraph.

In this case, the writer needs to explain how the 10-year-old boys served as spotters or lookouts. This is what makes this car theft unusual, and the public needs to be warned about it. If the writer lapses into the chronological in the second graph, the reader may lose interest and not finish the story.

If you promise something interesting, unusual or exciting in the first graph, come through immediately thereafter with what you have promised.

Backing In

Most readers want to know what is happening in the first few words of a sentence. If they get something that is not directly to the point, they may turn to something more interesting.

For example, a story starting like the following is sure to be a dud: "In their regular monthly meeting last night, the Fire Fighters Organization voted 6-5 to..." If you have only a few seconds to catch the reader's attention, your time is up.

Is the fact that the firefighters meet every month important to anyone except the firefighters? Why wait until the second typed line to say they had voted to form a union? Is that not more important?

Better to say, "The North Schenectady firefighters have voted to form a union, effective immediately."

A lot of national wire stories try to give the significance of the story first, and may lose the reader in so doing. "In a move designed to counter the German's lowering several key interest rates Monday, the Federal Reserve is considering a reduction in the prime lending rate in the United States."

Better to say, "U.S. interest rates may be coming down, as the United States tries to stay even with the Germans, who lowered rates last week."

On occasion, backing in is caused by using too many qualifiers. The reporter wants the reader to know that the decision was not arrived at easily, so he says "In a case that has drawn national attention because of its prolonged legal maneuvering, a Boise woman has been found guilty of supplying guns to a hermit white supremacist who lived high in the Rocky Mountains."

Or, "Delaware legislators, aware of growing voter resentment toward increasing spending for education, today refused to allocate more money for teachers' salaries despite an extensive lobbying effort."

It would be better to make two sentences. "The Delaware legislature has refused to vote more money for teachers' salaries. The vote came despite increased lobbying by the teachers."

Decide what you are going to say, without waffling about it, and say it directly.

Burying the Lead

An error of this type is not unusual for beginning reporters. They seem to want to start off slowly and then get to the good news when readers are ready for it. Little do they know that when readers start reading, they are ready for it. An example of this error follows:

> "The Murphy Motors management met yesterday at a retreat at Kelly's Lodge to plan for the future in a changing auto supply industry.
> "Murphy Motors has lost money for the last four quarters, after 16 straight quarters of profitability.
> "In a move designed to lower production costs, Murphy said today it would eliminate the third shift at its transmission plant in St. Louis, thus eliminating 200 jobs.
> " 'We will do everything in our power to help these people find work,' President R. R. Murphy said."

The problem here is that the most important news is that Murphy is laying off 200 workers. This should be the first half of the first sentence, as in, "Murphy Motors is cutting out its third shift, putting 200 men out of work."

Sometimes the information you get may come from a press release, in this case directly from Murphy Motors. The company may wish to put its own "spin" on a story. Your job as a reporter is to get the main news out first.

Here is another example:

"The West Canfield United Fund, faced with more demands for money in a difficult labor market, met for its first reporting meeting yesterday at the YMCA.

"Professional football player Bernie Coleman was guest speaker for the occasion.

"All but one canvasser was able to present a report. The reports showed that in the first month of the campaign, the United Fund has raised $210,000, which is $30,000 more than at the same time last year."

A better lead would focus on the specific amount raised. It would say, "The West Canfield United Fund is $30,000 ahead of last year's campaign, despite the problems in the local economy."

This should be followed by a statement from the local United Fund chairman or official giving his or her opinion on why the campaign was doing better than expected.

Not Finding the Uniqueness

Each news story is different from all other news stories, and no two bank robberies, accidents, or council stories are the same.

The reader wants to know why you are running this story, so you have to explain the uniqueness as soon as possible.

"Jason Montrose, *the oldest living county resident who served in World War I*, died today at 94."

"Police say a burglar *who returned to a house to get his expensive air-pump tennis shoes* was caught by police who were investigating the burglary."

"A man *who failed to tell his wife he was going into a restroom at a turnpike rest area* was reunited with her after she had driven four hours before noticing he was not there."

By thinking through each set of facts, and finding what is unique, the reporter goes a long way toward determining the lead. This thinking must be done before the writer begins putting words onto paper.

Use with Extreme Care—Quote, Question, and One-Word Leads

A lead summarizes an event or a story. On occasion, someone will give you a powerful quote that summarizes their feelings, and can be used as a lead by itself. But most people do not talk in powerful quotes, so a quote lead is an exception rather than the rule.

This applies as well for question leads. A good second-day lead on a murder might be, "What would make a normal-appearing 40-year-old father of two suddenly start shooting at his neighbors?" If the question has not been answered, and if the public is still wondering why it happened, it makes sense to ask it in the form of a question.

But once again, the audience watches, listens to, or reads the news because they want their questions answered. They do not want to play word games. They do not want to wade deeply into the story to get information that should have been at the top of the story.

And so for the most part, a question lead becomes more of a problem than a solution. The reporter's job is to provide answers, not questions.

The one-word lead is something students have started using more often in recent years.

"Horror.

"That's what the Zamboa family felt last Friday night when a drunken driver crashed his car through their picture window."

or

"Tahiti.

"The name brings up visions of South Sea islands, palm and coconut trees, and James Michener characters fighting a war that often never got to them."

Unfortunately, newspaper stories already have a headline attached to them before the reader starts reading the copy. The headline may give readers a hint before they get to the story.

And if the purpose of a lead is to summarize, one word alone won't summarize a thought. The shock value of one word standing alone will not help the reader understand what the story is about.

Putting Too Much in a Lead

How much can you put in a lead? More often than not, beginning reporters put too much into a lead.

Too much in a lead means all five Ws and an H. No lead can have them all. Writers have to pick the one that deserves the emphasis and build around it.

The other Ws and an H can be added in the next paragraphs as you logically explain the rest of the story.

Too much means that you have overloaded the reader's memory. Your sentence is so long that by the time the reader gets to the end, she has forgotten the beginning. The previous sentence is 20 words long, which could be about what you should shoot for.

Read *Reader's Digest* and *USA Today* to see how they run short sentences, often 15 to 17 words long. Remember that it takes more thinking, editing, and just plain hard work to write short sentences. Think the lead through again and decide what is not needed. It is much easier to write long sentences, but much harder to read them.

However, on occasion you can get by with long sentences if they are well-constructed, if the parts follow each other logically, and if they are put together in short sections so readers can remember the beginning when they get to the end. That sentence was 41 words, and you can see yourself running out of mental energy by the time you got to the end.

Nine times out of 10 a sentence can be improved by rewriting. But the writing itself is not the key—the key is thinking it through and deciding what you are going to say. If you develop a straight-forward declarative sentence, your problems are half over.

The length of the sentence is not as important as the clarity of the idea in your own mind. The problems come when you try to waffle, qualify, and add modifiers to a sentence.

Leads can often be shortened by putting identification materials in a separate graph. The lead could say "A local doctor has been named the top general practitioner in the state."

The second graph would say "He is Dr. Rolando Gomez, 40, whose office is at 4445 S.W. 14th Street. The award was announced today by the State Medical Association."

Trying to put name, age, address, etc., in the first paragraph would make it too long. The general statement the public needs would be in the first graph and the supporting details in the second. Readers could then decide if they wish to read more.

The Principles of Rank Ordering

Each news story has a different set of facts. Putting those facts in order of importance is called rank ordering; i.e., some facts get a higher rank than others.

Deciding which facts get a higher rank is the job of the reporter. The judgments are based on news values, the unique features of each story, whether similar stories have run recently, and countless other factors. To list them would be nonproductive, since local factors and timing play such an important part in each story.

You may recall how we rank-ordered the facts in the red-dye bank robbery story in chapter 11, Organizing a Complex Single-

Event Story. The principles are the same, but the facts change with each story.

Try this set of facts:

Students on the Jefferson High School campus have been taking weapons to school. In recent weeks, police have confiscated two pistols, a revolver, and three knives.

One student has transferred to a private school, and two others are making applications to private schools. Several students have been threatened, and others burned with cigarettes.

Five off-duty armed police officers have been patrolling the campus buildings for the past three weeks.

Last night, principal William Rose Hamilton told you that the board has adopted a new policy. "A child bringing a firearm, explosive, or other weapon to campus will be suspended immediately, pending expulsion."

Since the first three paragraphs are "old news," and may have been reported previously, you have to use the final paragraph in the lead because it is the newest information. A reporter starting a job may not know what has transpired in the past, but will have to get "up to speed" on the news as quickly as possible. A reporter with any news medium must know what his medium and his competition are running every day, lest he run "old news."

The most important information, then, is that students will now be suspended from school if caught with weapons, and the school will then try to have them expelled from school. Put this in your own words, which may not be exactly the same as the ones given here.

Remember, you must identify which school this is, and you cannot assume that all readers have been keeping up with this running story.

Therefore, your lead might be something like the following: "Students caught with weapons at Jefferson High School will now be suspended immediately, and efforts will then be made to expel them from school."

Or, you might paraphrase it slightly differently, as follows:

"Jefferson High School has had it with students carrying weapons into school. From now on, any student caught with a weapon will be suspended, and then expelled."

That would be your strong, straightforward declarative sentence that cannot be misunderstood. It might not be the first sentence that comes to your mind, but after you have written one or two, you will feel more comfortable with a strong declarative sentence.

After the lead, you need to deal with the other facts in the story. In this case, there are two main facts—the board making this decision, and events that led up to it.

Your second graph would then be "This is a result of a decision made by the school board last night and announced by principal William Rose Hamilton."

What you have left is a series of facts relating to previous incidents at the school, such as students transferring and police patrolling the halls. These could be placed into individual paragraphs in whatever order you think is appropriate. With items as similar as these, it becomes difficult to say that one is more important than another.

There are many other elements relating to how the lead ties in to the second paragraph, and how the second ties into the third, etc. We will discuss these in chapter 18, Organizing the Rest of the Story.

Tricks for Improving and Polishing Leads

First of all, there are no tricks. Rewriting is a difficult process, but the "trick" is knowing that rewrite helps.

Once you have done a lead, and after you are satisfied that the body of the story makes sense, then you can refine the lead. Putting the first lead onto paper or onto the screen commits you to a thought that you can then improve upon.

If you start out by writing the lead, and then go to the body of the story, you are likely to have troubles thinking it through. The lead comes first, but it may be written last.

We have already mentioned using your own words in the lead; i.e., paraphrasing, rather than the direct words of sources. This permits you to write a simple, straightforward sentence that summarizes the action in the story. Put your sentence into words the reader will clearly understand, and make as strong a statement as is permitted by the facts of your story. Don't qualify or "mealy-mouth" your statement if strong action is indicated.

Watch for ways to strengthen your statement and make it clearer to the reader. If you can use part of a quote from a source that pinpoints the statement, do so. As long as you do not mislead the reader, you can edit quotes; that is, use just parts of them.

Use specific facts and statements rather than vague or general statements. "A local man was fined $300 for driving his Corvette 134 miles per hour Saturday night" is infinitely better than "A local man was arrested for speeding on Route 27 Saturday night."

Focus on what the story means to the reader, not to the sources of the story. Reporters may tend to react to what sources tell them more than to what readers want to know. City officials checking the chlorine level in the water supply after a major flood is the source's side of the story. Whether the water is safe to drink is the reader's side of the story, and the one the reporter ought to be thinking and writing about.

Look at all of the qualifying statements or statements that weaken the main premise of the lead. Are you trying to "weasel out" of a strong statement? Do you need to check again with the source to be sure your stronger statement is correct?

Avoid using too many names in the lead. If the person is generally known by the public *before* his or her name appears in the paper, then it is permissible to use the name in the lead. If the person was not known to the public prior to the story, you should identify them as "a Doylestown author" or "a Ferndale resident." If the story is a continuing one, such as a court case, and the name has been used in the media for several days, then you can assume that the last name alone will be known by most people.

Your lead will be much smoother without all of the name, age, and address identification in the first paragraph. You will, however, use this material as soon as you can in the second or third paragraph, or as soon as possible.

Notice the difference in these two leads:

1. Albert Watson, 46, of 5786 Conestoga Way in West Millgrove, an accountant, has been charged with tax fraud by the U.S. Marshal's office in connection with international stock sales.
2. A West Millgrove accountant has been charged with tax fraud by the U.S. Marshal's office.

Example (2) comes straight to the point. Since the reader probably had not heard of the man before this story, it is proper to put his identification in the second or third paragraph. Example 2 is a much smoother, less complicated lead. Other details can be placed after the first straightforward, declarative sentence.

Try to avoid the common verb forms such as is, are, was and were in a lead. A lead is an action statement, and these forms of "to be" are linking verbs and have no action to them. It is better to say Jones was elected president of Rotary than to say Jones is the president of Rotary. The first form, "was elected," denotes a time and place and gives action to the sentence.

The "is" form of the sentence might mean he has been president for several years and is still president.

Each sentence, unless it has qualifiers, has only one verb. Your job is to find the most specific, most direct, and most accurate verb for that sentence. It takes time, but it is worth the extra effort.

Proper use of attributions (who said it?) is a problem in leads. As we shall see in the chapter on attribution, it is important to know who says something. A reader will very often judge the value of a statement by the reputation of the speaker.

The problem in using attribution is that some folks have long titles, and the entire title can take up a line of the two or three you have for the lead. We also have to consider whether that person is known to your audience or not. Therefore, you must use the source, but you need to keep the title short.

Instead of using the full title of Director of Foreign Study Programs for the Board of Higher Education of the Board of Education, United Methodist Church, a speaker would be referred to in first reference as "a Methodist spokesperson." Instead of referring to someone as the Director of the Investigative Services Division of the Regional Office of the Internal Revenue Service of the Department of the Treasury, the first reference to the person would be "An Internal Revenue Service official" or "an Internal Revenue Service investigator."

Beginning news writers tend to regard a name as sacred, and something not to be left out of the first sentence. This is not always true, because the person's job title or position might be the reason they are being interviewed.

When a writer includes the name and the title and a descriptive statement in the first sentence, the tendency is to slow down the reader by making the sentence long and complex. Note what a well-known writing coach has to say about this problem in the next story.

DEFINING-CLAUSE OVERKILL: IT NEVER GOES AWAY
by Harry Levin, *St. Louis Post Dispatch* writing coach
Coaches' Corner, March 1989, p. 12.

A while back, the coach complained about Defining Clause Overkill. The problem persists, so the nagging will as well.

The problem shows up as a common thread of bad writing in each of the following passages:

- Richard Teithorst, a partner in Condominium Property Inc., which manages the property, said...
- William R. Hirsch, attorney for the girl's parents, who filed the suit, said...
- Bernita Campbell, a secretary at the Sturm Funeral Home, which was making arrangements for the lawyer's funeral, said...

- C. Douglas Weizman, general manager of the Terminal Railroad Association of St. Louis, which owns the track, said...

In each case the subject is defined by a defining clause, which is in turn defined by a defining clause, which gives way—at last—to a verb. That sort of syntactical meandering often derails a reader's train of thought.

This sort of sentence results from a lack of forethought. The writer opens with the name, finds that the name must be defined, and then finds that the definition must be defined. By the time the writer gets to a verb, he has run the risk of leaving his readers behind.

The writer can choose from among three solutions, each of which eliminates one defining clause:

1. Break the fact into two thoughts, told in two parts.
   Condominium Property Inc. manages the property; a partner in the company, Richard Teithorst, said...
2. Remove the name and insert it later in the story.
   A secretary at the Sturm Funeral Home, which was making arrangements for the lawyer's funeral, said... The secretary, Bernita Campbell, said...
3. Remove the office, insert it someplace later in the story.
   C. Douglas Weizman of the Terminal Railroad Association of St. Louis, which owns the track, said... Weizman, the railroad's general manager, said...

As soon as the story permits, you would then give the individual's name and full title. Further references to that person would be by last name.

Whether you put the attribution at the beginning of the sentence or at the end is a debatable question. Is the statement more important than the identity of the speaker, or is it the other way around?

For example, a local college president might say that additional budget cuts by the state will force the university to raise tuition 10 percent. In this case, the fact that tuition may go up is so important that it should be stated first, with the name of the president at the end of the sentence. However, there are others who would say that since it is his opinion, the statement ought to start with the name of the source.

However, what would you do if the governor of the state made the same statement? Since the governor is closer to the policy-makers than the president, her statement would be stronger and more likely to cause a tuition increase. Therefore, the weight of her office would be behind the statement and her identification ought to be first in the story. Her political power is much stronger than that of a college president, for example.

There are a number of ways to polish a lead, make it more interesting, make it more powerful, and make it clearer to the reader. But unless you have a lead to polish, unless you committed something to paper or screen, you have nothing to polish.

Things to Remember

- The commonly used inverted pyramid lead is only one of several ways to go when writing a lead.
- The inverted pyramid carries with it the baggage of being the most common lead, and the most commonly misused lead. Find the form for the story you are trying to tell.
- Follow the most common mistakes made by students and learn from them. Do not let these problems show up in your copy.
- There is no answer to how long a lead should be. Make it readable and complete. Cover the essentials but avoid complicated phrases.

Exercise

1. Improve on the following leads, which contain some of the most common mistakes in newswriting.

   The Board of Trustees at City College met last night, in what was expected to be a long session. After four hours, the board voted to buy out the last year of President Harry Chapman's contract.

   At its regular monthly meeting Monday night, the directors of the Tri-City YMCA voted to raise entrance fees 15 percent, effective at once.

   A high speed police chase yesterday afternoon through downtown Ashland, with cars swerving and pedestrians heading for cover, resulted in the arrest of a Florida man for trying to elude police. No one was injured.

   Alfred Scallioni, 85, died at his home last night after a long illness.

Scallioni was born in New York City and moved here at a young age. He was graduated from the local high school and State University Law School.

He returned home to practice law, and got into politics. He had served as mayor of Central City for 20 years, longer than anyone else in history.

It was an exciting battle to the very end last night, as the Marine City Badgers pulled one out with three seconds left in the game. Jason Maki tipped in a rebound to give Marine City a 55–54 win over Attica West.

It was the 10th win in a row for Marine City, and the longest winning streak the team has had in 14 years.

A unique craft show will be held this weekend at the Farmer's Market, from 3:00 to 7:00 P.M. Saturday and 11:00 to 4:00 P.M. on Sunday.

Proceeds from the sale will go to support the American Red Cross disaster relief fund.

All of the crafts will be made by children aged nine to 12, who have been doing their work under the supervision of 4-H.

18
Organizing the Rest of the Story: Between the Lead and the Ending

"Most reporters' stories have a beginning, a muddle and an end."
—Jack Hunter, *Jacksonville Times-Union* writing coach.

In This Chapter

How thinking of news *as a story* helps solve organization problems.

Understand that writers have to move from one point to the next in a logical fashion, just as if they were telling a story. This is called transition or flow.

How to think through a story so that the paragraph following the lead answers questions that were left over from the lead.

Developing the body of the story using principle and example.

How to use specifics to prove a point—and to strengthen the body of the story.

WE HAVE discussed leads, and you have probably written several by this time. You know you have to find the focus, summarize the important facts, and tell what is important in an interesting way.

We have also discussed endings, especially for feature stories. Most writers try to save an anecdote or example to close on a high note in a feature story. In a summary or inverted pyramid, writers deliberately "slow down" at the end, leaving the least important facts for the last paragraph. In this way, these facts can be eliminated from the story if space is needed.

We have also talked about the importance of keeping opinion out of story endings, such as "Now that you have seen what Mary Manning has been through, we are sure you will feel she is a success in life." Show through facts, interviews, or in other concrete ways that this person is a success, or is likely to be a success. Do not tell readers that she is a success.

If you have not shown evidence of it, you have not proved it. Readers will not be convinced if you "lead cheers" for your own story.

The Rest of the Story

Even after writing the lead and the ending, as tough as they are, there remains a great deal more to do—everything between the first paragraph or two and the last. This is the majority of your story, and it does not just "automatically take shape" after you have spent a great deal of time on the lead. You have to think it through, and a few minutes thinking about it at the right time makes the job go much more smoothly and easily.

Just as you have a purpose in selecting the words for the lead and ending, you also have to decide on the content and organization of the rest of the story.

Generally speaking, the importance of organization, transition, and other facets is the same for formula and summary stories as it is for features. The approaches to the stories are different, but the essential ingredients are the same. Also, the problems with fleshing out the body of the story are the same for each type of story.

There are several ways to do this.

The Concept of Story

Every meeting you attend, every person you interview, and every game you report on has its own story. The citizens of a problem neighborhood want protection the council says it can't afford. The poster boy for the United Fund has overcome a serious disease and hopes to help others. The local football team, the Panthers, have lost eight in a row, but Bruiser Kenworth is back, and that might make a difference.

You must identify this central theme or story idea before you can grasp your lead. It may "come to you" in a flash of inspiration as you are interviewing, but more likely it will come to you slowly and somewhat painfully as you think through the information.

The lead is the sentence that comes to you when someone suggests you tell your Mom what you are writing about, or when an editor asks you what the story is about. Sometimes the problem is that we don't see the main points because we are focusing on details. Or you may be thinking about the form of the lead more than the substance; that is, you are worried about which words to use when you ought to be worried about the idea you are trying to get across.

Once you have the central theme, expressed in a straightforward sentence, you are ready to start, and not before. State it as clearly and interestingly as possible in your lead, then support it throughout the story.

If your story is about a local traveler returning from Southeast Asia, saying it was "a fascinating trip," you have to find out why it was fascinating. Develop a lead, and then go over the stops in the tour to tell why the traveler considered them facsinating.

If the story is about a medical breakthrough, explain what it might do for mankind in the lead. Then tell the readers why the researchers think it is a medical breakthrough—how it has proved effective in laboratory tests, how nothing else works in the same way, how soon it will be available,etc.

And, if Bruiser Kenworth proved to be a major difference in the Panther football game, compare their scores and offense with him and without him, and get quotes from the coaches to verify that he was indeed the difference.

Answering the Questions in the Lead

Beginning news writers often go astray in the first paragraph after the summary lead because they do not see this story as a story. They may see it as putting notes they have gathered into a story form.

The first paragraph after the summary or formula lead is designed to answer those questions you could not fit in the summary lead.

Your lead could say, "Three men were arrested Monday for shooting at Drug Enforcement officers during an early morning marijuana raid on the California-Oregon border. No one was injured."

Your next paragraph should identify who the men were, usually by name, age, and hometown. The reader needs to know who these people are.

A common mistake is to begin discussing the chronological details of the raid in the second paragraph, such as "DEA agents were acting on a tip and surrounded a house in coastal mountains just before dawn, ordering the men to come out."

This is valuable information, but it does not answer the question in the lead, namely, who are these people?

Let's take another case. Suppose the largest plant in your town has just named a new manager.

"Herbert J. Woodwin of Los Gatos, Cal., has been named the new manager of the Industrial Rubber and Supply Company in North Wilkesboro. He replaces Edwin J. Woodhaus, who is retiring at the end of the month."

The logical question to answer in the next sentence is, "How is this person qualified for this job?" You would not get to that by telling his life history, starting with where he grew up, where he went to college, and where he had his first job.

A good second paragraph would be something like "Woodwin, 55, has 20 years managerial experience in the rubber products industry, including the last four as assistant manager of the Ikebuko Automotive Supply division in Los Gatos, a suburb of San Francisco."

You would not start the second graph by saying, "Woodwin is a native of Zelienople, Pa., and has an engineering degree from Carnegie Tech."

The next graph should continue to state his qualifications, and later on in the story you can tell about his education, family, hobbies and interests, etc. But the first graph after the lead should include the material you cannot fit into the lead.

The Body of the Story

Remember, you are telling a story. You will need several paragraphs to explain the details of the story, to use quotes from sources that illustrate the point you are trying to make, and to add specifics, such as time and date, numbers, personal opinions, and other items that make your story strong and complete.

You are trying to make a point with your story. If the city doesn't think it has the money to pay for the project the citizens want, let the city officials say so. The reader is probably just as interested in the subject as the citizens who went to the meeting, and deserves to know what went on in the discussion as well as what the decision was. So include the discussion, watching for the most memorable quotes that would be of interest to the reader.

Follow the *Principle and Example* formula. The Principle is, the city doesn't have enough money. The example is, "We are facing new salary demands next month, and we are required to pay salaries. We can't pay for this project and more salaries, too."

The Principle is that Bruiser Kenworth made a difference in the Panther offense. The Example is that he ran for 12 yards each of the first three times he carried the ball, and he scored two touchdowns in the first quarter. Add both coaches' comments to this, and you are on the way to making the body of the story more complete and interesting.

If you remember the five Ws and an H from previous discussions, remember that including information about each of them also helps to fill out the body of the story.

Developing an eye for good quotes, anecdotes, and specifics is something the writer can do, but he or she must work at it.

If you listen for good quotes, you will find them. If you are not waiting for them, they will go right over your head.

Watch for people saying things in a colorful manner or with strength and power. A city manager saying "No one will tell this city how to spend its money!" has a lot of power.

A citizen in a public meeting saying "This city doesn't care for the poor one damned bit!" needs to be quoted fully to show the intent and the depth of feeling in the story. Identify who said it, interview him or her again after the meeting, but find out why that person feels so strongly on that issue.

Use that person's arguments and counter them with statements made by others at the meeting. Tell the reader who was not there what went on.

And don't just get the quote. A colorful quote may show emotion and feeling but it may not make a great deal of sense.

Reporters will often talk to a citizen in the halls outside a council meeting after that citizen has made a statement to the council. The reporter is taking a risk of missing something that goes on in the meeting while he talks to the citizen-speaker. But that must be balanced against the risk of not being able to contact the citizen later when writing the story.

Since very few citizens come to public boards and meetings, you need to find out what that person is thinking. For various reasons, the questions you might ask probably were not asked at the council meeting.

Dig for Specifics

Find out how much the project that the citizens want will cost. It is a major difference between $10,000 and $100,000. Do they have a ballpark figure if they don't have specifics? Has the project been studied by an architect or engineer? How many people are involved? Has there been a petition and how many have signed it?

In the case of Bruiser Kenworth, how big is he? If he is 220 pounds and a junior in school, this is a pertinent and important detail. That size may not be as unusual as it was 20 years ago, but to be a running back and 220 pounds is a specific that readers need to know. No wonder he gained 12 yards each of the first three carries!

Any story you do will have a beginning, a middle, and an end. It will also have quotes and details and specifics, but if it doesn't, your job is to get them. No matter what type of story you cover, you must have the information that sometimes doesn't "automatically" rise to the top.

The difference between a great news story and a poor one is usually the difference between the reporter who gets the details, quotes, and specifics and the one who does not.

The Concept of Flow or Transition

Not all stories get the reporter's juices flowing. You may be on a beat or at a media outlet for some time before you get to do the specific kinds of stories you like.

When you do stories you find enjoyable, editors sometimes refer to them as "having fingerprints all over them." They know you had extra enthusiasm and delight in doing that story, and it showed in the life and energy of the story.

Reporters sometimes call these stories "stories that write themselves."

There are not a lot of them, but these are the stories that are so easy to tell that they fall into place the first time through. You know that logic, facts, and writing skill have come together to make it an easy story to write, and probably an enjoyable story for the reader to read, as well.

When a story ties together nicely, it flows smoothly from the lead to the paragraphs in the body of the story and to the ending. It flows naturally from one paragraph to another, just as if you were telling a story to someone or a novelist were tying parts of her book together. A place for everything and everything in its place.

This happens rarely in real life. It would be nice if it happened more often, but students can make it happen more often by understanding transition.

The writer uses the concept of flow or transition to move from one paragraph or one topic to the next. This can be done "naturally" or "artificially." Each is legal, each is permitted, each improves a story.

Natural transition comes from having outlined the story or thought it through carefully, knowing from the start what you want to prove with the story. If you have the theme or main idea of the story in one sentence, you can do this. You know what you want to say. You know the specifics, details, and quotes that support your argument. You know how the story is going to end.

If you have not thought it through, or if you have not outlined the idea, you will focus on the lead and then struggle with transitions. Writers who do the lead first find they react to what is in the lead to do their next sentences, and this does not give them a sense of the whole story.

"Natural" transitions come from knowing where you are going with the story. They come from logical thinking that says this must follow that.

For example, you start with the name of the plant manager and the next paragraph tells why he is qualified for that job.

Or, you start with the fact that a neighborhood wants more police protection, and then you give the specifics (in their words) of why they want it.

Or, you can tell readers that the Panthers are on a winning streak, and in the next paragraph you tell the reasons for it.

"Artificial" transitions, while perfectly legitimate, do not come as smoothly. They come from using perfectly good transition words that help move the reader to the next thought, such as "then," "therefore," "however," "in contrast to," "shortly thereafter," and many others.

These transition words come in handy when you are trying to show how a story developed or how one argument countered another. You can tie your arguments together as you would a string through pearls. Each pearl in itself is fine, but when they are all tied together they are even more impressive.

In terms of newswriting, you have to want to tie a story together before it goes together. The tendency with beginning writers is to collect a series of actions or quotes or votes at a meeting and assume that this is a story. It is not a story until you make it a story.

It is not really a story unless it has purpose and transition. Spending extra time thinking about what you would like to have in the story makes the transition—and the story—come alive.

Things to Remember

- Good stories do not just happen. They are the result of careful planning and thinking through information *before* starting to write.
- A good story, carefully thought through, will be easier to write because the writer sees the information as a story, not a listing of facts.
- The reader will probably not see transitions in a story, saying only "Gee, that was fun to read." Good transitions mean stories are easy to read.

Exercises

1. Analyze a longer story in a national magazine or a Sunday feature in a newspaper. Is it clear that the story has been carefully planned, or do some facts and information just seem to have been "dropped into the story?"
2. Go through several news stories, watching especially for the transition words. Note which transition words are used, but more importantly, note how the story is held together by the transitions.

19
Attribution and Verification: Who Said That and Can You Prove it?

In This Chapter

The source of a statement is as important as the statement itself. The reader will judge the value of a statement by the reputation of the person who made it.

The writer must clearly indicate who gave a statement. Obvious statements, which anyone can verify by being there, do not need attribution.

Students usually worry too much about which words to use for attribution. Generally, "said" is the right word, at least three times out of four.

Handling full quotes and partial quotes.

How to deal with anonymous sources.

THE relationship between the audience and the media is based on trust. If readers trust what is read in the paper, heard on radio, or seen on television news, they will be back for the next issue or program.

But if the facts are known by the reader to be wrong, or if numbers or spelling are not correct, the audience loses trust.

Therefore every spelling, fact, and statement is important. The reporter is expected to "double check" every statement that is not common knowledge.

Mistakes in spelling, in names or in facts in one story cause the reader to be suspicious about all stories. Since the public does not distinguish between newspapers, radio, television, and magazines, an error in one is considered an error in all. This is obviously not fair, but the public clearly lumps all news organizations into "the media."

The legal problems of errors can be lessened by printing corrections, and many newspapers do print corrections. But they would much rather have the story correct the first time, rather than print a retraction.

And just as parents remember the one accident their child was in far longer than they remember the hundreds of times he got home safely, editors and the public will remember the one mistake you made much longer than they remember the stories you have done properly. You have to be eternally vigilant.

Please understand that this is not easy. Writers deal with ideas, which are complex and slippery, and with people, whose positions change as time goes on. They can only report what those people said on this issue on this day, and understand that people, issues, and ideas will change.

Readers expect writers to be as objective as possible. They

don't understand how complex the news gathering problem is, how many times writers may have to call for a simple report, or how little time they have to do the story. All readers want is something they can believe in.

Reporters can take steps to verify all facts and to be sure the quotes are accurate and reflect what the person said. These steps have to be followed *each time* the reporter makes a call, listens to a speech, interviews a source, or checks a name or fact. There is no letting up.

Remember that the reporter is a re-porter, she carries information back from someone else to the news operation to be relayed to hundreds, thousands, or hundreds of thousands of readers. The reporter, with the exception of those few who actually cover events live, is more likely to talk to someone else who has seen the event or has talked to the source.

Reporters more often talk to a candidate's spokespeople than they do to the candidate. For every presidential press conference there are dozens of daily briefings. For every accident you come upon on the highway, you will talk to police about hundreds of others they have investigated.

Therefore, you have to tell readers who actually saw the event, talked to the president, or investigated the accident. You didn't do these things yourself, so you must attribute them to someone else.

How you attribute statements to others and how you verify facts in stories are important enough to warrant a chapter in this book.

What Needs to be Attributed

The general rule is this: if something is obvious to anyone who was there, or is common knowledge, it probably does not need to be attributed. If it is someone's opinion, or if it is not obvious to all who were there, then it needs to be attributed.

If you can see it for yourself, should you be in the area, you do not need to attribute it. If it is a common fact found in a dictionary or encyclopedia, you do not have to attribute it.

If an elected or appointed official is making a serious charge, such as political corruption, embezzlement, or theft in office, it is that person's opinion and must be attributed. If the accused person is later convicted in a court of law, the verdict does not have to be attributed.

If the reporter is on hand and sees the football game or the airplane crash, she does not have to attribute what she saw. The reader will know by the byline and by the story that the reporter was present. If that same reporter talked to the football coach or the air crash investigator to get the facts, then she needs to quote that coach or official.

The reader wants to know who said this or that. The reporter needs to protect himself if he was not at the scene and got his information from someone else.

If the D&W drug store on the corner of Third and Main was destroyed by fire, anyone can see it by walking or driving by. The statement that the building was destroyed by fire does not need to be attributed.

But if the fire was caused by a chemical explosion in the back room, this is not obvious. You could not determine this by looking at the building, so the reader needs to know who said that was the cause. You must attribute statements about causes and since investigations take some time, you are often forced to say an investigation is continuing.

If there is a flu epidemic in the community, you need to have someone at the hospital state that there is an epidemic. As a reporter, you cannot determine that a large number of cases occurring at the same time is an epidemic because that is a medical judgment.

If you mention that Juneau is the capital of Alaska in a story, it is common knowledge that can be obtained from many reference sources. You do not have to attribute it. However, if you say Juneau has more government workers per capita than any other state, this is not common knowledge (if it is true) and it must be attributed to someone. Readers know that Juneau is the capital (or they can look it up), but the second statement needs to be attributed.

You can say that two persons died when their cars collided on South Ridge Road at about 2:00 A.M., but in all likelihood you were not there.

So you say two persons are dead without attributing it, but you must attribute the circumstances and causes of the accident to the agency that investigated it.

Any statement that is not obvious on its face, or that could be said by any of several people, needs to be attributed. Tell readers who said it, and let them decide if they should worry about that statement.

Some statements do not need attribution. "Polling booths will open at 6:00 A.M.," "The sun will rise at 7:42 A.M.," and "The Tigers defeated the Yankees, 6–1, yesterday" are statements of fact that can be verified independently.

However, if someone says, "I think polling booths ought to be open at 5:00 A.M. for those who go to work at 6:00 A.M.," then that needs attribution because it is an opinion. The sun rising at 7:42

A.M. is a fact, but someone stating the world will come to an end at 7:45 needs attribution. The Tiger-Yankee score is a fact, but someone saying the Tigers will win the pennant is expressing an opinion, and reporters need to tell the reader who that person is.

How to Use Direct Quotes

When should you use the exact words of the speaker or the source, and when should you use your own words?

Let's step back a minute. What are we trying to do? We are trying to tell the reader why this interview or this story is important to him.

Your lead paragraph or paragraphs must be your own words about what is important to the reader or viewer. Usually, but not always, these are not the direct words of the source, because sources don't always summarize what they are saying.

But you can use some of the words of the source in the lead; that is, a partial quote. Going back to the flu epidemic story, perhaps the doctor said, "Based on what I know right now, if things do not change, I expect a rather severe outbreak of flu in the next 10 days to two weeks." (Notice the qualifiers all careful medical people put into their statements.) If this information held up with other interviews, you could be justified in a lead that says: "The county health commissioner says Springfield can expect 'a rather severe flu outbreak within the next 10 days to two weeks.'" Or, you might say, "Springfield can expect a 'rather severe flu outbreak' in the next ten days to two weeks, the health commissioner says." You did not use the entire quote, but you did not change it in any material fashion. You did not use all of the qualifiers, but you did quote the source accurately. Partial quotes are acceptable if they do not change the meaning of the statement.

So in this case, you used a partial quote to strengthen your own words. The doctor said it better than you could have said it, or at least more directly and forcefully.

But if two doctors say they expected a flu outbreak and two others say it was too early to predict one, then you would have to use your own words. "There is no clear agreement on whether there is likely to be a flu outbreak in Springfield," is one way this could be done.

The general rule on using quotes is to serve the reader the best information in the shortest form possible. If the doctor says it better than you can, or in a more colorful fashion, use the doctor's words.

If a speaker uses colorful language, as long as it is in good taste, feel free to use his or her words instead of yours. It makes a better story because it tells you something about the source. If a political candidate calls his opponent "an ornery polecat," you might consider using that unless you think he is saying it just to get more publicity. If a scientist claims to have discovered "the secret to cold fusion without any doubt whatsoever" that would be a strong enough statement to consider using alone.

If you like the direct quote and think readers would like it too, use it. But the main point is to get as much information as possible into as clear a sentence as possible. If the quotes help, good.

How Do You Say "Said"?

One of the common questions beginning reporters have is about attribution words. Should you use said or some other word?

Beginning reporters try to find a fancier word than said. Perhaps because we try to impress others with our word choice (after all, we *are* in college). Perhaps we don't think the word "said" is strong or pompous enough. Perhaps we choose our attributive verbs more carefully in English themes.

Therefore, we find phrases such as, "the president stated," "the coach emphasized," "the governor explained," "the speaker averred" (declared with confidence, a good crossword puzzle word), and many others.

The rule of thumb in newswriting is simply this: what was said is more important to the reader than the attribution word. Use "said" three times out of four in general, though quite often "said" is enough for the fourth time out of four. Use a more specific word when it is called for under the conditions: "the coach shouted at his team," "the doctor whispered to his ailing patient," "the mother sobbed at a press conference."

Use the specific words when there is a specific reason to do so. But the old reliable is "said," because it gets the job done without calling attention to itself. The news and the source of the news are more important than the attribution word.

One other point is that when doing features, the writer often uses "says" instead of said. Said is for the past tense, as when someone said something yesterday or when being interviewed. "Says" means that the person interviewed for a feature, which does not have the same time frame as a formula or summary story, still has the same views as she did when being interviewed.

In "Johnston says the ozone layer problem is the most serious one the United States is facing," he meant it when he said it two or three days ago and he still means it. Past tense is not always appropriate in this situation.

325

Problems in Attribution

News media deal in facts and ideas. Facts can be verified; ideas are often someone's opinion and need to be attributed.

People running for or holding political office are news makers. The public elected them and the public needs to know what they are thinking.

Public officials and would-be public officials (candidates) have been known to throw statements around recklessly during campaigns. They have also been known to tell reporters their ideas about projects or ideas and then deny having said that if the public doesn't like the idea. These ideas are "trial balloons" and the press is, in effect, being used when it discusses them. But when a public official discusses public business, the idea needs to be reported. Except, however, that some politicians will try to weasel out if the idea turns out to be unpopular.

Reporters are well-advised to be sure their facts are straight. If there is any confusion about the story, reporters need to clear it up before leaving the interview. Be certain of what the source said by repeating the main ideas to the source and asking if this is what they indeed said.

Anyone who supplies you with information from a poll or survey needs to carry clarification a step beyond normal attribution. They need to tell you how the poll was conducted, when it was conducted, who the respondents were, what the margin of error was, and other factors. The reader needs to be able to judge how good the poll was to be able to tell how good the information was.

Poll information goes out of date as soon as a major event happens that relates to the opinions expressed in the poll. Too many times politicians, who have free mailing privileges, will give you results of a poll of their voters, without telling you the exact questions, the time the poll was taken, or whether the audience was a normal sample or friends of the office-holder.

One Source or Several?

In stories in which only one person is quoted, the use of attribution is straightforward. You use attribution when that person says something that is not commonly known, or when that person says something better or livelier than you can say it.

I once followed golfer Lee Trevino around 18 holes of a pro-am tournament, jotting down comments Trevino made while he was playing (Trevino makes comments in the middle of a swing, as many golf fans know). There was no need for many uses of "he said," because he was the only being quoted. Several paragraphs of direct quotes could be used with only one attribution. It was as if the speaker were talking directly to the reader.

In multiple-source stories, reporters sometimes have problems with "he said" or "she said." Several persons are being quoted, and reporters have to be certain it is clear who "he said" or "she said" refers to.

For example, let's take this story.

"John Monfrere was sentenced to 20 years for armed burglary by Appeals Court Judge Thomas Shingleton yesterday, and he finally got to tell his side of the story." (We clearly mean that Monfrere got to speak, but from the sentence construction it could be interpreted that the judge got his time to speak as well.)

Or, take this story.

"Marilyn Madison, Springfield's only Miss America, was in town yesterday on a promotional tour, and said she was delighted to be home again.

"Madison graduated from Central Houston high school six years ago. Her mother and grandmother still live in town. She was accompanied by her professional chaperone, Daisy Sherman, who is paid by the Miss America pageant to keep Miss Madison on schedule.

"She said her schedule is tapering off somewhat, now that the pageant is six months in the past, but is still as hectic as ever." (Who is "she?" Madison? Sherman? The mother? The grandmother? Usually the pronoun refers to the last person named.)

Remember that media style is to refer to the person with full name the first time, and by last name each time thereafter. This is called the "second reference" principle. In this case, the problem could be fixed by starting the third graph with "Madison said," or "Sherman said," or "Madison's mother said," or whatever is appropriate.

Anonymous Sources

A reporter may not be on the job very long before someone says, "Of course, all this is off the record. I was just giving you this for background information."

A reporter should ask a source, if there is any question, whether the information is not to be used—"off the record"—*before* the interview starts. A reporter with electronic gathering equipment or with a pencil and notebook is not asking questions for mere exercise, and the source should know this. All reporters must identify themselves to sources, and the source should never assume an interview is off the record.

If this occasion arises, reporters must check with their editors before granting "off the record" status. If you have called ahead to schedule an interview, and if the source knows you represent the media, she should not be asking for anonymity in the middle of an interview.

However, when this does happen, the person becomes the "anony-mess" source. This situation can lead to legal, deadline, and other problems. The reporter is best advised to stop the interview at that point, find other sources to verify whenever possible, and check with the editor immediately upon returning to the office.

While anony-mess sources usually happen at the state and national level more than the local level, persons at the local level will feed reporters information to get "even" with someone. Even if you can verify the information from other sources or through public records, you need to be very careful with this type of story. Check with your editors at each step so that you do not spend time or energy on someone else's business.

What About Bad Grammar?

What do reporters do if the source uses "ain't" or a curse word or says, "We is going to check this out?" Can they correct the grammar?

Remember that people do not have time to edit sentences as they are talking. They cannot stop to think if they have followed all of the rules of English 101 and 102.

Should reporters be able to change the "ain'ts" or "damns" in a quote as long as it does not change the essential meaning of the quote?

The Associated Press, which sets a media standard on word use because so many media belong to it, used to have a policy that said reporters and editors could change copy to avoid embarrassing a source who used bad grammar.

However, the most recent *AP Stylebook and Libel Manual* takes a tougher stance. "Never alter quotations even to correct minor grammatical errors or word usage. Casual minor tongue slips may be removed by using ellipses (. . .) but even that should be done with extreme caution. If there is a question about a quote, either don't use it or ask the speaker to clarify."

There is only slight variation to this, however.

"Do not routinely use abnormal spellings such as 'gonna' to convey regional dialects or mispronunciations. Such spellings are appropriate, however, when relevant or help to convey a desired touch in a feature."

If you wish to convey the special nature of the subject in a feature, and you can enhance this by using the way they speak to show the subject's personality, do it.

More about the *AP Stylebook and Libel Manual* in the next chapter on editing your copy.

Verification

It stands to reason that reporters should also verify the facts that they use in the story. While not directly related to attribution, they both demand a sense of fairness, accuracy, and completeness.

Attribute means to tell the reader who said something. *Verify* means to check with more than one source to be sure that the facts are correct.

No reporter should be happy to accept facts from one source. This person could be wrong, or this person might be using the reporter to "get even" with someone. Whenever possible, facts should be verified.

This does not mean that you need to verify that a double fatality accident occurred on South Ridge Road last night. What you need to be careful about is the spellings of the names of those involved, their street addresses, the types of cars that were involved, etc.

You cannot accept the word of the police on the spelling of names or addresses, for example. You are expected to double check. Police are heavily involved in investigating the accident, and may not be able to double-check spellings. You should compare the names with city directories, phone directories or whatever is available. Police and public officials are careful, but they have been known to misspell names, and the media are the ones who wind up embarrassed.

House numbers are critically important. Double check them with available directories and either check out discrepancies or talk to your editor about the problem.

Use whatever sources are available. If you are writing an obituary, check to see if your organization has a library file, or perhaps even now a computerized file, on this person. Not only can you verify that ages, spellings, addresses, etc., are correct, but also you may find a new angle about the person that should be included in the obituary.

Things to Remember

- Students are often confused and concerned about how and when to attribute statements from sources. They shouldn't be, and a few straightforward rules ought to help.

- Attribution (who said a given statement) is an important part of any story, and it gives the reader the chance to judge the value of any statement. Who said something is often the critical factor in whether that statement is believed or not.
- The most common attribution word is "said," and efforts to find fancier and more flowery words should be stopped. "Said" is a perfectly good word, and should be used three or four times out of four.
- Verifying a statement means getting someone else, preferably two or three others, to agree with a statement. No controversial stories should be run without due care in verifying all statements by at least two sources.
- In most cases, avoid people who say they will give you information, but only on an anonymous basis. Reporters deal with news as representatives of the public, and only in very rare cases should they agree to protect the names of sources. Check with the editor at every stage if someone asks for anonymity.

Practice

Write stories based on the following information, being careful to attribute properly.

Fact Set 1: Nursing Home

A press conference was held this morning at 11:00 A.M. in the lobby of the Magnolia Hill Care Center on Robinson Road. Present were Wilmer L. Robinson, owner and general manager, Darnell Valentine, builder, and Charles Jacob, director of the Chamber of Commerce. Mr. Robinson said he had just signed a contract with Valentine Builders to construct a new 100-bed community care center ("It's more than a nursing home") on property a mile west of the current nursing home. Bids were taken and opened yesterday and Valentine Builders was the low bidder. This center will have 24-hour medical care in the form of interns on the premises all day long, and will offer specialized diets and individualized care. It will cost $1.7 million and has all of the city, state, and federal approvals required. Mr. Valentine said that as a part of a different agreement, he will purchase the 40-bed Magnolia Hill home and convert it to senior citizen assisted-care apartments when the residents of Magnolia are moved to the new building. Mr. Jacob, the director of the Chamber of Commerce, said, "This is a good day for the city. We will have a new facility employing an additional 50 persons, and this makes us very proud."

Fact Set 2: Trashed

Bernie Hollingsworth is a retired investor who deals in coins, real estate, and industrial development. Yesterday, for reasons that are still not clear, Bernie got to the bank too late to deposit $30,000 in cash. It came from several commissions, from a sale of stock, and other sources. When Bernie got home, his wife was out shopping, and Bernie put the cash in his coat pocket and hung up the coat. He then went to sleep. When his wife came home, the coat had fallen to the floor, and "thinking he needed a new one anyway," she threw the jacket into the garbage. When Bernie got up, he asked about the jacket, which by that time had been collected by the city crew. Bernie, his wife and two retired friends spent 36 hours in the city landfill digging up the approximate spot where the city crew said the jacket should be. Bernie said he "could definitely be more careful and will get a key to the night depository next time." His wife said, "I am beside myself. This is ridiculous. I am so embarrassed." John Bennett, who manages the landfill, says "it is unusual for people to search for things, but I do remember a professor who spent several hours trying to find a dissertation once in the 1970s. He did eventually find it, however." And Bernie, by presstime, had found "about 90 percent" of what he had lost, and hadn't given up on the other 10 percent.

Fact Set 3: Casino

A year ago a major East Coast development company came to the resort area of northern Michigan and asked the city of Indian Village for permission to build a casino. The area has lakes and streams in the summer and skiing and hunting in the winter, and is popular as a resort. In addition, Native Americans live in the area and have permits to run casinos. Derek Hightower of the Atlantic Investment Company said Mayor Richard Fisher told him at that time that he would get legal permission for the casino "within six months at the outside." Fisher said he has all of the necessary permits except the governor's, "and it looks now like he is not going to budge on this. This would have been a major plus for this area." Hightower announced today that Atlantic Investment was seeking a new site in a southern state near a country music attraction to build their $2 million casino. "This is not a ploy. We have tried for a year and we cannot get permits. We have to go where we are wanted."

Hightower said a major national hotel chain, which did not wish to be identified, has already been working in the southern state to get permissions. A spokesperson for the governor said, "We have no comment at this time. We understand the situation here, but we do not think Atlantic Investment understands the mood of our state."

20
One More Time: Editing Your Final Copy and Catching Errors Before You Release Your Story

In This Chapter

When should you make corrections—as you write or after you
write?
The myth of the spell checking systems on computers.
Understanding the basics of Associated Press style.

YOU ARE now ready to turn in your story.
You have gathered the information, outlined and/or thought it
through, chosen the proper form, and written and rewritten your
copy.

You have used a form that is standard for media, double
spaced, one thought per paragraph, with some copy editing symbols
if it is in hard copy form. (See chapter 3 for copy editing symbols
and discussions on form.)

Now you want to check it one final time before turning it in to
your instructor or editor. What do you look for?

Write Straight Through or Edit as You Go?

The answer to this depends on whether you have been correcting
grammar and spelling on each draft. If you have, you may have only
minor changes to watch for.

However, if you have been correcting your grammar and style
mistakes each time (we will discuss Associated Press style shortly),
the writing progress will have been slowed down considerably.

When you begin writing rough copy, you ought to be thinking
about writing the story and telling the reader what the main point
and the supporting points are. If you stop in the middle of a
sentence to correct the spelling, you slow the thought processes and
ruin the smoothness of the story. Spelling is important, and it must
be corrected, but write your rough draft while the main story points
are fresh in your mind.

This permits you to think of story flow, transitions, quotes, and
examples while they are fresh in your mind. By the time you write
paragraph 10, paragraphs 2 and 3 are still fresh in your mind, so you
can tie the story together nicely.

Checking Spelling

If you have stopped several times between paragraph 2 and paragraph
10 to correct spellings or check grammar points, the story starts to
fall apart. It becomes a series of unconnected quotes, examples, and
facts, and you lose the strength and punch that story had to offer.

This applies especially to feature stories, which are more complex in their structure, and need to have a more complete sense of unity. It is also important when doing inverted pyramid and other formula stories since all parts tie together.

If your computer has a spell checking system, use it after you have been through several drafts, not with each draft. Remember that spell checking systems do not catch every error, although they do help enormously. A single letter standing alone, which may have been typed in error, is often passed as correct by many good spell checkers. Some do not differentiate between to, too, and two, and others will permit "the the" to pass uncorrected. You may have typed it twice, but each time it was correct. Spell checkers are a great advance, but they are not the final word.

There are countless problem words that are not recognized by spellcheckers—fire marshal (right) and fire marshall (wrong). One of the runners is (not are). The criteria are correct (the singular is criterion). Different from, not different than.

This is the time to look for Volkswagen, not Volkswagon, and the most troublesome sets in the English language—its and it's; its and their; and to, too, and two.

The to, too, and two situation is not that complicated. The writer needs to stop and check it each time.

Its and it's is a problem because it does not follow other rules of grammar. In my opinion, it is the most common grammar problem for students. It's means it is, plain and simple.

Its without the apostrophe is where the rule goes wrong. Most possessives have an apostrophe, but this one does not. So stop momentarily each time you proofread and ask yourself if the word is a contraction for it is (it's) or a possessive (its).

A very closely related problem is that its and their are not similar. The team held its pre-game meeting, but [each player made their own plans.] The word to use with groups is its, because a group is singular. The word to use with individuals is their, because more than one individual is being referred to, and they are making separate plans.

This is not meant to be a comprehensive section, but to remind you that you are now responsible for any grammar you missed earlier in school. Have the *AP Stylebook* on hand to check.

Change Once, Check Twice

Remember, each time you correct one part of a sentence, paragraph, or story, it may cause an error in another part of the sentence, paragraph, or story. If you change the lead to say, "Three men have been arrested" when you previously said two, you then have to change the second sentence to list three names rather than two.

Perhaps you are doing a story on deadline, and someone else is helping you. They give you updated information, which you just barely have time to include in your story, and you get it in. But if that update changes another part of the story, you are well-advised to read the copy one more time.

The number of times you read the story for final corrections depends on how much time you have—and how much patience. If you wait until the very last minute to write the first draft, you are going to miss a deadline because checking and correcting takes time.

Accuracy, Accuracy, Accuracy

Joseph Pulitzer, nineteenth century publisher for whom the Pulitzer prizes are named, once said the three most important things in newspapering were accuracy, accuracy, accuracy.

You have checked and verified your facts while writing the story, but you still have one final time to check spellings, street numbers, facts, assumptions, and any other element in a story. As you are writing, you may quickly go over a fact in the interest of completing the draft and making a coherent story. After the first draft is completed, you use the phone book or other directories to check addresses and names, use an almanac to check an important date, or call the police department again to verify the unusual spelling of a name.

Major national magazines have research departments that check facts, even the most mundane. Smaller outlets with very small staffs have no one but the reporter to check this information. In light of the growing number of lawsuits, the most important thing a reporter can do is check, check, check. "When in doubt, check it out" is a standard rule in newsrooms.

As you get close to turning in your copy, and control of what is on the screen passes from your hands to those of an editor, you must keep that person informed of possible changes. If someone is going to call information in, or is checking on something, tell the editor. If the spelling is unusual, tell the editor and tell him which sources you used to check the spellings.

Whenever possible, check your library, usually called the morgue, to see if other stories have been done on this person or event. This also helps verify spellings, dates of birth, previous honors, and other stories. These libraries are now being transferred to computers, and in the foreseeable future, reporters will be able to check the "morgue" files from their own computers. It saves a lot of time, but adds that much more responsibility to the reporter.

Computers are much faster than manual typewriters. But because they are faster, most reporters are required to check facts, set style and size of type, write heads, and do more of the proofreading than ever before. This adds to the deadline pressure, with the reporter doing jobs that ten to 20 years ago were done by two or three persons in the newsroom. You must factor this in when you get down to the last few minutes before deadline.

Cliches, Redundancies, and Related Problems

We have previously discussed cliches (the good ole days, giving 110 percent, experience is the best teacher) and redundancies (Easter Sunday, Jewish rabbi, own your own home). This is the time to check for these and other grammatical and word problems.

Keeping Opinion Out

This is the last chance to check that you have not used a cheerleading ending, or called something "exciting" or someone "exceptional." Most adjectives and adverbs, in the words of Mark Twain, need to be "killed on the spot." They add nothing to a story, and they put the reporter on the hot seat.

Reporters should try to be as objective as possible, and words of this nature do not belong in a story.

Story Form and Structure

Make sure you do not have paragraphs that are nine or ten lines long on the computer or the typewriter. These paragraphs· will translate into twice as many lines in newspapers, and they will be too long for radio and television.

With computers, it is easy to cut paragraphs down to size, eliminate unnecessary words, and keep the story moving. Try to keep to one clear thought per sentence, and perhaps two or three sentences as a maximum for each paragraph.

Associated Press Style

Although this discussion appears at the end of this chapter, you may need to study AP style much earlier in the semester.

Associated Press style is the standard for uniformity and consistency in copy and word usage in the media, although each paper and station may have some local variations. You are advised to understand AP Style as thoroughly as possible in your first course, and to have a copy of the *AP Stylebook and Libel Manual* with you when writing news stories.

Keep it right along with your dictionary and thesaurus, and no one will ever look down on you. No one can spell all words correctly. Smart media people check those words they are not 100 percent sure about.

"Style" as used in this sense has nothing to do with flair or elegance in writing or in clothing. It pertains to consistency, such as agreeing on a spelling where two spellings are permitted in the dictionary. It has to do with everyone using numbers in the same fashion so that copy sent from New York, London, or Tokyo can be understood and processed at any AP member throughout the world. Style refers to everyone being "on the same page" as far as common usage problems are concerned.

The 340-page *Stylebook and Libel Manual* is organized like a dictionary. It covers countless words that need to be defined or clarified. (How much is in a long ton? Do you need to use California after Los Angeles? Which countries are called the Low Countries?)

It also has the generally accepted rules on when to use capital letters and when not, when to abbreviate and when not, a review of punctuation rules, a section on libel, and sections on how to file stories on the AP wire.

It also includes a special section grouping entries on sports, another on business terms, and a third on computer terms, since so many have been added to our vocabulary in the past ten years.

The "trick," if there is one, to understanding the *AP Stylebook* is to know that like a dictionary it cannot be memorized. [Understand its major sections and know which section to turn to.]

Beginners will spin some wheels trying to find the proper term to use, whether attorney or lawyer (either is permitted); ax or axe (use ax); or pistol, revolver, or Saturday Night Special (they are not interchangeable).

The student who first turns to the *AP Stylebook and Libel Manual* may be confused. However, when the student begins to realize that words have particular meanings and many of them are very specific, she will begin to look upon the *AP Stylebook* as a referee or the last word in a discussion. It is easier to check things out quickly in the *Stylebook* than to try to memorize too much.

However, the student should also know that there are some general rules that will make life much easier in the newswriting business.

338

Please note these are simplifications and each section should be checked carefully for specific rules.

Abbreviations

Journalists try to get expert sources or eyewitnesses to tell what happened at an event. The reader wants to know who this person is, or what his or her title is. In general, abbreviate the title before the name, and spell it out after the name. "Lt. Col. William Farnsworth, information officer of the 530th Gunnery Command, said . . ." However, it would be "William Farnsworth, a Lieutenant Colonel in the 530th Gunnery Command, said . . ." Abbreviate titles before the name, spell out after the name.

Addresses

AP style for consistency is to abbreviate the words "avenue," "boulevard," and "street" only if there is a number accompanying the address. You would abbreviate 1600 Pennsylvania Ave., but you would spell out "He lives on Pennsylvania Avenue." This is important because these words are often used in identifying who a person is, where he lives, or where certain accidents or other actions took place.

The words "drive," "road," "alley," and "terrace" (which are not that long anyway) are always spelled out, whether accompanied by a number or not.

Capitalization

In general, use as few capitals as possible. Use them with proper nouns or company names; with specific names (Democratic Party in caps, but a political party in lower case); the Arkansas River, but a nearby river (no specific name); and in all accepted punctuation cases (the first word of a sentence, etc.).

Numbers

In normal usage, either the word "one" or the numeral "1" would be correct. Media usage, however, is not that easy. Unless otherwise specified, numbers below 10 are spelled out, numbers from 10 to 999,999 use the numerals, and a different rule exists for millions and above. Because adding numerous zeroes would confuse most readers, AP style is to use 1.24 million, or $45.6 billion.

But there are many exceptions. Do not start a sentence with a number, except if it is a year, as in "1984 was a good year for the Tigers."

Ages are expressed in numerals, even below 10, as in "a 6-year-old daughter," and temperatures below zero are expressed as minus 10, not −10.

Punctuation

Admit it or not, no one knows all the rules of punctuation. The *AP Stylebook* has a special section, starting with ampersand, apostrophe, brackets, and colon, and concluding with periods, questions marks, and quotation marks. Reporters can brush up on what they need to know in a matter of minutes before they turn in their copy.

This well-organized section also includes the troublesome commas, hyphens, semicolons, and apostrophes that many writers have troubles with.

Trademarks and Brand Names

I once wrote a headline using the words "Who's Who," a shortened form of Who's Who in American Colleges and Universities. Within three days I received a letter from a law firm telling me that Who's Who was a protected, copyrighted name that referred to an organization other than the one I had referred to. A clarification was requested, and was run within the week. Other papers have become confused over the difference between Realtor, a member of the National Association of Realtors, and a real estate agent, which is the term AP style prefers.

America has a very competitive business environment. To refer to someone's Reeboks rather than tennis shoes may harm the Reebok firm, and they could ask for a retraction. Brand names are widely promoted and heavily advertised, and owners of these names are anxious to protect their investments.

There are hundreds and hundreds of brand names, trademarks, and service marks. The reporter is urged to watch for lists of them available in many trade publications, and to use generic terms whenever possible.

Use soft drink, not Coca Cola or Diet Pepsi.
Use chocolate cookies, not Oreos.
Use tear gas in an aerosol container, not Mace.
Use simulated leather rather than Naugahyde.

The annual "Trademarks and the Press" special section in *Editor and Publisher* magazine reminds reporters and editors that *all* of the following are brand names and should not be used generically:

Professional Secretaries Week (not National Secretaries Week); Weight Watchers; Realtors; Chanel; Xerox (use copying machine); Vise Grip (use pliers); Gore-Tex; Kleenex; Crayola; Nabisco; American Express; Kodak; Weed Eater; Little League; and Sweet N'Low.

Unless there is a definite reason for using the brand name, as in the description of a crime scene or the background in a feature story, stick with the generic terms.

It is important to know that all copy must be accurate, correct, and follow AP style. But it is up to you as to how and when to check for accuracy and how and when to check for AP style.

If you worry about grammar and style as you are writing each draft, it will slow down your progress and probably ruin your concentration and flow.

You are advised to learn and use AP style and have it become second nature to you. The quicker you learn it, the less trouble you will have in your newswriting career.

However, you must also know how to write well, quickly, and with interesting quotes and examples. If applying AP style each time you write harms you, your effort should be on writing first and editing for style after your final draft.

Be sure you allow enough time to do the editing after your final draft. This means budgeting your time in a manner most reporters have not yet mastered. It also means developing ulcers and stress when they could possibly be avoided.

Things to Remember

- You can never check your copy too often, but you only have a certain amount of time. Use it wisely.
- Do not stop writing a story to make a correction.
- If you make a correction, be sure there is not some related part in a story that must also be changed.
- Know that Associated Press style will be the basis for consistency and accuracy in your writing throughout your career. Learn it, refer to it, and keep a copy of the *Stylebook* with you wherever you work in the media.

21
Personalizing and Foreshadowing: Adding Life and Depth to Your Stories

Don Lee

In This Chapter

Two key concepts can help you write with more power and interest almost from the beginning.

One is personalizing, the idea of telling a story through people, of using their individual stories as examples of a larger concept.

Another is foreshadowing, telling the reader early that there is going to be a problem later in the story.

THIS IS a step beyond the beginning newswriting manual, but writers need to know how to make copy as good as it can be. They also need to know some special advanced techniques that can be incorporated into their stories. These techniques are not that difficult, but they require students to think about their stories in terms other than formula or feature.

These steps include *personalizing* or using the human element; *foreshadowing* or "warning" the reader what is likely to come; a *sidebar* or additional story that adds new or related information to the main story; and *continuing* or second and third day stories.

We will start with personalizing, to make the story more interesting and readable for your audience.

Please notice that the stories used as examples for specific items are also examples of good writing. These stories demonstrate how a longer story develops, and the specific benefits of details, quotes, attribution, numbers, repetition, etc.

Personalizing

Turn on the national television news some evening or read your favorite national magazine. Watch how they handle feature stories. Follow what they do to make written or electronic stories jump out and get the attention they deserve.

Television networks and national magazines are excellent at humanizing stories, of giving the people angle of a story. You can do this with feature stories, issue stories, and meeting stories—if you pay attention.

Personalizing works as follows:

If you are doing a story on a new federal program cutback, talk to someone who will be influenced by the cutback. If veteran's benefits are to be reduced, talk to a local veteran's association, find out what an individual person will have to do when the program changes. For example, if the payment to veterans will go down by 20 percent, ask how much that will be for a veteran, and what it will mean to him.

Here's another example. Many campuses have an office to help students work out plans for a semester or a year on another campus. Most students do not know of these opportunities because they don't read the fine print in the catalogs.

You could personalize this story by talking to students on campus who have come from other states, and you could find out how many of your school's students have gone to other campuses. Some of them are likely to be back on campus, so you could interview them. Explain the program by showing how people have become a part of that program, and use their words to tell others the strengths and weaknesses of being at another campus.

This is showing through experiences, not telling about programs. The difference is huge. Showing people's experiences makes a program come alive. Rewriting material from a brochure puts readers to sleep.

People are the most important ingredients of any story, yet reporters who cover government, schools, or businesses often focus on policies or procedures. Technically, these writers are correct, because the media have to understand what plans or changes government and businesses are considering. But readers will understand it much better if you put it in people terms.

Robert Davis, now with the *USA Today* news section but then with the *Fort Collins Coloradoan*, won a medical reporting award for Gannett Newspapers in 1991 for a seven-part series about a man who waited more than a year for a heart-lung transplant. The first of the seven articles, describing the problems and pluses with organ transplants, was entitled "Into your hands I commend my spirit."

Davis personalizes the story and foreshadows the problems that might develop later in the story.

> Dave Benefiel's skinny arms are outstretched so that doctors can poke needles into his veins.
>
> He lies on the cold operating room table with a cloth over his groin.
>
> He prays: "Into your hands I commend my spirit."
>
> The 31-year-old Fort Collins man is about to undergo a heart-lung transplant.
>
> [The first four graphs indicate the seriousness of the situation. Clearly placed clues such as "skinny arms," prayer, and transplant give readers an idea of the up-to-the minute situation. Davis then provides a brief look at Dave Benefiel's medical history with the next three paragraphs.]
>
> A genetic lung disease has destroyed his heart and lungs.
>
> After a lifetime of failing health, he has put his life into

the hands of God and transplant surgeon Dr. Jim Narrod.

Narrod says Dave has a 30 percent chance of making it. Dave hopes if he dies, God will take care of him.

Heart lung transplants are rare and risky.

This will be the fourth time the procedure has been attempted in Colorado. The first two patients died soon after surgery. At the time of Dave's surgery, on the afternoon of April 21, the third has survived almost two months.

Dave is one of four people in Colorado and more than 250 in the country waiting for a heart-lung transplant.

[These specific facts tell readers about the extent of the problem.]

Of the 13,290 transplants performed across the country in 1989, 70 were heart-lungs.

For comparison, kidneys are most common. There were 8,886 kidney transplants performed last year. Colorado hospitals transplanted 129 kidneys in 1989.

Each day more than 20,000 people hope their transplants will come before their death.

[This series was a long time in the writing, and Davis is careful to place the story in its proper context by giving appropriate figures and numbers. Despite the odds, which have been given, there is still a reason for going through this kind of difficult surgery. Davis outlines that next.]

Dave's chances at a new and improved life free of debilitating disease is possible because of a death.

In some other Denver hospital, a heart and a set of lungs are being surgically removed from a person who, for some devastating and sudden reason, has lost it all—a job, a family, good health.

Somebody who hours or days before had everything Dave Benefiel wants.

Life.

The heart and lungs that Dave Benefiel almost died waiting for now have his name on them.

And the surgeon Dave trusts with his life will haul the Fort Collins man's future back in an ice-filled Igloo cooler.

But while Dave and his wife, Linda, march into the transplant center at St. Luke's Hospital in Denver confident and full of hope, a family in another hospital mourns.

Bob Kourtakis of Westchester-Rockland Newspapers in New York wrote a program anniversary story on Title IX's first ten years when he worked for the *Port-Huron (Mich.) Times-Herald*. Title IX is the law Congress passed in 1972 to provide equal opportunity for women athletes. (Mr. Kourtakis died in 1993.)

For the most part, Kourtakis found, the act has worked well because women athletes have been given more equal opportunities.

But women coaches and administrators in colleges have been replaced by men in many cases.

Kourtakis personalizes his story by comparing two athletes. Let us follow the development of this story to see how it is constructed and how the writer supports the conclusions he made from his study.

Glen Rice and Tonya Edwards have followed an uncannily similar road.

Both were basketball stars at Flint Northwestern High School. Both parlayed their talent into athletic scholarships, Rice going to Michigan and Edwards to Tennessee. Both played on teams that won national championships this month.

But their paths are about to part.

Rice's future in sports includes an array of possibilities—the National Basketball Association (he is with the Miami Heat) coaching, or perhaps some related administrative job.

Edwards' road in sports is nearing a dead end.

Ironically, it is a dead end that was paved with the best of intentions.

[This is the nut graph, also foreshadowing what is coming ahead. These graphs must be located within the first few graphs of the story so that readers have an idea of what is going to happen next, or why the story is being written or produced. Next, Kourtakis brings readers up to date on the history of the program—not too much but just enough.]

In 1972, Title IX promised a new era for the female student-athlete.

Congress passed the law to allow equal opportunity for the woman athlete, and the 10,000 scholarships available to females each year—compared to none before Title IX—is evidence of its impact.

The basic objective has been met. Women's athletics have never had more prestige, more power, more opportunities.

But an unforeseen side effect has emerged: Many doors to careers in sports after graduation today are being slammed shut.

In the 17 years since Title IX's birth, the percentage of women in control of athletic programs has shrunk drastically and dramatically.

Call it the ultimate irony. As women's sports grows bigger, the role of female coaches and administrators is diminishing.

[This is not opinion. It is a statement of fact to be supported shortly by figures.]

"Title IX has been disastrous to women interested in sports careers," says women's athletic director Donna Lopiano, who leads one of the country's top female programs at the University of Texas.

[Attributed quote from someone recognized nationally for her experience and leadership in this specialized area.]

There's no question it has severely worsened their situation in terms of employment of women who want to continue in sports after college.

Many critics blame sex discrimination for the decline.

Whatever the reason, the statistics are alarming. Consider:

- In 1972, nine out of every 10 collegiate women's teams were coached by a female. Now the figure is four out of 10.
- In 1972, 90 percent of women's programs were led by females. In 1988, only 16 percent of the women's collegiate athletic directors were female.
- Of all administrative jobs within collegiate women's programs, only 29 percent are held by females.
- In nearly a third of all women's collegiate programs, there is no female in any administrative or coaching job.

The exclusion of women has trickled down to the high schools as well. In 1976, nearly 60 percent of Michigan's girls' high school teams were coached by females. Today, that has been cut in half to just 29 percent.

And the situation is only getting worse.

For example, the number of jobs available for coaches of women's teams increased by 42 last year. Women, though, held seven fewer jobs than in 1967.

"I can't really say that Title IX has helped the overall picture," says Annalies Knoppers, a volleyball coach at Michigan State before Title IX. "There's more opportunity for women to participate now, but the positives are only for the players. After you play for four years, that's it."

[Reinforcing a thought given at the end of the lead.]

"It's actually limited the opportunity."

Or, as Kentucky women's athletic director Kathy DeBoer put it, "The bottom has fallen out of the coaching market."

Many point to the shrinking numbers of women in high level positions as clear evidence of discrimination.

Fifteen complaints of sexual discrimination have been received by the Department of Education's Office of Civil Rights in the past year from 11 schools.

"The reason for the decline is sex discrimination in employment—it's that simple," Lopiano says. "Women are just as qualified, if not more, to coach, yet men are unwilling to hire them.

"The fact is that if you are a male athletic director, you won't even consider a woman for a job. They (men) would rather go to the old-boys system, where white males call on other white males to fill vacancies.

"You can apply all you want, but in the real world when you have a position to fill, you don't sit and wait for the resumes to come in. You go out and get the person you want and get them to come."

Discrimination remains just one prong of a complicated problem.

[Transition to a related subject, getting the reader to ask "What is the problem?"]

Michigan State women's basketball coach Karen Langeland says her team is made up mostly of business majors—thus the odds of one of her players moving into coaching is slim.

St. Clair County Community College women's basketball coach Dave Seddon has just one physical educational major among his 10 players, but says two others have expressed interest in coaching.

"I've always encouraged my players to continue in athletics after their playing days are over," he says. "If they're qualified, they'll get a job. There is a great need for women coaches right now.

"Some of these girls need a female role model that they can look up to. In many cases, that's missing right now."

[Excellent quote, helps justify why there are more women needed in coaching.]

DeBoer, who also coaches volleyball at Kentucky, sees the same problem with her team.

"Socially, the woman is still considered the one who brings up families," she said. "We should be getting more candidates because we now have this large feeder system, but many of them do not want to go into athletics because it doesn't pay enough or because it is too time-consuming. They take other roads.

"I don't have one single kid in education or physical education. So where are the new coaches going to come from?"

Title IX's ironic dilemma has gone largely unnoticed because it occurs during a period of unprecedented interest and funding of women's collegiate athletics.

[This introduces a section on positives about women's athletics to help balance the story.]

More than 156,000 women will participate in women's sports this year. Before Title IX passed, that number was just 16,000.

Additionally, there are now 10,000 scholarships in 24 different sports available for the woman athlete, compared to virtually none in 1971.

"I remember giving out one or two scholarships for $1,000," Knoppers says. "Now they are all full-ride or half-ride. Those are some great strides."

Another sure sign of progress: Women's basketball programs are suddenly big business on campus, drawing the same money-making demands from athletics directors as their male counterparts have for years.

In the process, budgets for women's athletics have mushroomed. The University of Texas, for example, set aside $70,000 for women's sports in 1976. Today, the Lady Longhorn's women's program works with $3.5 million annually.

This new popularity also spills over into network television coverage. ESPN televised six regular season games and four tournament games last month while CBS's live Sunday afternoon telecast of the Tennessee-Auburn final drew a 5.4 rating. CBS's Cleveland-Boston NBA game, which preceded it, drew a 4.7 rating.

[Note the specific details, which add strength to the argument.]

"There isn't as big an audience as for the men's games," ESPN spokesman Dave Knegler says, "but there is an audience."

The interest isn't confined to the television screen either. Perennial women's powers such as Texas and Iowa average 10,000 fans a game.

"If you would have told me 10 years ago that we would get this kind of exposure and attendance, I would have said you were crazy," Michigan State's Langeland says. "It's amazing the way the sport has grown.

"Title IX opened the door to this in all sports."

Still, Title IX is seen as a disappointment in the eyes of

administrators and coaches who experienced the inequality of the early 1970s.

So much more was expected. And, they feel, so much more needs to be done.

"From the standpoint of the participant, there is no doubt there has been progress," Lopiano says. "But when you begin thinking about coaching and administrative possibilities, you begin to ask, 'At what price?'"

[Kourtakis leads the reader to develop his or her opinion. Do you think the price has been too high? Is the jury still out?]

Foreshadowing

A lot of reading is for enjoyment. Writers who understand this know that the good reader is willing to go along with them as they build suspense into a feature story, but only so far.

If you expect a reader to go along with you through a story, you need to give hints about what is coming. No one wants to read a happy story about someone, only to find out at the very end that the person has died. The reader deserves to be told that this is an obituary story that celebrates the person's life but also respects the finality of death.

The writer does this by giving clues early in the story. These clues tell the reader that this is a special story because it has a special conflict—a struggle between man and disease, man and alcohol, or man and man, as the following three stories indicate.

What follows are three extended sections of three outstanding news stories. Two are from the same paper, the *Roanoke Times & World-News* in Virginia. Note not only the foreshadowing but also the excellent writing techniques.

Mary Bishop of the *Roanoke Times & World-News* did a series of stories on the use and control of pesticides in the state of Virginia. The series was a Pulitzer finalist and won the George Polk Award for outstanding journalism. You know from the headline ("Pests, toxins and risks: Fumigation 'loaded gun,' experts says") that the series is about pesticides.

Watch as she leads into her story by telling the reader about the victims and one incident that made the entire series important. Note also the short sentences, the clear thoughts and the careful use of every word.

GALAX, Va.—Hubert and Freida Watson's house was one of the showplaces of Galax.

They designed the white-columned brick colonial in the early 1970s with architectural details they got from trips to Williamsburg and a Tidewater plantation.

They furnished it with Victorian antiques. An out-of-state professional decorated it.

They installed an elevator.

Solid walnut paneling went into the dining room.

The den was paneled with wormy chestnut.

Hubert Watson cut and dried the wood himself so it would be just right.

Wood, after all, was his life's work.

Until they retired, Hubert Watson owned Sawyers' Furniture Co. here. Freida Watson, the company vice president, ran the office.

So it was no small matter when a man with Orkin Exterminating Co. in Roanoke told them that wood-boring beetles were eating their house.

[Foreshadowing]

The Watsons gave the go-ahead for an $8,000 fumigation.

On Sept. 25, 1986, the men from Orkin put a huge red-orange tarpaulin over the Watson's five-bedroom house at the corner of Roseland Lane and Bona Vista Lane.

It was an astonishing sight—like a giant fluttering piece of fabric art. The Watsons' next door neighbor took a picture.

The Watsons abandoned their home—usually buzzing with their 13 grandchildren—and stayed with a daughter overnight.

Orkin workers pumped the house full of Vikane, or sulfuryl fluoride. The colorless, almost odorless gas permeates wood—furniture, woodwork, everything—to kill wood-eating bugs.

The former Orkin sales supervisor remembers reassuring the Watsons about the fumigation when he settled with them on a price.

"...I met the people and the last thing I said to the people before I left their home was, 'It's not dangerous, don't worry,'" Emmette Lee Farmer testified in an unrelated lawsuit that year.

[Foreshadowing]

Another Orkin worker said that the Watsons could move back in after 3 the afternoon of September 26. And they did.

Within a few hours, according to federal court documents, the Watsons were sick. They experienced nausea, chills, weakness—all symptoms of Vikane poisoning.

On Sept. 28 Hubert Watson had a severe spell of coughing. His wife called the rescue squad, but he was dead by the time he got to the hospital. Hubert Howard Watson was 73 years old.

Richard Haskin, a neighbor who visited Freida Watson shortly after Hubert Watson died, recalled that she needed help in getting to the phone to take her condolence calls. Haskin said she was weak and coughing.

By the time of her husband's funeral, Freida Settle Watson, 65, lay dying in Twin County Hospital. She died Oct. 2.

A state medical examiner says Vikane killed the Watsons.

"...A state pesticide inspector testified that Orkin workers acknowledged not using an air monitor to see if the Watson's house was safe for occupancy, as recommended on the Vikane label."

This is just one part of a several-part series, but notice the clear, short sentences, the lack of any opinion, and the definite statement of the problem. Readers feel as though they know the people involved in this tragedy.

A tragedy of a different sort has overtaken the Crow Indians in Montana. While their basketball teams have been very successful, the players have not done well in life after basketball. Gary Smith uses the foreshadowing technique extremely well in this excerpt from the beginning of a 12-page story that appeared in *Sports Illustrated* on the plight of this group of Native Americans.

SHADOW OF A NATION
by Gary Smith
John Papanek, managing editor; Chris Hunt, story editor.
February 18, 1991

[Smith describes how on March 24, 1983, an eight mile caravan of cars headed from the Valley of the Big Horn in Montana to Billings for a state basketball tournament.]

The boys stared through their windows at the caravan. There was bone quiet in the bus. It was, as if, all at once, the boys had sensed the size of this moment...and what awaited each of them once this moment was done.

In one seat, his nose pressed to the window, was one of Hardin High's starting guards, Everette Walks, a boy with unnaturally large hands who had never known his father. In a few weeks he would drop out of school, then cirrhosis would begin to lay waste his mother. He would wind up pushing a mop at 2 A.M. in a restaurant on the Crow reservation.

In another seat sat one of the forwards, an astounding leaper named Miles Fighter. He too had grown up with no father, and recently his mother had died of cirrhosis. In just a few weeks, he would be unemployed and drinking heavily.

Not far away sat the other starting guard, Jo Jo Pretty Paint, a brilliant long range shooter, a dedicated kid—just a few minutes before a game with Miles City, his coach had found him alone, crouched, shuffling, covering an invisible opponent in the locker room shower. In two years Pretty Paint would go out drinking one evening, get into a car and career over an embankment. He would go to his grave with a photograph of himself in his uniform, clutching a basketball.

Hunching nearby, all knees and elbows and shoulders, was Darren Big Medicine, the easygoing center. Sixteen months after Pretty Paint's death, he would leave a party after a night of drinking, fall asleep as he sped along a reservation road, drive into a ditch and die.

And then there was Takes Enemy. . . .

"Thunder in the Coal Fields," is a story by Dwayne Yancey, a 1990 Pulitzer Prize finalist, also from the *Roanoke Times & World-News*. The paper published a 16-page supplement April 29, 1990, recapping an 11-month strike by the union coal miners in the western tip of Virginia. It was concluded after many bitter incidents just before midnight on New Year's Eve of 1989.

There were 13 parts to the series in the supplement. This is the beginning of Part 1, and note how it foreshadows the coming of the strike in personal terms.

The day Richard Dishman figured out there was going to be a strike is as vivid in his memory as a jagged flash of lightning.

It was one day in 1985. He was working second shift at the Hurricane Creek mine in Russell County. He was running the supply motor when his supervisor, Earl Hess, hollered at him and a buddy to come and share supper.

[Note the tone in the writing—"hollered at him and a buddy to come and share supper." This is colloquial, this is the way they talk, it is appropriate for the story. It does not make anyone look foolish. Don't paraphrase to something formal like "his supervisor had asked him and a co-worker to speak with him over lunch." This is coal mining country and readers not only know something is going to happen but also they are gettin' it straight from the writer.]

Hess didn't like to eat alone. He also didn't like to lie. Hess was a preacher and he didn't want to be a part of what he knew was coming.

[Foreshadowing]

"He just up and told us," Dishman recalls.

[Yancey gives readers a brief background on union-miner relations in the area.]

It was the damnedest story Dishman had ever heard. Pittston Coal's roots ran as deep as the precious mineral itself. Dishman had worked for Pittston nearly 30 years: his daddy 42 years before that—"long before they were union" is the way his son remembers it. The United Mine Workers had had troubles with Pittston over the years, sure, but no more than with any other coal company. By now, the UMW was a way of life in Southwest Virginia, as rugged and durable as the little country churches like the one Earl Hess pastored.

[Here is the nut graph, the summary graph the writer has been leading up to.]

Now, Hess told Dishman, the company planned to change all that. Pittston had been dealing with the union as a part of the Bituminous Coal Operators Association, a nationwide group set up to sign a single contract with the UMW to make sure that all companies, and all workers, got the same shake. The UMW's new president, Richard Trumka, recently had negotiated an extension of the BCOA contract until February 1988—without a strike, the first time that had happened in more than 20 years. But when the contract expired, Hess now said, Pittston intended to pull out of the BCOA. Moreover, Hess told his men, "they were gonna bust this union."

The mere mention of such a thing was enough to make a man shudder.

[Yancey uses examples to show, not tell, why the union men felt so strongly about the union.]

Throughout Appalachia, the UMW is revered as the institution that lifted miners from poverty and into the middle class. To hear miners tell it, it's also the only thing that keeps them from slipping back to the days of working for a dollar a day and owing their life to the company store.

"I remember when I was a boy, my daddy left before daylight," Dishman recalls. "He'd come in way after dark and he'd be so tired, he'd just lay in the kitchen and we'd rub his back."

In those days, miners were paid by how much coal they loaded, not by the hour. If a roof caved in and a miner had to spend days hauling out rock before he could pick his way back to the seam, that was tough luck. Dishman remembers once his father was sloshing around in water up to his knees and begged a foreman to pump the mine dry. The boss refused. "There's another barefoot man waitin' to take your job."

Dishman didn't need to be reminded what the union had brought him. He grew up in a company house that wasn't much better than a shack. Now he lived in a nice house on a hill, overlooking the Clinch River. He was able to send a son to college. He could look forward to pension and generous health benefits. Things were comfortable, as comfortable as life can get in the coalfields.

These are the first ten paragraphs of the 16-page supplement. They focus on individuals who reappear throughout the story and they summarize the depth of their feelings, which helps explain the length and difficulty of the strike that followed.

But this lead works in an interesting way, letting readers relate to the people who are involved and see the story from their side. The other side is also presented as the story evolves.

A team of *Dallas Morning News* reporters used personalizing to help tell the story of an entire section of the United States, the 11-state area known as the Great Plains. The series was a winner of the 1991 Oscars in Agriculture award.

A team of journalists covered 15,000 miles of Plains highways, meeting with and photographing more than 400 residents. The region's problems are grave. Some of the towns in the heartland probably will die. But places that historically have been closed are opening to outsiders in an attempt to blend new ideas with old-fashioned survival skills.

THE PLAINS: NEW VISIONS OF AN OLD FRONTIER
Dallas Morning News
by Thomas J. Watts and Steven H. Lee;
project editor John H. Ostdick,
photographer Catherine Krueger

Chard Hirsch has conquered the anxiety that ripples across much of American's vast Great Plains.

She remembers looking out the window of her shop that day in 1984 when so many people were gathered around the bank she thought it had been robbed.

It was worse. The bank had failed.

During six months in the mid-1980s, the outlook for this community of 3,900 residents was as bleak as the Sand Hills surrounding it. Twenty-six businesses, including the two other banks, closed. Other companies were threatened. Friends began moving away.

Broken Bow fought like hell to survive.

It's succeeding. And it's not alone.

[To introduce a section on how tough life has been on the farm in the last 10 years, the authors personalize.]

The 1980s were not good for Kiefer Cauble.

A college-educated cotton framer, he followed the bigger-is-better dictum a decade ago and expanded his farm to 1,500 acres of red soil near Roby, Texas, bought new tillage equipment, and installed new fertilizer tanks. Bankers were very supportive.

But overproduction severely depressed prices in 1981. He lost $100,000.

The next year, his crop was destroyed twice by hail. He suffered more losses.

By the end of the decade, Mr. Cauble said, he had lost more than $500,000. He was bankrupt and out of farming. He now works as manager of his brother-in-law's grocery store in Roby.

He is embittered by federal agricultural policies and private financial practices that he said ultimately pushed many farmers and ranchers off the land.

The last of his farm equipment was scheduled to be auctioned off Saturday. "At the end of 1989," he said of farming, "I started hating it . . . it played on your mind."

There were other victims on the Plains. In the past decade:

- Thousands of people moved out of the sometimes-desolate rural areas, leaving fewer to work the farms and fewer customers for the remaining shopkeepers. Only the eastern slope of Colorado gained population, everywhere else in the Plains county after county watched their populations recede.
- More than 1.1 million farmers left the land nationwide, primarily because of economic problems or old age. By the end of the decade, nearly 55 percent of farm family income came from non-farm jobs.
- Declining school enrollment forced 411 districts to

consolidate, and the schools were the only unifying force in many communities.

But there are success stories as well:

A Nebraska farmer tills copies of the *New York Times* into his land to aerate the soil and return some organic matter.

A North Dakota farmer practices sustainable farming by plowing his fields to the contours of the land and growing his crops organically. He speaks widely to conferences and seminars.

A doctor at the West River Regional Medical Center in Hettinger, N.D., pushed his philosophy of providing medical care outside the limits of the town. His clinic now has 14 physicians who treat patients from four states, a model of rural health care.

A Texas researcher developed a new irrigation system that cuts the amount of water used by 50 percent.

The former owner of a lumberyard in West Texas now works with a friend producing wooden birdhouses and recently won a contract to provide them nationwide for Wal-Mart.

Jack Kresnak of the *Detroit Free Press* has won the James W. Byers award for reporting on the juvenile justice system three times from the National Council of Juvenile and Family Court Judges. He has been with the *Free Press* 24 years. He uses personalizing to bring home dramatically the problems of youngsters and drugs.

MOM'S LOVE SENDS SON, 13, TO JAIL FOR DRUGS
July 23, 1991
by Jack Kresnak
***Detroit Free Press* Staff Writer**

About four months ago, she noticed a change in his attitude. At 13, her handsome only son had become surly and defiant, spoiling for arguments.

Then he came home wearing expensive gym shoes, claiming he bought them with money from selling drugs.

Saturday, his two sisters said he drove by in a car, boasting that "some crack head" had let him use it in return for drugs.

Later, he walked into his home with a plastic bag sticking out of his pocket. His mother grabbed the bag and found more than a dozen dirty white rocks of crack cocaine.

"I always told him that if I ever caught him with drugs, I'd call the police," the woman said.

And she did. But the police wouldn't come.

So the mother brought her son to them, turning him in along with the crack to officers at the 9th Precinct on Gratiot, near her home on Detroit's east side.

The mother, 34, fought back tears as she told her story Monday in a stairwell at the Wayne County Youth Home while waiting for her son to have a hearing in juvenile court.

"He's totally out of control," she said, agreeing to be interviewed only if names were not used. "He doesn't do anything I tell him to do.

"He's only 13 and he's been a good kid," she said. "He was getting straight As before all this started. I feel that he's still salvageable. I truly believe that, but I know I can't do it myself."

The woman said her son did not resist when she decided to take him in, but he did cry "when I sat him down and told him I was doing this because I loved him."

The mother works two jobs to support her three children. She spoke with frustration about trying to steer young people away from the easy money of the drug trade, and with anger at adults who supply the illicit merchandise.

"If I had my way, they'd be in jail or dead," she said. "They take good kids and they turn them into this.

"My son and I talk a lot. He's very anti-drug, supposedly, very anti-violence. He claims he does it for the money."

She said the boy's sisters are a year older and younger, and the 12-year-old "worships the ground he walks on; if he gets away with this, she'll be out there doing the same thing."

The mother said police initially were reluctant to take her son into custody, even with the drugs she gave them.

"I had to literally cry and beg the police to take him." she said. "I want somebody to make that child understand that for every action, there's a consequence. He has never seen that."

Precinct Commander George Merritt said youth officers don't normally work weekends and that special laws for juveniles prevent police from locking them up if they pose no immediate danger.

"She did the right thing" to bring him in, Merritt said.

"I'd like to commend the mother. We need more of them to turn those kids in and put them into the system."

At Monday's hearing, attorney Marcia Covert asked Referee Seymour Weberman to set a personal bond, saying "Obviously, he has a parent present who is quite supportive and will insure that her son will stay out of trouble."

But Weberman set bond at $2,000, requiring $200 to be

posted for the youth's release pending a hearing July 31 on charges of drug possession and incorrigibility.

The mother, who got a quick kiss from her son before he was led out of court, wasn't sure she would post the bond.

"He wants to get out of there," she said. "But I will have to think about it."

Sidebars

Sidebars are stories that pick up on an angle of a nearby story. The first story may be just right as it is, and the sidebar adds more information. It is usually run the same day as the main story, and usually alongside it, or as close to that position as possible, therefore a "side-bar."

On Bob Kourtakis' Title IX story, his paper ran a sidebar about a local girls' basketball coach who "never got the chances her students did" and thus gave some perspective to the dramatic changes taking place.

In the pesticide series, two sidebar stories ran the same day. One gave the history of the family who died from the pesticide and another gave an overview of what was to become a theme in the series—how minimal the penalties were for those convicted of misusing the dangerous chemicals.

Sports uses many sidebars on football games. One writer will cover the game highlights, another will talk to the player or players who made the key plays.

If a president visits a community, the main story will cover the speech, and sidebars will be on reactions people have to the visit. There are usually too many things happening for one story to cover it adequately.

Government meetings also are ripe for sidebar reporting. The main story covers the meeting, and sidebars cover public reaction, the reasons behind decisions, history of events that resulted in votes, and public reaction to government decisions. The public needs to know the decision, the reasons behind it, and what other people think about that decision.

Some papers have decided to run several stories from city council meetings rather than one long story. Each item on the agenda, or each item that comes up for discussion, is covered in a separate story. This gives readers the chance to scan the headlines of the meeting and pick the stories they want to read. Which is the main story and which is the sidebar is really moot at this point, because readers choose the stories most important to them.

Second Day Story

A second day story is a journalistic term for a continuing story. If a summary story is written on one day, another story can be written the next day if important events occur in the mean time.

If a major political figure dies, second day stories will be written about world reaction, funeral plans, or successors in the job.

If someone is arrested in a murder investigation, a second day story will cover any new angles that have developed or might get further information about the nature and length of the investigation. Police are often unwilling to give information that will later come up in a trial, and reporters will have a difficult time finding things out. Good reporters thrive on this challenge, and get stories when no other reporters can.

The problem with second day stories is in knowing how much of the first day story to repeat.

Let us say, for example, you do a thorough story on a decision to fire the school superintendent the day the announcement is made. When you run a story the next day about the procedure for finding a new superintendent, how much of the "old" information do you have to repeat?

There are two rules on this. First, you have to understand that not everyone read the first story. So you have to tell who the new superintendent will replace and when the decision was made to fire the previous one.

Second, remember that each story is new and that you should use enough of the "old" information to justify the current story. You may be able to get by by saying, "The new superintendent will replace William J. McFerrin, who was fired yesterday. The replacement is scheduled to start work August 1."

Things to Remember

- Think of people before policies or procedures. It is easier to get people interested in a story about a person who will be hurt if a new law goes into place than it is to get them interested in the procedural aspects of the story or the political reasons for the new law.
- When doing longer stories, remember the reader needs to know early in the story that something important is likely to happen later. This is called foreshadowing, and it warns the reader that something is coming up later in the story.

Exercise

1. Read a Sunday feature section of a regional newspaper, and see how many examples you can find of personalizing and/or foreshadowing.

Practice

Write a story based on the following information, using the foreshadowing technique.

Fact Set 1: Foreshadow

Mary Keller is a registered nurse at City of Angels Hospital, and she is starting a support group for people who have the same illness she has. Mary had a normal childhood except for a battle with polio when she was ten years old, before the Salk vaccine was available. As a result of the polio, her left leg is slightly smaller than the right. The polio has not caused her any problems in the last 30 or more years. About a year ago she began feeling extremely tired but decided it was because of the extensive walking she does as a nurse. When she did not get stronger, she went to the doctor. The doctor reviewed her medical history and advised her that physicians in recent years have gained a greater understanding about persons who earlier in their lives had polio. These persons do not regain strength as quickly as non-polio patients, and must be advised to curtail some activities so as not to deplete their strength. A meeting was held in an adjoining county for people who suffer similar symptoms and more than 100 persons showed up. Mary is now publicizing the condition and the need for understanding by starting a support group in this county. She can be reached at 352-7899. A meeting is planned for the first Monday of the month at the Community Hospital meeting room for anyone interested in learning more about this condition.

22
First Person Stories: The Cutting Edge

In This Chapter

There are a few times when the reporter needs to tell his or her story. When readers and audiences understand that reporters have feelings, they can benefit from special insights in certain cases.

R EPORTERS are advised, and properly so, that they should keep their opinions out of the story. The reader wants to know what the source said, not what the reporter said.

Striving for objectivity is almost a fetish with newspapers, but as times change, the media are changing as well.

There are an increasing number of first person stories in newspapers and the electronic media, and there may be more in years to come.

If a reporter is personally involved in an issue, and if that reporter has insights that will help a reader understand an issue, the reporter should be encouraged to speak up. The story must be clearly labeled as opinion or as a feature, and bylined to indicate who is telling the story.

REPORTERS CARE, TOO: LET THEM SAY SO
by Lucille deView, writing coach, *Orange County Register*
Coaches' Corner, March 1986, p. 4

One of [newspapers] credibility problems is that readers perceive reporters as cynical, heartless people with little sympathy for human dilemma. Are there ways to show this isn't true?

Once when two reporters came into the office after a long vigil for some teenagers who were missing, they shared their grief that the bodies were found in a lake. They felt close to the families with whom they waited; they, too, had hoped against hope. I suggested that one of the young reporters write a column to share with the readers the heartache of covering tragedies involving children. The column, well written and poignant, was well received. It communicated to readers that reporters do care.

At year's end, I asked a few reporters to submit an essay on "the story I liked best—and why." They came up with stories of personal courage and unexpected joy, and added important insights into their personal reactions to these quietly heroic people. Not only could readers feel upbeat about the people in the stories, but they could also discern that reporters are sensitive human beings. We must cling to our objectivity most of the time but on occasion it is good to practice exercising our personal views. It makes for good writing.

These kinds of stories will continue to be in the minority, not as numerous as the standard news stories or feature. Often they are included as columns with the picture of the writer included.

The purpose for including a small sampling of these stories in this introductory textbook is two-fold:

- Students should realize that these stories are rare, and that personal experiences often fall flat with readers unless they carry a great interest for society.
- Personal experience stories require the same qualities as good news stories—something new, well-written, with details, examples, and anecdotes.

The only major difference is that they carry the opinion of the writer to a greater extent than in other stories.

Bill Falk, a former columnist for Gannett Westchester (N.Y.) Newspapers, now with Long Island's *Newsday*, writes with compassion and sympathy about the problems of AIDS. He won an award from Gannett for outstanding work as a columnist in 1989 and also for outstanding achievement by an individual.

WHEN AIDS HITS HOME: IN MEMORY OF A BROTHER

I lost my brother 11 days ago. He died of AIDS.

A year ago we were together in my car, inching through Easter traffic on the West Side highway. We were headed home to see my parents. We sat in silence, our small talk swallowed in the blackness in my chest.

My brother's pants hung loosely on legs that once bristled with muscle. His hair, once a thicket of curls, was as fine as an 80-year-old man's. An alien thinness haunted his face...

This was the first time I'd seen my brother since discovering he had AIDS. Byron hid his illness from us for months, putting off face-to-face contact with our family through a long winter. He said, later, he wanted to spare my parents the agony...

Once, a long time ago, we were close. Separated by less than three years, we grew up locked in a fraternal wrestling match of love and envy, allies against the world and competitors for its approval. I remember us hunched over games, sharing secret vocabularies, fighting desperately. I remember him waiting for me outside kindergarten, so that I, a third grader, could take his hand and escort him safely home.

In our teens, a space opened up between us. It widened as we went off in search of our own places in the world. By our mid-20s, our lives intersected only at holidays and special occasions, otherwise running on parallel tracks separated by many miles.

I knew, and my parents knew, that Byron was gay. But it was not openly discussed. He was more comfortable not talking about it. We were more comfortable not hearing it. My parents loved him, and tried to hide their puzzlement and disappointment. This was not, of course, the way it was supposed to be. This was not what they expected.

Many times, I promised myself I would talk to Byron, to close the gap, to prove to him that it didn't matter. I longed for a breakthrough. But it didn't have to happen, then, and it didn't.

But last Easter Sunday, as we drove past men selling baskets of spring flowers, I had run out of reasons not to speak. "I haven't been much of a brother," I started.

"Well, neither have I," he said. He said that we were equal partners in the awkward conspiracy. He wanted me to know it was not my fault. This was the first of gifts we'd exchange, small gifts that surpassed any breakthrough I'd imagined.

So much has happened in the year of our knowing. Byron Carl Falk died on March 15, at age 31. Much of what we experienced, of course, was horrible. AIDS is most cruel, not only in its indifference to youth but in how it inflicts an endless succession of scourges. Strength goes first, then flesh, then sight or reason—a vibrant person deactivated, one plug at a time. In a condensed span of months, my brother suffered a lifetime's pain and indignity...

I knew, when I first saw my brother's gaunt face last year, I was beginning the most agonizing year of my life. I didn't foresee that it would also be the most wondrous and the most miraculous.

All that had gone unsaid between my brother and my family, that formidable blockage of words and emotions, dissolved. One day our differences were too fraught to discuss. The next, they were irrelevant. All that mattered was that he was under attack, and that he was ours—my brother, my parents' son, our flesh and blood . . .

I am relieved his suffering is over. I wish I knew, though, how to think of him now. I see his handsome face, his radiant smile, and I wonder: Where is that wonderful energy now, and in what form? I know that I will have to live with this mystery, as we all do.

And I know this: Though Byron, my little brother, is gone, he will be part of me all of my days.

When the Gulf War broke out, it reopened vivid and painful memories for Marney Rich Keenan of the *Detroit News*. Her brother had been killed in Viet Nam, and it made her think about the horrors of all wars. In the death toll of the Gulf War, she hears echoes of her family's pain, remembers a brother killed in Vietman . . . and asks why.

A MESSAGE TO MICHAEL
by Marney Rich Keenan
The Detroit News, March 2, 1991

At 8:30 A.M. on Wednesday morning Nov. 6, 1968, two Marines knocked on the door of our home in Bloomfield Hills. Having thrown an election party the night before, my mother would later think it providential that she had let us sleep in on a school day, and thus was not home alone when the news came that her oldest son, Michael Robert Rich, had died 12 hours earlier in Vietnam.

She stood in the foyer facing the concrete gazes Marines are taught to effect, flanked by my brother Chris, then 21, and Rob, then 17. I was 14 at the time. Vietnam seemed as far away as the moon to me. Mike was 22 years old and had just graduated from the University of Notre Dame.

He taught me how to do back flips off the dock. He took me to see the Beatles at Olympia Stadium. He bought me the first album I ever owned. I never considered that he might not come home.

My younger brother, Paul, then 12, and I sat on the steps, out of view, bracing for the wrecking ball to swing in our direction. "Mrs. Rich, the president regrets to inform you . . ." the voice began, and my screams were summoned more from fear than grief.

The Marine said that Michael was killed while on patrol in

Quang Nam Province. He was leading his platoon to an objective area when they came under intense and accurate fire. Even though a medical corpsman rushed to his aid immediately, his wounds proved too severe and he succumbed almost instantly. To my mother's comfort, the Marine said that Michael was given last rites by a Navy chaplain.

My mother did not break down until my father arrived home from the office. They fell into each other's arms in the doorway. The sounds of their sobs was devastating. My parents held each other in that open doorway, oblivious to the November chill, for what seemed to be an eternity. The sight of them is permanently etched in my mind.

My father had tried to persuade Michael not to join the Marines. He felt Michael was joining as some sort of rite of manhood, a test of bravery on the front lines. "And I knew, the moment Michael told me, that this was it," my father said in retrospect. That he was gone. That he would not come home. He had lost the argument and his first-born son.

Twenty-three years later, I am jolted by headlines of newspaper boxes, their headlines blaring out like air raid sirens: BLITZ STUNS IRAQ.

All the dilemmas of war are agonized over again: Is the loss of life proportionate to the gain? When you've lost a loved one, the balance is thrown out of whack, the scales overturned. When the frontlines reach to your doorstep, no justification seems adequate, not even to stop a madman.

The memories flood back. I can see now the Marines coming up the walk. I can hear my brother's halting voice: "Mom, there are two Marines downstairs." I remember the two-week wait for his body to be shipped home, the day I saw my mother bury her head in her arms in the kitchen table, letting a check from the insurance company drop to the floor. I remember the newspaper headline four days later that read: "Death of GI cancels meeting with son," referring to a South Vietnamese orphan Mike had adopted through Foster Parents Plan and had hoped to meet.

[In perhaps the greatest possible understatement of the war, Mike had written Foster Parents shortly before his death apologizing for delays in paying his fee, saying: "Please be patient—things are in somewhat of a scramble here in Vietnam. I shall mail the check ASAP."]

And finally, I remember the prophetic letter he'd written home that was read at his funeral:

"These troops have some unbelievable family records;

most of them contend with incredible personal problems. I see them everyday and I can only think about how lucky I have been to have been born into the family I have. These kids see other families every day that they would rather have been born into. And I, in my 22 years, have yet to see any family that might have for me one tenth of what mine already has. Even all my friends, without fail, have mentioned to me, at one time or another, how my parents and my family were the greatest they have ever known. How all my newlywed buddies work to reach the goal of a Rich-type marriage.

"I've just been unbelievably lucky being a brother to Mern and my brothers. If my life were to end tomorrow, I will have lived a fuller life than any friend of mine, no matter how long he or she hangs around.

"Anyway, I want you to know how I feel. I'm completely unafraid, because if I lost everything I'd still come out miles ahead of anyone I know outside the Riches. I only wish you could feel the same way and not worry. Remember that if something were to happen, I'd be in heaven long before you ever hear about it."

The morning after the first U.S. strike on Iraq, my mother calls: "It brings it all back," she says...

In chapter 12, we recounted some of the stories of the firestorm that raged through the hills around Oakland, California.

Another of those stories is used in this chapter. It is a first person account of the fire by the editor, whose home was destroyed in the fire his paper reported. Mr. Maynard died in 1993.

KINDNESS OF NEIGHBORS AND STRANGERS
Robert C. Maynard
Editor, *Oakland Tribune*

Disasters can have deceptive beginnings. Nothing about our peaceful morning forewarned us of the conflagration that was to come. Nothing except the wind. I went to open a French door. The wind blew it back in one fierce gust.

Our youngest would be playing a Little League game around noon. We were reading the Sunday papers when the phone rang about 10 A.M. A friend told my wife there was a fire up on Grizzly Peak. This is more than a mile from our home on Upper Rockridge.

From the vantage point on our roof, I could see a thick

plume of smoke rising on the horizon. A helicopter was making a water bombing run every 5 to 7 minutes.

As the day turned out, that image of that helicopter would form the basis for a bitter irony. It would eventually be the equivalent of thimbles of water trying to quench the flames of Hades.

Hell came to the neighborhood at a little after noon. A house on the hill above our house burst into flames. Then, as my older son and I took pictures on the roof, we watched the flames come roaring over the hill and down the Broadway Terrace corridor toward Lake Temescal.

My wife took a tour of the neighborhood and drove home with the urgent message. "We have to get out. Now," she said, "Let's just go."

We grabbed the dog and one of the three cats, Tommy-Cat. Percy, the black Persian and Abigail, the calico cat, were nowhere to be found, but they were streetwise cats so we were confident they would avoid harm on their own. (They were found later in the week.)

After Nancy and the children were settled in our office, my older son and I went back to the neighborhood. It was like a visit to Hell at Ground Zero. Cross Road, the little street on the north boundary of our property, was a ball of flame. Every house on both sides of the street, more than a dozen in all, was engulfed in flame.

It was an eerie scene. The wind howled down Cross Road and the flames sprang from tree to tree, from roof to roof. This little street, the one my Little Leaguer and I used to head to school on every day, was now a blazing inferno.

Earlier in the afternoon, Jeff Langer called. His parents, our neighbors Bob and Michael Langer, were traveling. They have lived here for a quarter of a century in a house that was built in 1912. Could I look out for their house? he asked.

I told him I would do what I could. Now I was standing transfixed as the flames roared through the Langer's lovely home. They were already beginning to devour the Fujita's house. Ours was next.

What added to the eerie nature of the scene at Cross Road and Broadway Terrace was the total absence of any fire equipment. The neighborhood was going up in flames, and there was not a firefighter to be seen at that moment.

My older boy and I were trying to decide if we dared try to rescue our family valuables by going back into the house. It hadn't caught yet, but it was bound to go at any minute.

Just then, two Oakland police officers came screaming to a halt in front of our home. "You only have five minutes," said Officer Smith. "Come on, I'll help you get some of your valuables out."

Smith and I raced up the stairs, I headed to our bedroom. Without electric power I was grabbing things in the dark. I reached for a suitcase to pack them.

"No, no," said Smith, "there's no time for that. You have to do it as if you were a burglar robbing this place."

I stood dumbfounded. "Like this," Smith said. He began helping me pile valuables and clothing onto the bed. When we had everything worth grabbing, Smith showed me what a burglar does. He grabbed the four corners of the bedspread and it became one huge bundle. Away we went.

Outside, Peter Haidt was in his car with his wife, his dog and a few valuables. Theirs was a particularly touching story. Their house, at the top of Cross Road, a few hundred yards above ours, had been vacant until last weekend. The Haidts bought it and moved in 8 days ago.

"I'm trying to get a picture of the house we never got a chance to live in," Haidt said. With that, he went charging up Cross Road, his wife shouting at him to come back. In seconds, the flames, the heat and the heavy smoke drove him back.

Neighbors came to ask how they could help. When I told a total stranger about two large paintings I was afraid would be lost, he said "I was an art major. I can't stand the thought of losing valuable paintings."

He and I ran into the threatened house. We saved two masterpieces by Elizabeth Turner Hall, one of our favorite painters. My wife, who had returned to the house, joined our son and me in shoving those paintings in the truck as our last family act before we fled.

On the day last week of the anniversary of the terrible Loma Prieta earthquake, we had made no particular mention of it in our house. It was not a memory that we wanted to relive in any prolonged manner.

Instead, on that day, we were engaged in an act of supreme optimism. We erected a scaffold to begin painting our 81-year-old house. This is a remodeling and redecorating job we have been planning for more than five years.

Now my son and a friend of our family were using the scaffolding to get water on our roof. I watched their heroic effort. It was similar to the efforts I had been witness to all afternoon. Hundreds of my neighbors were out with garden hoses, pouring water on their roofs.

I called them down from the scaffold. It was a futile effort. The temperature of the flames rose so high as to disdain something as inconsequential as a damp roof. The sun was hidden by the smoke. The howling wind and the crackling flames in the trees and the houses next door seemed out of this world. It felt as if we had visited Dante's Inferno.

As we made our way out, still uncertain of the fate of our home, some firefighters were struggling with a hydrant, trying to get enough pressure to fight at Broadway Terrace and Clarewood Road.

It was another display of that old futility. I remembered the first helicopter I had seen at 10:30 that morning. These paltry human efforts, a garden hose here and a bucket of water under a helicopter there, were no match. This was a disaster of extraordinary proportions that began on an otherwise ordinary Sunday morning.

On occasion, one single incident can move a writer to ask "what is going on here?" Such a case is recounted by Dave Nordstrand of the *Salinas Californian* in one of his columns. He was honored by the Best of Gannett for a selection of his work. Notice the short sentences and powerful, urging language.

BUSY MOTORISTS COULD LEARN
FROM BOY'S HEROISM

You'd think seeing an 8-year-old boy with blood on his face along the roadside would signal trouble to the adult world.

Yet motorists sped past Salinas' Jimmy Hubbard as though he were a fence post.

Waving frantically, the boy stood on Alisal Road.

At the bottom of a nearby 10-foot ditch lay a yellow pickup. Trapped inside and unconscious was Jimmy's mother Kate Hubbard, 26. With her was Jimmy's brother, Cody, 4. Momentarily distracted, Kate had lost control. The truck had gone over the edge.

"I remember thinking, 'Oh my God, all this blood,'" Kate said. "It was in my hair and on my face."

Then she passed out.

Jimmy escaped by squeezing through a broken window.

From outside, he peered back into the cab. He pounded on the windshield. His mother did not move.

He scrambled up the embankment and began screaming at passing cars. He was acting under the childhood expectation that, given an emergency, adults will respond.

"Nobody stopped," he said.

Out of desperation and anger, he picked up stones and began throwing them at cars.

"Finally one guy came back," Jimmy said. "He helped us. He waved his hands at other cars. They stopped."

The man pulled Cody from the truck and put his jacket over the boy. Rescuers had to use the "jaws of life" to peel back the roof and free Kate.

She and her sons had been wearing seat belts, she said.

The accident was Thursday 8 P.M. At noon Saturday the family was gathered in Kate's Salinas Valley Memorial Hospital room for a party.

It was both to celebrate being alive and to thank Jimmy for his efforts.

It had taken 14 stitches to close the cuts on his face. Cody had a leg fractured and the right side of his face was swollen.

Balloons, one reading "Congratulations Hero," were tied to Kate's bed.

Jimmy sat there in jeans and T-shirt and sipped a soda. He didn't feel like a hero.

Maybe not.

But the adult drivers who passed by that night could learn a thing or two about responsibility from Jimmy's actions.

Some of life's daily frustrations can be packaged nicely into personal features—with answers to the problems. If you had lost four car stereos to thieves, perhaps you would feel the same way as Rich Warren of the *Chicago Tribune*. His July 12, 1992 story was entitled, "After too many thieves, car alarm looks good."

I lived on the 50th floor of a high-rise overlooking Lake Shore Drive. On windy nights, the cars in the outdoor parking lot serenaded me like a choir of demented angels.

The wind seemed to trigger the motion detectors of every car alarm in the lot. The alarms protected most of their owners handsomely. My quiet Toyota and the silent Ford next to it paid a pirate's booty in car stereos to the local thieves.

Altogether I have donated four car stereos to the outlaws.

More annoying than the hole in the dash is vacuuming the broken shards of glass that litter the car interior—not to mention that the window costs as much to replace as the stereo.

When I purchased my new Nissan Maxima, I swore that its Bose sound system would not be the first on the shopping list of any creep armed with a brick. Educated thieves know that the Maxima, along with most other expensive autos, comes with a factory alarm system.

However, these factory alarms protect the entire car better than they protect stereos or the wheels.

So, I succumbed and joined the crowd of wailing sirens, honking horns and flashing lights that used to annoy me so much.

But finding the right alarm system, and getting it installed, wasn't as simple as picking out a favorite CD at a music store. I started by surveying the alarm peddlers at the recent Consumer Electronics show at McCormick Place.

Today's alarms do everything but perform a citizen's arrest. Some even emit screams and tell intruders to back off in plain English or Spanish.

They still can't prevent a skilled, determined thief from taking or breaking into your car, but they do separate the amateurs from the pros and make the pros think twice.

Each company exhibiting at the show had several levels of alarm security. Some protect a few points in the car, others protect every orifice. Deluxe models place an invisible shield around the car that warns away intruders.

Directed Electronics Inc. of California markets the most models, with menacing names like Viper and Hornet. Other companies include Bulldog, Mongoose and Python.

The most novel alarm is a teddy bear that sits benignly on the front seat. Touch it or move it without disarming it, and an ear-piercing alarm drives the would be thief from the car. It also could deafen a child by accident.

Insurance companies love alarms so much they'll give you up to a 15 percent discount on your premium. That means if your policy normally costs $1,000 a year, your insurance discount will pay for the alarm system in about three years.

All practical car alarm systems use a microprocessor, which is a computer on a chip. This intelligent alarm reduces false alarms.

It analyzes signals from the car's sensors and determines the appropriate reaction.

You or your installer program it to your preference. For example, it might immediately lock the ignition and chirp a warning, or set off the entire Armageddon reaction.

Unlike primitive early alarms, if someone taps your bumper while parking, the alarm won't immediately sound. But if someone keeps tapping your bumper—such as a thief connecting a tow truck—the alarm will scream bloody murder.

You control the alarm from a small key fob transmitter that has two or three buttons. A few fobs transmit infrared light like your TV remote control, although most transmit a digitally coded radio signal. An enterprising thief could bring a laptop PC to the scene to work through all the codes without success.

Even if he or she eventually stumbles onto the code, most alarm systems will lock up for half an hour after a few incorrect attempts to disarm.

After conducting research at the electronics show, I had plenty of unfamiliar manufacturers' names in hand but still no clear sign which alarm was best for my car. So I turned to a pro who had installed many of my car stereos following their predecessor's crowbar removals. Corky Peterson of Autosonics in Highland Park recommended Alpine, the familiar name of the company that had manufactured my last car stereo.

Alpine makes superb car stereos, and as I discovered, the security systems to protect them.

On the surface, the system looks beguilingly simple. In reality it takes a professional about three to four hours to install one. The system costs $500 installed.

The installer can wire the Alpine 8040 Digital Radar Security System to work in tandem with the car's factory security system.

This double security blanket still can't prevent a thief from smashing a window, but it will more than likely insure that you'll find your car where you left it.

The 8040 is a small black box with an accompanying siren and key fob controller. It transmits a field of microwaves in and around the vehicle, which work like radar. If any object interrupts the security field, the microprocessor immediately begins calculating the number, type and duration of the intrusion(s).

Initially, it chirps four times as a warning. You don't want to hear the 123-decibel siren when the 8040 gets serious.

A strong wind won't set off the alarm accidentally.

However, one day my sunglasses slipped off the dash and triggered the alarm. So be sure to keep large insects and small rodents out of your car.

The only switches set the sensitivity of the exterior alarm field. The key fob remote programs all the other settings.

Incidentally, that remote has a possible 5,000 trillion cubed code combinations.

A hidden switch installed near the black box deactivates the alarm for valet parking.

Mike Marzigliano, who installed the alarm, covered the driver's seat with plastic, and like a deep sea diver, descended to inspect my car's nether regions under the dash near the steering column. The 8040 disappeared into this void that drivers never see.

When I picked up my car, the only evidence that the Autosonics crew had been spending my money was a conspicuous flashing red signal in the middle of the dash.

The signal flashes a code that tells you everything you need to know about the alarm, including whether someone has tampered with your car while you were gone. It also informs thieves the alarm is armed.

So that I could receive the maximum insurance discount, Marzigliano set the alarm to arm automatically one minute after I leave the car. It will even lock the doors, if you desire. The car also chirps and flashes its lights affectionately to confirm arming and disarming.

As a convenient bonus, pushing a button on my remote also pops open the trunk.

My alarm has been on duty for a month and my radio remains in the dash. On windy days my car never joins that choir of demented angels. I've parked in some Maalox spaces, such as Lower Wacker Drive at night, and returned to find the red signal winking confidently at me. It suggests to the thief that another car on the block might be easier pickings.

Considering the cost of a car, or even a good car stereo, a few hundred dollars beats losing your wheels or windows.

Things to Remember

- Although for the most part the reporter is supposed to be objective, there may be times when their insight is unique and important. The reporter and the editor should feel free to use a column or a by-lined commentary to make a point. Readers will be better off after reading this carefully considered opinion.

23
Reporting Cultural Diversity: The World as We See It Versus the World as It Is

In This Chapter

> The world is changing, and reporters need to understand those changes to report on them.
>
> Not all groups in society are similar to the group to which the reporter belongs. The press has a duty to cover all elements of society.
>
> National commissions in the 1940s and 1960s said the media need to work harder to report more fully on all aspects of society.
>
> Racial and ethnic minorities cover more than 20 percent of our population.
>
> Specific steps can be taken to see that minorities are reported on fairly, and that misconceptions are not perpetuated.

WHAT ARE the responsibilities of the press and how well does the press do what it should? Is the press reporting on and writing about the things the world needs to know?

This is a continuing question, and constantly changing as society changes. As soon as reporters think they have it figured out, the makeup of society changes. A reporter is a member of one or two groups in society but must report on all of the other groups.

Students go from one group of friends in high school to another in college, and soon to yet another in the "real" or working world. Being social creatures, they develop friendships among people with the same backgrounds and interests as their own.

If you work on the college student paper or radio station, for example, there is a high probability that you will go out socially and perhaps even date (and often marry) other members of the staff. Life is hectic in college and after, and your close friends tend to be those you live and/or work with.

But as a reporter, your job is to interpret the community to everyone else in the community. It is not enough to write about your friends or relatives, and in fact, doing so ruins your credibility with the reader (and with most editors). The reader expects you to be as objective as possible, and we are not objective about our friends and/or our family.

Mixing in the Community

A major study of newspaper reporters and editors several years ago reported that editors and reporters were "out of touch with their communities" (Stein 1982).

The study found, and few stepped forward to argue, that

reporters and editors were in their own little world. Daily deadlines, nightly meetings, and other pressures of the business gave them little free time outside their work. What free time they had was spent with other reporters and editors; they really did not mix with other members of the community as much as they should.

Now, just a minute, you might say. Is it not true that other groups socialize with their kind, that business people fraternize with other businesspeople, that lawyers and doctors play golf or go to parties with other lawyers and doctors, etc? True enough.

However, the role in society for reporters is different from the roles of business or professional people. Businesspeople, lawyers, and doctors practice specialties or sell goods and services. Their job is not to interpret what is going on in the community to the rest of the community. They do not necessarily need to know how society is structured, or which groups are represented in a community.

Reporters need to know this. They need to recognize that racial and ethnic minorities are 20 percent of the population in the United States and much higher in many communities. If a newspaper or television station does not report thoroughly on a Hispanic population that may be 30 percent of its community, it is not doing its job.

Reporters also need to understand that their families may differ from other family structures. The so-called nuclear family, with a mother and father and one, two, or three children, is no longer the majority unit in our society. Single parents with children, or single persons living alone, are major factors in all communities, and have special needs that most print and broadcast media do not address.

Unfortunately, while minority populations have been increasing in communities throughout the United States, the percentage of minorities working for the media has not increased proportionately. Often, if there is a significant black or Hispanic population in a reading or viewing area, papers or stations may not have blacks or Hispanics to cover those groups.

The media are making efforts to attract more minorities to work with them. Progress is slow, but must continue.

Reporters must understand the racial and ethnic makeup of their community, and they must make efforts to report on those significant groups in their community.

By minorities we do not mean race or national heritage alone. Questions of gender, or proper coverage of women's issues; discussions of sexual preference, lifestyle, gay, and lesbian issues; and religious issues are also included. The percentage accorded to each of these and other minority groups should be based on the percentage of minorities in a readership or viewership area.

Recent History

The issue of the social responsibility of the press was raised by the Hutchins Commission in 1947 after World War II. Among other things, it said that freedom of the press also has responsibilities. Those who benefit from telling others about society have an obligation to use those freedoms for the benefit of everyone, not just the reporters, publishers, and their friends.

In fact, the most important thing the media do is to promote the welfare of society. The Hutchins Commission said this can be done by giving a "truthful, comprehensive and intelligent account of the day's events—in perspective." Just the facts and impartiality is not enough, reporters need to *explain* to the readers what is happening in society and why. To know what is happening in a given community, the reporter has to know that community.

Most important for this discussion is the Hutchins Commission suggestion (remember, this was 1947) that the media provide "a representative picture of the constituent groups in society," i.e., tell the audience what life is like in all aspects for the different groups in society. This is not easy, and it means doing more than covering police reports, meetings, and speeches. It means getting to where the people live and reporting on their lives.

With the urban riots of the 1960s, it became clear that the Hutchins Commission recommendations had not been met, and that much of America did not really know what had been happening in the urban areas, nor why it happened.

The Kerner Commission was appointed by President Lyndon Johnson to investigate causes of the riots of the 1960s in Detroit, Newark, and Watts, among other cities. The commission found the media, especially television, had reported the riots fully and properly, but was still missing something important.

The media, according to the commission:

> have not communicated to the majority of their audience, which is white, a sense of the degradation, misery and hopelessness of living in the ghetto. They have not communicated to whites a feeling for the difficulties and frustrations of being a Negro in the United States. They have not shown an appreciation of a sense of Negro thought, culture or history.
>
> When the white press refers to Negroes and Negro problems it frequently does so as if Negroes were not a part of the audience . . . such attitudes in an area as sensitive and inflammatory as this, feed Negro alienation and intensify white prejudices (Emery and Emery: 494).

Over the past 20 years, the subject of race relations may have been the most discussed topic in and for the media. Steps have been taken, but more steps need to be taken. Since the United States is a nation of immigrants, different cultural minorities are now asking for the same respect that African-Americans have been seeking for years.

While there has been some improvement in the number of minorities in newsrooms, after a great deal of hard work, it is not clear that the percentage of minorities is much higher than before. It is clear that the percentage of minorities in the newsrooms does not equal the percentage of minorities in the population.

The goal of the media should be to cover the same kinds of news about minority Americans as about white Americans and to show minority people with the same diversity as white people—affluent, middle class, poor. Every effort must be made to avoid dealing in stereotypes about minorities.

Specific Steps to Consider

Reporters can take the following steps:

The problem may not be the reporting techniques, because good reporting is good reporting. The problem is getting the student or reporter to understand that these groups must be covered as diligently as the sometimes overcovered groups like the city council or the school board.

A student journalist must go out of the way to interview people other than close friends or usual sources on a beat. When looking for story ideas, seek out minorities, handicapped, or elderly persons. Look for people who have grown up in different circumstances, such as broken homes, inner cities, or in areas known for drug problems. Seek out persons to tell their stories when assignments are due in your classes or on your beats.

Remember that editors, too, have close personal friends and group ties. They may not understand specifically how a community is changing, since they are wrapped up in everyday production problems. Seek out features that tell the story of persons with AIDS, victims of child abuse, or minorities whose life styles you do not really understand. Enterprise features of this sort are much appreciated, and are generally well-accepted in contests that reward insights into how society operates.

Identify a person by race only if that identification is critical to the story. Reporters and editors will have to discuss whether it is critical to the story.

If police have a description of a person wanted in a crime, and they are asking public help to find that person, then race is important, whether white, African-American, Hispanic, Native American, Asian-American, etc. Some media outlets do not mention the race of persons accused of crimes because that mention reflects on the race itself, which is not a factor in the crime, and tends to continue stereotypes.

In this case, the crime itself is the important thing, not the race, and perpetuating a stereotype demeans an entire race and causes people to overlook important information because they associate it wrongly with a given group.

Preferences change for the name a group uses to identify itself. Consult an editor or the stylebook for the preferred term to identity a group of persons. A group name is a part of a person's identity or personality, and must be treated with respect.

Identify a person by race if the story is about racial conflict and the person identified is a key source in the story. Use the race to make sure the story is understandable, not to add some incidental information or because you feel you have to put in every fact that you have.

For example, if the reporter is doing a search of public records to find out whether housing costs as a part of income are higher in certain minority neighborhoods than in other neighborhoods in the city, race is clearly a part of the story.

If you are reporting a speech and the topic of race is a part of that speech, report it as it is given, and get reaction to the comments from others attending the speech. Then-Vice President Spiro T. Agnew in Hawaii once referred to a person as a "Fat Jap." Unfortunate as that remark was, it was made by the vice president of the United States and was widely reported at the time. Statements made by elected or appointed officials in public meetings or on public occasions need to be reported so that the public understands the nature and intent of the officials, in this case, one who was one heartbeat away from being president of the entire country.

Understand that all persons of a given racial group do not think alike, just as all residents of a given city do not think alike, and that all Democrats or Republicans do not think alike. The word "monolith" is often used (having a uniform, massive, or intractable quality or character) to show that not all members of any minority (or majority) are the same and do not think alike.

Specifically, reporters must treat minority sources with the same care and diligence as all other sources. Do not call one or two persons of a group, for example, and ask for their opinion, and then report it as the opinion of this group. You would not ask two residents of one ward what they think and then report this as the opinion of all residents in the city, and you would not ask two members of Congress what they think and report this as the opinion of Congress. Treat minorities with the same care and respect.

Find a spokesperson for a group, and report that this spokesperson made this statement (identifying the position and the group), but do not assume that one random opinion of one person represents any group.

Understand that members of minorities are important, integral, and indispensable members of your audience. If you ignore them, they will ignore you. In days of increasing competition in the media, it is good common sense and good business sense to report on *all* significant groups in your audience. Not only will the members of the group be pleased that someone is paying attention to them and their concerns, but society will be able to understand how and why these groups operate and think. Every customer, audience member, or subscriber will benefit.

Some statisticians indicate that during the twenty-first century, the minorities in this country will be the majority of the population. David Lawrence of the *Miami Herald* has said that diversity in the newspaper business is "both a moral issue—providing a voice to all people in society—and an economic one; what's at risk is nothing less than survival of newspapers as a mass medium with a real and substantive role in the democratic marketplace of ideas... The very best and most successful newspapers will be those reflecting the full rainbow of human experiences" (Lawrence 1990: 25).

Report on issues, not personalities or incidents. Jesse Jackson said in 1989 that the American press is out-of-touch because it covers incidents of racial divisiveness and ignores examples of racial harmony. A balanced reporting on society as requested by the Hutchins and Kerner commissions would cover both situations.

A coalition of minority journalists meeting in Los Angeles after the 1992 riots said, "journalists need to look at class and socioeconomic issues and rely less on dramatic conflict and sexy issues. Journalists should seek out more minority experts and question the media's traditional values" (Iwata 1992: 10).

Jay Harris (1992), vice president of the media conglomerate Knight-Ridder, said Americans were surprised at the Los Angeles riots because the media had not done a good job of covering racial issues.

A panel at the University of Missouri stressed the need for changes in the way the media portray women and minorities. Nancy Woodhull, a former newspaper editor with *USA Today*, accused the press of "symbolic annihilation" of minorities and women by "picturing faces and quoting people who are mainly from one group and ignoring the issues about which other groups care" (Stein 1992: 68).

Above all, students must understand the common stereotypes about minorities and care enough to deal with them in a fashion which will permit society to understand itself better. Do not treat all members of a minority group (or a majority group) as if they think alike.

What follows are stories about minorities in America. Those represented in these varying stories are African-Americans, Japanese-Americans, gays, and a religious minority, the Amish. They represent different minorities and they come from different parts of the country. Some of the problems discussed are not new, others are.

As you read these stories, watch for the following:

- You may be shocked when you read some of these stories. Shock is one technique writers use to get the reader's attention.
- These are primarily feature stories, which contain all of the things we consider important in features—detail, quotes, story line, anecdotes, etc. In some cases, the details and the quotes are more difficult to obtain, and you should know that a great deal of time and work was involved in getting the information.
- There is no higher calling in journalism than to report on the problems of others so that the rest of society can understand them and do something about them. These stories are some excellent efforts to help society understand itself better.

Writing about Japanese-Americans

In the economic competition between the United States and Japan, stereotypes have developed on both sides of the story. Americans have a mental picture of Japan, and Japanese have their own ideas about American society. Many of these stereotypes are discussed in a story called "Sold on America: Japanese couple in Elyria enjoy mix and pace of U.S." This was written by Fran Henry of the *Cleveland Plain Dealer* and ran on Page F1, February 29, 1992.

Notice how she deals with the stereotypes right up front, and then squashes them in the third graph.

ELYRIA, O.—Keep in mind that some Japanese businessmen work 18-hour days and think Americans are lazy; and Japanese housewives are shy women, happy only when pushing their children to excel.

Also remember that the Japanese are terribly formal, and don't entertain guests in their home; instead, they meet at restaurants to dine on seaweed and raw fish.

Then spend some time with Steve and Ako Okushima, and kiss your Japanese stereotypes goodbye.

He is a senior member of a Japanese contingent of 15 assigned to USS-Kobe Steel Co. in Lorain. His wife is a community volunteer, as well as homemaker and talented cook.

In 1989 they moved to Elyria from Kobe, a bayside city about 350 miles west of Tokyo, and brought with them a desire to spark as much Japanese-American exchange as possible.

"I was the most senior of the 15 Japanese, and I told them 'Do not live together,' because I did not want to have a Japanese community. We came to America to work for an American company, and we should understand the American culture, surround ourselves with American people all 360 degrees.

"Of course it would have been more comfortable for us to live together, but that is wrong," he said emphatically. He was also a proponent for distributing the Japanese in all divisions at USS-Kobe, instead of grouping them in an engineering division of their own.

"We live separately, but we tell the people if they need us, we can help them anytime," said Ako, 47. "For them to get along with a new life, it takes about a year. They're very happy now."

The first time the Okushimas had to grapple with culture shock was in 1971 when they moved to Stockholm, Sweden, so Steve could study on a scholarship from Kobe Steel. They met the challenge, he said, because "we were young (30 and 27)...and very curious."

They lived there a year and a half, then went back to Japan. When Steve was transferred to the New York City office of Kobe Steel from 1980 to 1984, they lived in Westchester County.

"My philosophy is to have a sense of curiosity about that which I don't know," said Steve.

Steve, 50, has a high opinion of Americans. "The quality of the American people is fantastic," he said. "They are very eager to work to make the company better and support the community." He admits that he hasn't shaken a 12-hour workday.

"When that Japanese politician made that stupid comment about American workers (being lazy), I don't think all the Japanese people are thinking American people are that way."

That's the attitude that keeps the Okushimas from getting upset over "Japanese bashing." They simply do not believe that the newsmaking bashers represent all the people.

"You American people are so open, you should be proud of that," he said. "This is totally different from Japan," which, he explained, was totally closed to other countries until this past century. The isolation kept its people homogeneous.

It would be hard to consider Ako a stereotypical Japanese mother. She combined her mothering of Atsushi, 18, and Hiroshi, 22, with her personal interests.

The boys attend a combination high school-college near Kobe, sparing them the brutally intense competition associated with college admission in Japan.

"We wanted them to learn other things, be in sports and have many experiences. That's important for our kids," said Ako.

Hiroshi lived in Stockholm with his parents and both boys lived in New York. Atsushi vacationed here last year and Hiroshi spent five weeks of his two-month vacation last summer with an Elyria family.

"He could not improve his English if he lived with us," said Ako, who takes a weekly private English lesson. She and Steve speak Japanese at home.

The Okushima's find day-to-day living comfortable, especially since they are finding that "everything is cheaper in the United States."

As a master cook, Ako especially appreciates the grocery prices and selection. In Japan she took lessons for 20 years in Chinese cuisine, gaining the proficiency to be a cooking teacher.

Chinese food? That's simply her preference. She prepares elaborate Chinese meals at their frequent dinner parties with ever-expanding guest lists. "We want to have as many friends as possible," Steve said.

They met many through the Cleveland Ballet, thanks to the influence of their landlord, Barbara Evenchik. She is a member of the Cleveland Ballet Council.

"Steve says I remind him of his mother," said Evenchik, 67. "We've gotten to be like family."

Even so, they have had to deal with cultural differences, such as greetings. "My husband, Marvin, said I shouldn't come on too strong—which is something I do." Evenchik's inclination is to include hugs and kisses with her "hellos," while Japanese custom excludes such physicality.

"So we've compromised and each come half way. Now we brush cheeks. That is one thing I have to get used to," she said.

And Evenchik said Ako has been gung-ho since she arrived here. "She'd call me and ask where I was going that day, and she'd go along, like to the ballet council or the Opera League. Soon she was a participant."

Volunteer work was a new outlet for Ako, who said that except for PTA, Japanese women rarely volunteer.

Steve is the newest trustee of the Cleveland Ballet; and Ako, a council member, has been a prime-mover in designing the trip to Japan for a ballet benefit auction March 7. At last year's benefit, she and Steve volunteered to serve hors d'oeuvres she made.

Ako was also instrumental in having traditional Japanese tea ceremonies in the ballet council and the Cleveland Museum of Art. Another ceremony is planned for this fall at the Garden Center of Greater Cleveland.

"If we were the kind of people who kept to ourselves, things like that would never happen," said Steve.

Ako says her only problem in the United States is being away from her children. "But it's very important to live with my husband and have the same experiences, so I chose to come with him."

Happily, their shared experiences have been positive. "They really put themselves out . . . They are a warm, wonderful and generous couple," said Evenchik.

Their outgoing natures are not typical of the Japanese.

That's the big difference: "Here everybody has his own opinion," said Steve. "They've got it whether it's right or wrong, and they speak out. But in Japan being silent is more appreciated.

"Here if I say nothing, you would think of me, 'He knows nothing. He's a downer.' But in Japan if we speak too much, the Japanese would say, 'I wonder who the hell he is,'" he said.

"We're very Americanized. I'm very comfortable."

Ako nodded. "I like to express my opinion. I feel very accepted here," she said.

Writing about the Gay Community

Laura Pappano of the *Patriot Ledger* in Quincy, Mass., did a three-part series entitled "Emerging community: Gays in the suburbs."

It won the Publick Occurrences award for superior journalistic achievement in 1991 by the New England Newspaper Association.

Excerpts from her series show the depth of feeling on the issue, and demonstrate perspectives we may not be used to.

"The way we lead our lives is not very different from the way people in these other houses lead their lives.

"We go to work, we come home and watch TV and go to bed. On the weekends, we worry about the lawn.

"It is a lot like Ozzie and Harriet. Except it is Ozzie and Ozzie."

"I am determined that by the end of the summer everyone (in my family) but my parents will know," said Patrick, 23, of Canton, who in January began telling members of his large family that he is gay. "And it is not like I am *asking* to be accepted—I expect it. I demand it."

"People who are openly gay are not wanted in so many sectors of life," [David] said. "When I meet someone, there is always the dread that they will find out or I will tell them, and I will lose the positive regard of that person.

"Losing a job is something I can deal with, but feeling someone doesn't like me is hard."

The advent of the AIDS epidemic, local gays say, has taken its toll in lost lives and in lost support from some in straight America.

"The AIDS thing has put us back 20 years," Diane said. "The gay community has come together more, but the straight community has backed off."

[The gays] want acceptance, or at least peaceful coexistence. But they know that will not happen overnight. Already, they want the straight world to know, homosexuals are among their teachers, clergy, lawyers, doctors, store owners, business leaders and friends.

"I would like to wake up someday and have all the gay and lesbian people turn green," said George, sipping coffee in his Marshfield home.

"Then there would be no question. We would all know who we are."

Gays in the suburbs say that the myth that all homosexuals lead fast paced lives is just that, a myth. "People think because you are gay, you do all these wild, wonderful things," said Diane, a 47-year-old bank administrator who lives on the South Shore and sometimes goes to the Randolph Country Club.

"We do what everybody else does on a Saturday night."

Patrick, 23, who grew up in a large Catholic family in Canton, is still struggling to reconcile his sexual preferences with his Catholic upbringing. "I've spent many endless nights in the corner of my bed balled up crying about that," he said. "But I know being gay is not something I am going to hell for."

Writing about African-Americans

Perhaps the most important problem between groups is a lack of understanding. Those who do not see, talk or read about people of other races or colors, religions, or sexual preferences do not and cannot understand them. The conflicts that arise from this lack of knowledge have dogged American society for hundreds of years, and still trouble it.

Stories about this conflict, this lack of knowledge, this "racism" are important to lessening the problem.

Kathy Ann Moilanen, a staff reporter for the *Ann Arbor (Mich.) News* won a 1991 Clarion Award for Outstanding Reporting from the Women in Communication, Inc., for her balanced coverage of an explosive issue—racism in a rural county in Michigan.

The first story in the series was entitled "Livingston grapples with racist image" and was printed in April 29, 1990.

Notice the power, bluntness, and directness in the first several paragraphs. Personalizing, anecdotes, and strong writing get the reader right into the story.

Despite her name, Karen Livingston-Wilson has little in common with Livingston County, where she works.

She is black. Livingston County is 99 percent white.

She says that at least once every couple of weeks someone yells a racial insult at her on the streets of Howell. The Ann Arbor resident is an attorney at Citizens Insurance in Howell but refuses to live in the community which she otherwise describes as "charming."

Blacks cannot even drive through Howell, the county seat, without worrying about what would happen if their cars break down and they have to stop, she says.

That image is strong and widespread. Case in point: A state trooper pulls over a bus of Detroit second graders travelling I-96 with a flat tire.

"The kids start screaming because they knew they were in Livingston County and thought the officer was going to arrest them all," relays Dan Rose, Livingston County assistant prosecutor.

Many people who live or work in Livingston County agree the county has the reputation of being racist.

Others say the reputation is undeserved. The key difference is that Livingston County has been unable to shake a reputation rooted in being home to a former Ku Klux Klan leader...

[Moilanen also covers the other side of the story, talking to blacks who live in the county.]

Gerry McClure is a tall, bald man who would stand out in a crowd even if he weren't black and living in an all-white subdivision of $100,000 to $180,000 homes. His soft-spoken wife Verna apologizes: "I'm sorry we don't have any horror stories for you."

Perhaps that depends on the definition of horror.

While riding a bike in his neighborhood, Gerry McClure says he has been followed by state police, "Taking a close look at me like I do not belong."

Verna McClure has also been offended when visitors at her home have asked her: Is the lady of the house around? She also mentions a grocery store clerk who asked whether she would be paying with food stamps. She says she responded: "Did you ask the person ahead of me about food stamps?"

"We've just had isolated incidents that you, as a minority, would experience anywhere," Gerry McClure contends.

[She also talks with another black person living in the county.]

Louise Nettles' home in Brighton Gardens puts her two minutes from work at Spencer Elementary, a Brighton school with one black student.

For a few hours each day, Nettles serves food and milk in the lunchroom and supervises the playground.

She always spreads hugs and concern. Each year she takes a couple of kids under her wing, says principal Carol Owoc.

"I think she allows children to have a very positive, black female role model. She is also very kind and kind of 'mothers' the kids," Owoc said.

Nettles is 77 and has lived in Brighton since 1943. She recently shared her experiences in the civil rights movement with a group of spellbound third-graders at Spencer. She proudly shows off a stack of thank-you notes on double-lined green paper.

Asked whether she has experienced racism in her hometown, Nettles says the answer is mostly no.

"Back in the early 60s, there was a flare-up, but we got a coalition and it was straightened out. I personally haven't had any problems. But I know that racism exists here. I believe it."

Racial injustice is sometimes difficult to prove. Carolyn Tuft and the staff at the *Belleville (Ill.) News Democrat* spent four months sorting through 175,300 traffic tickets investigating whether blacks got a disproportionate share of traffic tickets in her city. Tuft won a national Investigative Reporters and Editors award for her stories.

Were police harassing blacks in Belleville? A four-month investigation into 18,681 traffic tickets showed blacks received 42 percent of the tickets in west Belleville compared to 8 percent in the rest of the city.

Tuft searched by hand to pull out 18,681 specific traffic tickets from a total of 175,000. Traffic tickets are public records but were not yet computerized in St. Clair County.

For the 5,040 tickets written in west Belleville, the race of the arrested, the ticket location, the name, address, age, sex, date, time of stop, violation, and arresting officer was recorded. (Belleville police wrote the driver's race on the top of every ticket, even though a space is not provided for the information.)

The information was coded by the newspaper, entered into a computer, and analyzed by Dr. Won Chang, a professor of graduate studies in journalism and statistics at the University of Missouri.

After all this work, the lead of the story was relatively simple:

BLACKS IN BELLEVILLE

Blacks receive a disproportionately higher percentage of traffic tickets in west Belleville than elsewhere in the city, an investigation by the *Belleville News Democrat* shows, and former and current officers say that blacks received 42 percent of the tickets in west Belleville and eight percent in the rest of the city.

A separate study of 390 tickets more than a year later showed blacks six times more likely to be ticketed in west Belleville than in other parts of the city.

Police chief Robert Hurst formed the special patrol shortly after he became chief in 1985, and it operated until some time in 1988, former and current police officers allege. They said it was a four-man detail that was assigned to stop, ticket and harass black motorists in west Belleville.

"This was a way Chief Hurst had, he thought, to legally intimidate and harass black people for all to see and (to have them) go back and tell their friends, 'You better not go to Belleville or they'll stop you,'" said Timothy Roeper, a Belleville patrolman from 1984–90.

Belleville's black population is 6.75 percent. West Belleville borders East St. Louis, which is 97 percent black.

[Other excerpts from the series include the following:]

The police chief said, in a certified letter to the newspaper (he declined to be interviewed) that he had created a mobile unit but denied the intent was to harass blacks.

"The unit was organized to stop a rash of burglaries that were taking place in the Signal Hill area" (also on the west end of Belleville).

However, Roeper said the purpose of the unit "was basically to stop black people, that's all. The chief ordered it. Nothing goes on up there without the chief ordering it."

The ticket information was analyzed by computer experts at the University of Missouri-Columbia. Among the findings:

- Blacks received twice as many of their tickets in west Belleville—2,086—as in the rest of the city—1,027—while whites received four times fewer tickets in west Belleville—2,931—as they did in the rest of the city—12,566. City-wide, blacks got 17 percent of the 18,861 tickets issued.

  Whites received 58 percent in west Belleville, compared with 92 percent in the rest of the city. Other ethnic groups received 23 tickets in west Belleville and 48 in all other areas—less than one-tenth of one percent in both cases.
- The ratio of tickets given to blacks compared with whites was four times greater in west Belleville, where blacks received four in 10 tickets, compared with one in 10 tickets in the rest of the city.
- All drivers were more likely to be ticketed during the 3–11 P.M. shift, the hours Roeper and other officers said the special unit operated. Of the 2,780 people ticketed on the west end during those hours, 45 per cent, or 1,238, were black.
- In the year after the special unit folded, blacks still received 37 percent of the tickets in west Belleville and nine percent in other parts of the city.

Eugene Kane of *The Milwaukee Journal* uses analysis to let his readers understand race relations. His 1991 piece on the movie "Boyz N the Hood" was entitled "Films, rap capture the hard core." Kane is a columnist and entertainment reporter and has written several articles on black cultural issues for the *Journal*.

The motto of today's black urban youth—using their own words—appears to be: "It's gotta be hard core."

Hard-core, as in loud, blaring, hard-hitting, confrontational. You can see it in their fashion, hear it in the music and language.

For many young people, this fascination with the hard-core is only a posture, a way to freak out their parents, as teenagers have been hassling parents for generations. Many who adopted the subculture are not even from tough, inner-city backgrounds, but are solidly middle-class. Some are even white.

But for another group—a low income, high desperation segment of young people—hard core means violence: as in violence against women, violence against rival gang members, violence against anyone who gets up in your face—on the street, at concerts, in movie theaters. And not merely the mano-a-mano confrontations of the past—too often the equalizer is the bullet.

Check out any newspapers for evidence of that credo. Chances are there will be at least one incident involving a young, poor, black man's desire to earn his "hard-core" badge of honor.

Currently, two representations of this hard-core subculture are in the face of the mainstream public: The best-selling rap album "Niggaz4life," by self-proclaimed "gangsta" rappers N.W.A. (Niggers With Attitude) and "Boyz N the Hood," a new film by young black director John Singleton.

Amazingly to most journalists who previewed the film and praised it, showings of "Boys N the Hood" have been accompanied by violence—in Racine and Milwaukee and around the country.

But the historical context is that this happens a lot with films about gang culture or violent urban youths regardless of the film's intent. From "Warriors" in 1979 through "Colors" in 1988 to "New Jack City" earlier this year, such films have resulted in disturbances in and around movie theaters. Rap concerts, too, have been affected with some regularity.

The violence may come in part because the films bring out a crowd that theaters and their security systems are not used to dealing with in large numbers. Both "New Jack City" and "Boyz N the Hood" also combine film and rap attractions through the presence of Ice T in the former and Ice Cube in the latter.

The violence may also come because of the hard-core attitudes and expectations being brought to the event—and how those attitudes are being presented in our culture is worth exploring.

Let's deal first with N.W.A. Simply put "Niggaz4life" is an assault on the ears and sensibilities of anyone over 25; this is gritty, non-accessible rap music that strikes to the core of what this rebellious art form is supposed to represent. A reviewer for the *Los Angeles Times* called it "the best sounding rap record to come along in some time" while simultaneously decrying its violent imagery and misogynist rantings.

In N.W.A. parlance, every black woman is a "bitch," every black man is a "nigger," every confrontation should be resolved with gunfire. The group defends its material by claiming to be "street reporters," artists from the inner city who simply document what they see around them.

The language on "Niggaz4life" proved so raw that virtually no commercial radio stations were able to play any of the cuts over the airwaves. But the album's hard-core pedigree attracted enough young buyers, black and white, that it became the No. 1 album in the country. Not the No. 1 rap album, but the No. 1 album *of any kind*.

In "Boyz N the Hood," 23-year-old director Singleton takes a different tack. His coming-of-age tale about a trio of young black men growing up in South Central Los Angeles depicts a neighborhood where gang members ride around in boom-cars with shotguns, and police helicopters circle overhead constantly. The film makes no attempt to sugarcoat this environment, or pull its punches, but instead seeks to present ghetto violence for what it is: a deviant lifestyle that corrupts young minds and creates a cycle of early death.

The main character, Tre Styles, played by newcomer Cuba Gooding Jr., is an intelligent young man who realizes that the gang activity and drugs that rule his neighborhood represents an unacceptable choice. The violence is presented as senseless mayhem that does nothing to address the greater issue of decaying neighborhoods being attacked from within and without by powerful social forces.

One of the most telling commentaries in the movie is one character's lament about the benign attitude of the powers-that-be when it comes to inner-city violence: "Either they don't know, don't show, or don't care what's going on in the 'hood."

The truth is that "Boyz N the Hood" is as hard-core as anything N.W.A. covers on "Niggaz4life," but with a major difference. The indiscriminate violence is presented in its proper context, and the gang lifestyle is not glorified. What is stressed is the humanity of the people involved, and the message is that whenever people are placed in insane situations, anarchy will reign until someone decides to stand up and bring the madness to an end.

In cities like Milwaukee, where a generation of young blacks are struggling with their own insane situation filled with senseless violence, that's a hard-hitting, hard-core message that can't afford to be lost.

What happened during the film's opening last week suggests that, in many instances, the most mindless side of hard-core won out over sensible message and hard human truths.

A *Toledo Blade* story by Rhonda B. Sewell brought out the facts on "Crisis of the black male," subtitled "For a variety of reasons, the young black male is becoming an endangered species." The story ran on October 4, 1992, Page F1.

Notice the powerful use of statistics and statements by persons well versed in the field.

"One out of every 21 young black males in the United States will be murdered in their lifetime. Half of them will be murdered at the hands of another black male."
—Opening written statement in the 1991 film "Boyz N The Hood," by film writer-director John Singleton.

The gunshots ring loud. The bullet pierces his body and blood streams out. The killer dashes from the scene of the murder. Observers scream and sirens are soon to follow.

The victim is buried. A suspect is captured, charged, tried, convicted, and put behind bars for life.

This could be the perfect story line for a made-for-TV movie, but unfortunately this scenario is reality for scores of black men, especially young ones, who live in the war zones of urban America.

The Centers for Disease Control report that homicide is the No. 1 cause of death for black males aged 15 to 24.

And, according to a book by Richard Majors and Janet

Mancini Billson, *Cool Pose: The Dilemmas of Black Manhood in America* (Lexington Books/Macmillan, Inc.), the problems black males now have are not new, they've just gotten worse.

The authors reported that in 1977, more black males died as a result of homicide than perished in the Vietnam War from the years 1963 to 1972.

Today there is a 1 in 21 chance that a young black male will be murdered by the time he reaches his 25th birthday, they add.

In addition to homicide, the black community is losing its men to crime and incarceration, stress, heart disease, and even suicide, which is now the third leading cause of death among black males in the 18 to 29 age group, according to the *Journal of Black Studies*.

In Toledo alone, out of 36 violent deaths to date this year, 20 were black males. They include:

- Roger Gordon, 30, who was stabbed to death by Juan Vail, 24, in May in front of the Underground Cocktail Lounge, 401 Junction Avenue, after attempting to break up a fight. Vail had earlier been ejected from the lounge after another fight.
- Frederick Carter, 18, shot by police in April. He was holed up in a North Toledo motel, holding a Tec-9 semiautomatic pistol. Police were attempting to serve warrants; he was wanted for aggravated robbery and escape. He was shot nine times, with one bullet piercing his skull. The coroner ruled his death a suicide.
- Farley Bell, 35, was stabbed to death in September with a butcher knife, in the middle of a near west end street. Stephanie Saunders, 24, was charged with the murder. An autopsy showed Bell had cocaine in his system when he died. Police believe Bell lent his car to Saunders and gave her $80 so she could buy some crack cocaine; they add that Bell had been looking for the woman and when he found her, began beating her. Saunders' attorney said she will plead self-defense.
- Deon Williams, 19, was shot by police in a controversial killing in March. He was holed up in a South Toledo motel, holding a Tec-9 semiautomatic pistol and threatening suicide. Police were trying to serve numerous warrants. A police firearms review board found that police were justified in shooting Williams. The ruling followed an investigation by the Lucas County prosecutor's office that reached the

same conclusion. Marches organized by concerned citizens, Williams' family, and the Rev. Floyd Rose were held after his death, to call for an investigation.

- Nathan Anderson, 22, shot to death in August along with James Sawyer, 24. Both were found on the ground with gunshots to their heads in front of an apartment complex at Parkside Avenue. Anderson, Sawyer and two others friends were walking out of their apartments when they were ordered by a gunman to empty their pockets and lie on the ground.

Rev. Floyd Rose, a local civil rights leader, began a fast in September, saying he was distressed by the execution-style slayings of Anderson and Sawyer and the arrest of Attila Turner, the 19-year-old black youth charged in connection with those murders.

Rev. Rose later ended his 18-day fast, during which he took only water and fruit juices. He said he discussed issues with black youth held in the Child Study Institute, in jail, and on street corners. He said God sent him a spiritual message on how to end black-on-black violence. Some of the minister's proposals included economic empowerment and spiritual renewal.

Some describe black men as the new endangered species, and many view the crisis as a conspiracy by the white power structure that wants to keep them at a low level, socially and economically.

Whatever the explanation, all agree that what's happening to black males in America is a tragedy.

The statistics are disturbing, but black men on the local and national level say there are solutions if society would wake up to the reasons behind the crisis.

Noted black psychologist Alfred Poussaint, associate professor of psychiatry at Harvard Medical School who studies juvenile behavior, told *The Blade* that there are various reasons behind the problems of black males.

"I would say that what it amounts to is that so much of the problem begins with neglect. They're being neglected in their own families, by parents, and the same neglect is in the schools," said Dr. Poussaint, a former advisor to the defunct TV series, *The Cosby Show*.

"Then they develop a subgroup with their friends because they begin to feel left out. Some of them do OK and do well, but others are on an anti-social course. We see them on the TV news and you see statistics that say we have a serious problem.

It's not all black males in the inner city, but it's a high percentage of them."

Dr. Poussaint added that years of poverty and institutionalized racism have had serious effects on generations of American black men.

"There's a devastating future for the black male. They lose hope and don't see any way out of their situation. There's more annihilation, and they become more indifferent to other people. There's no value on the lives of other people. There's the lack of opportunity . . . [in] the educational system that exists— very early they are shunted aside.

"There's a stereotype about black males . . . that they are all criminal or violent. They [mainstream society] don't like their cultural styles, don't like the way they walk, the way they talk, they don't even like their color."

Author Richard Majors, an associate professor of psychology at the University of Wisconsin in Eau Claire, said more government-supported assistance is needed.

"There's a lot of apathy, a lot of hopelessness, a lot of despair with the black males and among the black community," said Mr. Majors, co-founder of the National Council of African American Men and co-founder and consulting editor of the *Journal of African American Male Studies,* to be released in two weeks. (The journal will keep and generate statistics and facts on black males.)

"While the black community could always do more, I think they have been doing a lot. You see, there's a difference between a helping hand and a handout," he said. "I don't think the black community has ever looked for a hand-out. The government needs to do a lot more in terms of developing programs and funding and providing activities for young males who are in crisis."

To critics who claim black males are not in crisis and that their problems have been sensationalized by the media, Mr. Majors says:

"Some of the things that tell me it is a crisis [are], *The New England Journal of Medicine* in 1990 said that black men in New York, in Harlem, have a lower life expectancy than men in the third world country of Bangladesh. The Department of Health and Human Services said that black men have a shorter life expectancy except for one category of people and that is those 65 and older.

"I don't care what category you are looking at, whether it's homicide, cirrhosis of the liver, heart disease—black men are the lowest [in life expectancy] in all of those categories."

Mr. Majors, also author of a book to be released next year, *The American Black Male: His Present Status and Future,* said black men are trying to do something about the problem.

"There have been more organizations and committees and task forces since 1988 than ever before. I'm co-founder and past chairman for the National Council of African-American Men, which is an umbrella group for black males created in 1990. The purpose is basically to be an advocate for the 14 million black males in this country and to create social policies and initiatives for solutions."

During the group's convention in August, its members targeted 80 young black males nationwide for whom the members could serve as role models and offer assistance.

"We are also developing manhood training for young black boys," said Mr. Majors.

Bernard Clayton, a local bank manager and Baptist minister, said he felt empty inside when he heard about the recent murders of Sawyer and Anderson— both murdered on Parkside Boulevard near the church where he preaches, Friendly Missionary Baptist Church.

"It bothered me because there are so many senseless killings going on. The picture that's being painted raises the question, 'What's going to happen to us as a race of black men?' Especially if we don't wake up and do something."

Rev. Clayton, who held a special service in his church shortly after the murders, said the black church needs to get back into community outreach programs to help guide black males.

At one time the black church, which has long been the backbone of the black community, used to serve a multifaceted function, he said.

"We did that outreach then, now when there's a murder we don't say anything. Now we're building half-a-million-dollar churches and we lock them out. With our young men, we can't get them all, but we can save some before they slip through the cracks."

He added that opportunities are very few for black men, even in corporate America.

"The black man isn't the one that's bringing the dope into the country, but we are consistently destroying ourselves. We need to stop killing each other, and there have to be other avenues to make a decent amount of money so they can live."

As an executive of a local bank, Rev. Clayton said that the

demeaning stereotype of black men isn't confined to inner city youths.

He recalls one incident. He was about to get on an elevator when a white woman already on it looked up and screamed when she saw him.

"When the doors opened she screamed—there's a fear that's built into [American society]. It's just harder for black males and sometimes it makes you just want to quit, you get so frustrated."

Toledoan Avery Sutton, 25, who describes himself as very spiritual, said he is not going to just sit back and watch the crisis grow.

"When I was in the navy they taught you self-control, or preventative maintenance. You get to the problem before it happens. We need more programs to help more people so we can prevent the homicides...so the black men and the young people on the streets that don't have anyone at home, they will have somewhere to go and someone to talk to at a program—there's not enough of that in Toledo now," said Mr. Sutton, who now serves in the naval reserves and plans to attend college.

Mr. Sutton, who said he was raised in the central city, added that the lack of education, black male role models, and community programs, and the availability of drugs are just some of the many reasons for the problems encountered by young black men his age and younger who live in urban environments.

"But I think education is the key, and I think it all starts in the home. I'm going to school to further my education, maybe law or something. I'm capable of doing it, so why not go for it. Then I can help the black community."

Ben Johnson, assistant managing editor of the *St. Petersburg Times*, made these remarks while he was executive director of the Multicultural Management program at the University of Missouri-Columbia. They were reported in *Coaches' Corner*, Dec. 1986, p. 6. Despite the time lapse since these comments were delivered, "these remarks are every bit as current today as when I gave them," Johnson said.

REPORTING ON BLACK AMERICANS: HOW WE ERR IN COVERING BLACKS

There has been progress (since the Kerner Commission report of 1968) but, all in all, little has changed. Consider these examples:

Item: The *Columbia Missourian* reported this spring on the police investigation of an armed robbery, stating that police were looking for "two black males...in their 20s." No other description was provided but the story requested that anyone with information about the robbery or the robbers should call police.

The newspaper subsequently, after protests, reinstated its policy that race should be mentioned only in complete descriptions and gratuitous use of race should be avoided in news and feature stories.

Item: On the eve of the National Association of Black Journalists conference in Louisville, Ky., in August, 1981, a story in the *Courier-Journal* about a black political rally began with this lead:

"They were dancing and eating fried chicken and watermelon."

Upon seeing the offensive, stereotypical depiction in print, *Courier-Journal* editors ordered the story recast and the paper recalled.

Item: During the late '70s, the *Detroit Free Press* carried a weekly feature called "Best Cook on the Block," highlighting the favorite recipes of a local cook and including his or her picture. The feature ran several months with no black "best cooks"—this in a city with one of the highest percentage of black residents in the country.

Item: In a premier issue of its slickly redesigned Sunday magazine last September, the *Washington Post* included a cover story about a black "rap" disc jockey charged with killing a drug dealer. A column defended Washington-area store owners who discriminate against young black shoppers because of the perception that they are most likely to be robbers and shoplifters. Also none of the many advertisements in the magazine featured black models.

In a signed column, Don Graham, *Post* publisher, lauded the magazine's new look and said the magazine would report on the best of the Washington area.

Black organizations and citizens responded by returning thousands of copies of the magazine. Many were dumped unceremoniously on the front steps of the newspaper's office.

Executive editor Ben Bradlee apologized and promised that the magazine and the newspaper would do a better job of covering minorities in the future...

My many years in this profession lead me to believe we can do a better job of covering minorities and reducing stereotypes when our news staffs and management ranks more closely resemble the ethnic and cultural makeup of the communities we are supposed to serve...

Use common sense. Imagine how much anxiety would have been relieved if a reporter or editor had shared that *Courier-Journal* feature story or that *Washington Post* magazine article and column with a minority staffer.

Use the resources in your newsroom. If something you are writing or researching doesn't feel right, ask someone else. And that other person doesn't always have to be Asian, black, Hispanic or Native American.

One of the unfortunate tendencies of the media is to focus on the negatives in a society. Where there are problems, discussion is important to see if the problems can't be resolved.

The other side of the coin, however, is that where there are positive influences, these, too, need to be brought out. Readers who are surveyed often talk of "bias" in the media, and really mean they feel there is a bias toward negative news. Positive stories also need to be reported, and the *Cleveland Plain Dealer* did this with a section called "To be a local hero: A teacher of great expectation" by Margaret Bernstein on February 16, 1992, p. G1.

Retired teacher Elizabeth Clarke remembers the day her principal said he was nominating her for a Master Teacher award.

"I said forget it. They don't give it to blacks," she said.

But Clarke, 83, then a teacher at Miles Standish Elementary, was the barrier-breaking exception.

In 1970, she became the first black to win the award from the Martha Holden Jennings Foundation and received an expenses-paid trip to study in Africa.

But a better reward for the 32 years she spent in her Glenville classroom had been watching her former students achieve.

Carolyn Gordon, who wrote a glowing nomination letter about her fifth-grade teacher, said Clarke "expected us to produce our best."

Clarke reeled off a list of Clarke's former students who have done just that: Mayor Michael R. White, WKYC news anchor Leon Bibb, and Connie Kennedy Calloway, Ph.D., a Warrensville Heights school principal.

The many accomplishments of Clarke's students are "a living legacy," said Gordon, a Cuyahoga Community College English professor who recently earned a Ph.D. in education.

"She has continued to nurture young people in whom she saw promise and opened doors for them."

Clarke said that all she expected of her students was excellence, regardless of what career they followed.

"It was rewarding to me to see these youngsters grow up and have useful lives. Many of them have become very fine parents, and active in their churches and their communities," she said. "I'm just as proud of them as I can be."

Her students, who stay in close touch with Clarke, prove that teaching isn't always a thankless job. White invited her to his mayoral inauguration and wrote her into his speech.

"With one furrowed brow she could scare me and my classmates half to death," he said in the speech. "But Mrs. Clarke refused to settle for less from me and would never allow me the luxury of drifting into mediocrity."

He thanked her "for making the difference in one child's life."

Her teaching style, which emphasized African American heritage, was a precursor of the multicultural education movement. Clarke traveled to Africa 15 more times after that 1970 trip.

Her sister had arranged a surprise on her first trip to the continent: Louis Stokes, then a freshman congressman, was on his way to dedicate a Liberian hospital and was her seatmate.

"And another black man was with him," she remembers. It turned out to be the late Alex Haley on his way to Africa to research "Roots."

Knowing little about Africa, she had packed flashlights in case she found herself in a place without electricity. Upon arrival, they received a welcome she'll never forget. As she stepped off the plane, a band struck up and the Liberian president stepped up to greet her. A military escort stood by.

She and Stokes stepped into a waiting, chauffeured Mercedes Benz. "I thought about those flashlights in my luggage," and threw away all the stereotypes," she said.

She visited 52 schools in eight African countries and brought back to Glenville a new perspective steeped in African culture. In 1971 she began a series, "Let's Look at Africa in the 1970s." Her sixth graders studied the history and culture of Kenya, Liberia and Ghana.

"They were very interested. The blacks wanted to know more about themselves," she said. The lessons on Africa helped her instill self-esteem in her black students. "Teachers are very important in building self-esteem, as important as the parents," she said.

An accomplished pianist and choir director, she also used music in her lessons.

She retired from teaching 13 years ago, and is a consultant for the East Cleveland schools. Two hundred of her former students showed up when she initiated a college scholarship for young people at her church, St. Mark's Presbyterian.

"Mrs. Clarke made sure that we realized we were citizens of the world," said Bibb, who remembers the songs in French, German and other languages that she drilled into his memory. "She helped us expand our horizons to realize we could be whatever we wanted to be."

Writing about Native Americans

Understanding minorities includes developing a new perspective on the Native American cultures that first settled in what is now the United States. Paul DeMain says American Indians are the most misunderstood segment of North America's population. A journalist, he has been the Indian Affairs policy adviser to Wisconsin Gov. Anthony Earl.

REPORTING ON NATIVE AMERICANS
LEARNING ABOUT AMERICAN INDIANS
by Paul DeMain, Great Lakes Indian News Bureau, Hayward, Wisc.
Coaches' Corner, December 1986

The headline read "Wooden Indian theft is heap big mystery" and the cutline under a cartoon called the comic figure of an American Indian slumped in a chair "Chief Sitting Bull." More than one letter writer called for (and received) an apology for such insensitive treatment, but the slurs go on in newspapers across the land.

Journalists should understand the following:

* Use tribal names where possible. A history teacher asked if we prefer to be called American Indians or Native Americans. I said we prefer to be called by our native names whenever possible. Why not use Lakota, Menominee, Seminole or Oneida, many of the names Indian people call themselves. After all, the tribes of North America were as different culturally, politically and economically as are the nations of Europe, from France to Italy.

Recently, there has been a trend by tribes to identify themselves by their more traditional names rather than the derogatory, often warlike names attached to them by historians. The commonly known Sioux now refer to themselves as Lakota; the Chippewa of the Great Lakes region as the Anishinabe; and the Papago of the Southwest as the Tohono O'Odham.

- Acknowledge the role of women. Indians are amazed by the rudeness and incompleteness of American history as written by male Caucasian historians whose perspective is that women had little or no role as leaders within a tribe. This ignores the tremendous impact Clan Mothers and their Medicine Societies had on the political and religious structures of their societies.

  Among the Iroquois of the eastern shores, the women owned all assets of the community and controlled the decision to declare war against an enemy. And in other tribes, it was the women who helped groom and choose the hierarchy of male leaders and chiefs.

  The male Caucasian, unlikely to have access to the structure of women, spent time with the chiefs and macho warriors who boasted of several wives. Historians reported these boasts without knowing the wholeness or tradition of such marital relationships.

- Avoid historical errors. The discovery of America by Columbus is replete with historical errors, including his reference to "Indios," a Spanish term meaning "children close to God." And recent anthropological evidence suggests that tribal societies in North America numbered some 20 million strong in 1492, not 5 million, as history books suggest. The rampage of European diseases took their toll, as did slave snatching and wars, reducing the indigenous population to fewer than 250,000 by the turn of this century.

- Avoid stereotypes of appearance, life styles. God gave Indians blue eyes, too. In modern society, we look and dress like everyone else. We are often asked: "How much Indian are you?" We are called upon to prove our tribal pedigrees based on affiliation, residency and ancestors. This is offensive, especially when we do not suggest blood quantums as the basis of citizenship for emigres to this country.

- Correct myths of a simple, unsophisticated society. Our modern democratic form of government was borrowed from the Iroquois Confederacy. American Indians contribute to every aspect of modern life—medicine, art, agriculture, science, law, politics. Many served with distinction in the Armed Services.
- Take time to know us. During the 1975 occupation of the Alexian Brothers Novitiate near Gresham, Wis., by the Menominee Indian reservation, the new owner of the local paper was appalled to find that his staff used the news wires to report on major events taking place 15 miles down the road. Small wonder few people know to any extent the true Menominee nature and all their beautiful, powerful contributions.

Writing about Religious Minorities

Some minorities lead entirely different lifestyles. The Amish, who live in Ohio, Indiana, Pennsylvania, and other states, want to be left to their own lifestyle and their own rules. But on occasion, the dominant society intrudes on this quiet, peaceful, farming group, and they make news.

The *Lorain (O.) Journal* on June 28, 1988, reported this clash between cultures in "Old order faces new threat: Amish fight back in Nova," by Dick Hendrickson, Journal Bureau Chief.

The story started with an editor's note that set the tone: While many people would be pleased to have their lives and views featured in a newspaper story, an Amish person would see it as a source of deep embarrassment, calling attention to himself in a prideful way. Because of that, the Amish interviewed for this story are not named.

(Notice how Hendrickson tells readers of the conflict between the new and old ways of life, and also weaves in details most readers do not know about the Amish and their way of life. It is a story with present-day and age-old conflicts in lifestyles, all wrapped into one.)

NOVA, O.—The work day is already three hours old when the silver and blue truck rolls up and its driver exchanges the milk cans in front of a farm a few miles east of here. It is a scene repeated many times each morning, but only at certain farms, the ones without wires, without electricity.

The milk is one of the few links to the outside world for the Amish. It is taken, in cans, to a dairy processing plant, eventually to be made into cheese, rather than being bottled for the stores.

Because they insist on using the cans, the Amish are limited to the cheese processing market and are paid less for their products than their neighbors, dairy farmers with electric-powered refrigerated, bulk milk handling and storage systems.

The Amish are content with that because the alternative, the modern way of those they call "the English," is to be feared more than the economic hardship. It is in the old order of things, a 16th century European peasant lifestyle, that the Amish find happiness.

Their wish is inherently American, to be left alone with their lives, their families and their religious beliefs.

But now there is a serious threat to the Amish here, so serious that they have done the forbidden and unthinkable: they have stepped into the spotlight of the media and politics.

- A few months ago, a few Amishmen drove their buggies through the crossroads of Sullivan, past the cameras of television and newspaper journalists, cameras Amish have traditionally avoided, and handed a petition to U.S. Sen. Howard Metzenbaum.
- A few days after that, two Amishmen appeared at a press conference in Columbus with another petition signed by the heads of 4,000 Amish families.

In both messages, they expressed their great alarm over the proposal by a regional firm to build and operate a hazardous waste incinerator just outside this crossroads town in the northeast corner of Ashland County.

"We must live in fear that something could happen to endanger our health," the Amish said. "We earnestly pray for our safety, and not for us alone, but for everyone..."

If the plant is built on a 292-acre site just west of Nova, tank trucks will rumble past the Amish buggies on US Rt. 224, bringing the wastes of industry— hazardous solids, sludge or liquids such as paint thinners, chemical solvents and poly-chlorinated biphenyls, or PCBs—to be burned into ashes that will be buried in vaults.

The equipment manufacturer, International Technologies Corp., insists the operation will not pose a danger to the community. Opponents are just as certain that they will.

For the Amish, who have put generations of hard work

into the farmlands around here, it is the battle of a lifetime, a 20th century disaster for a 16th century people.

They have been able through personal, family and church discipline to keep out the influences of modern conveniences such as chrome-plated microwaves and shiny painted automobiles. But they fear they soon will be powerless to stop the waste products from the manufacture of those things, chromium and paint thinners, from invading their lands and homes through the air and water.

[One] Amish farm is downwind and downstream from the incinerator site. One of the source tributaries of the Black River flows through the property nearby. The farmer can't stop his cows from drinking the water. "If that water becomes polluted, I'm in trouble," he declares.

[Additional graphic examples of how the Amish way of life differs from the rest of the Americans.]

The Amish get most of their horsepower from real horses. There are no tractors. They do not own or operate automobiles, though they will ride in them under certain circumstances, usually depending on the practicality of it.

The rules vary from community to community. Those who live around Olivesburg, in central and western Ashland County, are willing to use belt-driven elevators to move the hay into storage. Those near Sullivan and Homerville in northern Wayne and southwestern Medina counties do not.

Both groups in this area are considered to be among the most conservative of the Amish in America.

The Amish have large families—a couple with 10 or 12 children would not be unusual—and it is understood that as the parents get older, they will be succeeded by and supported by the sons. At first the young married couples will live in a small house next to the main house. Later, as the new family grows and the older one diminishes, the two switch homes, a very practical move.

The Amish do not pay for or receive Social Security, both because they feel they do not need the benefits and because to do so would mean accepting Social Security numbers.

They will pay taxes, based on Christ's answer to a question about taxes in the Bible, but they are fearful of Social Security numbers. "We don't know if the numbers are those referred to in the Book of Revelation," says an Amish church leader.

A group called Citizens Against Pollution tried to get the

Amish to donate their popular home baked goods for a fund raiser to fight the incinerator. The Amish declined to be involved.

"We hope that you understand that we are not for the incinerator in this area, and it is not that we can't afford to donate baked goods for your festival. We feel if we do something that would hinder our peace in the church. It would do more harm than good," the bishops of the church said.

There are no church buildings for the Amish. Worship services rotate from home to home. Each church group, of about 25 families, meets at one of the homes for services every other week. On the alternate week, the people are free to go to the services of another, neighboring group of families.

The services are long and all in a German dialect. There are two sermons separated by scripture reading and followed by testimonials. The congregation sings, but the hymns are from the 16th century and almost chant-like.

A bishop explains that it is not electricity that is feared, but the changes that come with it. The modern conveniences would corrupt the families and disrupt their simple—and successful—lifestyle.

Things to Remember

- Understand that your lifestyle is not the only one on your campus or in the community. It is your responsibility to know the major groups in your community and to report on them completely.
- Know the sensitivities that result in names applied to groups, and how those groups prefer to be named. Be current on what are the acceptable names for groups.
- Understand that one person does not represent any group, much less a minority group. Do not ask one person for an opinion and assume all persons in that group feel the same way.
- In the past, the media have not covered society in a way that helps society understand itself. It is a difficult job, and must be constantly worked on.

Exercises

1. Go to your campus library. Find the racial and ethnic mix in your community by using government documents or other reference materials. Based on what you have learned, do you

think all groups in your community get fair treatment in the newspapers or on television?
2. Invite someone from your Affirmative Action office, or a leader of a minority group on campus, to your class. Find out if this person thinks minorities in your community or on your campus are covered fairly and completely. Does this person have suggestions for improvement in news coverage?

24
The Visual Attitude:
Help Me to Understand

Don Lee

In This Chapter

The reporter must understand that words alone, while important, cannot tell the story as quickly and effectively as words with visuals.

While most reporters do not take photographs, they should be expected to help the photographer by suggesting good photo ideas.

Even though reporters are not expected to do charts, graphs, and illustrations, they should be able to suggest ideas to editors and graphic artists.

For the television reporter, integrating moving photographs into a news report is a fact of life.

Print media reporters must realize that in an era of very intense competition, they need to present a complete package of information—words, photos, and illustrations—to compete with the electronic media.

FOSTER DAVIS (1988) of the *St. Louis Post-Dispatch* tells a powerful story about improving copy by using a story from the *Philadelphia Inquirer*.

Gene Roberts of the *Inquirer* (now at *The New York Times*) calls visual writing "making me see." He tells the story of his first editor, a blind man, having Gene's stories read to him.

"And many days—I still wince at the thought of how many—he would summon me into his cubicle after having heard my stories word by word and say 'You aren't making me see: make me see.' "

Not "make me see" literally but make my imagination work.

Television cannot do this. When you watch television, you watch someone else's imagination. When reading absorbs you, your imagination is at work.

How to do it? It is a trick, really. The writer allows readers to provide most of the information. Well-chosen details tickle their memory banks, which spill more details, colors, sounds, scents even, to fill out the picture.

The strategy is to nudge readers' memories, by evoking something they are familiar with, be it clouds scudding across gray harbor water or the sight and sound of a trowel in an old man's hand digging into red clay. Readers add the details that complete the picture.

One reader may imagine New York harbor, another

somewhere else. One reader may dress the old man in faded khakis, another may see the set of the jaw. Their imaginations are at work.

A modest example: We published a story about what dogs do when they are home alone. One entry: "4 P.M. The rain starts again. Socrates sleeps curled like a cashew."

When you read these sentences, they tickle your own memory of rainy afternoons and sleeping dogs. You fill in all sorts of things the writer did not say. And you read with absorption.

As William Strunk put it, "The greatest writers...are effective largely because they deal in particulars and report the details that matter. Their words call up pictures..."

A good way to help a writer see what is necessary is to ask this question: "If you were making a movie, what would the pictures be?"

A movie is a collection of images in motion. For the newspaper story to work well, it must have motion just like the movie.

Let's say we are doing a light little story about someone who is a whiz at raising artichokes. What do we take word pictures of? Perhaps the gardener at dawn, sipping coffee. On the kitchen wall is a picture of the ultimate, unattainable artichoke. Perhaps the second scene is the gardener on her knees, plumbing up the earth around the artichoke seedlings.

We must report so we can write sentences and paragraphs that will evoke pictures—and sounds and smells and tastes and touches, for that matter—in reader's heads.

Don't try to make me fall in love with the story on the council subcommittee recommendation for a sewer line. Heed instead, the readers' prayer: "If it must be dull, please God, let it be short."

But where there is the opportunity, engage the readers' imaginations. It will improve your newspaper.

The editor meant that he could not visualize this person, that he could not get a good feeling for what this person was doing, that the writer needed to draw a better "picture."

Making someone see, or helping them to understand, involves more than words, though words are a critical part.

In this book, we have talked about many ways to improve understanding through writing, including:

• Using dollar amounts instead of mills to help the reader

understand just how much 4.7 mills for 10 years will cost him in dollars and cents;

- Personalizing, or telling a story in terms of the people who will be impacted by the story, rather than talking about the problems of the government putting the policy into effect;
- Developing appropriate leads, which tell the reader almost immediately what the most important parts of the story are, so the reader who scans quickly can use time wisely;
- Foreshadowing, or warning readers in advance that something is going to happen later in the story, and they should be prepared for it;
- Attributing, or telling who said something, so readers or viewers can judge for themselves whether the source is reliable.
- Using direct quotes, so readers can tell exactly what the person said.

But beyond "making me see" through words, there are additional dimensions to helping someone see important events in today's world. These are the aspects that literally help readers to see something better, in more detail, or in a "new light."

The World of Visuals

They are called photographs, charts, visuals, maps, or graphics. And while the reporter may not specialize in them, he or she must understand the growing role of the reporter in providing visual information to the reader.

A young metro editor recently told of a new reporter who had interned at one of the country's largest newspapers before working for the medium-sized daily after graduation. The reporter protested that at the huge metropolitan daily, the reporters did not bother with arranging photographs or talking with photographers about assignments.

The editor put it very succinctly: "With a good picture, this will run on Page One. Without any art, figure on page eight or nine." The message came through and the reporter called the source to ask if she would be willing to be in a picture, then worked out details with the photographer as to when and where the picture should be taken, and what angle was needed.

There can be no doubt that this is a visual world. We see hundreds of thousands of meticulously prepared television ads each year, and we have grown used to color and movement and clever slogans and the pink bunny going and going and going.

Reporters must realize that in a competitive news media

environment, when it seems everyone is using color and graphics and heavy doses of pizzazz, they are automatically behind in the competition for the audience if they do not.

Words alone, as important as they are, do not do the entire job of helping the audience to understand the world around them. Just as important, photos, graphics, or charts alone usually will not do the job either.

There has to be a combination of the best words and the best art (a generic term which means photos, illustrations, charts, cartoons, and other visual elements other than words alone). Here is where the reporter comes in.

The visual element is the most obvious in television. Reporters must not only do a story but also they must have either a visual background for the story (a standup on the site of the story) or an interview of the persons making the news on the site where the news is being made. This puts an extra demand on television reporters that is not present with radio or print reporters.

For one thing, the print reporter has to get the name spelled right, the radio reporter has to get the pronunciation right, but the television reporter has to get both the spelling and the pronunciation right.

Radio reporters cannot be as "visual" as television, but they can use sounds of the event and actual voices of the sources, and they can "paint word pictures." This means they should describe the scene they are reporting from to give listeners the feeling that they are on the scene as well. They can also use the writing principles discussed previously to help listeners understand the story.

Newspaper reporters, who for hundreds of years have focused solely on the written word, have the greatest challenge. They must add "visual" to their vocabulary, and they must realize that words alone may not be enough. Visuals are not possible in every news story, but whenever they can help the reader understand the story better, they should be included.

The print reporter on smaller papers may be required to take photos. This is a demanding task, but it can be conquered with persistence and imagination.

On larger papers and in most magazines, the reporter is not likely to take photos, but they must do at least three things to adjust to the new realities of print journalism.

Requirements for Reporters

Reporters must respect the importance of visuals; be prepared to understand the news requirements of charts, photos, and illustrations;

and understand the needs of and be willing to cooperate with photographers, artists, and graphic designers.

The Importance of Visuals

The print reporter must understand that quick-scanning readers may not even look at a story unless there is a visual to stop their scanning.

The story about a new person in the community is much more effective with a photograph. A sports game story is much more valuable if a small chart includes individual statistics. The story about the restoration of a 200-year-old downtown landmark should be accompanied by an exterior or interior shot, or a street locator, so the reader is sure they know which building is being discussed. If a new golf course opens, a road map showing how to get to it is appreciated by most readers.

Readers need a reason to stop scanning and be pulled into a story. And if they are pulled into the story, they need to understand it fully, and that understanding is usually improved by photos, charts, or graphs.

The New Requirements of Providing for Art

This puts an additional burden on the reporter. In addition to writing the story, she must be concerned with finding statistics to be used in a chart, helping an artist draw a graphic of the murder scene, selecting pull quotes that can be used in the story, or identifying people in a photograph. The extra work will help the reader understand the story better.

The print reporter is also responsible, in many cases, for cutlines or captions under pictures that go with his story. Very often, this means getting the names of everyone in the picture, and providing information that readers would not get simply by looking at the picture. For example, if the photo shows a football player crossing the goal line, the cutlines should mention that this is a record-breaking touchdown. Or, if a photo shows a tropical island in a travel story, the cutlines should point out this island is considered one of the hemisphere's best travel bargains. Try not to repeat information in the headlines.

Working with Photographers and Graphic Designers

Reporters must understand how to work with photographers and designers. All persons in a newsroom are professionals, but many have different specialties. Understanding that the needs of the reader are paramount will help them to work together. The feelings between reporters, photographers, and designers should not be competitive, but cooperative.

Each newsroom person has a natural feeling that their contribution to the story may be the most important. Letting these feelings dominate a person's thoughts will mean competition where there should be cooperation.

For many years, the old cliche, "A picture is worth a thousand words" has made its way into conversations between photographers and reporters. Articles have attempted to justify the value of photographs by comparing the space a picture takes with the space 1,000 words would take.

Nothing could be more distracting or irrelevant than a conversation of this sort. First, it is a distortion of the philosophical statement that "One look is worth a thousand rumors," which is used to advise people to verify their statements before spreading rumors. (Not bad advice for beginning reporters, either.)

Secondly, the argument is counterproductive. Words without pictures are usually far less effective than words with pictures. And pictures without words may also have little value.

One illustration showing earthquake damage, or a map showing where the earthquake was, or a chart listing recent earthquakes—all can add immeasurably to an earthquake story. "You've got to see it to believe it" may be the motto for persons using photos of natural disasters. Since the world is connected by television satellites and pictures can be sent anywhere, those who do not use them suffer competitively.

Process in Taking Photos

The reporter should think of the process the photographer goes through when taking a picture. It is similar to the process the reporter goes through in writing a story.

Think of it. A reporter gets an idea for a story, talks to sources about it, collects notes, outlines material, finds a focus for the story, and writes and rewrites to get a completed story.

The photographer develops an idea for a news picture, goes to the scene or arranges to meet someone to take a picture, and takes several shots from different angles. The photographer is looking for the angle, literally, that will give her the best picture, just as the reporter is looking for the angle which will give him the best story.

The photographer is bound to take more pictures than she can use, just as the reporter should take more notes than he needs.

When they get back to the office, they both talk to the editor about the angle and the size of the expected product, and then they go to work.

The reporter focuses on the person or situation that will make the story understandable and interesting. The photographer also focuses on the best picture she has, and crops out extra material that does not pertain to the main point.

The photographer tries to avoid cliche photos, such as four or five people lined up facing the camera, just as the writer avoids cliches in use of language. The photographer tries to show what is different and newsworthy in this photo, just as the reporter does.

Both then refine and polish their product to present the best material to the editor for inclusion in the paper.

Both reporters and photographers are looking for messages that will help people. They just go about it in different media, so to speak. The important thing to understand is that they complement each other, and by working together can "make me see," can help the audience understand.

The reporter, usually so involved in telling a story in words, is the one who has to adjust to the changing situation. He or she must understand that words alone are not enough, and make suggestions to the editor about pictures. Being on the beat or on the scene almost every day, the reporter knows what is changing and what is newsworthy better than the editor (who by definition leaves the office less often), or the photographer (who can't know everyone's beat).

If the reporter and photographer on a newspaper know what makes good pictures, they can overcome the technical advantage of television by running the story before it becomes common knowledge, or by finding and focusing on the most important angle.

Newspapers have space that can sometimes be expanded whereas television and radio usually have defined time limits. They must anticipate what other media are likely to cover and get their stories first to eliminate the technical advantages of radio and television. Newspapers usually have larger news staffs as well, so they can and should be more flexible in what they cover.

Reporters and photographers must guard against stereotypes in photographs as well as in stories. All members of a given group should not be written about as being similar in thought and action just because they belong to a group. And all photographs of a group should not project them as being poor or rich, hopeless or helpless, or similarly stereotyped just because they are all members of the same group.

Things to Remember

- Reporters may not think of photographs as being their responsibility, but in a competitive world all news department members must work together.
- The reporter should be thinking of photo and illustration possibilities while doing a story, and should suggest ideas to editors and photographers.

References

Bradbury, Ray. "Words from the wise." *Coaches' Corner* (December 1991): 10.

Caughey, Bernard. "The popularity of obituaries." *Editor and Publisher* (April 23, 1988): 46.

Clark, Roy Peter, and Don Fry. *Coaching Writers*. New York: St. Martin's Press, 1992.

Cutlip, Scott M., Allen H. Center, and Glen M. Broom. *Effective Public Relations*, 6th ed. Englewood Cliffs, NJ: Prentice Hall, 1985.

Editor and Publisher. "Survey: Juries hiking libel penalties." (September 5, 1992): 13.

Emery, Edwin, and Michael Emery. *The Press in America*, 5th ed. Englewood Cliffs, NJ: Prentice Hall, 1984.

Flower, Linda, and J. R. Hayes. "A cognitive process theory of writing." *College Composition and Communication* 32 (December 1981).

Giles, Bill. "Stress has significant presence in newsrooms." *Editor and Publisher* (Nov. 12, 1983): 12.

Goodman, Ellen. Quoted in *Writing for Your Readers*, by Donald Murray. Chester, CT: Globe Pequot Press, 1983, p. 115.

Hairston, Maxine. "The winds of change: Thomas Kuhn and the revolution in the teaching of writing." *College Composition and Communication* 33 (February 1982): 76–88.

Harris, Jay. "Bearing the burden of blame." *Editor and Publisher* (May 9, 1992): 11.

Iwata, Edward. "A new sense of mission." *Editor and Publisher* (June 27, 1992): 100.

Kendall, Robert. "Public relations employment: Huge growth projected." *PR Review* X:3 (Fall 1984): 13.

Kopehaver, Lillian Lodge. "Aligning values of practitioners and journalists." *PR Review* XI:2 (Summer 1985): 17.

Laakaniemi, Ray. "An analysis of writing coach programs on American daily newspapers." *Journalism Quarterly* 64 (1986): 243, 569.

Lawrence, David, Jr. "Broken Ladders/Revolving Doors: the need for pluralism in the newsroom." *Newspaper Research Journal* (Summer 1990): 25.

Lesher, Tina. "Writing coaches offer lessons for teachers." *Coaches' Corner* (September 1987): 8.

McLean, Deckle. "Move to clear and convincing proof as libel standard gain for the media." *Journalism Quarterly* (Autumn 1989): 640.

Morton, Linda. "How newspapers choose the releases they use." *PR Review* XII:3 (Fall 1986): 22.

Moyer, Marilyn. "The coach as editor—Part 1." *Coaches' Corner* (September 1991): 3.

Murray, Donald. *Writing for Your Readers*. Chester,CT: Globe Pequot Press, 1983.

Olson, Lyle. "Effect of news writing instruction in English composition classes." *Journalism Educator* (Summer 1992): 50.

Parsegian, Elise Keolian. "News reporting in the midst of chaos." *Journalism Quarterly* (Winter 1987): 721.

Pitts, Beverley. "Protocol analysis of the newswriting process." *Newspaper Research Journal* 4:1 (Fall 1982): 12–21.

Richman, Alan. "Five hours for five days of work?" *Coaches' Corner* (Sept. 1989): 11.

Scanlan, Christopher, ed. *How I Wrote the Story*. Providence Journal Co., 1983: 1.

———. "Riding the roller coaster: The emotion in good writing." *Coaches' Corner* (Sept. 1988).

Schierhorn, Ann. "The role of the writing coach in the magazine curriculum." *Journalism Educator* (Summer 1991): 46.

Stein, M. L. "Managing editors hear newsroom study results," Editor & Publisher, Nov. 13, 1982, p. 13.

———. "The Year 2008." *Editor and Publisher* (May 2, 1992): 68.

Wolf, Rita, and Tommy Thomason. "Writing coaches: Their strategies for improving writing." *Newspaper Research Journal* 7:3 (Spring 1986): 43.

Zahler, Rick. "Rich Zahler: the coach as counselor." *Coaches' Corner* (March 1986): 3.

Zinsser, William. *On Writing Well*, 3d ed. New York: Harper and Row, 1985.

Zinsser, William. "Zinsser: On Writing Well—and Rewriting Well." Speech to Wisconsin Educational TV, 1986, reported in *Coaches' Corner* (March 1986): 4.

Zinsser, William. *Writing to Learn*. New York: Harper and Row, 1988.

Zurek, Jerome. "Research and writing process can help journalism teachers." *Journalism Educator* (Spring 1986): 19.

Credits

The following stories have been excerpted in the book and appear with permission of their respective authors and publications.

Alexander, Keith, and Adrianne Flynn. "Teens sling slang. You say 'no way' can you interpret their lingo? Yes, way!" *Dayton Daily News* (May 9, 1992): 1.

Bernstein, Margaret. "To be a local hero: A teacher of great expectation." *Cleveland Plain Dealer* (Feb. 16, 1992): G1.

Bishop, Mary. "Pests, toxins and risks: Fumigation 'loaded gun,' expert says." *Roanoke Times & World-News* (Aug. 21, 1988).

Bohannon, Jim. Collection of radio news stories from "America in the Morning" and "The Jim Bohannon Show."

Bowles, Scott. "Scary 'cat': New drug creeps in from the U.P." *Detroit News* (Sept. 27, 1992).

Brand, William. "Deadly siege near UC; Two dead, 9 wounded in assault." *Oakland Tribune* (Sept. 28, 1990).

Brubaker, Bill. "Where have all the athletes gone?" *Washington Post* (March 29, 1992). © 1992, The Washington Post. Reprinted with permission.

Davis, Foster. "Making me see is the key to visual writing." *Coaches' Corner* (Sept. 1988): 7.

Davis, Robert. "Into your hands I commend my spirit." *Fort Collins Coloradoan* (Aug. 1, 1990, to Sept. 23, 1990).

DeMain, Paul. "Reporting on Native Americans: Learning about American Indians." *Coaches' Corner* (Dec. 1986): 7.

DeSilva, Bruce, "Cliches that cling: Should we avoid them like the plag . . ." *Coaches' Corner* (Dec. 1990).

deView, Lucille. "Reporters care, too: Let them say so." *Coaches' Corner* (March 1986): 4.

Fagan, Kevin. "Smoking ruins dash most hopes. But a handful of homeowners find a miracle." In "FIRESTORM: The week the hills burned." *Oakland Tribune* (Dec. 2, 1991): 17.

Falk, Bill. "When AIDS hits home: In memory of a brother." *Westchester-Rockland (N.Y.) Newspapers,* in Best of Gannett, 1989: 38.

Francis, Beth. "Addiction: Why some get hooked, others walk away." *Fort Myers (Fla.) News Press* in Best of Gannett, 1991: 32.

Fry, Don. "Lead writing by the numbers." *Coaches' Corner* (June 1990): 4.

Gottschalk, Marina. "Many suburbs vulnerable to fire." In "FIRESTORM: The week the hills burned." *Oakland Tribune* (Dec. 2, 1991).

Grabowicz, Paul, and Bill Snyder. "Ruins look like hills were under aerial bombing." In "FIRESTORM: The week the hills burned." *Oakland Tribune* (Dec. 2, 1991).

Gust, Kelly, "Gunman was man of extremes." *Oakland Tribune* (Sept. 28, 1990).

Heller, Jonathan. "The solitary death of Suzan Carter." Edited by Ina Chadwick. *The (Westport, Conn.) Fairpress* (Oct. 31, 1991).

Hendrickson, Dick. "Old order faces new threat: Amish fight back in Nova." *Lorain (O.) Journal* (June 26, 1988).

Henry, Fran. "Sold on America: Japanese couple in Elyria enjoy mix and pace of U.S." *Cleveland Plain Dealer* (Feb. 29, 1992): F1.

Johnson, Ben. "How we err in covering blacks." *Coaches' Corner* (Dec. 1986): 6.

Kane, Eugene. "Films, rap capture the hard core." *The Milwaukee Journal* 1991.

Keenan, Marney Rich. "A message to Michael." *The Detroit News* (March 2, 1991).

Kepple, David E. "Lesson's dividend: $100,000. Custodian's estate goes to seminary." *Dayton Daily News* (Dec. 3, 1988).

Koperdak, Carolyn. "Boy, 11, held in robbery: Loaded gun aimed at Dairy Mart clerk." *Lorain (O.) Morning Journal* (Sept. 8, 1992).

Kourtakis, Bob, "Title IX's first 10 years." *Port-Huron (Mich.) Times-Herald* (April 23, 1989).

Kresnak, Jack. "Mom's love sends son, 13, to jail for drugs." *Detroit Free Press* (July 23, 1991).

Kurilovitch, Mike. "Crack: Drug tightens grip on country." *Niagara (N.Y.) Gazette* (May 28, 1989).

Levin, Harry. "Defining-clause overkill: It never goes away." *Coaches' Corner* (March 1989): 12.

Lipton, Jeff. "Bank robber betrayed by loyal dog." *The Virginia Gazette* (June 6, 1992), p. 1.

Macy, Beth. "Mudcat the Maverick." *Roanoke Times & World-News* (Mar. 17, 1991).

Mahoney, Brett. "Luxury cars melt down. About 2,000 cars damaged; wrecks fetch $50 as scrap." In "FIRESTORM: The week the hills burned." *Oakland Tribune* (Dec. 2, 1991).

Maynard, Robert C. "Kindness of neighbors and strangers." In "FIRESTORM: The week the hills burned." *Oakland Tribune* (Dec. 2, 1991).

McCartney, Scott. "S&Ls on Main Street, effect of S&L crisis on homeowners, investors and vacationers." *Associated Press* (Sept. 8, 1990).

McCarty, James, and Ulysses Torassa. "Judge not by name alone: 92 lawyers crowd ballots for courts." *Cleveland Plain Dealer* (Feb. 17, 1992).

Moilanen, Kathy Ann. "Livingston grapples with racist image." *Ann Arbor (Mich.) News* (April 29, 1990).

Nalder, Eric. "Trials of taxol: Promising cancer drug is stalled in the forest." *Seattle Times* (Dec. 15, 1991).

Newton, Eric, and Roger Rapoport, editors. "The Bay Area at war." *Oakland Tribune* (Feb. 15, 1991).

Nordstrand, Dave. "Busy motorists could learn from boy's heroism." *Salinas Californian*. Best of Gannett, 1991: 41.

O'Connor, Matt. "Cop guilty of aiding son's drug ring." *Chicago Tribune* (May 9, 1992): 5.

———. "You've got 10 seconds, then I fire." *Chicago Tribune* (July 14, 1992).

Pappano, Laura. "Emerging community: Gays in the suburbs." *Patriot Ledger* (May 4–7, 1991).

Pardue, Douglas. "Madeline Adams Tate: Now she is just a number." *Roanoke (Va.) Times & World-News* (Jan. 26, 1985).

Parziale, Eva. "Agents shot." *Associated Press* (Apr. 11, 1986). Copyright © 1986 by the Associated Press.

Poole, Monte. "Three strikes fired at Jackson." In "FIRESTORM: The week the hills burned." *Oakland Tribune* (Dec. 2, 1991).

Prendergrast, Jane. "Graduates bracing for tough job market: Some college seniors expect the worst." *The Cincinnati Enquirer*. (May 8, 1992): 1.

Rathje, William, "Rubbish!" *The Atlantic Monthly* (Dec. 1989): 99.

Riepenhoff, Jill. "Parents hustle to see twins graduate." *Columbus Dispatch* (May 11, 1992). Reprinted, with permission, from the Columbus (Ohio) Dispatch.

Robinson-Haynes, Ellen. "Adam Rhodes and his battle with leukemia." *The Sacramento Bee* (Mar. 11, 1990).

Scanlan, Christopher. "Riding the roller coaster: The emotion in good writing." *Coaches' Corner* (Sept. 1988).

Seigerman, Dave. "Basketball star maintains poise under pressure." *Jackson (Tenn.) Sun*. Best of Gannett, 1991: 35.

Sewell, Rhonda B. "Crisis of the black male." *Toledo Blade* (Oct. 4, 1992): F1.

Sherborne, Robert, and LaCrisha Butler. "Brave Nashville woman foils kidnap attempt." *The Nashville Tennessean*. Best of Gannett, 1989: 20.

Smith, Gary. "Shadow of a nation." *Sports Illustrated* (Feb. 18, 1991), p. 62.

Smith, Tim, William Fox, and Jeannie Faris. "Supreme Court rules USC foundation a public body," series, *The Greenville News* (Feb. 12–June 26, 1991).

Staats, Craig, and Carolyn Newbergh. "Day 1. Eastbay blaze destroys hundred of hillside homes." In "FIRESTORM: The week the hills burned." *Oakland Tribune* (Dec. 2, 1991).

Stapler, Harry. "The one sentence, long sentence habit of writing leads." *Newspaper Research Journal* (Fall 1985): 17.

Taylor, Jeff, and Mike McGraw. "Failing the grade: Betrayals and blunders at the Department of Agriculture." *Kansas City Star* (Dec. 8–14, 1991).

Tuft, Carolyn. "Blacks in Belleville." *Belleville (Ill.) News Democrat* (May 12–June 4, 1991).

Wallick, Merritt. "CFCs: DuPont's safety whitewash." *Wilmington (Del.) News-Journal* (Aug. 25–28, 1991). Copyright © 1991 by the Wilmington News Journal.

Warren, Rich. "After too many thieves, car alarm looks good." *Chicago Tribune* (July 12, 1992).

Watts, Thomas J., and Steven H. Lee. "The Plains: New visions of an old frontier." *Dallas Morning News* (Apr. 28, 1991).

Yancey, Dwayne. "Thunder in the coal fields." *Roanoke Times & World-News* (April 29, 1990).

Index

Index